STORE FRONT NYC

STORE FRONT

**JAMES T. &
KARLA L. MURRAY**

FOREWORD
Chris Stein

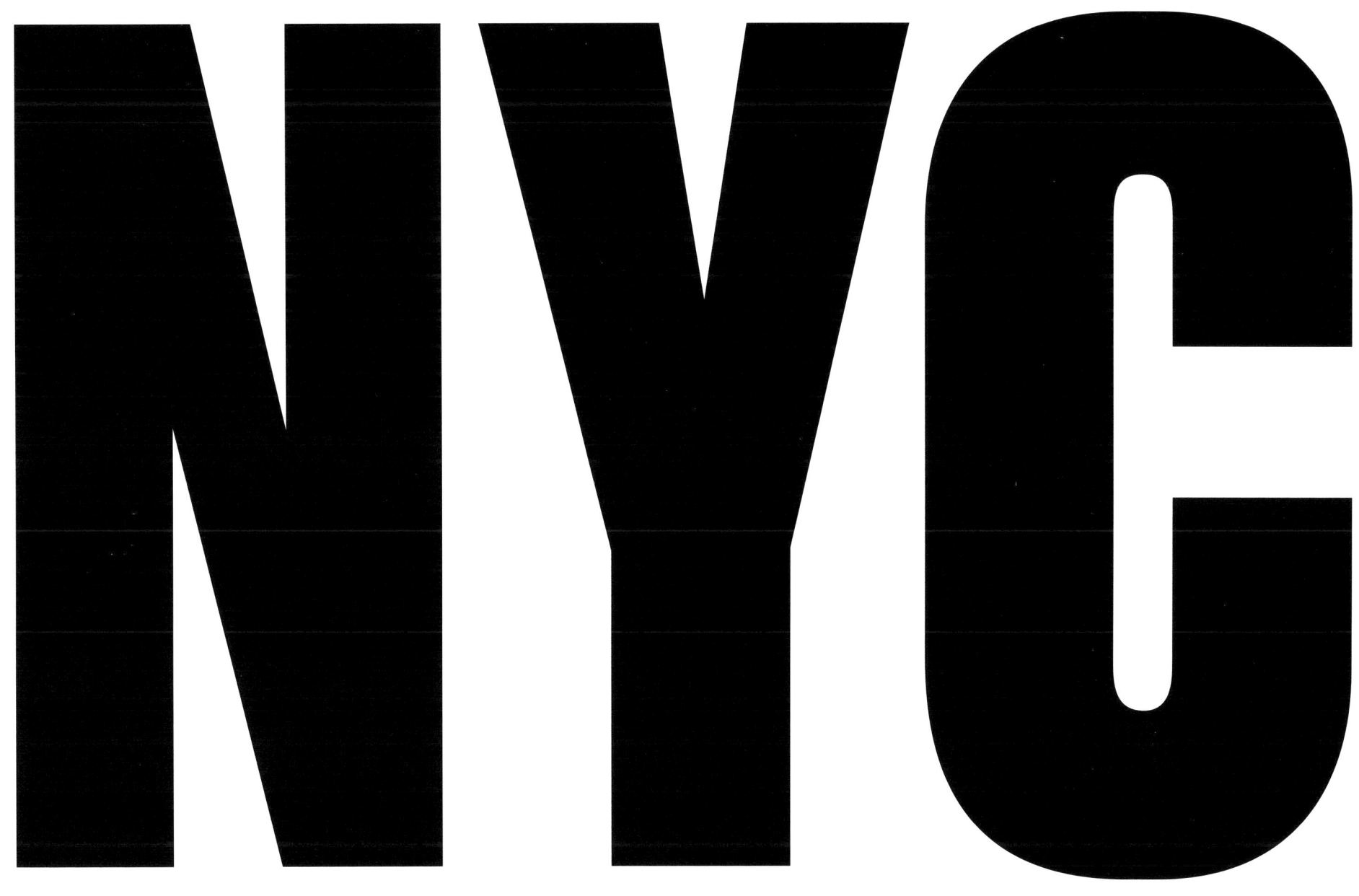

NYC

Photographs of the City's
Independent Shops, Past and Present

PRESTEL
Munich · London · New York

FOREWORD: SIGNS

Chris Stein

Growing up in Brooklyn, I got caught up in various musical genres at around age ten, in 1960. By the time I was twelve or thirteen I was a fan of jazz, folk, and film soundtracks. The funny thing is that my relationship with the pop music of the day was somewhat strained. I considered things like the massively popular Shangri-Las "too commercial" to consider worthy of my affections. "I Will Follow Him" by Peggy March was omnipresent and seemed to stay at number one for months. I even questioned the Beatles at first before being drawn in.

So it came as somewhat of a personal revelation when, in later years, dealing with my own band, Blondie, I suddenly found myself greatly enamored of songs and styles that I had derided as a kid. I had a particularly abrupt reversal regarding the Shangri-Las. Working on my own music somehow caused me to now think "Leader of the Pack" was genuinely and unironically brilliant.

Spending years—the 1950s to the '80s and onward—on the streets of Manhattan and New York City's other boroughs perhaps led me to a similar consideration (or lack thereof) of the urban commercial sprawl that I was embedded in. I would of course breathlessly appreciate some bit of baroque architecture like The Alwyn on 58th Street, but the day-to-day signage and more "mundane" little shops and store fronts didn't quite register as integral and vital—until they started disappearing. It was eye-opening to then see them being presented in a new context by people like James and Karla Murray, whose photographs I discovered online.

The Papaya Kings, pizza places, cafés, and restaurant fronts that had been just background material for it all I now find charming and distinctly original. "You don't know what you've got till it's gone" philosophy is a component. The city is in constant flux, and at the same time corporations mine personal nostalgia in order to hypnotize consumers, they still miss the target when it comes to recreating the atmosphere of the past.

The trend leans away from individual shops and cafés and in toward chains and online supply. I live in the West Village, and the turnover of shops and small businesses on Bleecker Street, for example, is fast and furious. I've seen boutiques come and go in the space of literally a year or less, and each iteration of consumerism is more modern than the previous. I'm all for plowing ahead, but I find it fascinating that some old location that I might have ignored for its normalcy I now see as vital, and representative of a totally fresh antique context. The flat, undecorated lines of 1960s and '70s architecture really has the same appeal for me now as an old iron-front loft building in SoHo.

Photography is time travel, and the past surrounds us even as it's absorbed. Great that somebody is keeping track.

Chris Stein is the cofounder, songwriter, and guitarist of the iconic punk band Blondie. His photographic work has been featured in galleries and press around the world, and published in the books Negative: Me, Blondie, and the Advent of Punk *(2014) and* Point of View: Me, New York City, and the Punk Scene *(2018).*

INTRODUCTION

James T. & Karla L. Murray

Every city has its own tale to tell, and for us, the story of New York's time-worn, generational mom-and-pop stores is an important part of what makes it a unique and remarkable place. Yet unfortunately, the neighborhood shops where New Yorkers buy a cup of coffee, the morning newspaper, or a loaf of bread; where they get their shoes repaired or a haircut, or purchase anything they could ever want or need, are becoming increasingly threatened.

The idea to thoroughly document small stores came about when we were photographing the city's streets for a project involving the graffiti art scene in the late 1990s. Our work took us to all corners of New York City as we traveled not only through Manhattan but to distant neighborhoods in the outer boroughs. We would often return to the same streets, sometimes months or even weeks later, and despite the short time frame between visits, we noticed that some blocks looked drastically different. Many stores with charming hand-painted and neon signage had closed and the whole look and feel of the area had changed; much of its individuality and character had faded away. We made it our mission to meticulously catalog these independently owned businesses when we first began to notice the alarming rate at which they were disappearing. Today, over 80 percent of the stores we photographed for our first book on the subject, *Store Front: The Disappearing Face of New York*, published in 2008, have vanished. Even with our follow-up volume, *Store Front II: A History Preserved*, which was published in 2015, nearly half of the stores we photographed have already closed.

This book is arranged into five main chapters corresponding to the five boroughs of New York City: Manhattan, the Bronx, Brooklyn, Queens, and Staten Island. We have also loosely organized our photos by neighborhood within each borough, and every neighborhood included is briefly described at the start of each chapter. The location of each store front—cross streets and neighborhood—is captioned below the image, along with the year the photograph was taken. The boundaries of New York's neighborhoods are in flux, and sometimes disputed; we've relied upon Kenneth T. Jackson's *The Encyclopedia of New York City* to delineate the city's neighborhoods and map our work.

When selecting the photos for this publication, we knew we had to include store fronts that we photographed in the 2000s, some of which are no longer in business but are so fondly remembered, while also bringing in updated photos of older store fronts still in business, reflecting what their facades look like today. We also chose to include many previously unpublished photos of store fronts that continue to play vital roles in their neighborhoods.

Throughout all five boroughs there are numerous distinct regions. But the small stores that make up each area, contributing to the spirit and cultural diversity of the streets, have been threatened by economic pressures, the takeover by chain stores with their uniform branding, and rapidly changing demographics. The local store has always been a foothold for new immigrants, a comfortable place where familiar languages are spoken and traditional food is served. These shops are lifelines for their communities, vital to the residents who depend on them for a multitude of needs. When these shops fail, the neighborhood itself is affected.

We hope that our project acts as an artistic intervention to help draw attention to and preserve the small shops whose existence is essential to the distinctive, colorful atmosphere of the city's streets.

MANHATTAN

When most people envision New York, they think of Manhattan, the smallest in area of the city's five boroughs. Manhattan is a long finger-shaped island, surrounded by the Harlem River to the north and northeast, the East River to the east, the Upper New York Bay to the south, and the Hudson River to the west. It is the oldest and densest of all the boroughs and contains the city's most famous attractions, buildings, and cultural institutions.

Most of Manhattan is easy to navigate because of the well-executed grid plan of 1811 that imposed a kind of waffle-iron system of order on the streets north of Houston Street. Twelve major avenues, each 100 feet wide, run north and south through uptown and downtown, and most are numbered. Fifth Avenue divides the east side from the west side, with 1st Avenue all the way to the east and 12th Avenue all the way to the west. Broadway is an exception to the rule, as it is the only major avenue that doesn't run strictly vertical, but cuts a diagonal path across the island. Streets intersecting the avenues at right angles run east and west between the East River and the Hudson River and are numbered consecutively as they proceed uptown from Houston Street. The grid plan, however, does not apply to many neighborhoods south of 14th Street, including SoHo, TriBeCa, and Greenwich Village, which were constructed before engineers instituted the plan.

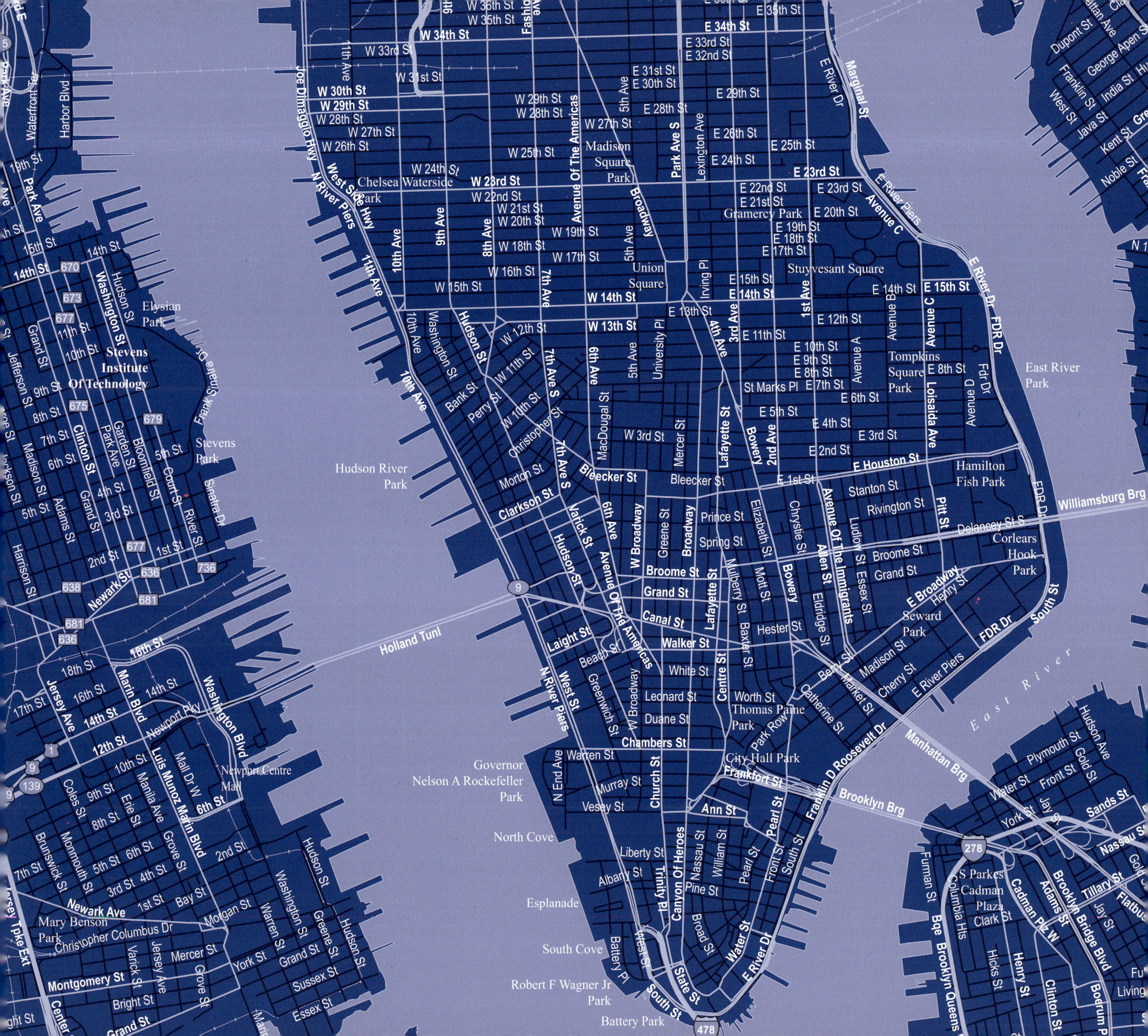

BELOW 14TH STREET

GREENWICH VILLAGE — EAST VILLAGE — SOHO — LOWER EAST SIDE (including NOLITA, LITTLE ITALY, CHINATOWN) — TRIBECA

The area of Manhattan bounded to the north by 14th Street, to the east by the East River, to the south by New York Harbor, and to the west by the Hudson River, is commonly known as "downtown." At one point in time, this southern tip of Manhattan *was* New York, as everything north of 14th Street was farmland and wilderness. Downtown encompasses many diverse neighborhoods.

Greenwich Village is bounded to the north by 14th Street, to the east by 4th Avenue and the Bowery, to the south by West Houston Street, and to the west by the Hudson River. By the late 1930s it was known as a bohemian enclave, and during the 1950s it became a center for the Beat Generation. Despite widespread gentrification and escalating real estate values, Greenwich Village—which is historically known for embracing the artistic and unconventional—still retains some of its countercultural vibe.

The **East Village** is bounded to the north by 14th Street, to the east by Avenue D, to the south by East Houston Street, and to the west by the Bowery and 3rd Avenue. Starting in the 1830s, large numbers of German immigrants moved into the area. But, when the wealthiest families left in the early 1900s and moved uptown to Yorkville, Eastern European Jewish immigrants from the overcrowded tenements of the Lower East Side moved in. In the 1960s, the area changed radically when intellectuals and artists who were being priced out of Greenwich Village began moving east. In the 1970s, drugs brought about a general decline, and a massive abandonment of housing resulted. The area's Spanish-speaking population increased throughout the 1980s, and by the '90s, it had become home to the largest community of Ukrainians outside Ukraine. Today, the East Village is a thriving, diverse neighborhood.

SoHo, an area whose name is an abbreviation for "South of Houston," is bounded to the north by Houston Street, to the east by Crosby Street, to the south by Canal Street, and to the west by 6th Avenue. In the mid-1800s it became known for its factories, warehouses, and large retail businesses, a number of whose buildings were constructed from cast iron with elaborate ornamentation. However, the neighborhood suffered economically in the early 1900s, after many businesses moved uptown to 5th Avenue. Between 1960 and 1970, artists seeking low rents and large spaces for their studios and living quarters transformed SoHo by converting the empty warehouses and manufacturing spaces. During the 1980s, the area became one of the city's trendiest neighborhoods, and many of the artists who had reclaimed it were no longer able to afford the increasing rents brought about by gentrification.

The **Lower East Side** is a large region of lower Manhattan bounded to the north by East Houston Street, to the east by the East River, to the south by Fulton and Franklin Streets, and to the west by Pearl Street and Broadway. Within its boundaries are the neighborhoods of **NoLIta** (known as such due to its geographical location "North of Little Italy"), **Little Italy**, and **Chinatown**. The Lower East Side has a multi-ethnic history as the first home for many immigrants seeking a better life for their families in the United States: initially it was the Irish and the Germans, followed by the Italians and Eastern European Jews, and finally various Latino and Asian immigrants.

TriBeCa, which stands for "Triangle Below Canal Street," occupies a trapezoidal region bounded to the north by Canal Street, to the east by Broadway, to the south by Murray Street, and to the west by the Hudson River. The area, which once contained a fruit and produce market as well as warehouses for the dry goods, textile, and mercantile industries, has since transformed into one of the city's most fashionable residential neighborhoods, lined with shops, restaurants, and bars. It is largely made up of former industrial buildings that have been transformed into high-end lofts and apartments.

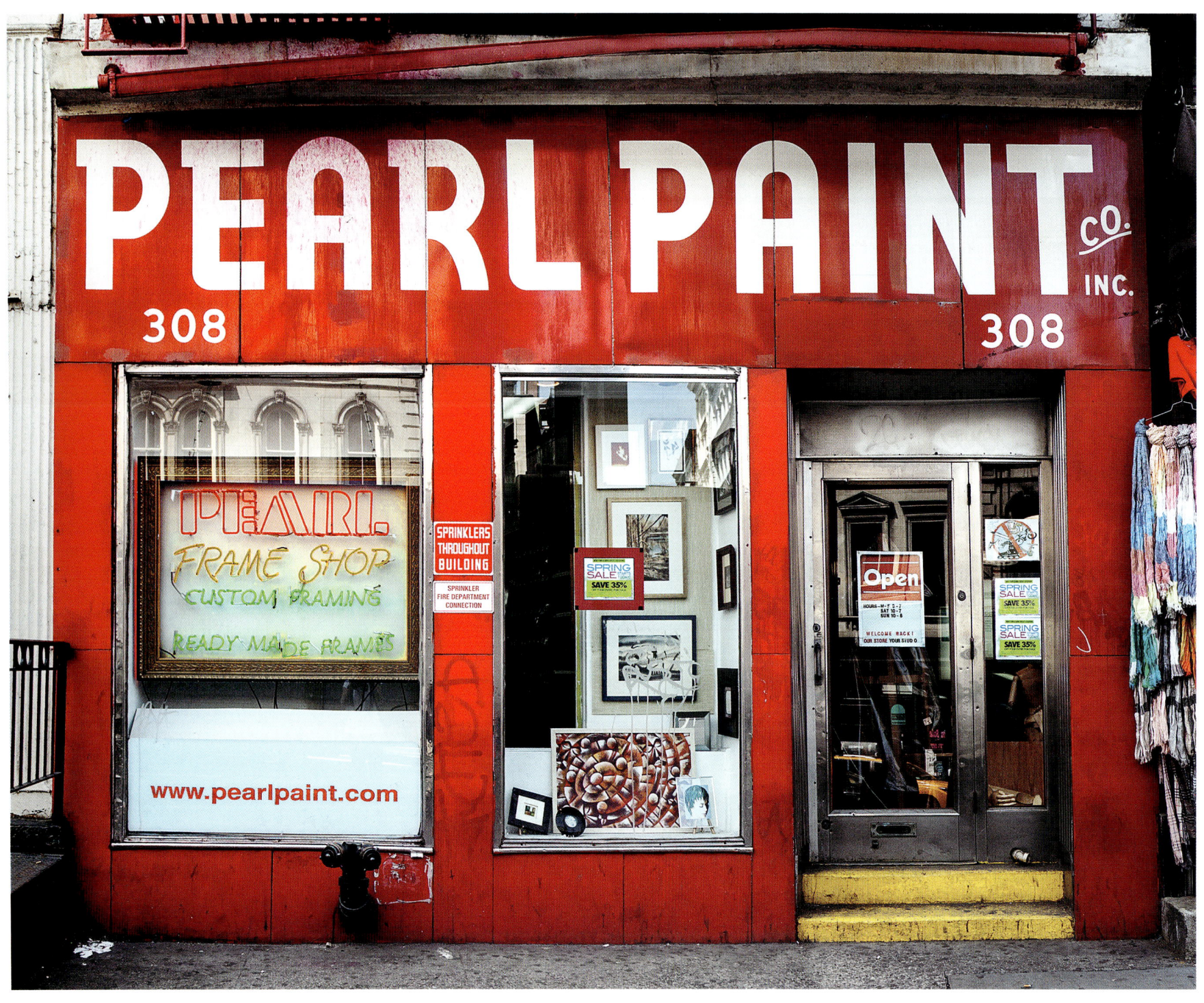

12 PEARL PAINT
Canal Street at Mercer Street, TriBeCa, 2014

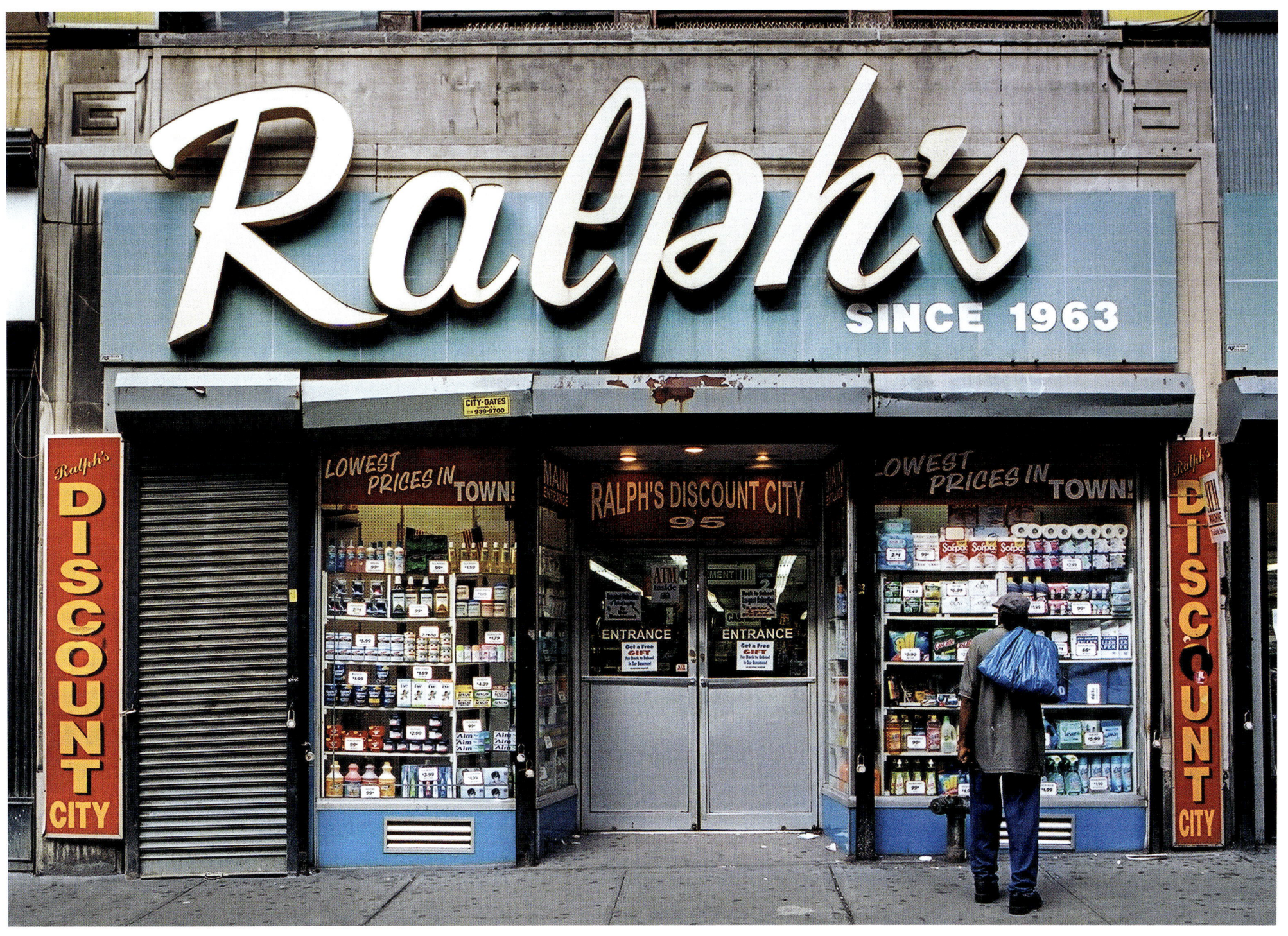

13 RALPH'S DISCOUNT CITY
Chambers Street near Church Street, TriBeCa, 2004

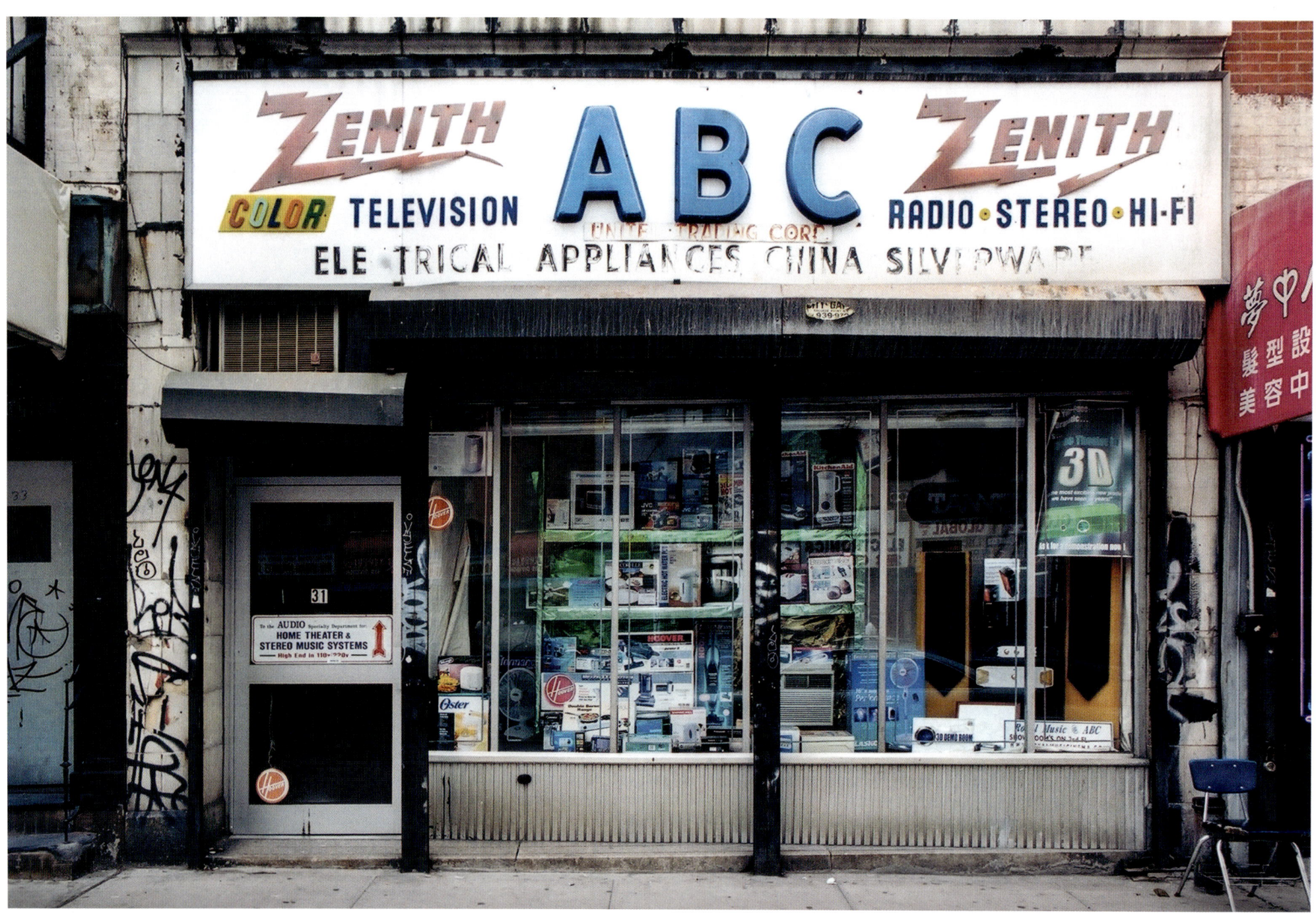

14 ABC TV
Canal Street near Essex Street, Lower East Side, 2004

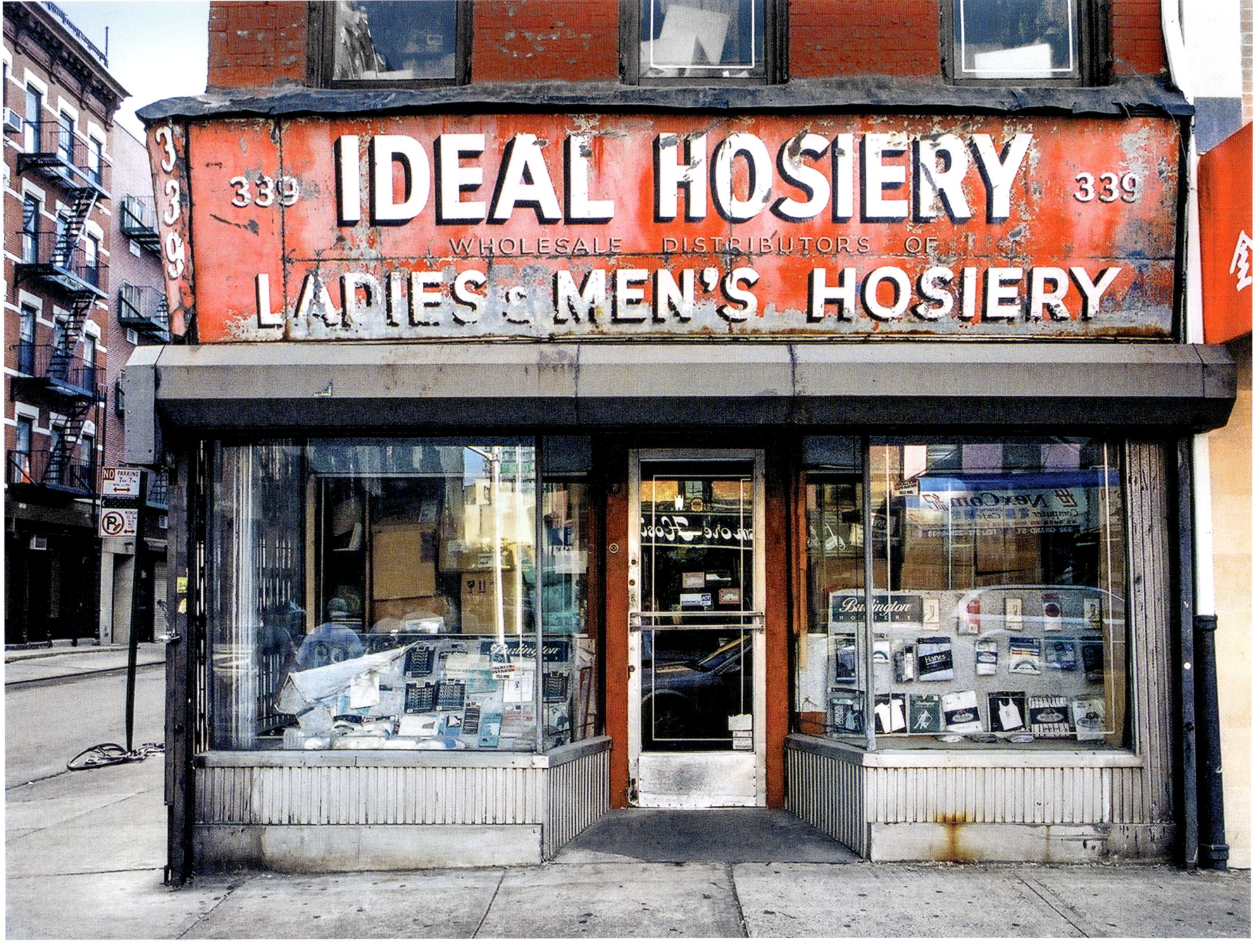

IDEAL HOSIERY
Grand Street at Ludlow Street, Lower East Side, 2004

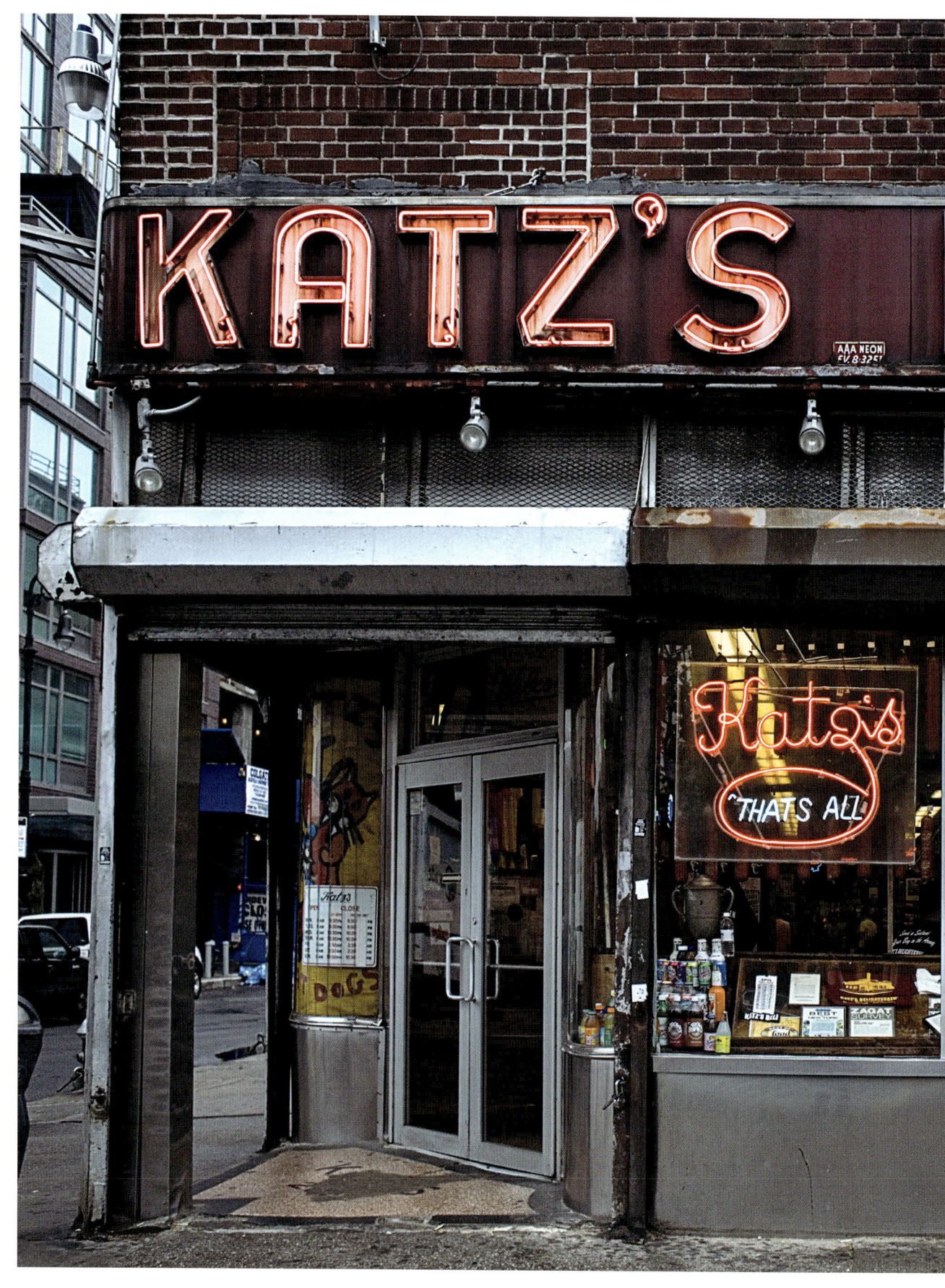

KATZ'S DELICATESSEN
East Houston Street at Ludlow Street, Lower East Side, 2008

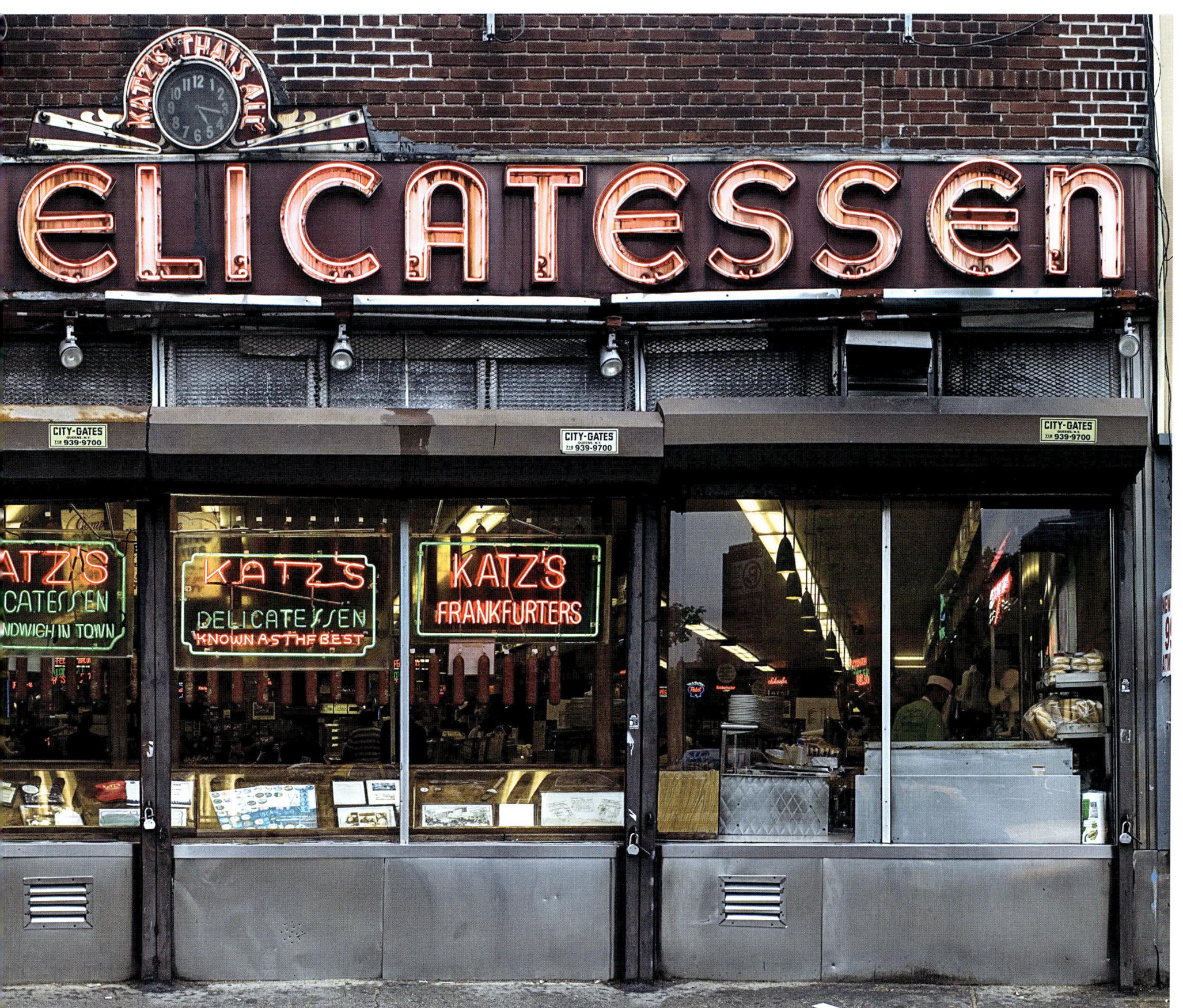

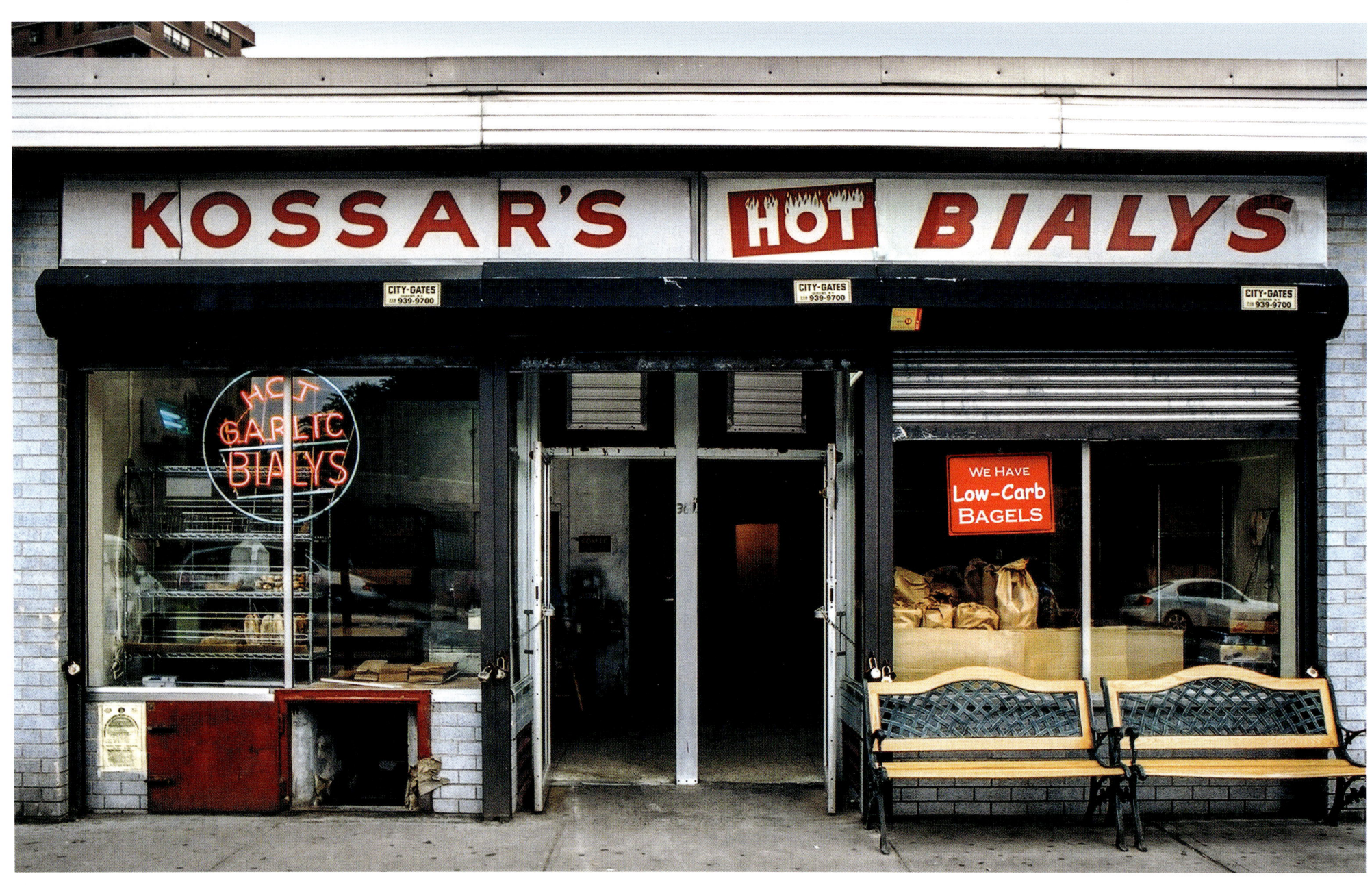

KOSSAR'S BAGELS & BIALYS
Grand Street near Norfolk Street, Lower East Side, 2005

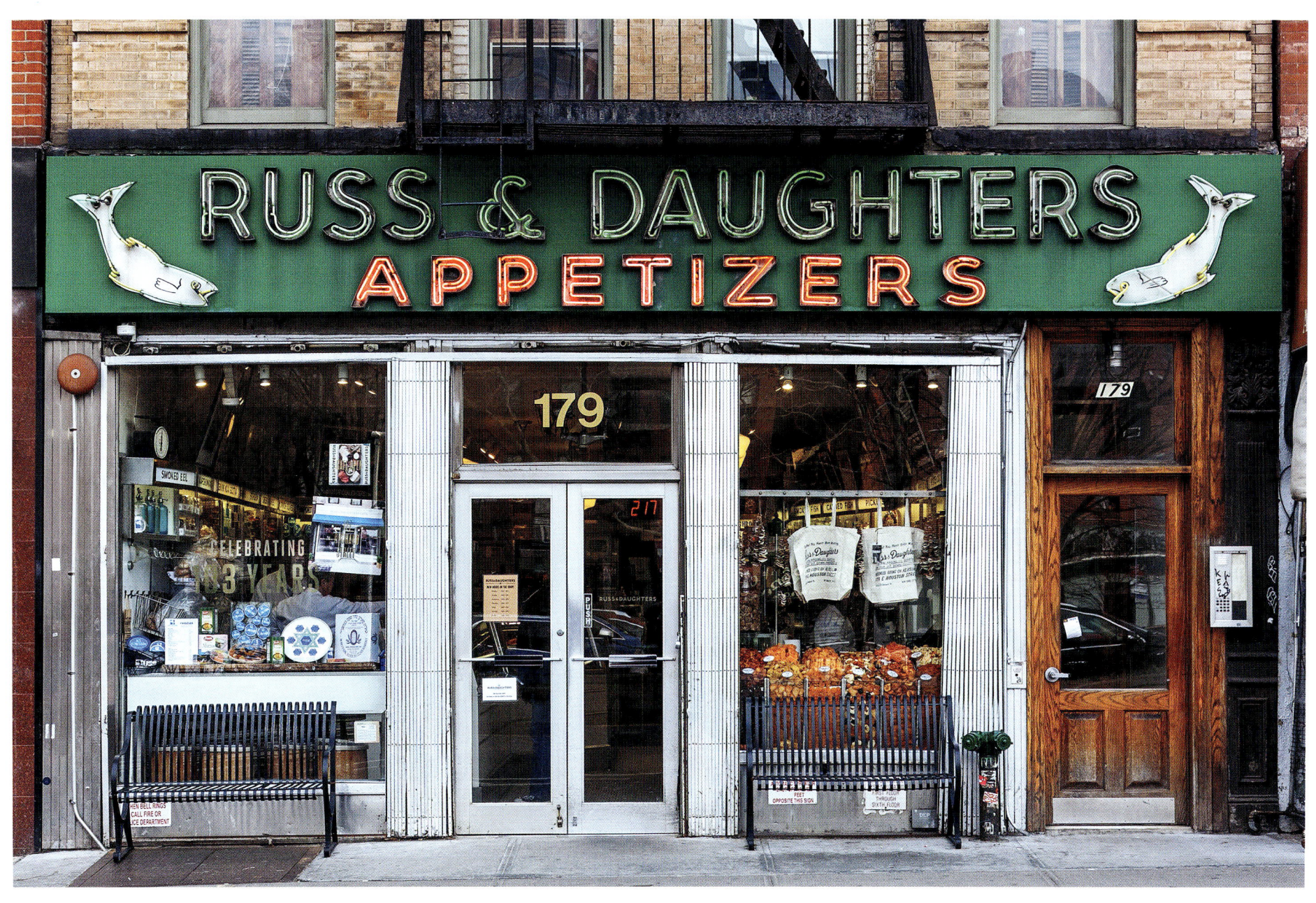

RUSS & DAUGHTERS
East Houston Street near Orchard Street, Lower East Side, 2018

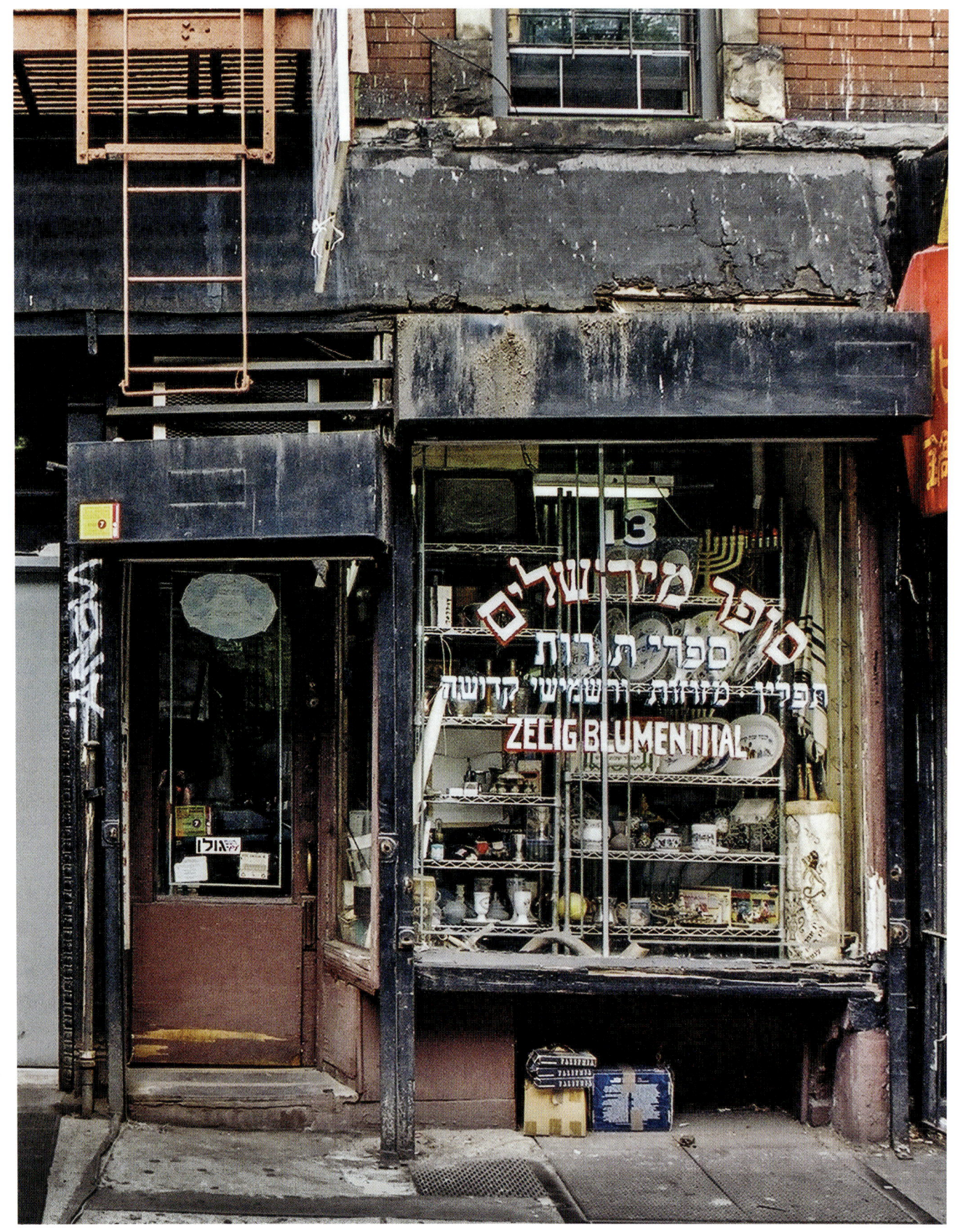

ZELIG BLUMENTHAL
Essex Street near Hester Street,
Lower East Side, 2004

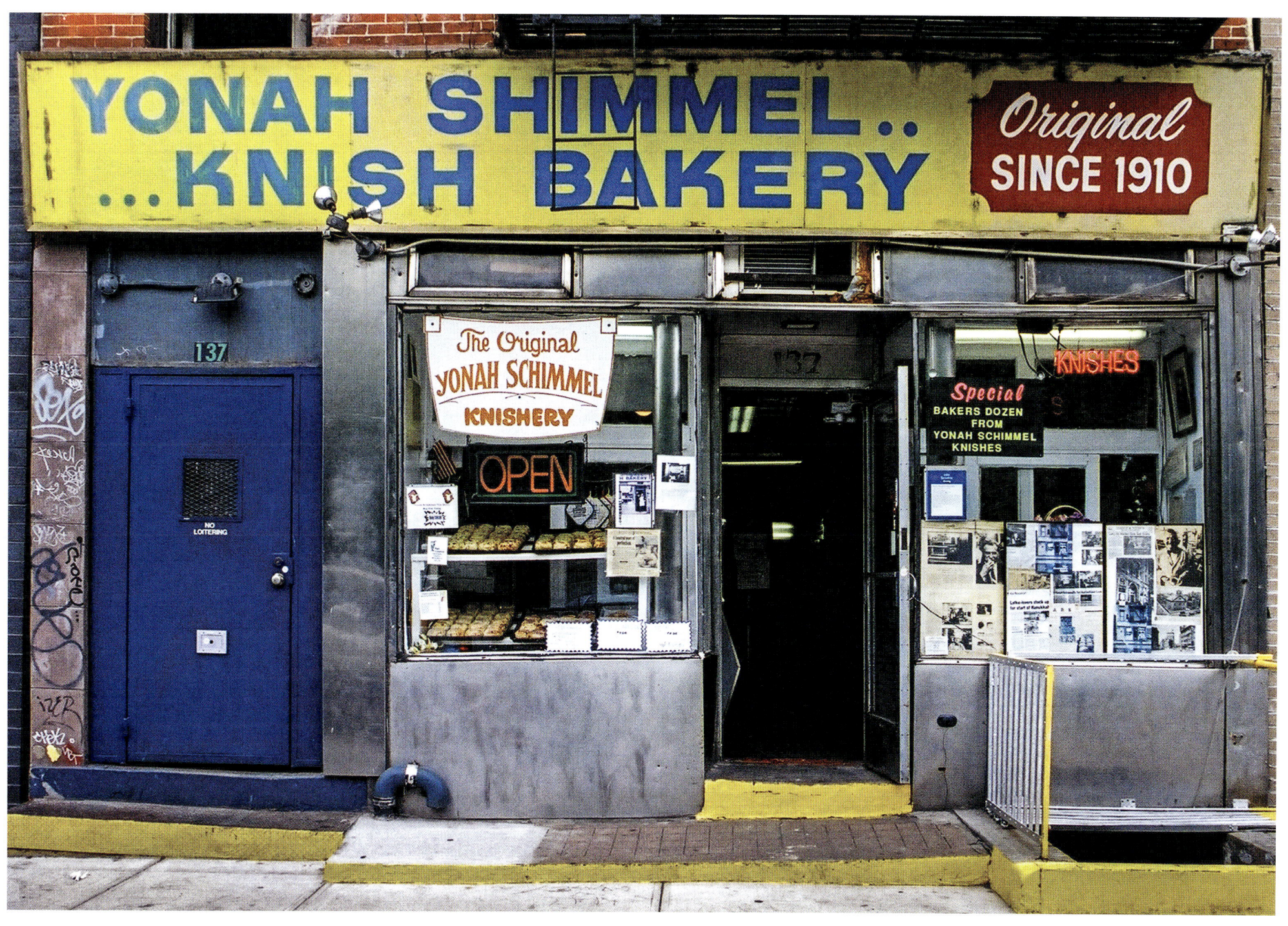

YONAH SCHIMMEL KNISH BAKERY
East Houston Street near Forsyth Street, Lower East Side, 2004

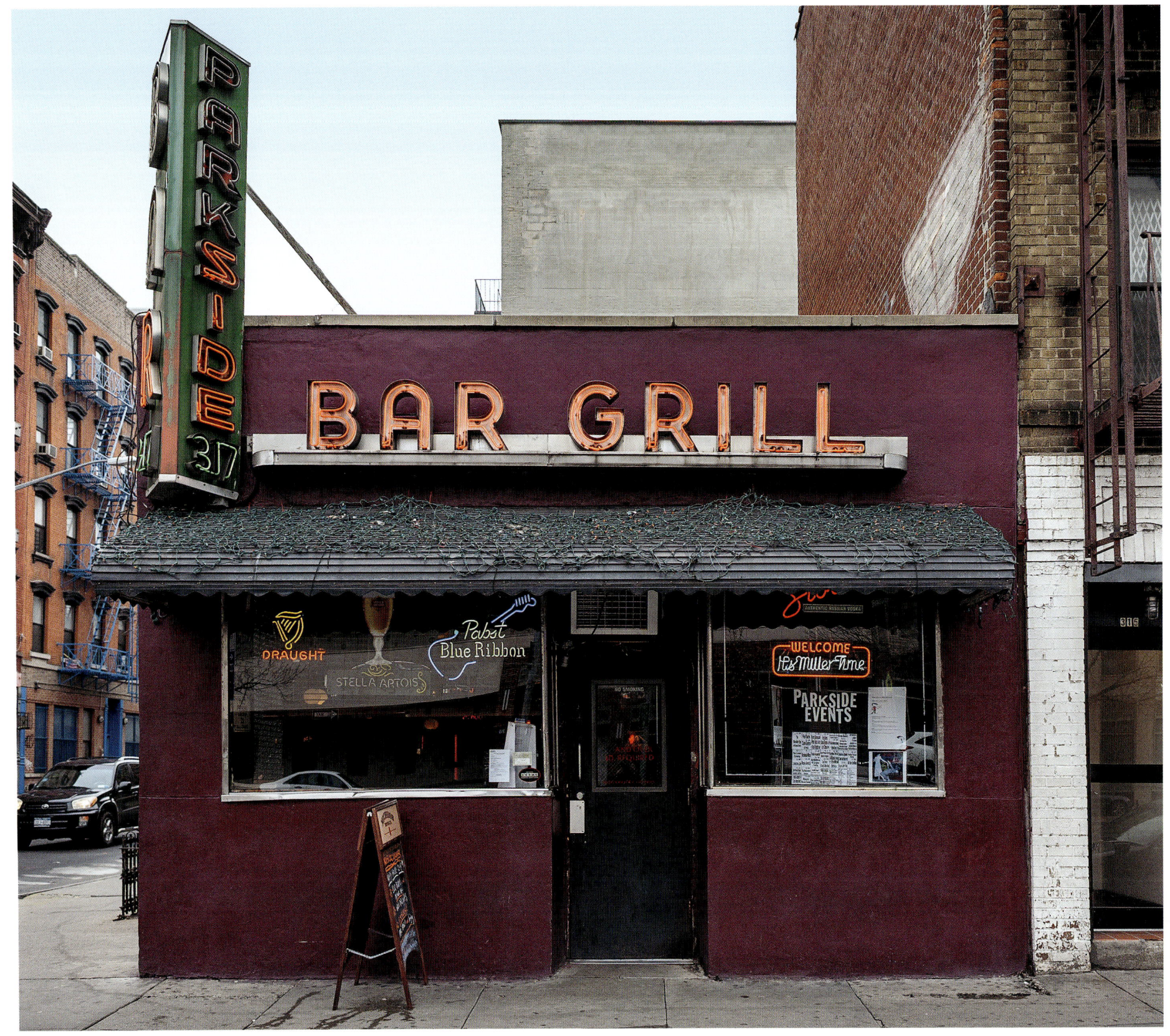

PARKSIDE LOUNGE
East Houston Street at Attorney Street, Lower East Side, 2009

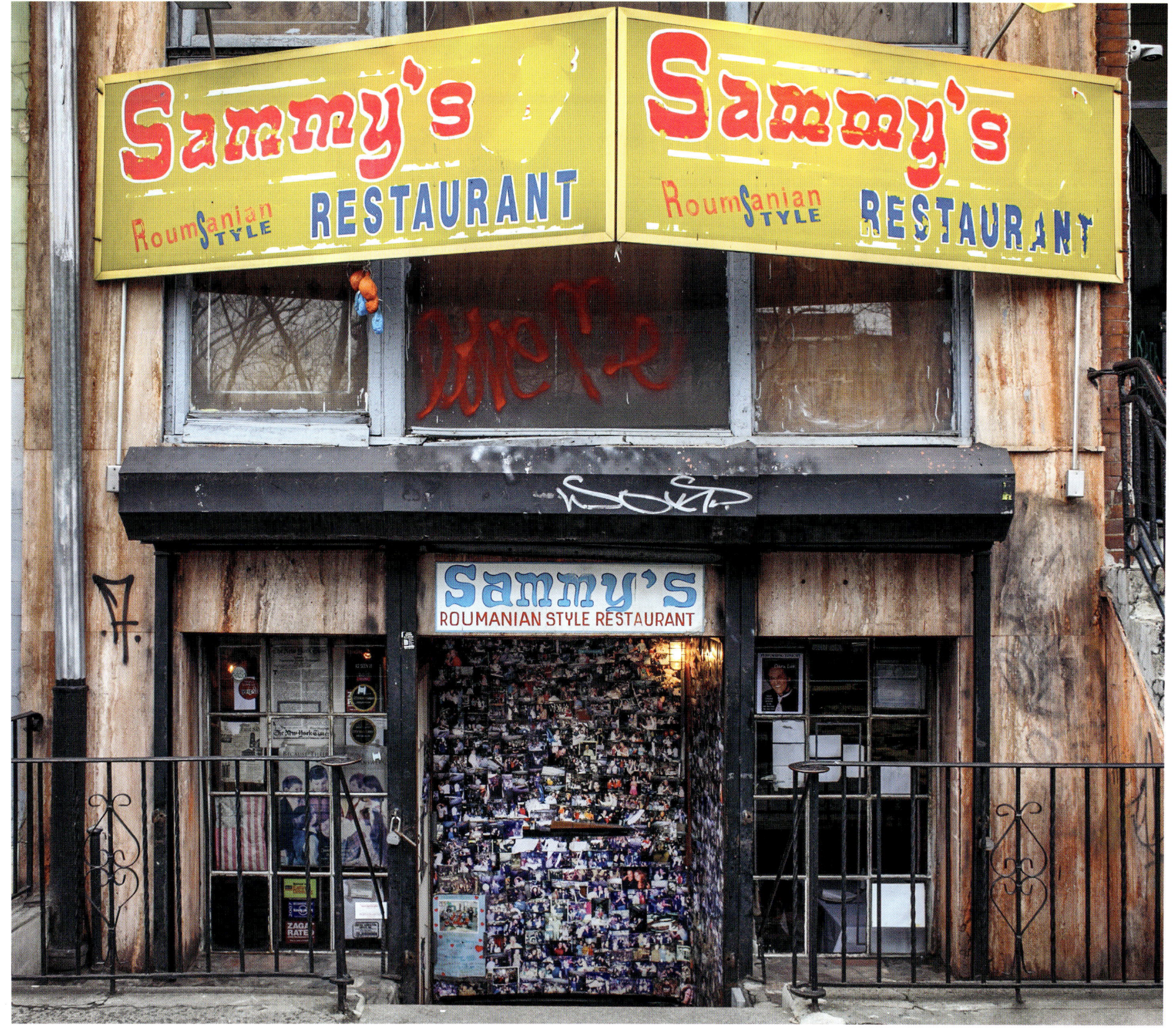

SAMMY'S ROUMANIAN STEAKHOUSE
Chrystie Street near Delancey Street, Lower East Side, 2010

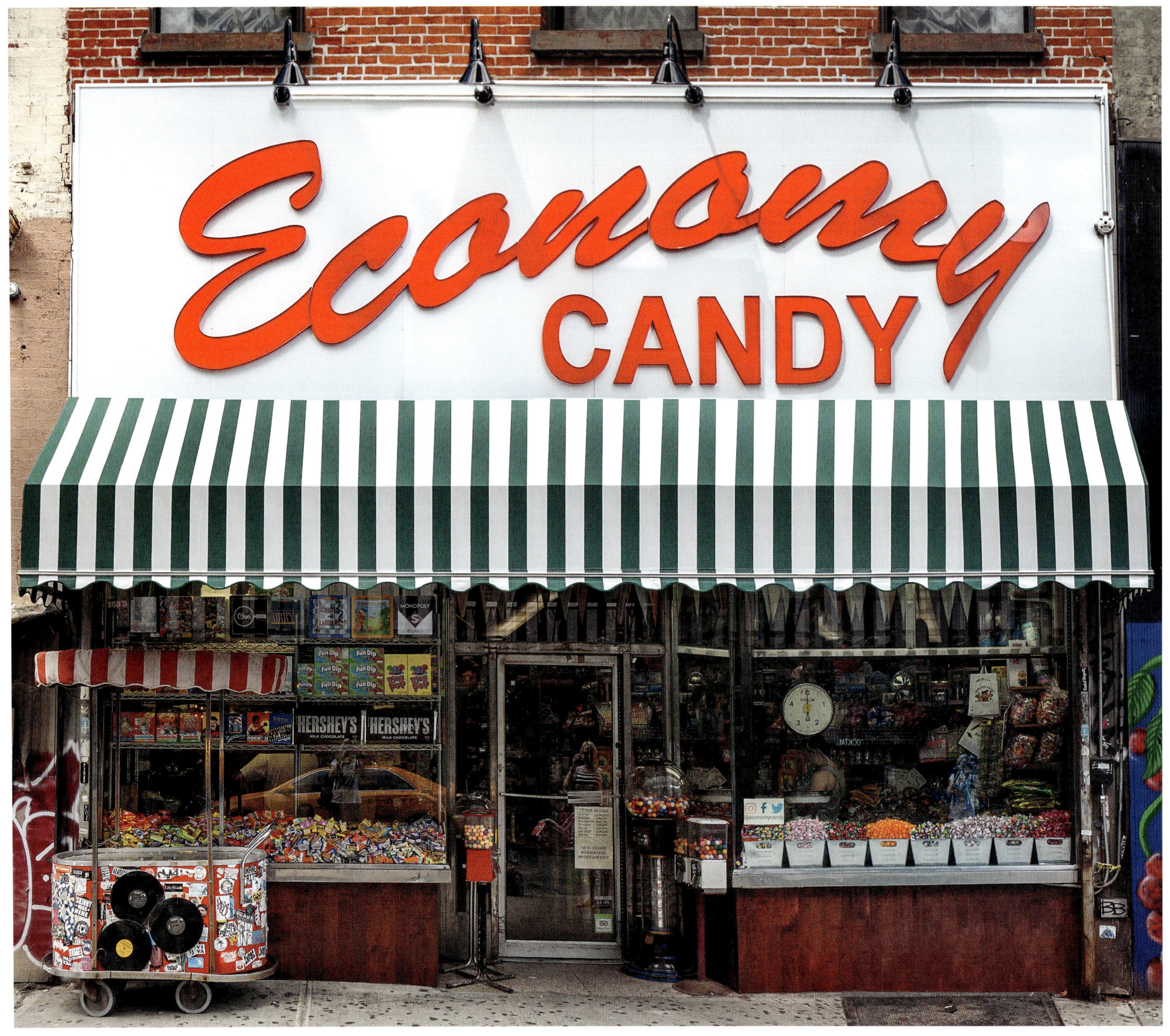

ECONOMY CANDY
Rivington Street near Essex Street, Lower East Side, 2017

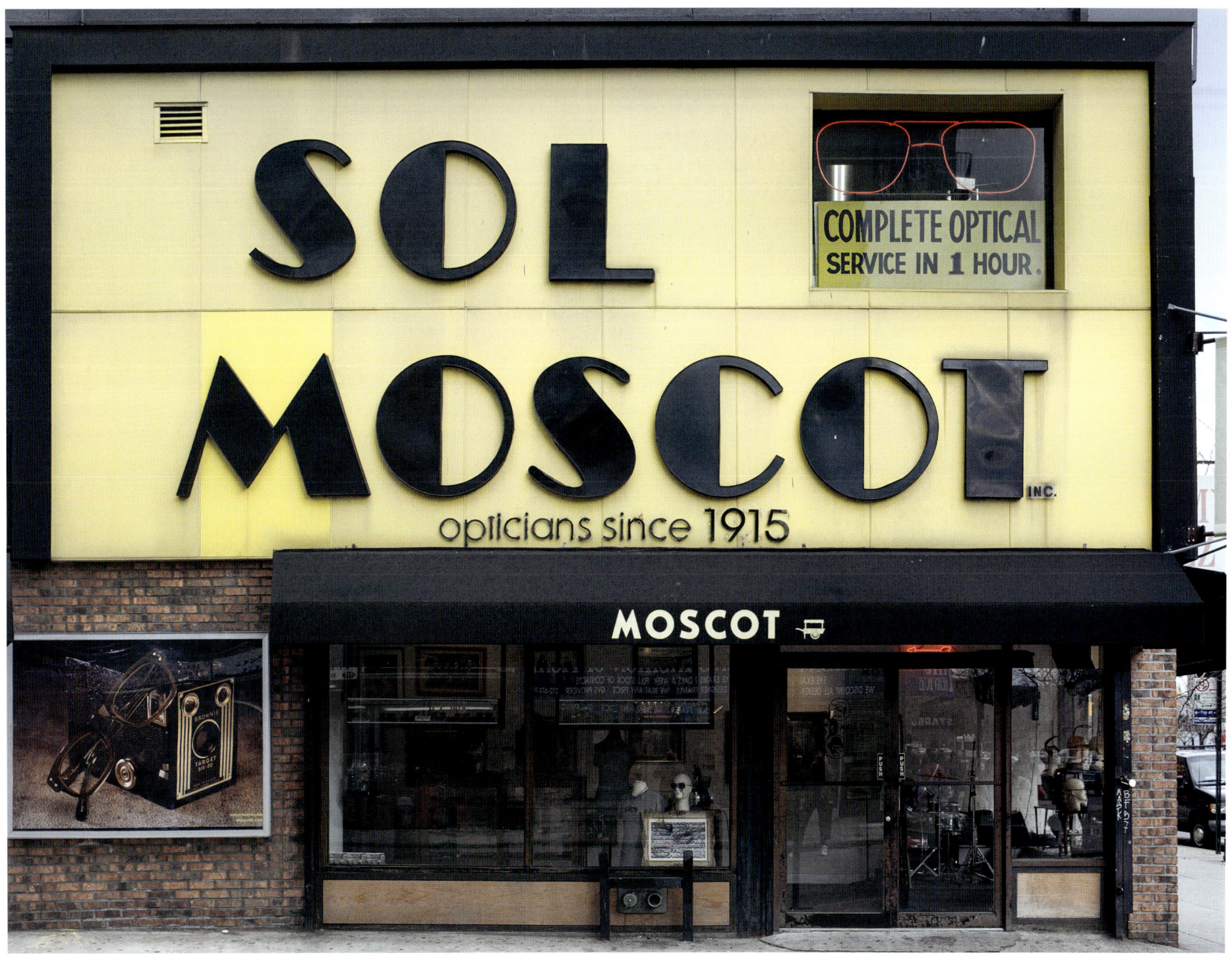

SOL MOSCOT
Orchard Street at Delancey Street, Lower East Side, 2011

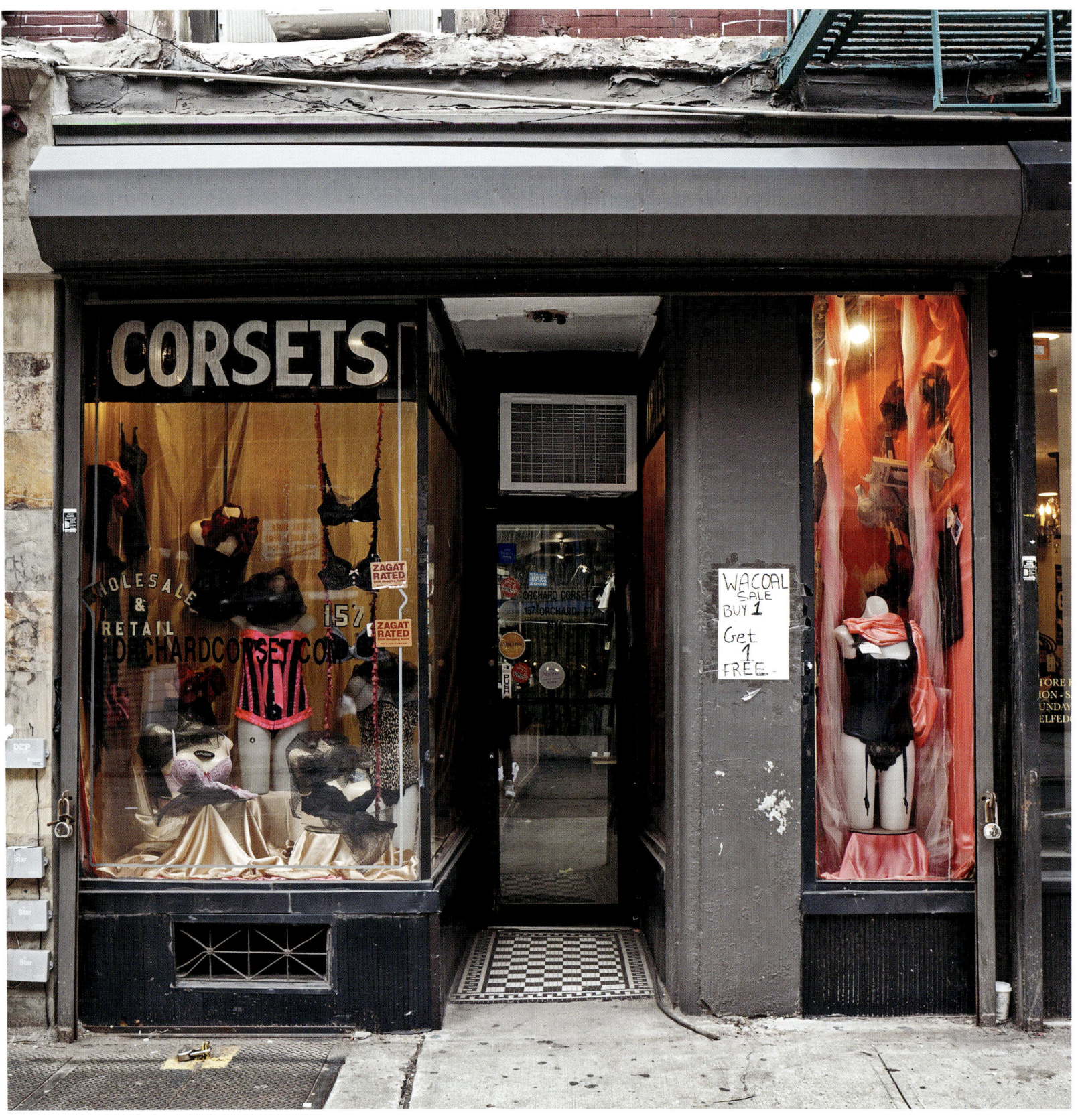

26 ORCHARD CORSETS
Orchard Street near Rivington Street, Lower East Side, 2011

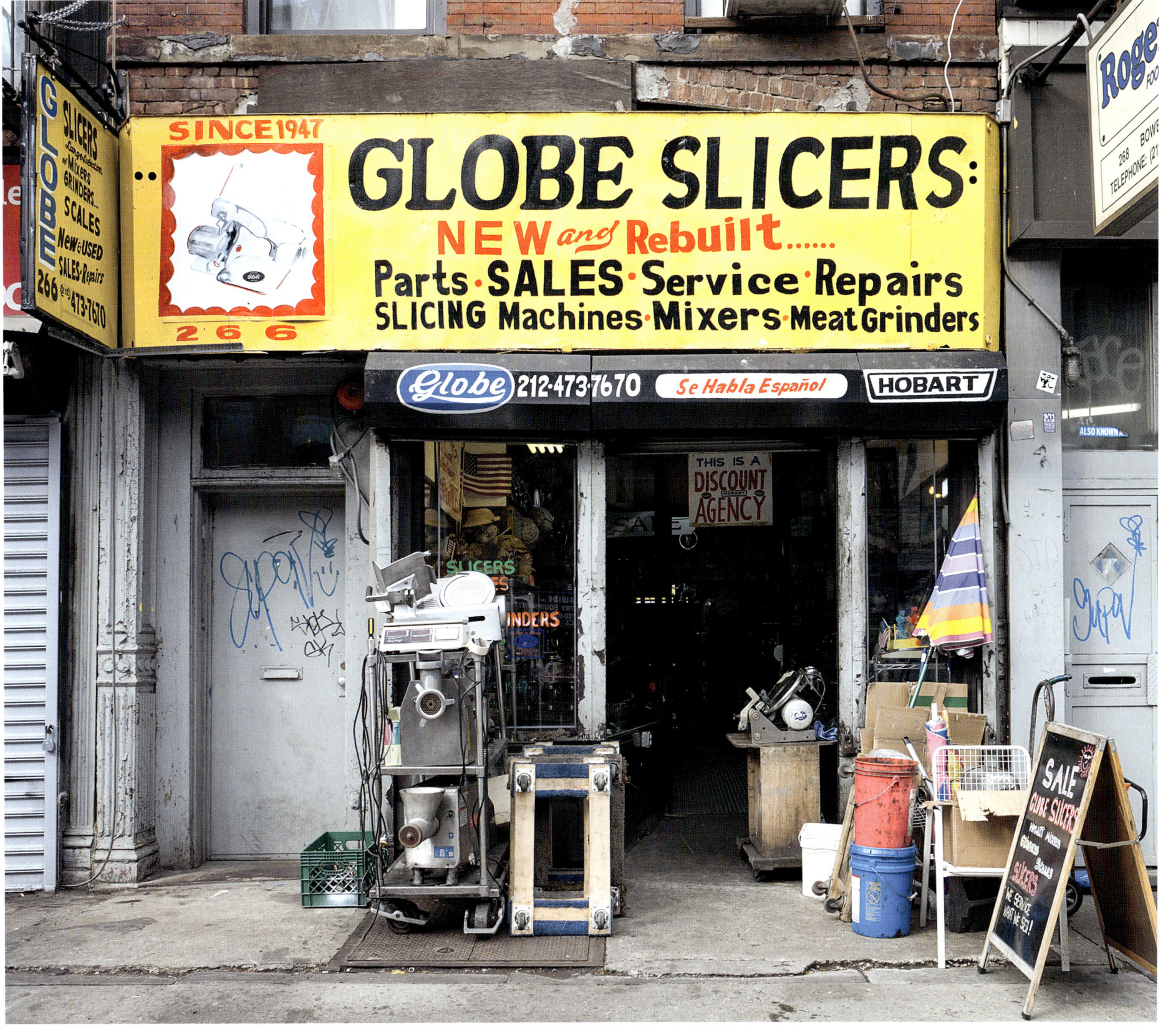

GLOBE SLICERS
Bowery near East Houston Street, Lower East Side, 2010

MANHATTAN

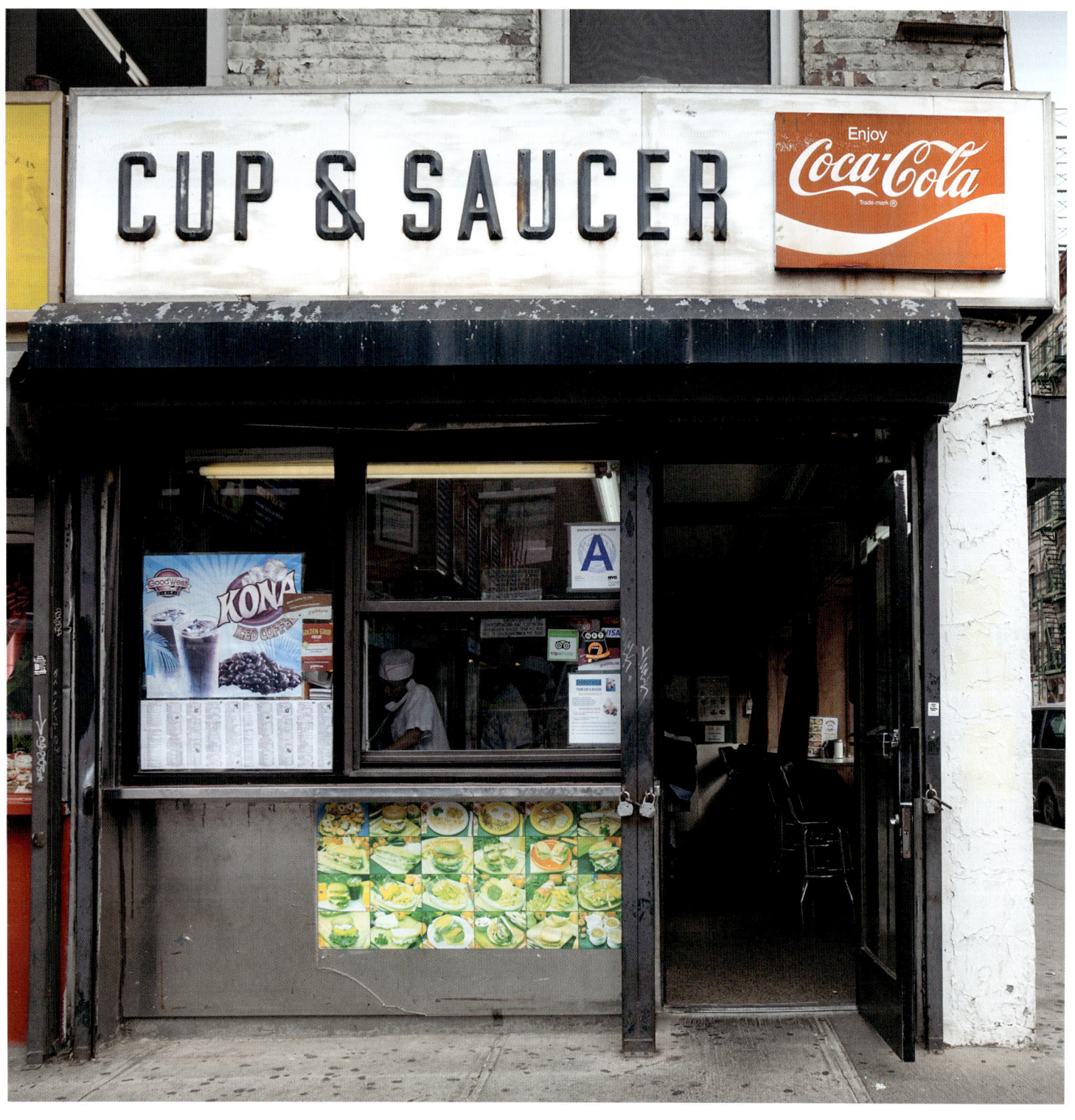

CUP & SAUCER
Canal Street at Eldridge Street, Lower East Side, 2012

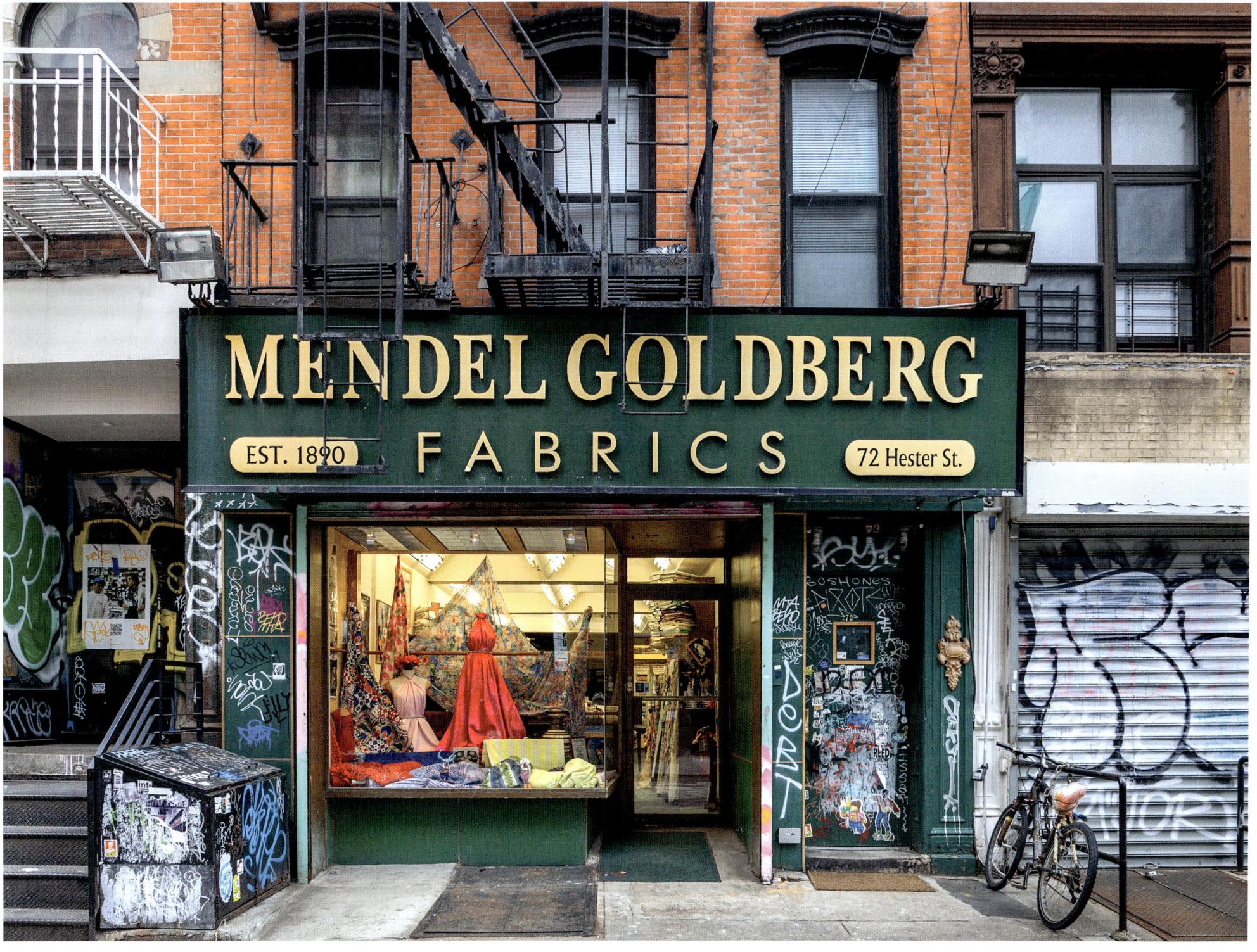

MENDEL GOLDBERG FABRICS
Hester Street near Allen Street, Lower East Side, 2018

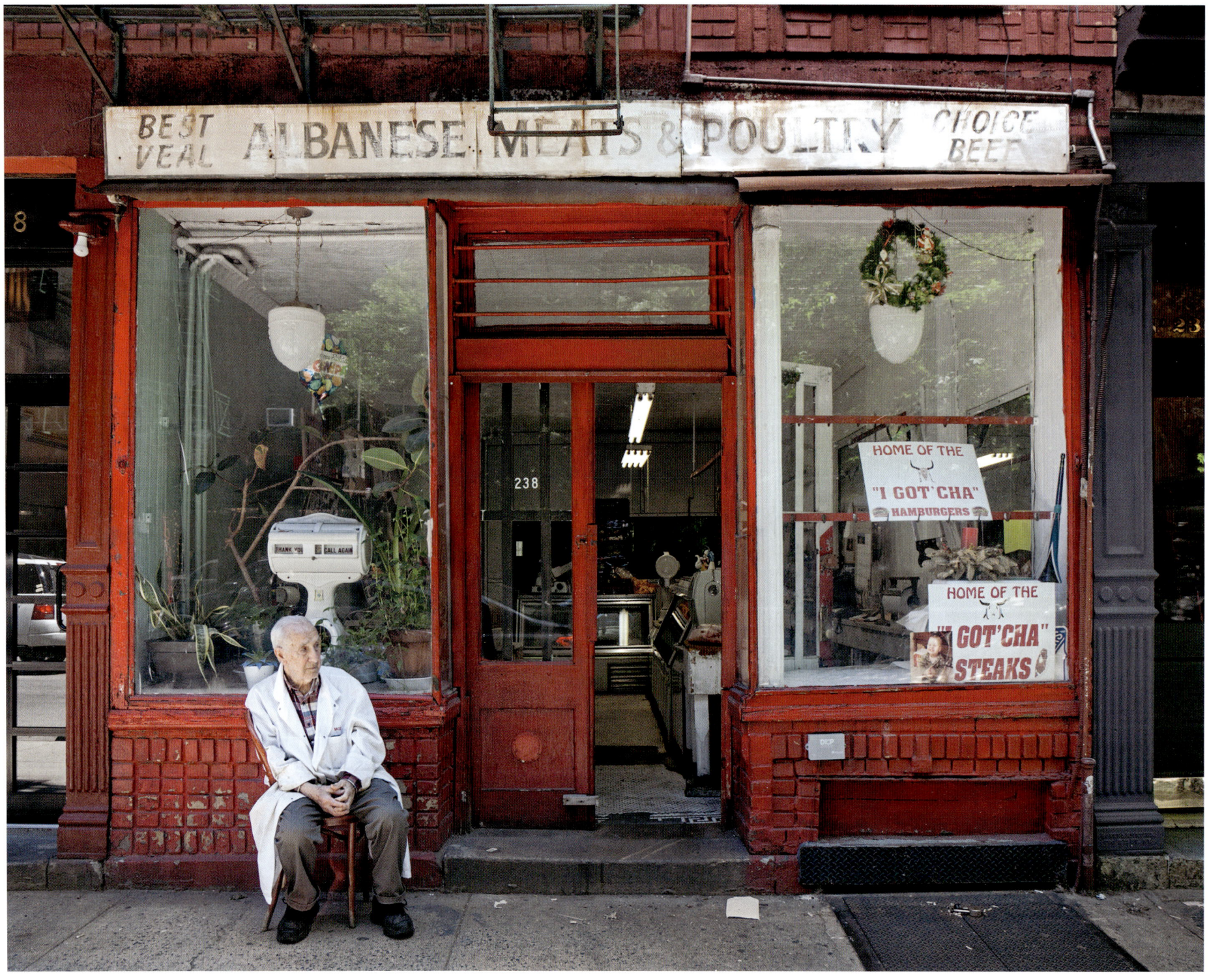

ALBANESE MEATS & POULTRY
Elizabeth Street near Prince Street, NoLIta, 2017

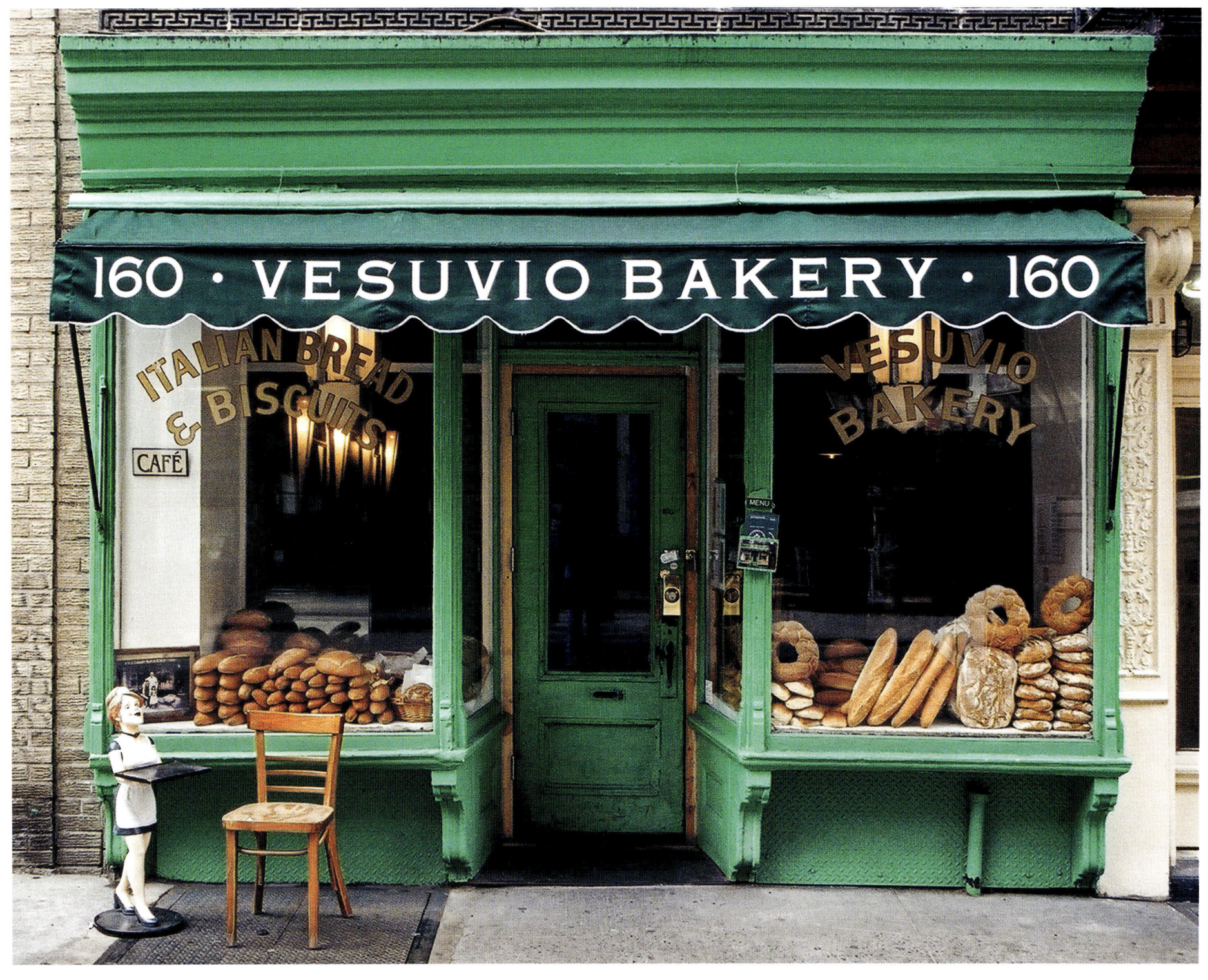

VESUVIO BAKERY
Prince Street near Thompson Street, SoHo, 2004

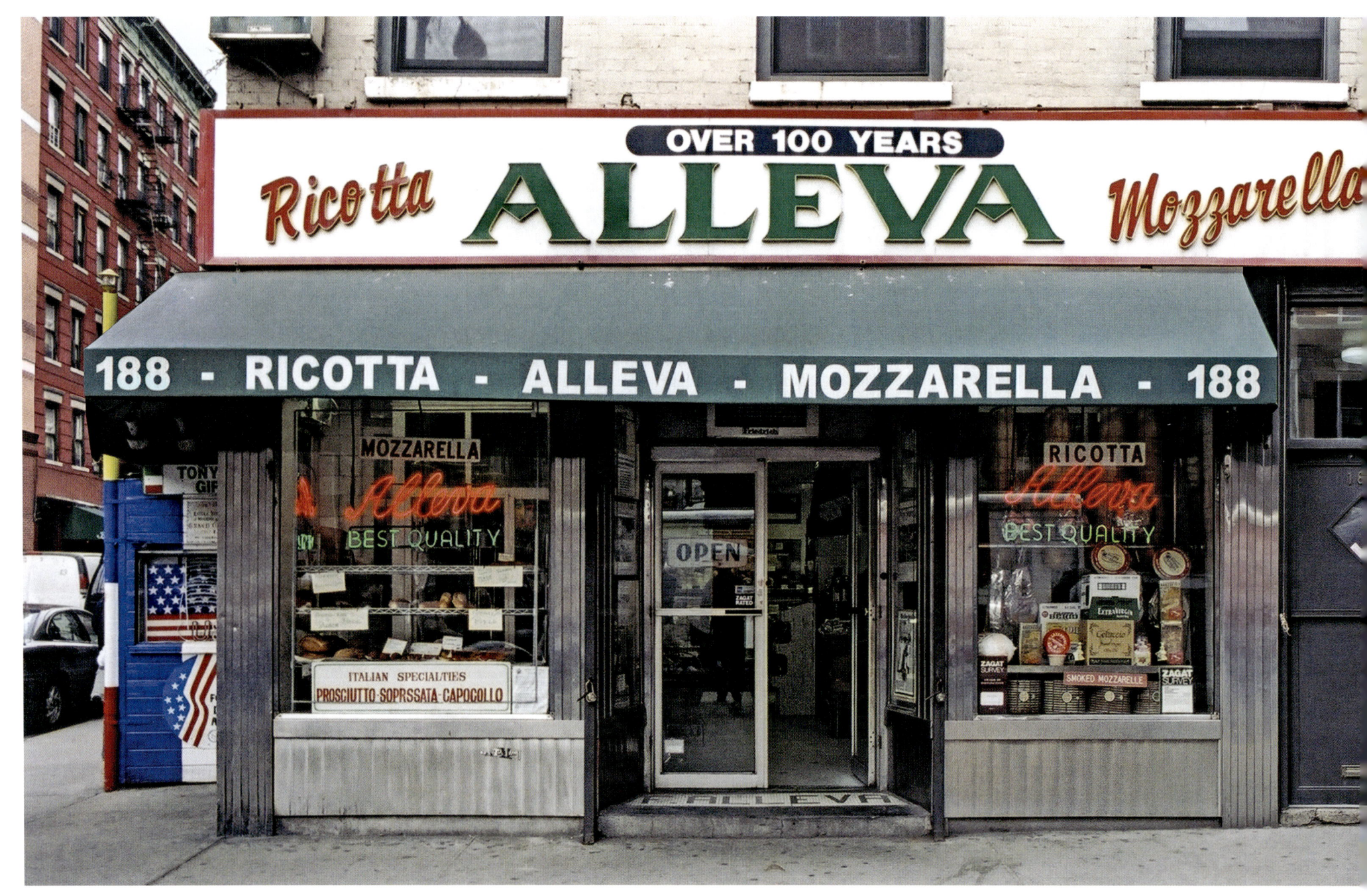

32 ALLEVA DAIRY AND PIEMONTE RAVIOLI
Grand Street at Mulberry Street, Little Italy, 2005

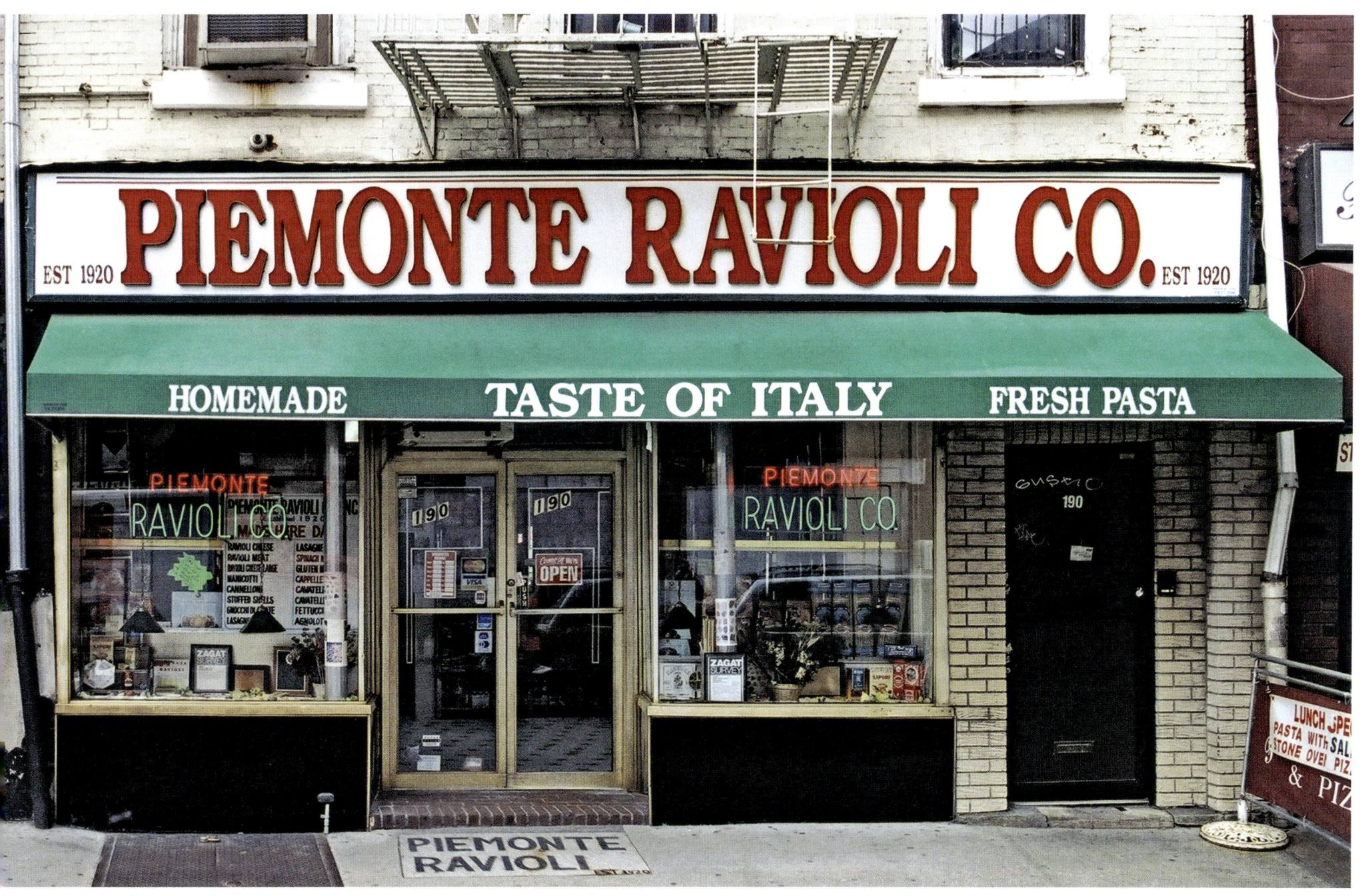

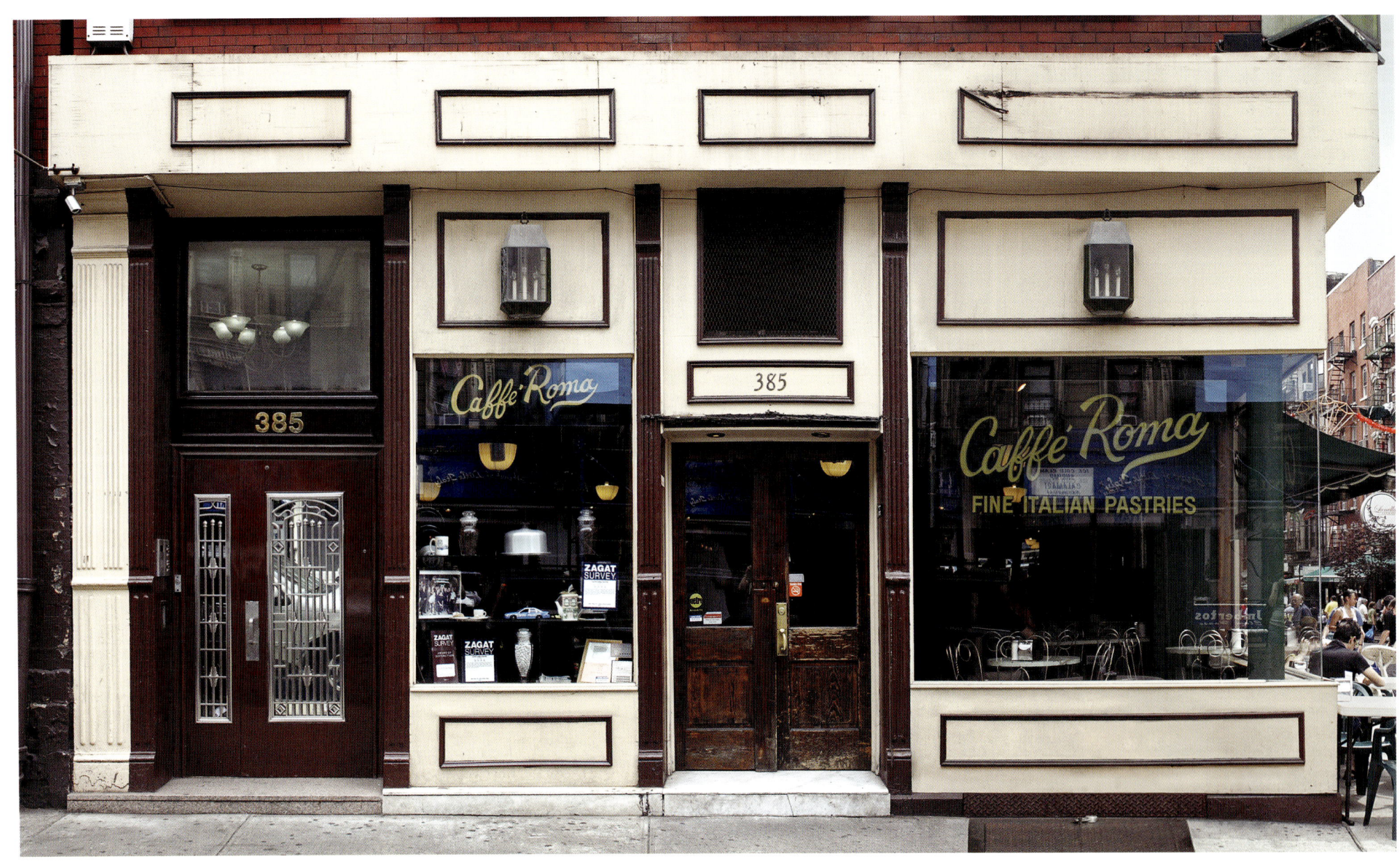

34 CAFFÉ ROMA
Broome Street at Mulberry Street, Little Italy, 2010

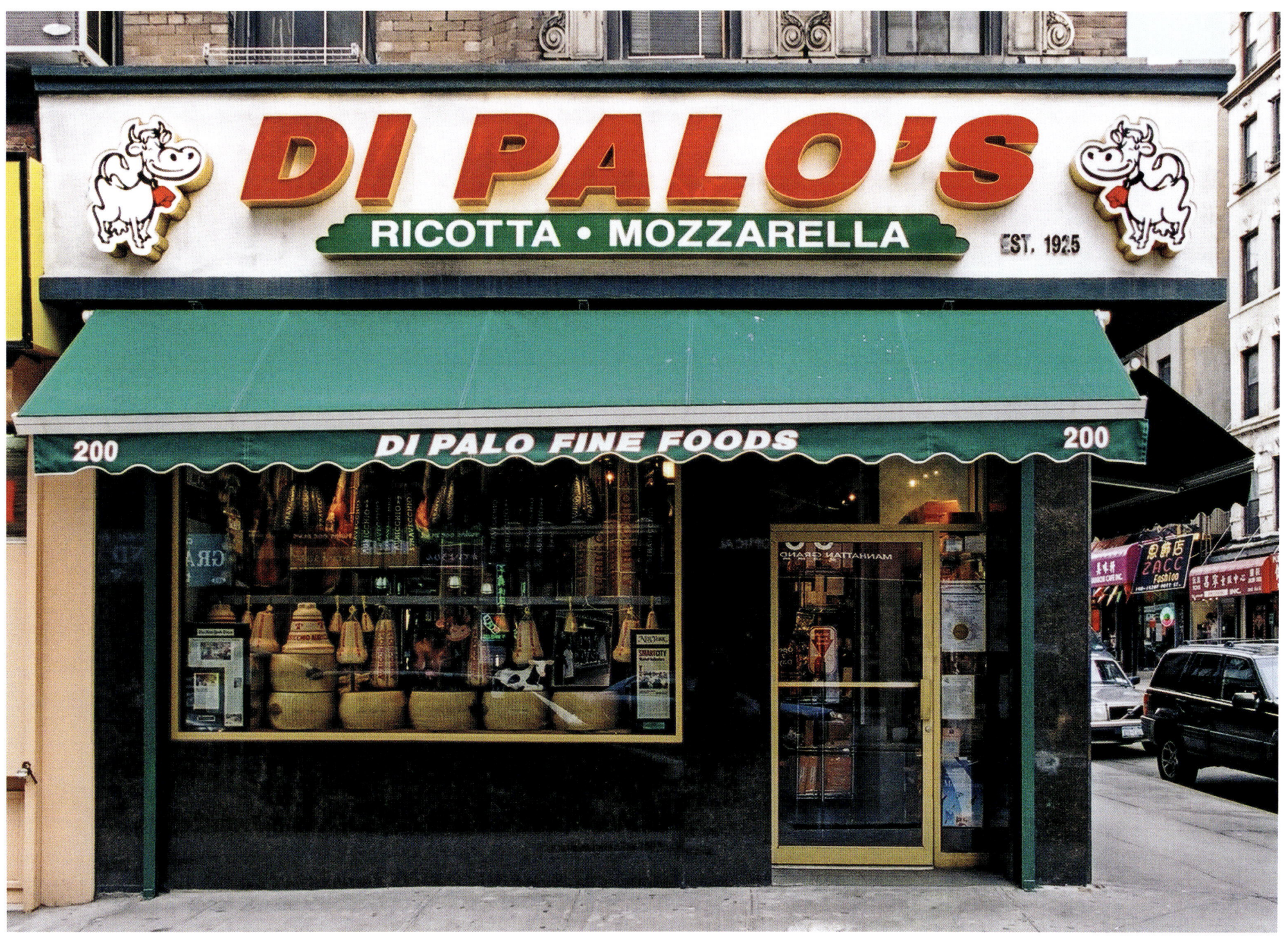

DI PALO'S FINE FOODS
Grand Street at Mott Street, Little Italy, 2005

MANHATTAN

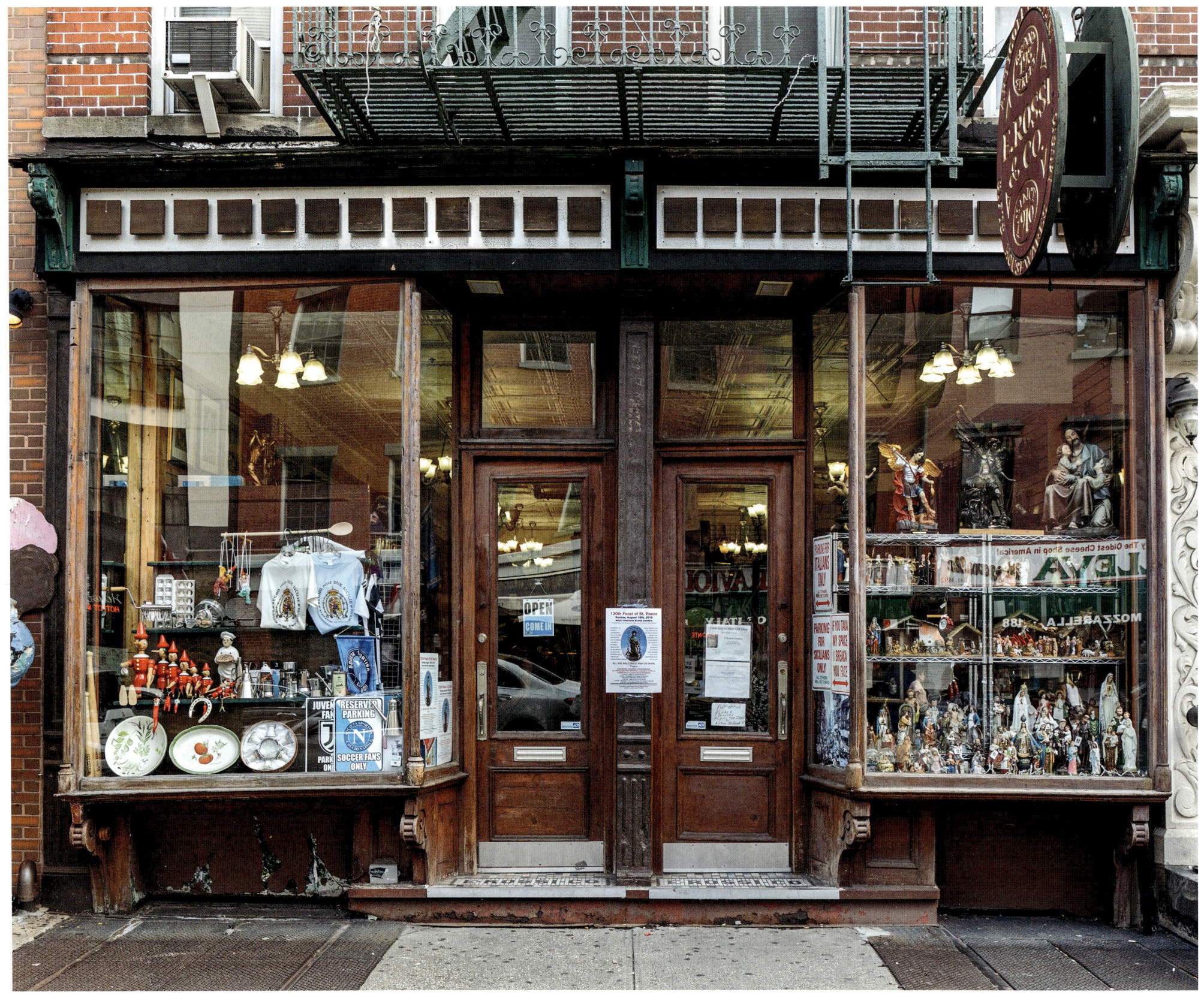

E. ROSSI & COMPANY
Grand Street near Mulberry Street, Little Italy, 2019

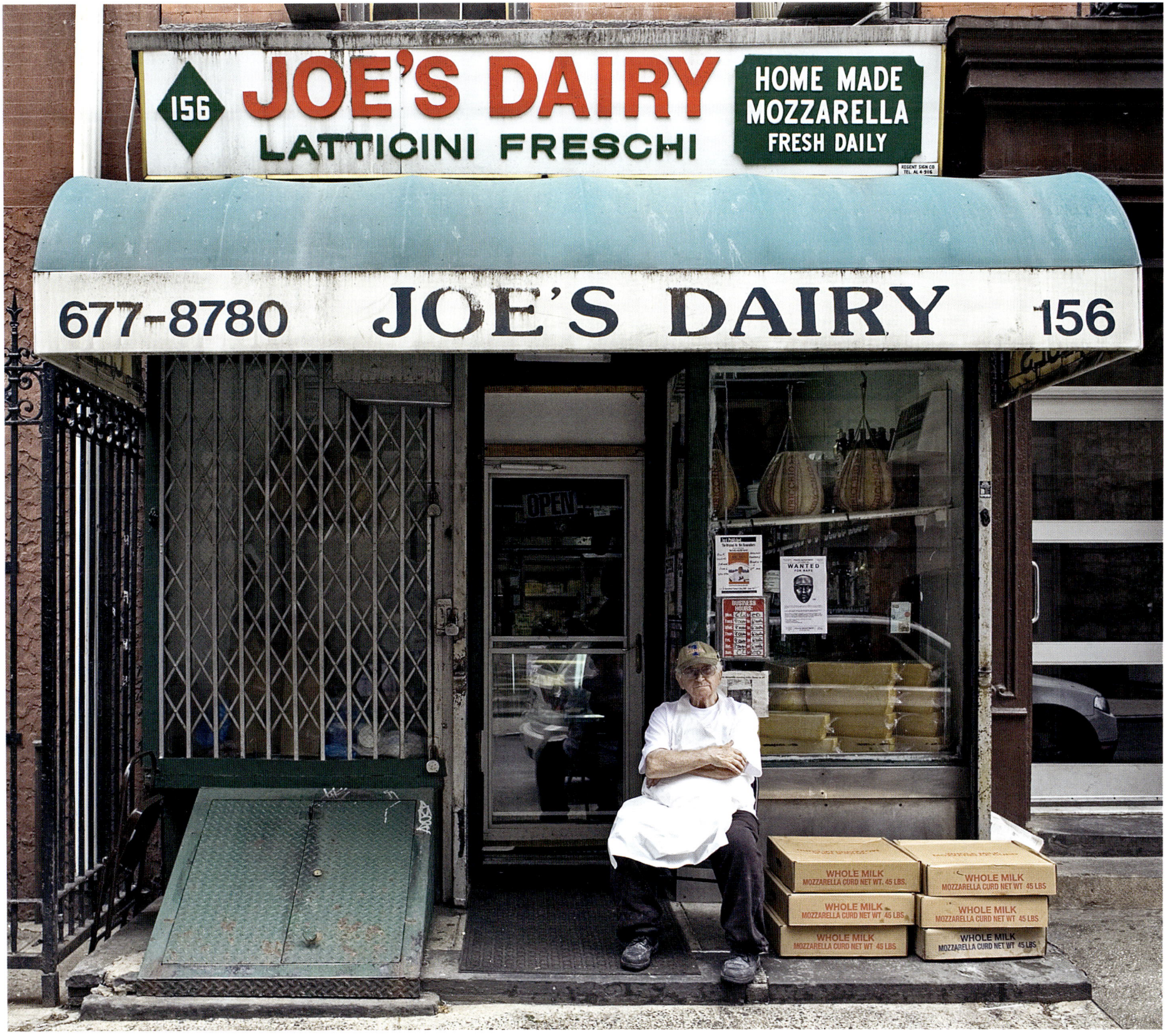

JOE'S DAIRY
Sullivan Street near West Houston Street, SoHo, 2008

MANHATTAN

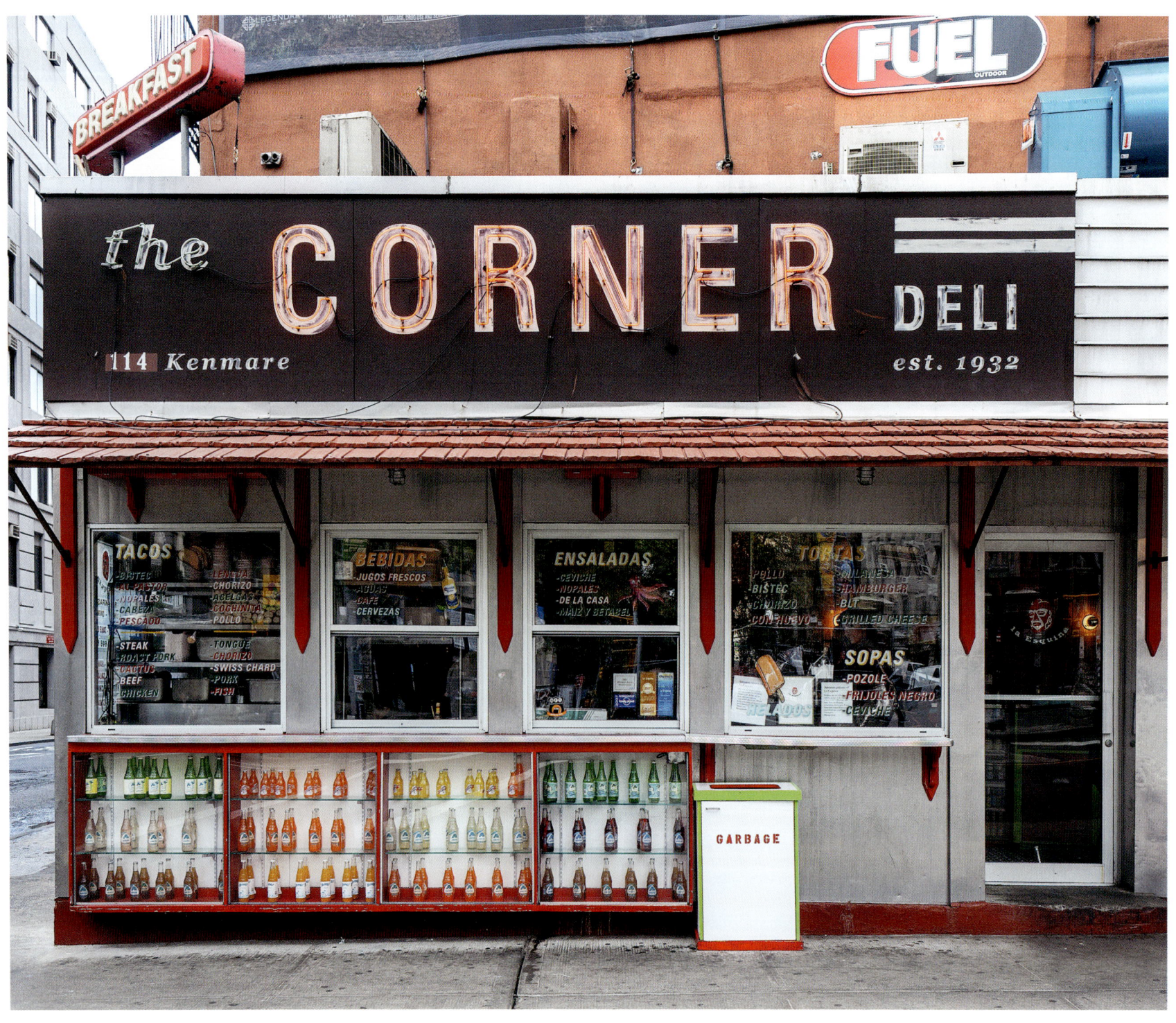

38 LA ESQUINA
Kenmare Street at Lafayette Street, NoLIta, 2010

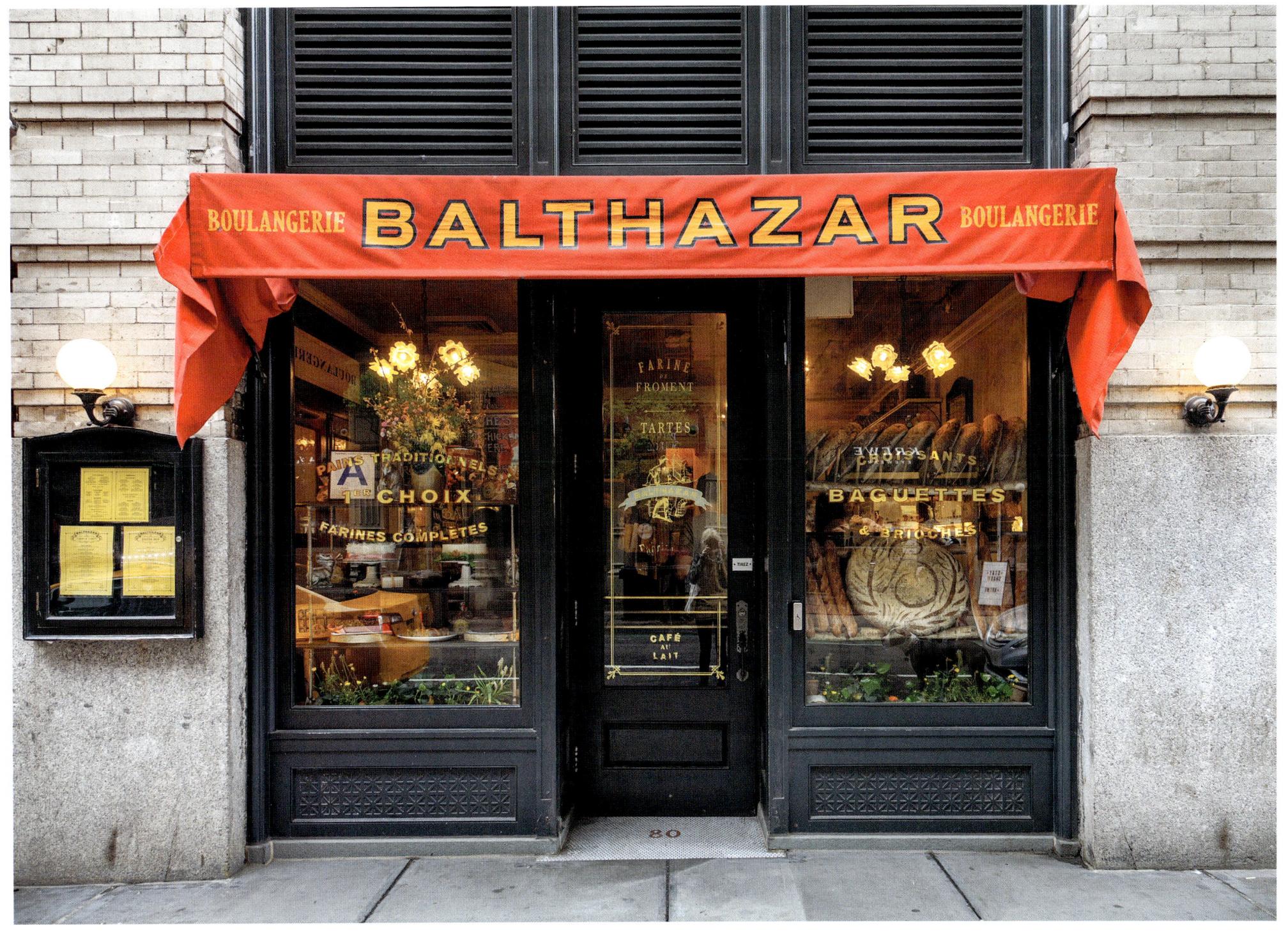

39 BALTHAZAR
Spring Street near Crosby Street, SoHo, 2019

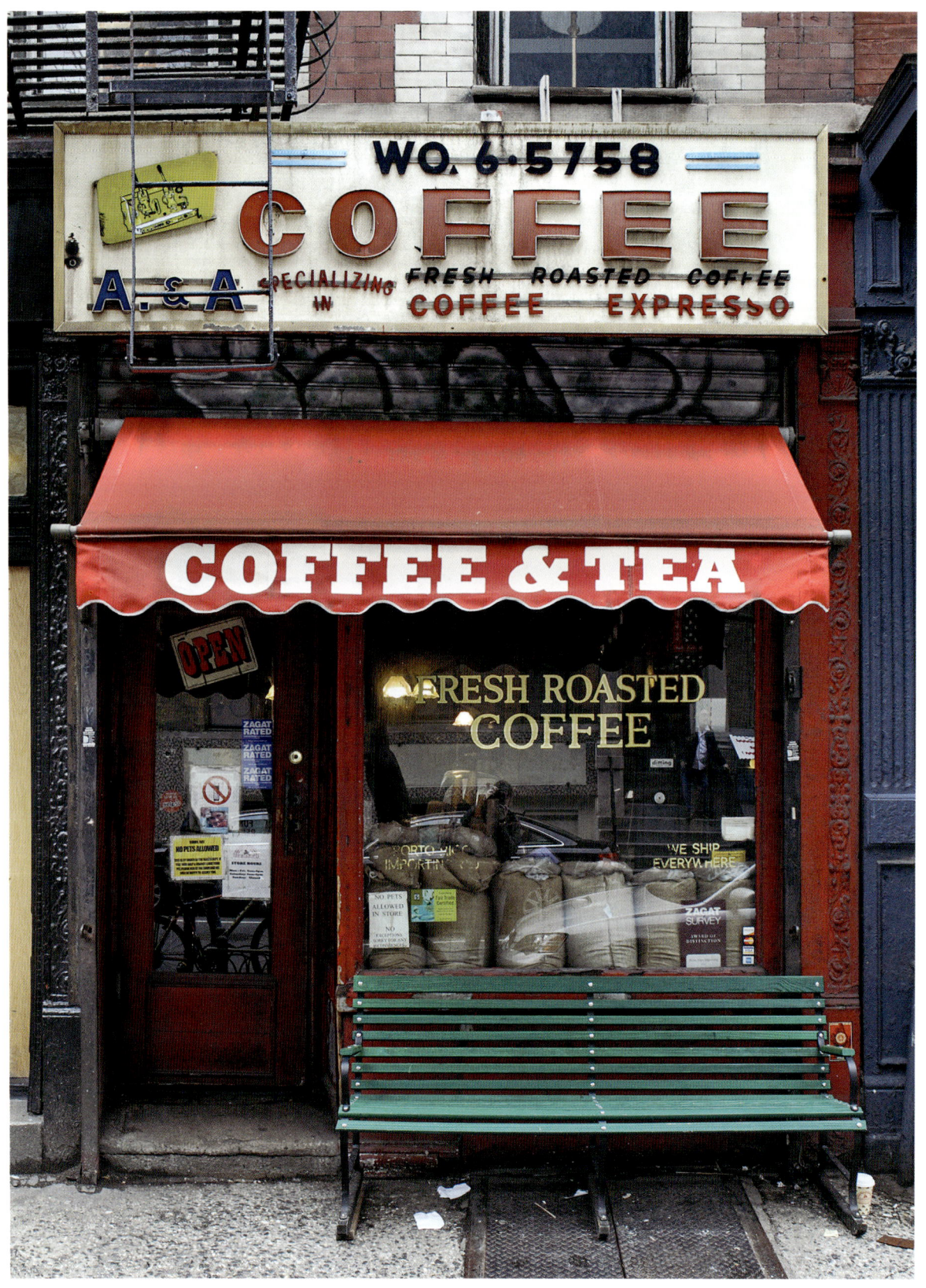

AUGGIE'S COFFEE
Thompson Street near Prince Street, SoHo, 2010

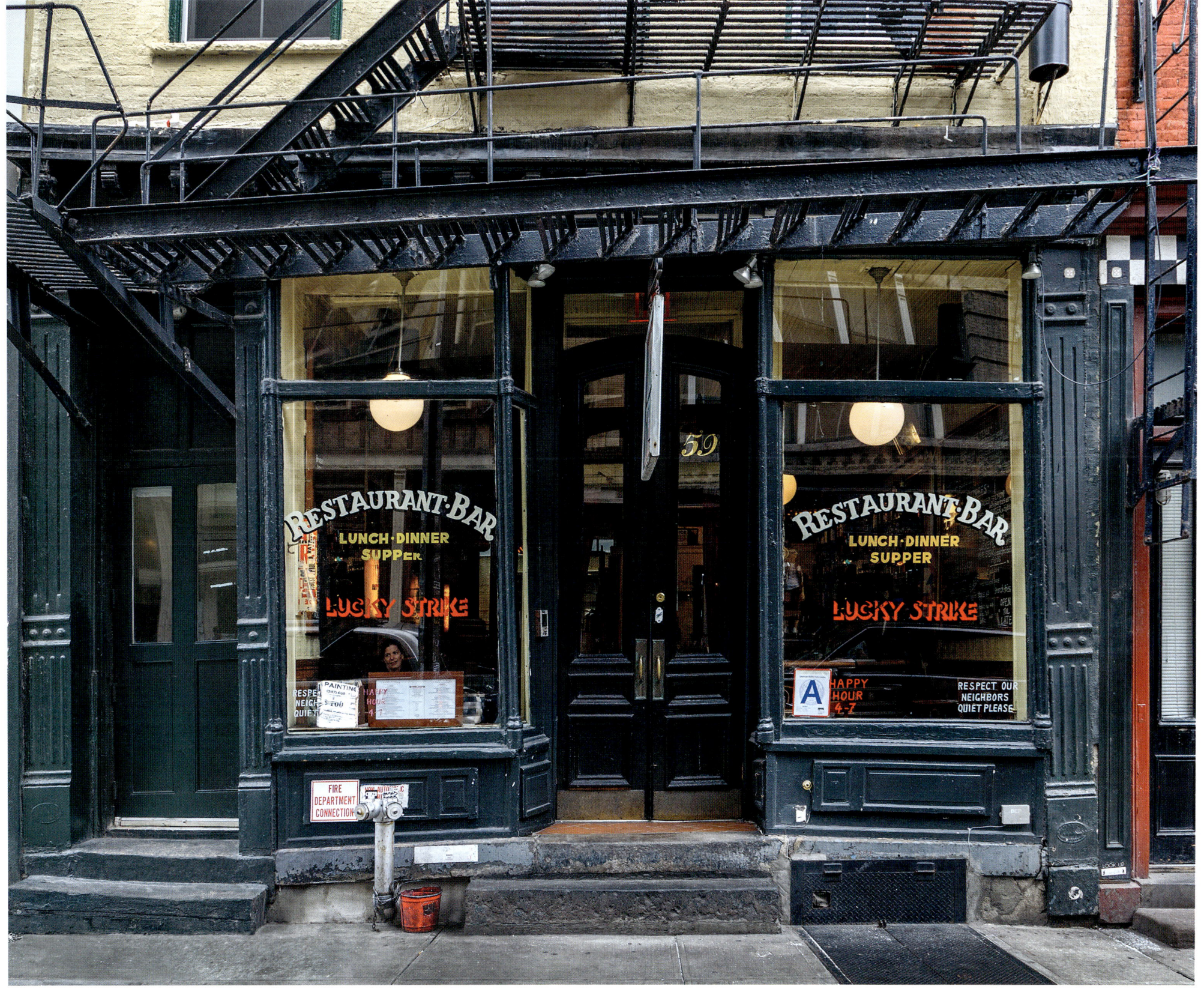

LUCKY STRIKE
Grand Street near West Broadway, SoHo, 2016

MANHATTAN

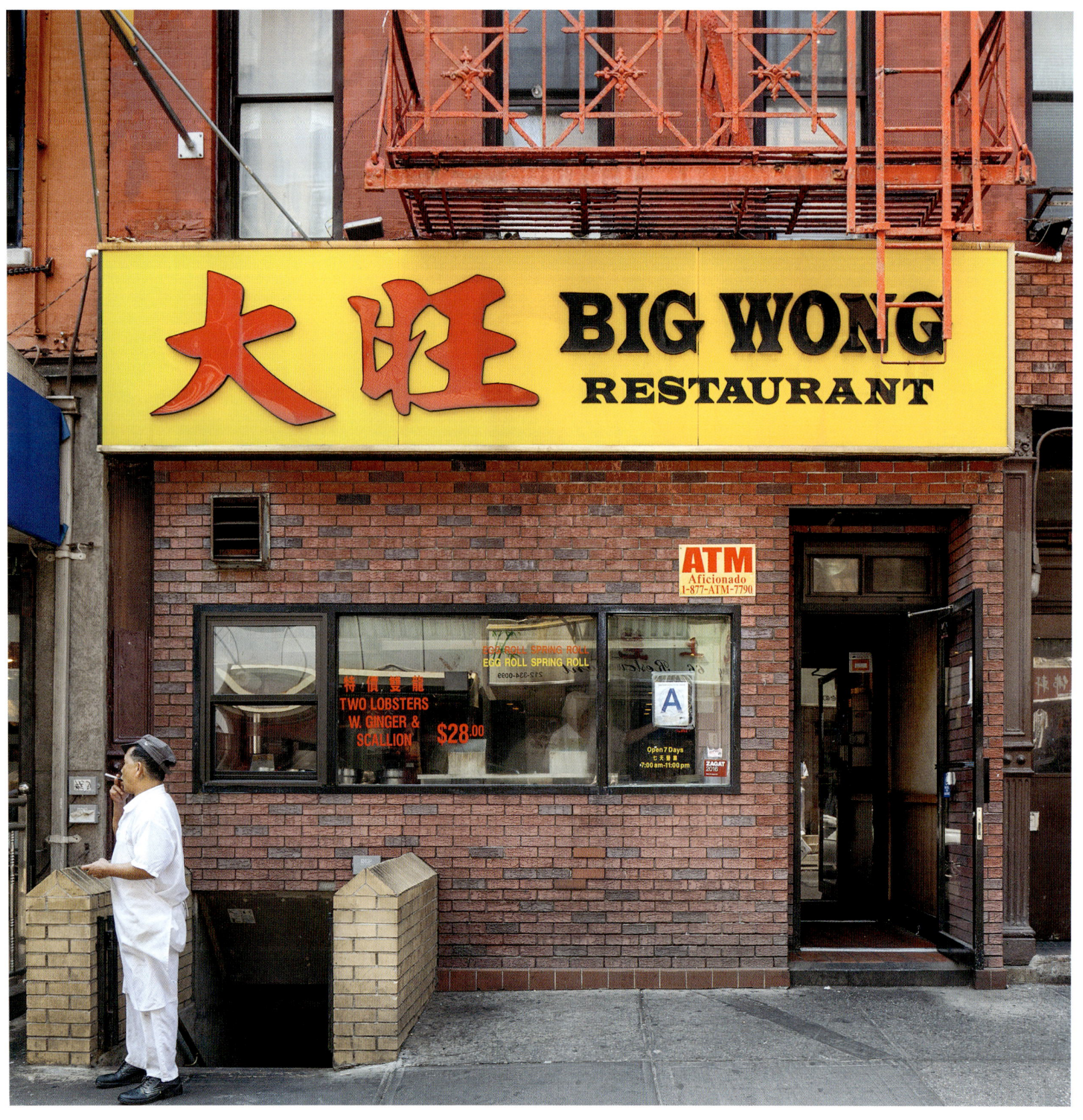

42 BIG WONG
Mott Street near Bayard Street, Chinatown, 2016

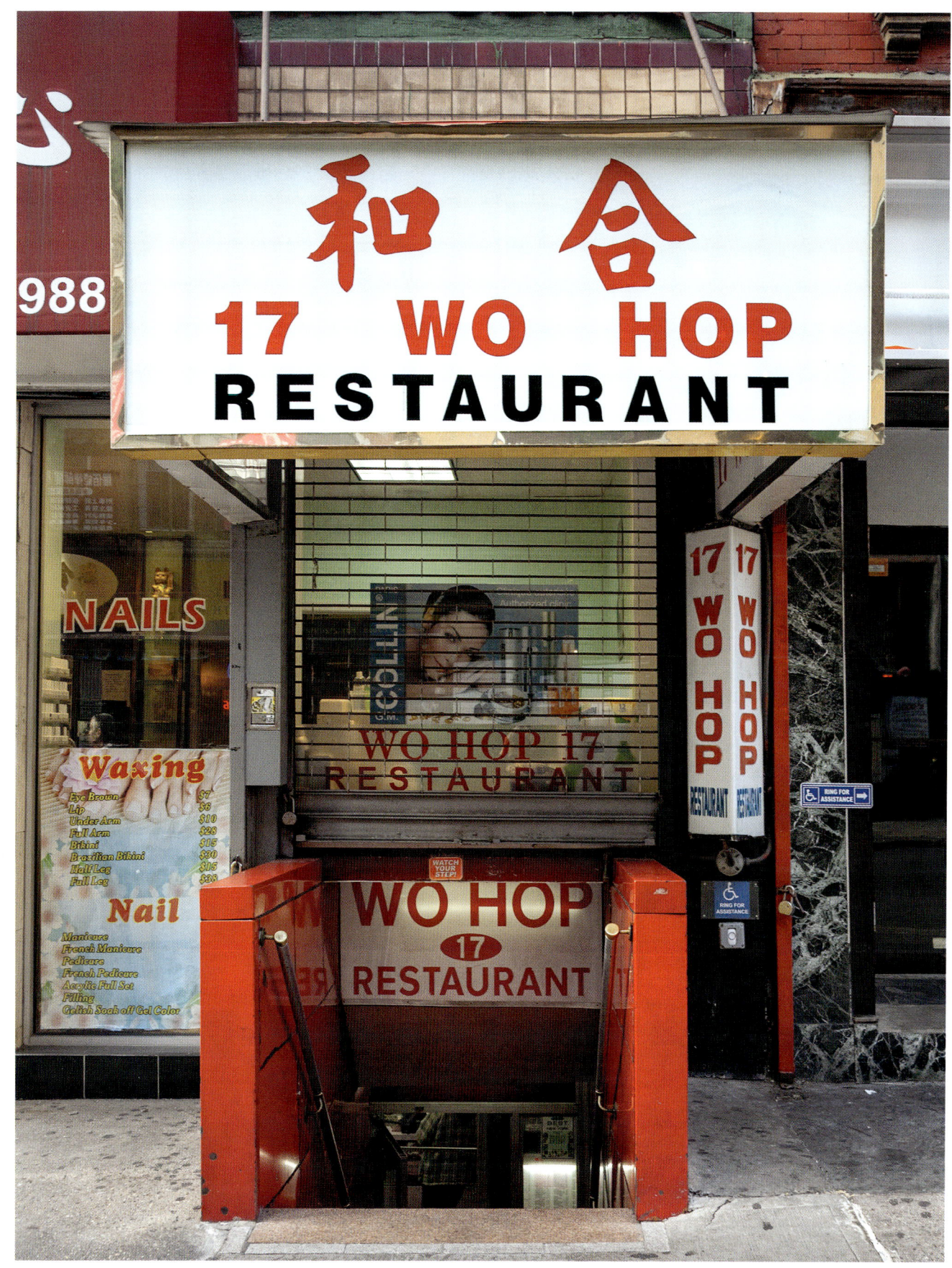

WO HOP
Mott Street near Mosco
Street, Chinatown, 2019

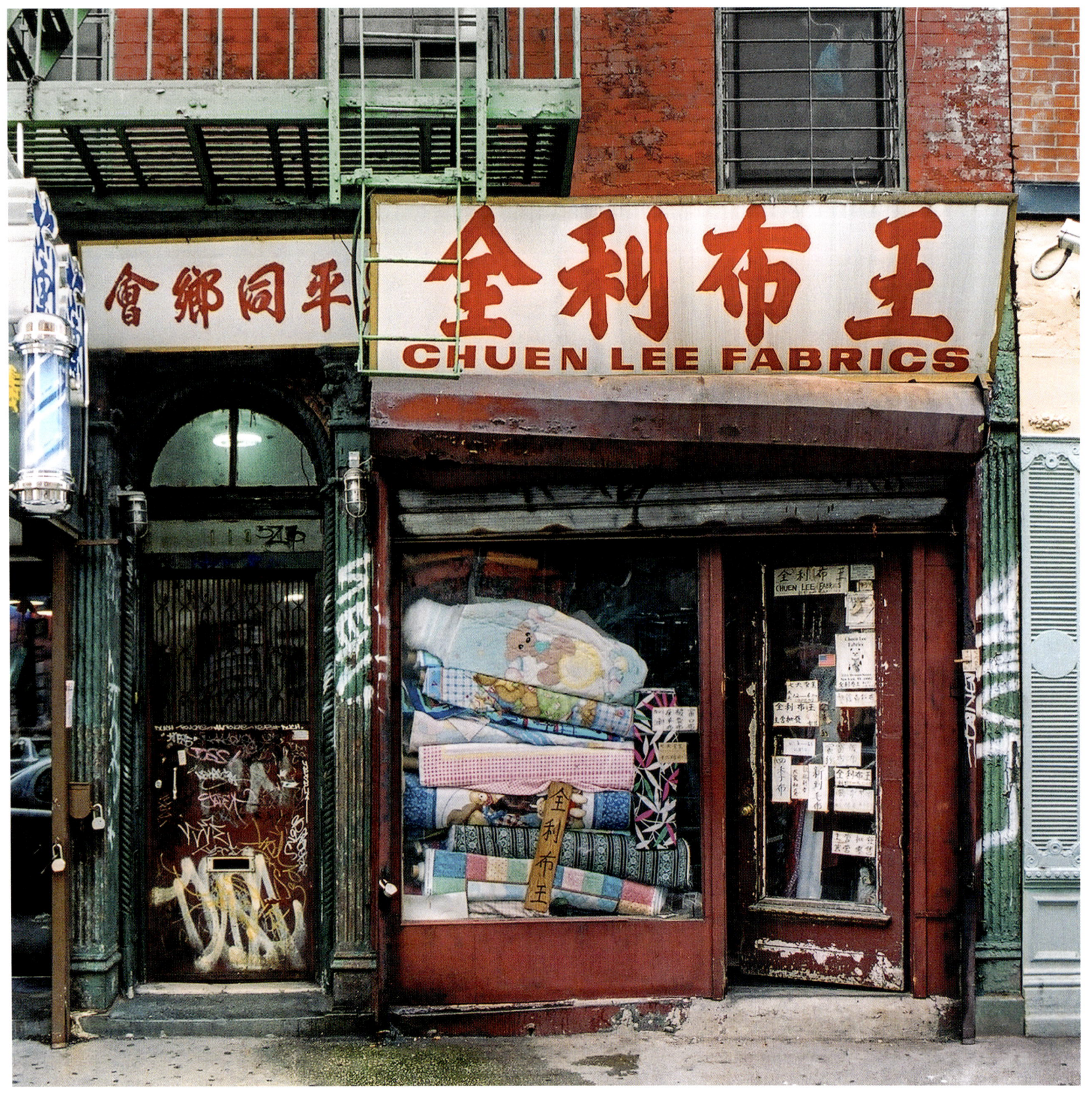

CHUEN LEE FABRICS
Division Street near Orchard Street, Chinatown, 2006

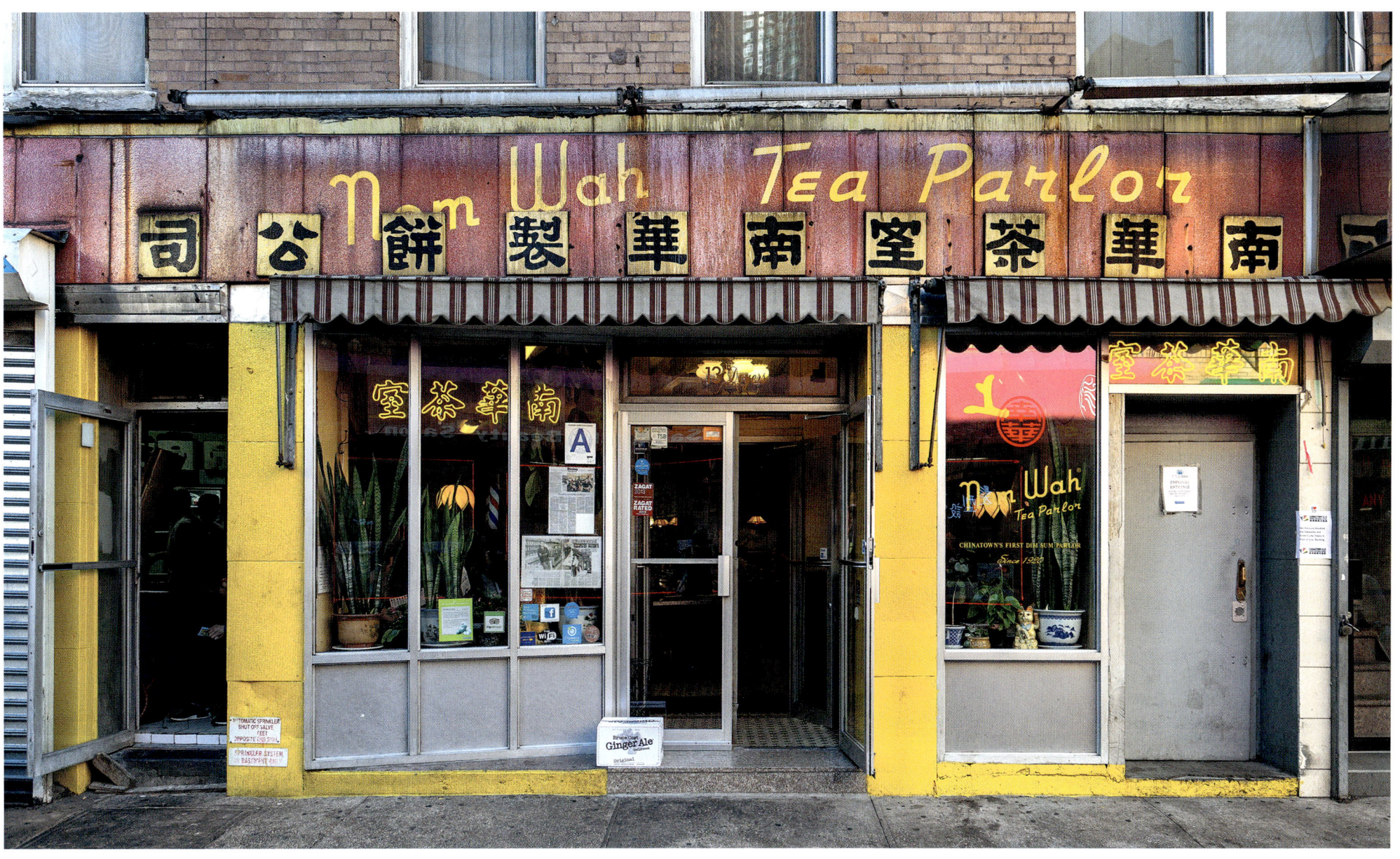

45 NOM WAH TEA PARLOR
Doyers Street near Pell Street, Chinatown, 2016

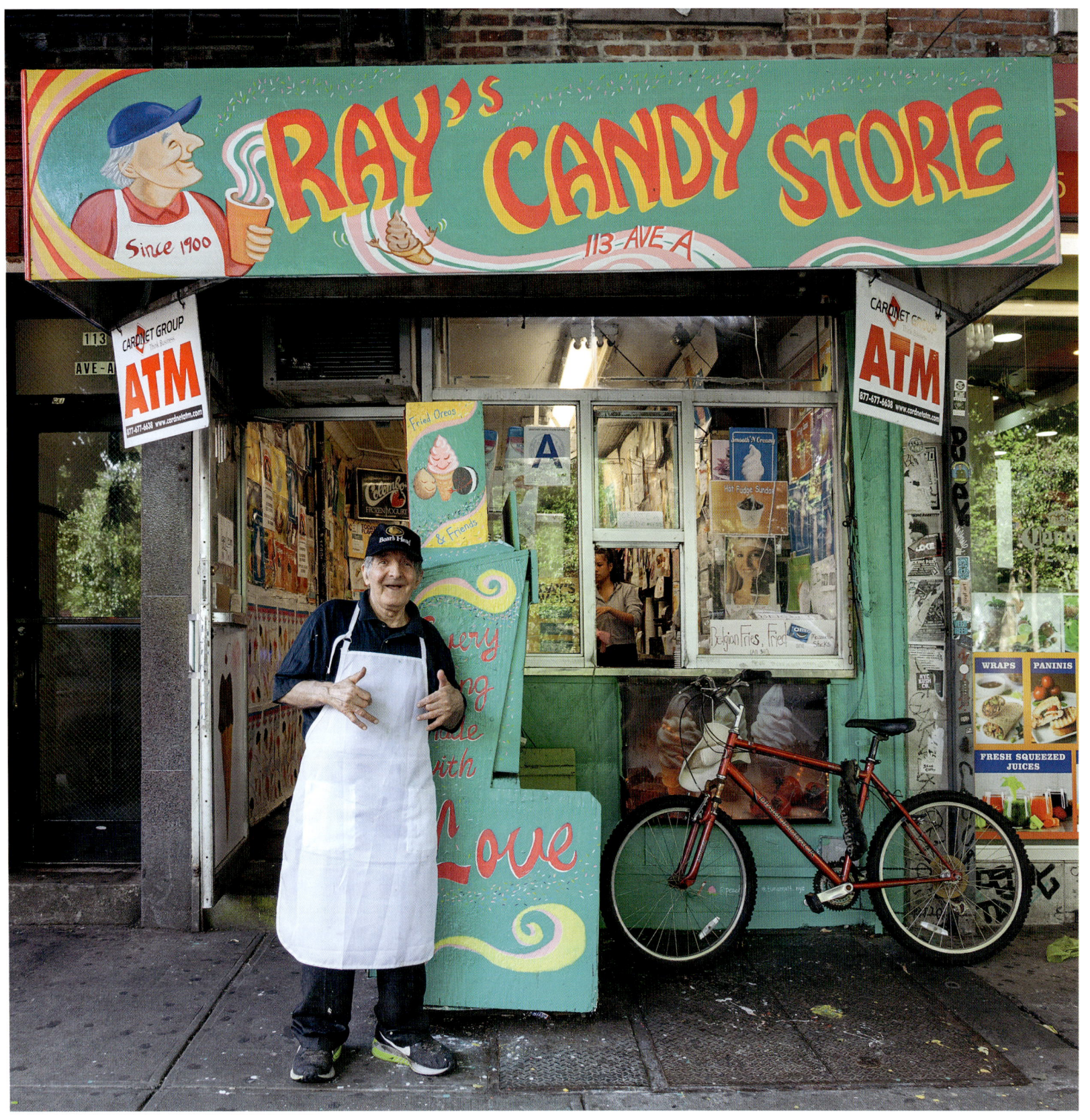

RAY'S CANDY STORE
Avenue A near East 7th Street, East Village, 2019

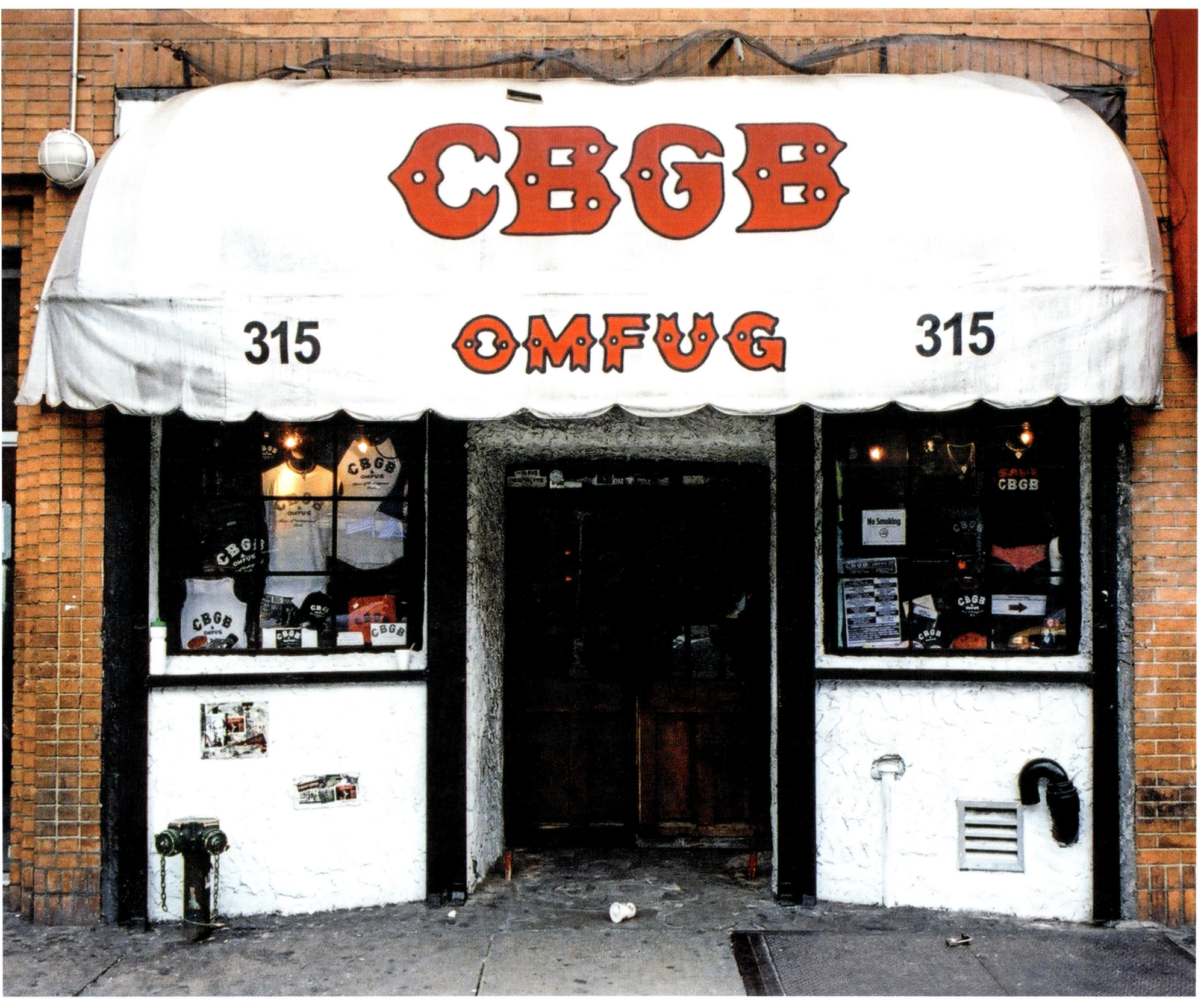

CBGB
Bowery at Bleecker Street, East Village, 2005

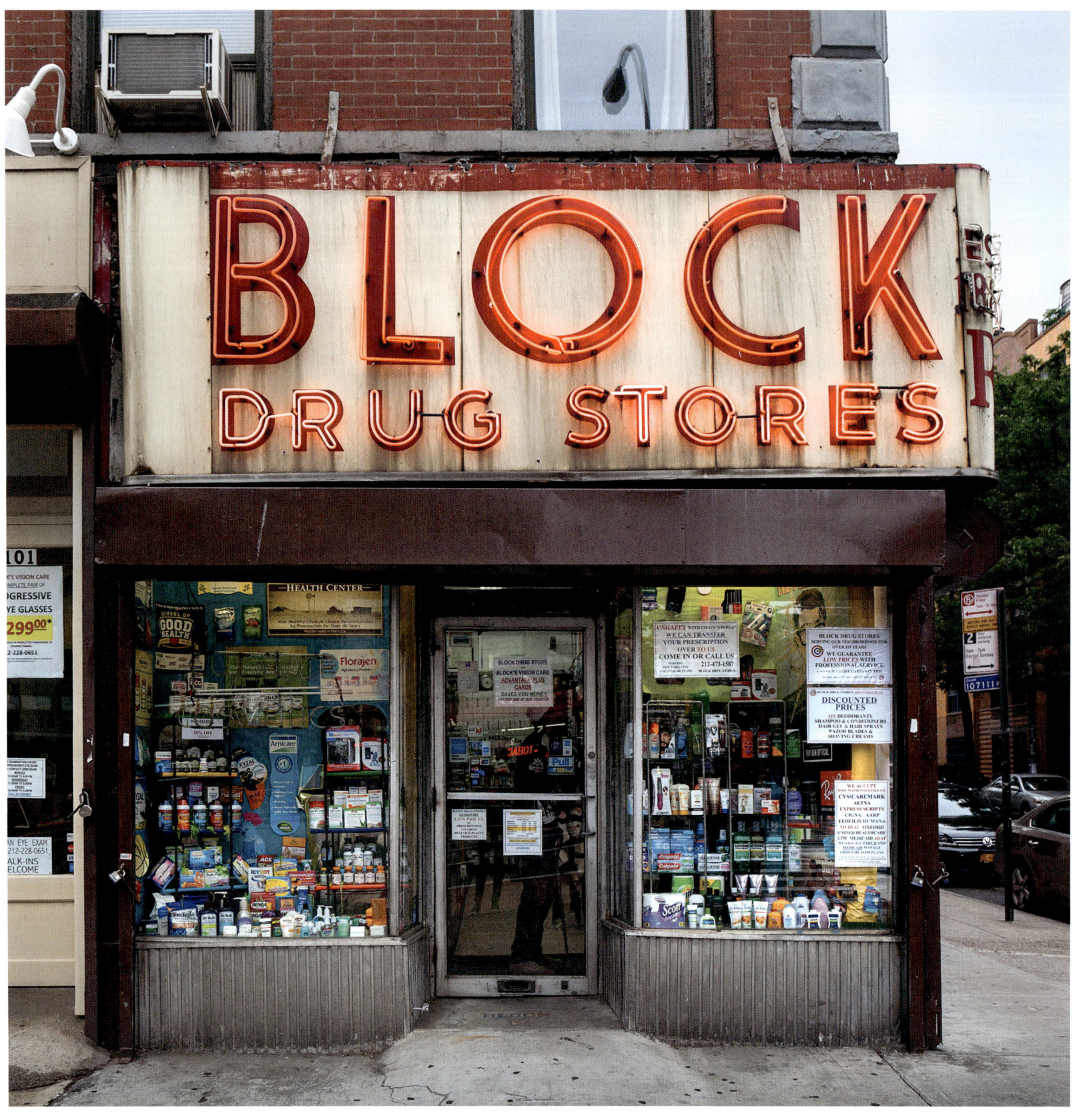

48 BLOCK DRUG STORES
2nd Avenue at East 6th Street, East Village, 2004

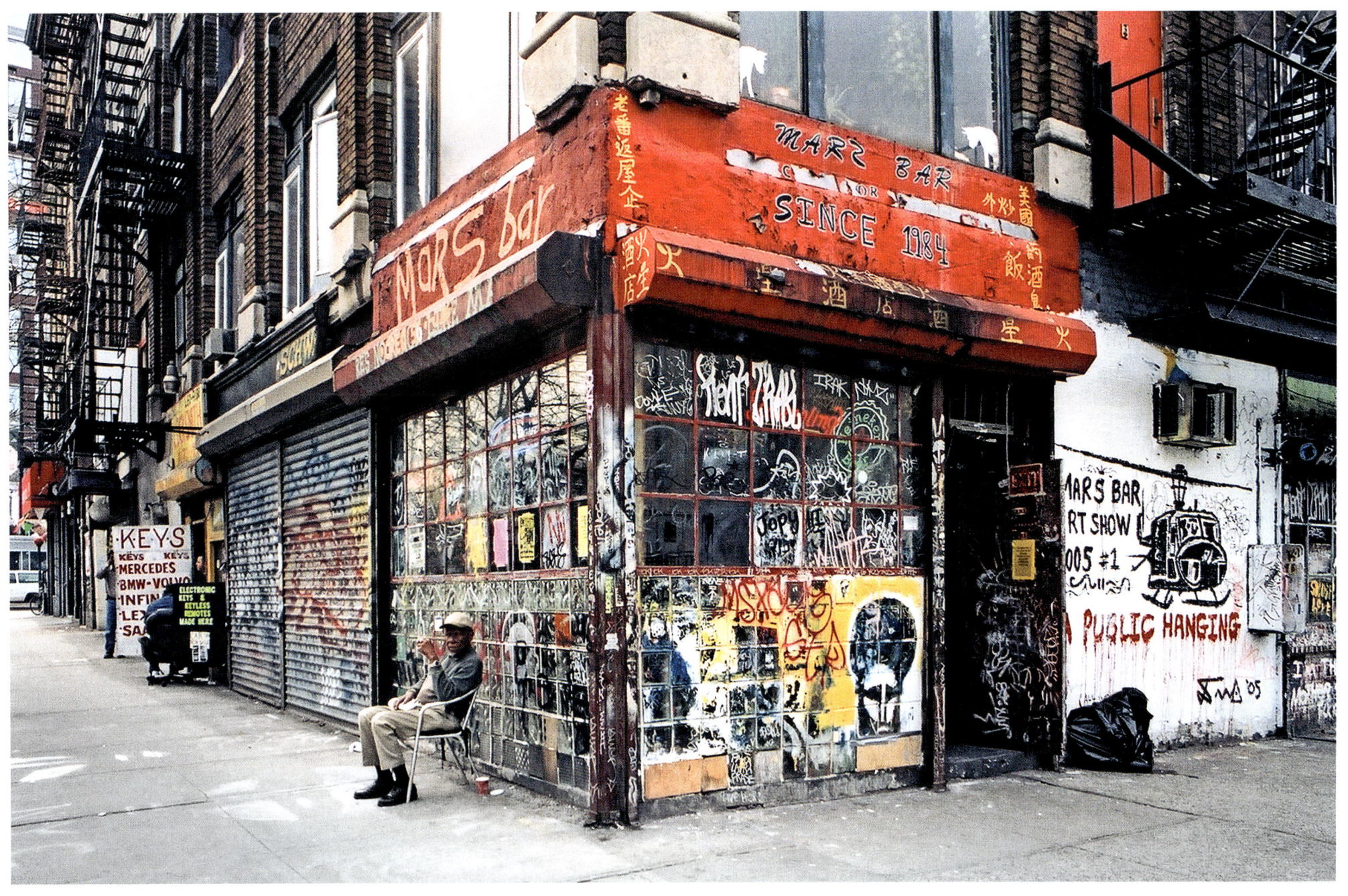

MARS BAR
East 1st Street at 2nd Avenue, East Village, 2005

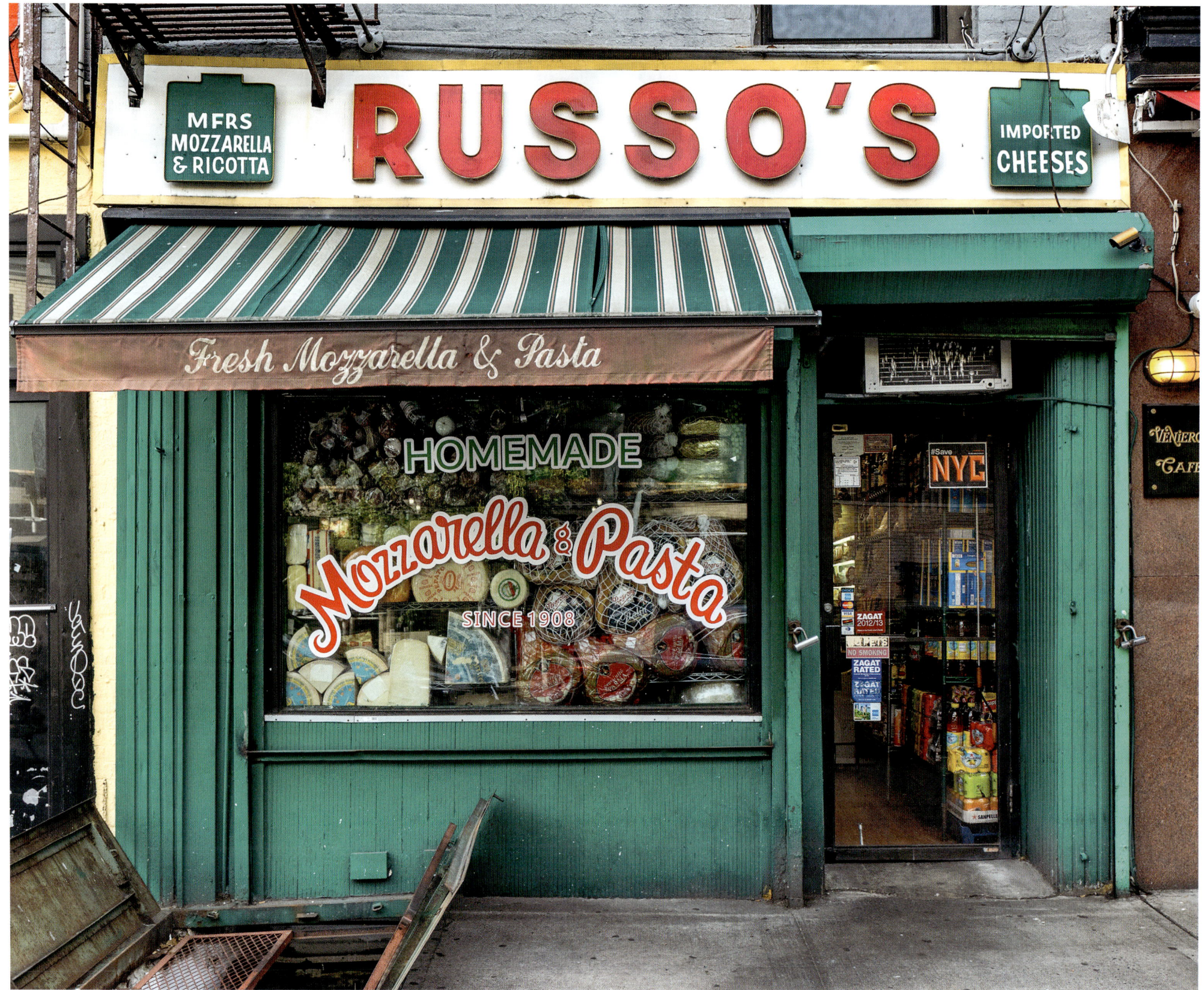

RUSSO'S MOZZARELLA & PASTA
East 11th Street near 1st Avenue, East Village, 2020

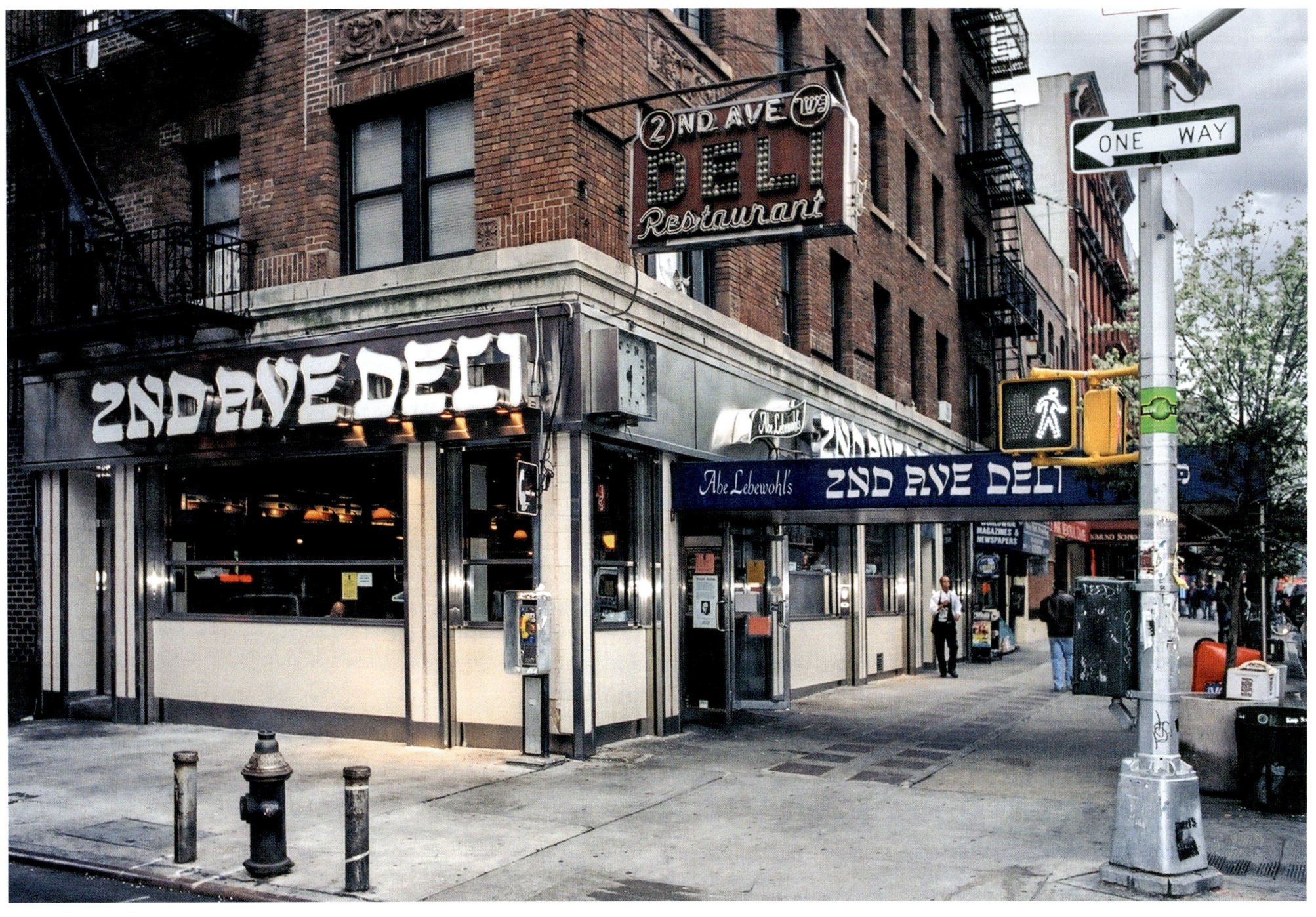

2ND AVENUE DELI
2nd Avenue at East 10th Street, East Village, 2005

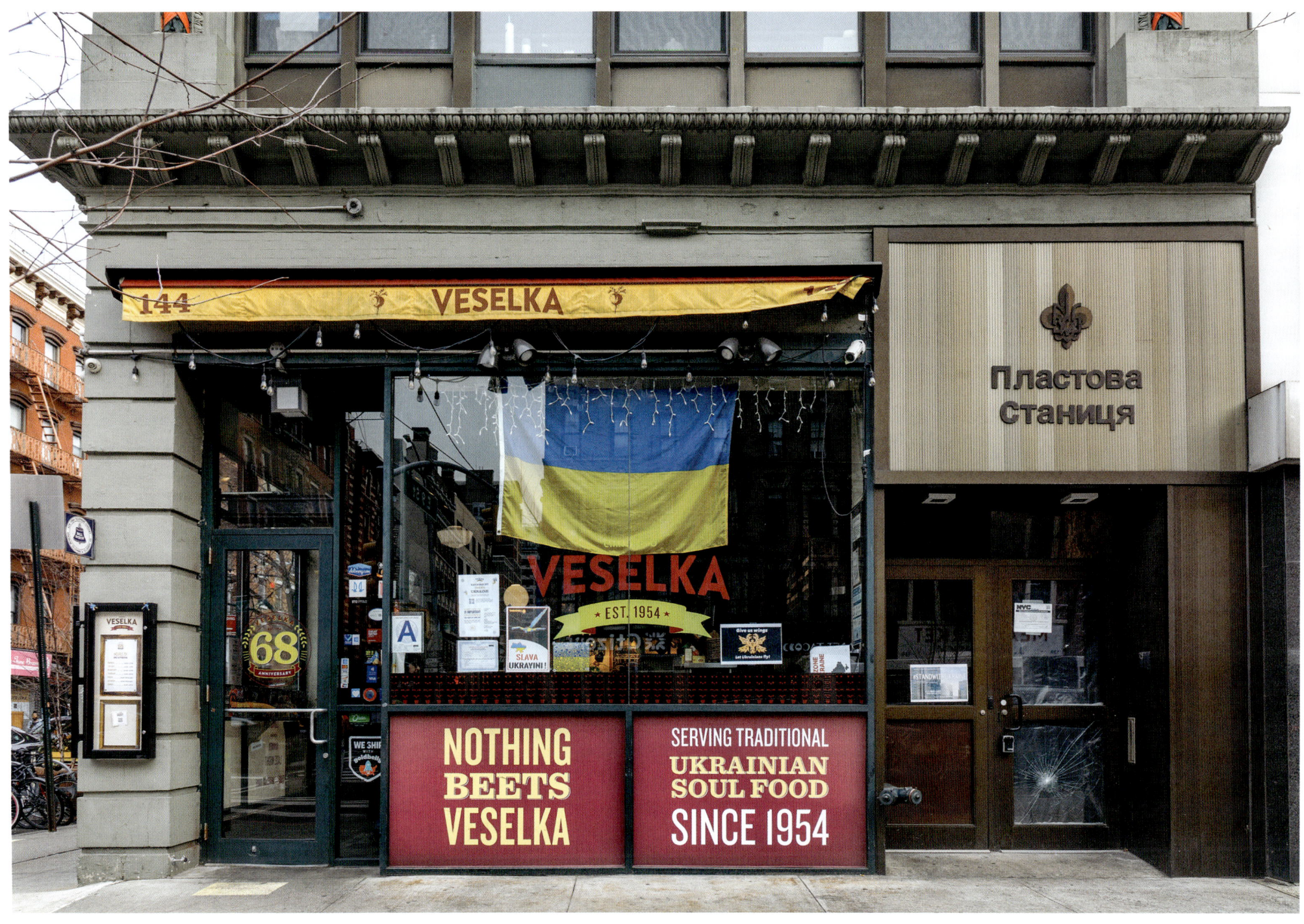

VESELKA
2nd Avenue at East 9th Street, East Village, 2022

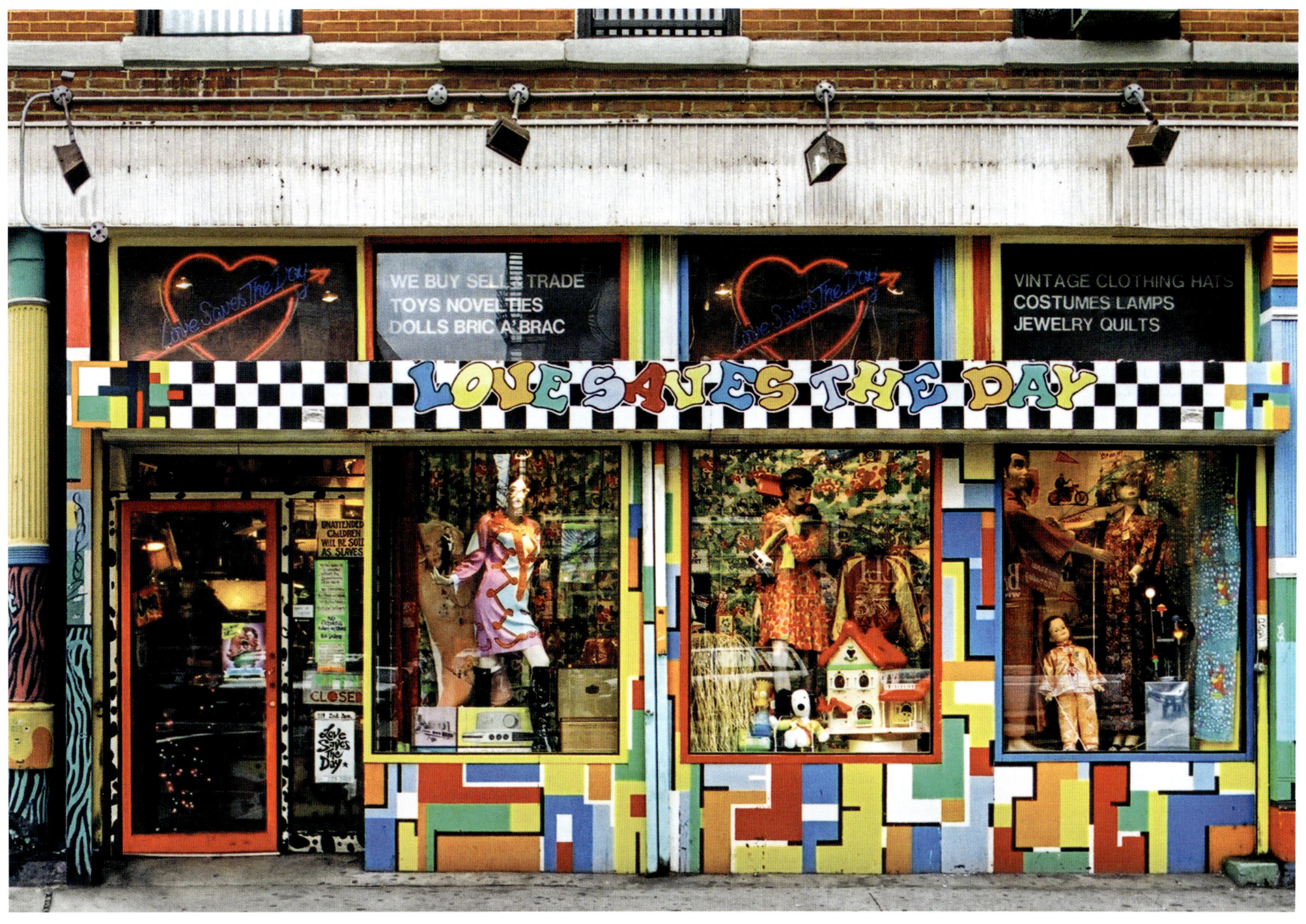

LOVE SAVES THE DAY
2nd Avenue at East 7th Street, East Village, 2001

MANHATTAN

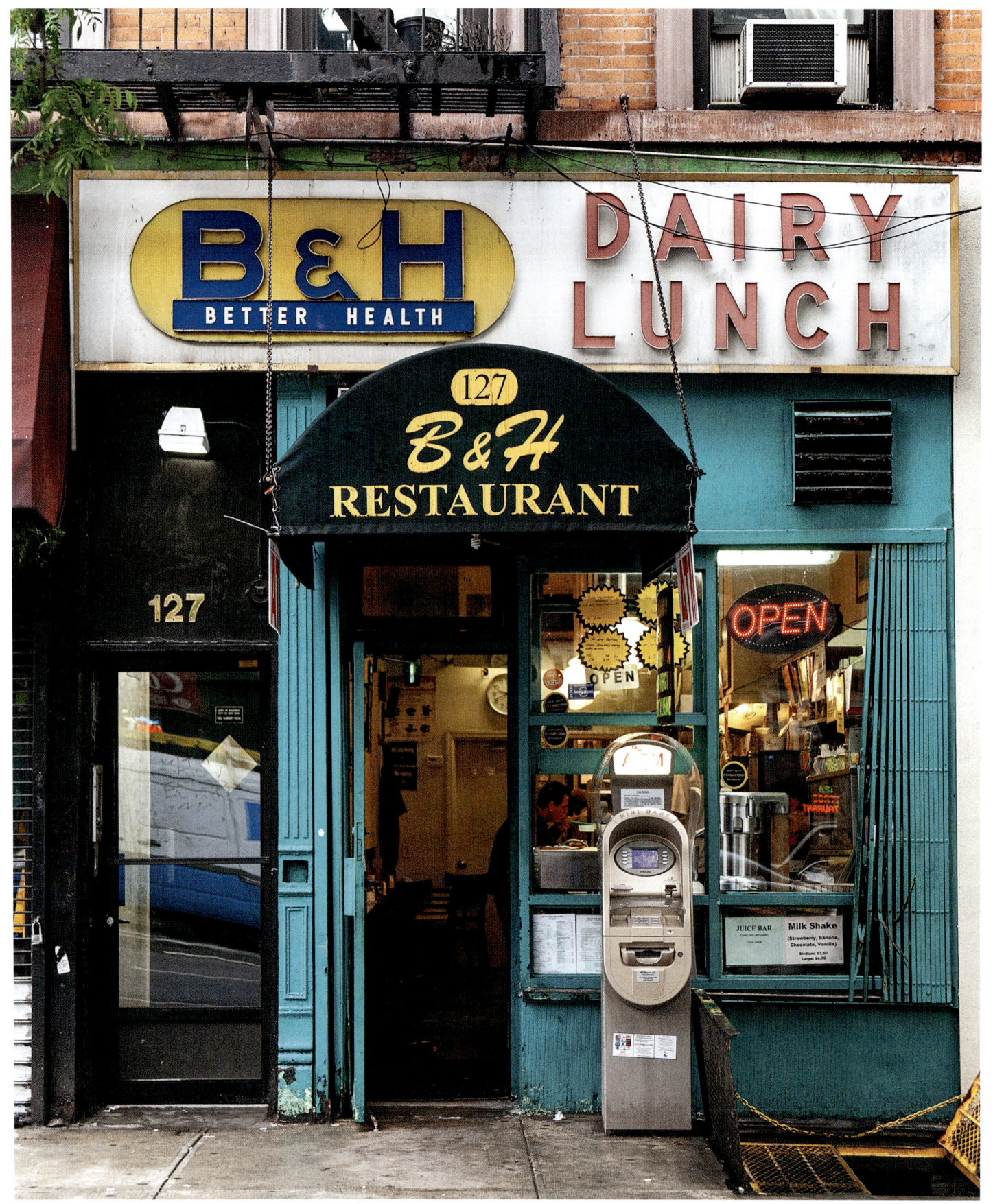

B&H DAIRY
2nd Avenue near St. Marks Place,
East Village, 2008

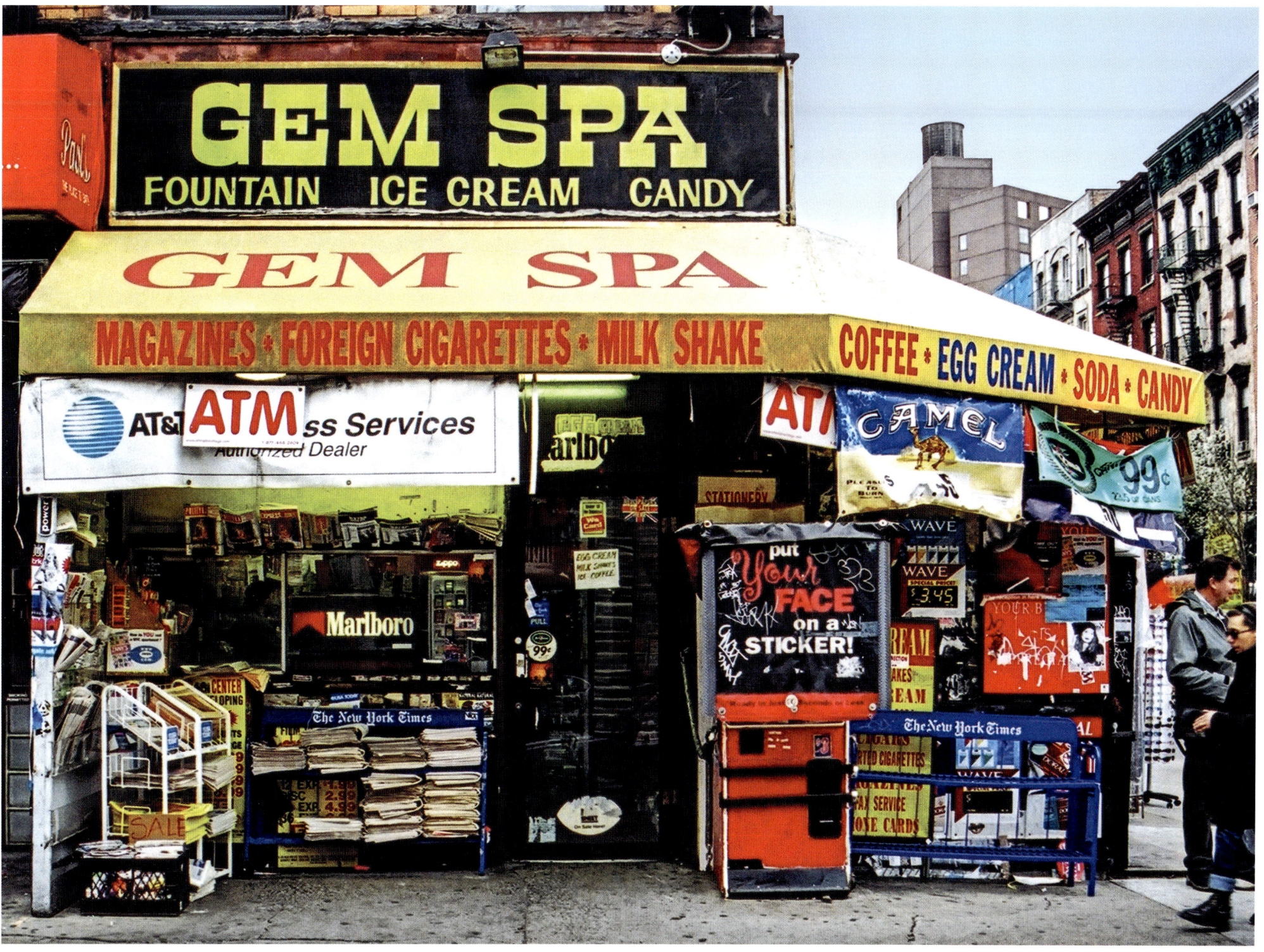

GEM SPA
2nd Avenue at St. Marks Place, East Village, 2001

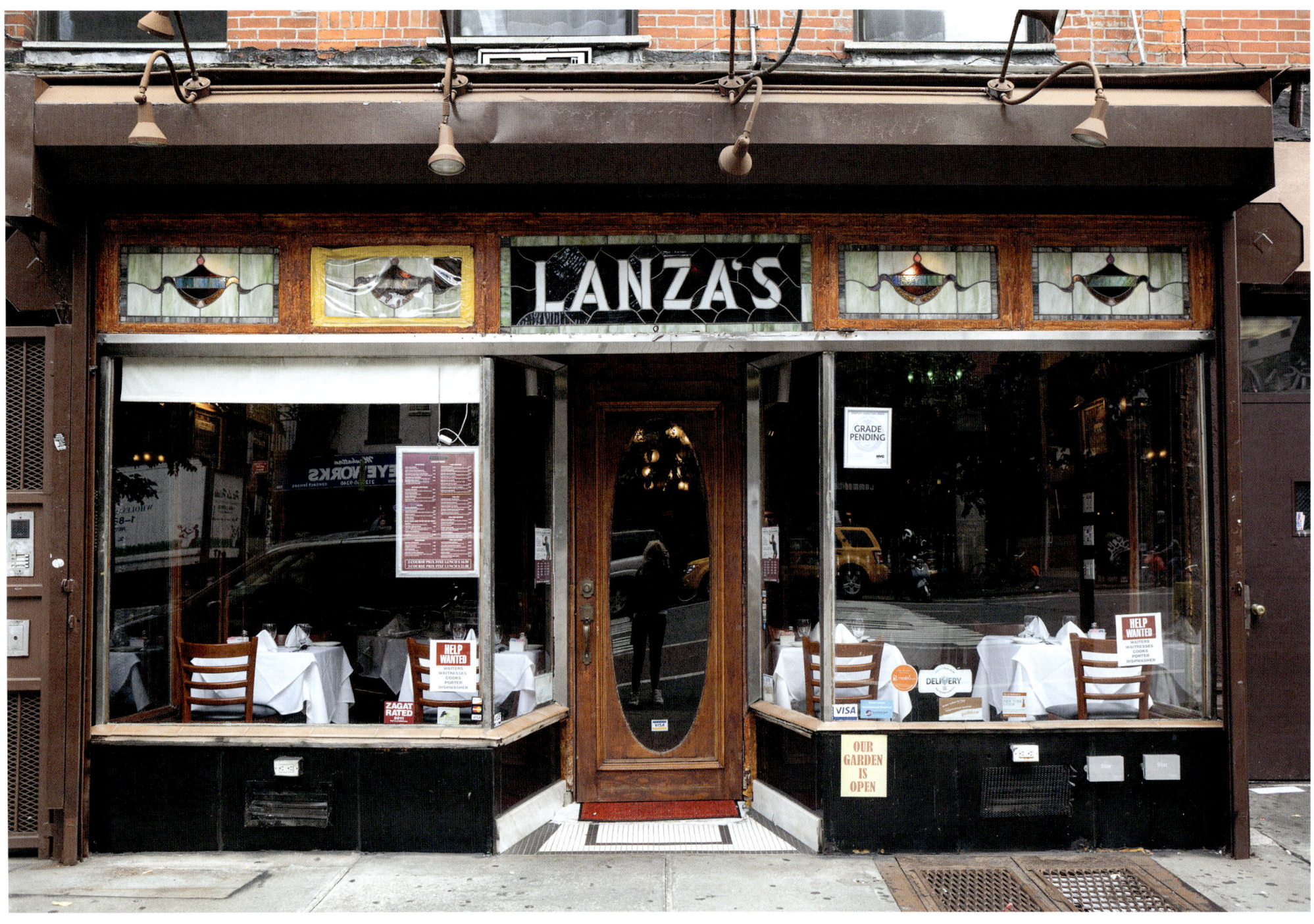

56 LANZA'S RESTAURANT
1st Avenue near East 10th Street, East Village, 2012

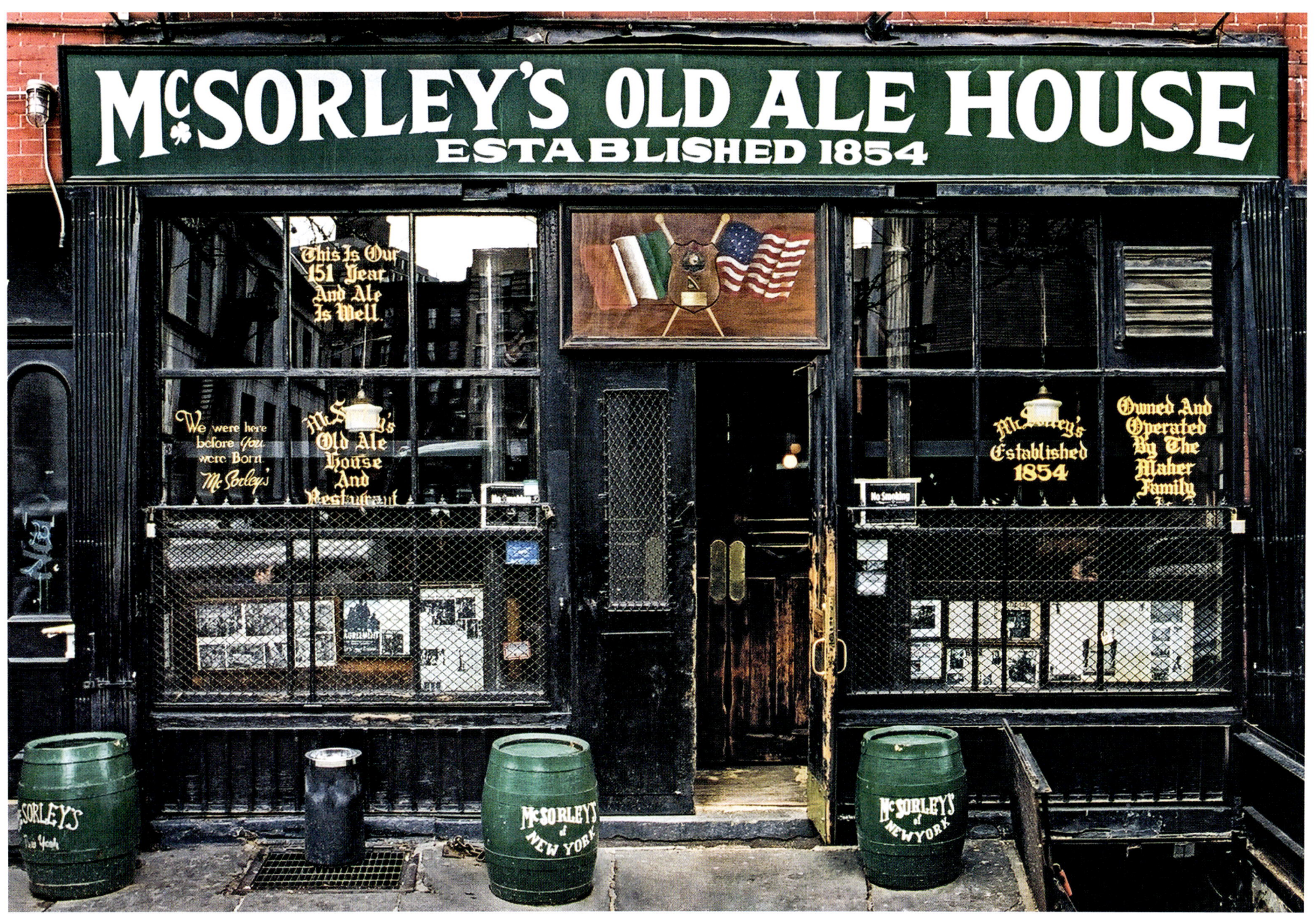

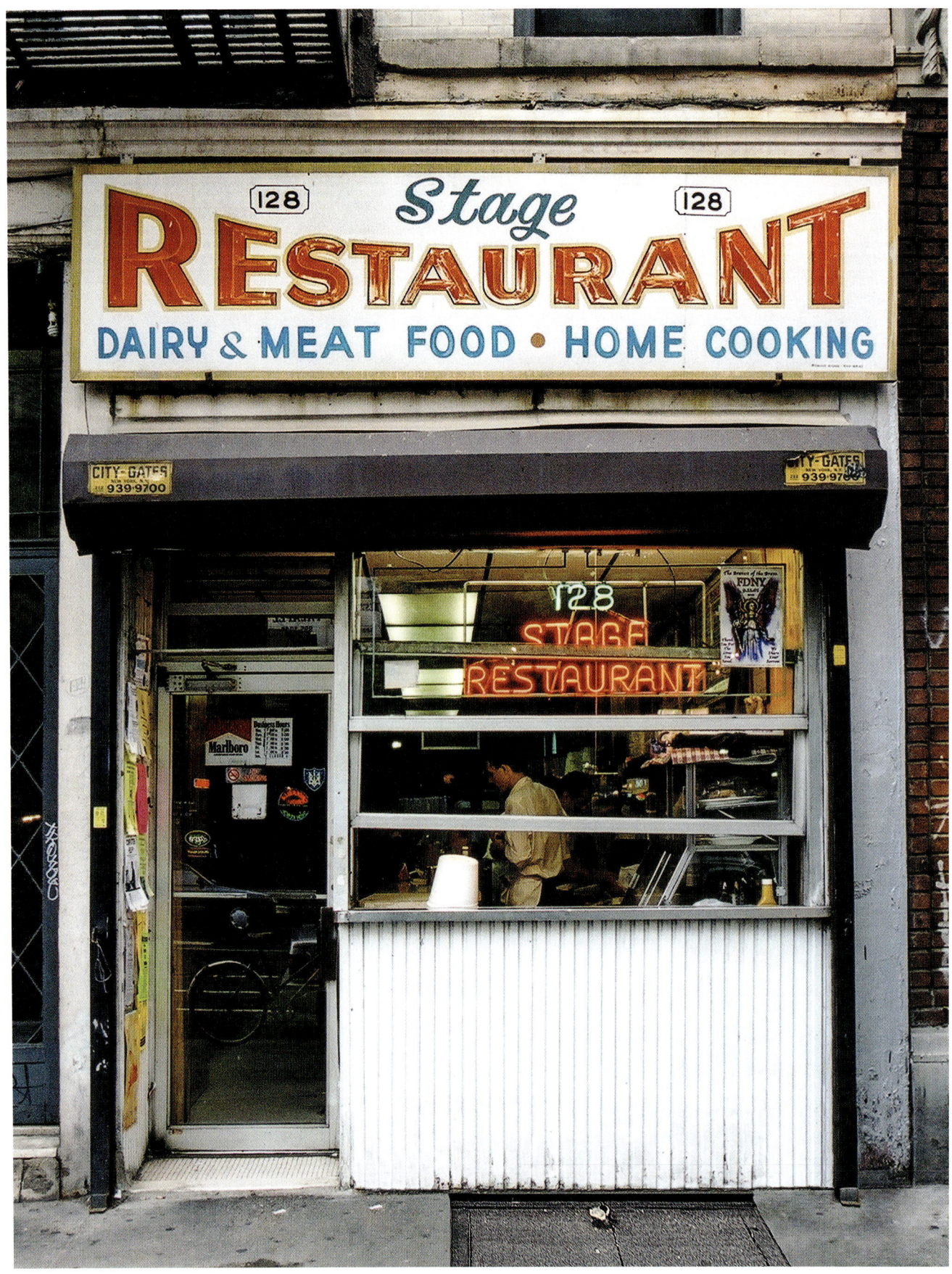

STAGE RESTAURANT
2nd Avenue near St. Marks Place,
East Village, 2003

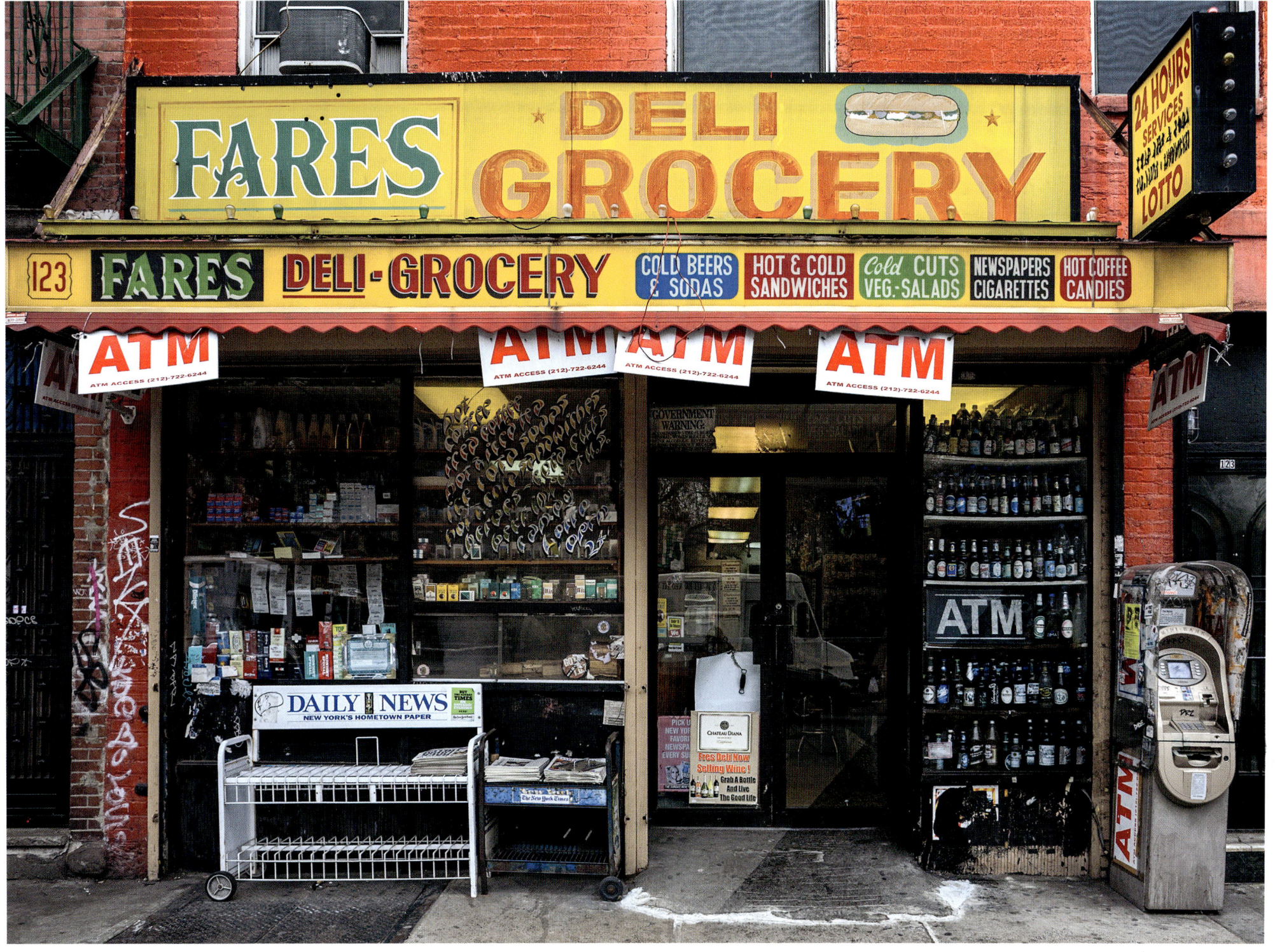

FARES DELI
Avenue A near St. Marks Place, East Village, 2009

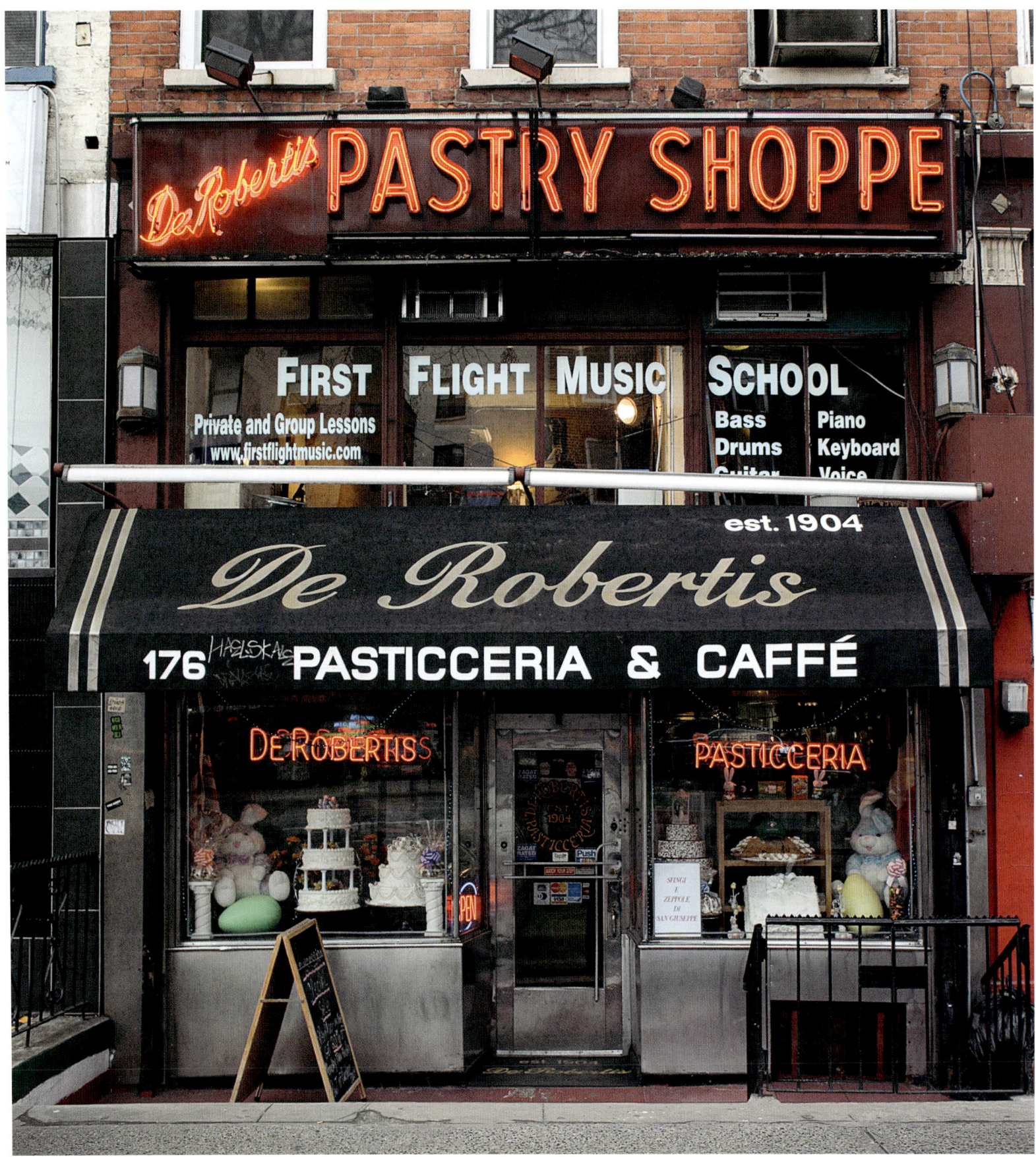

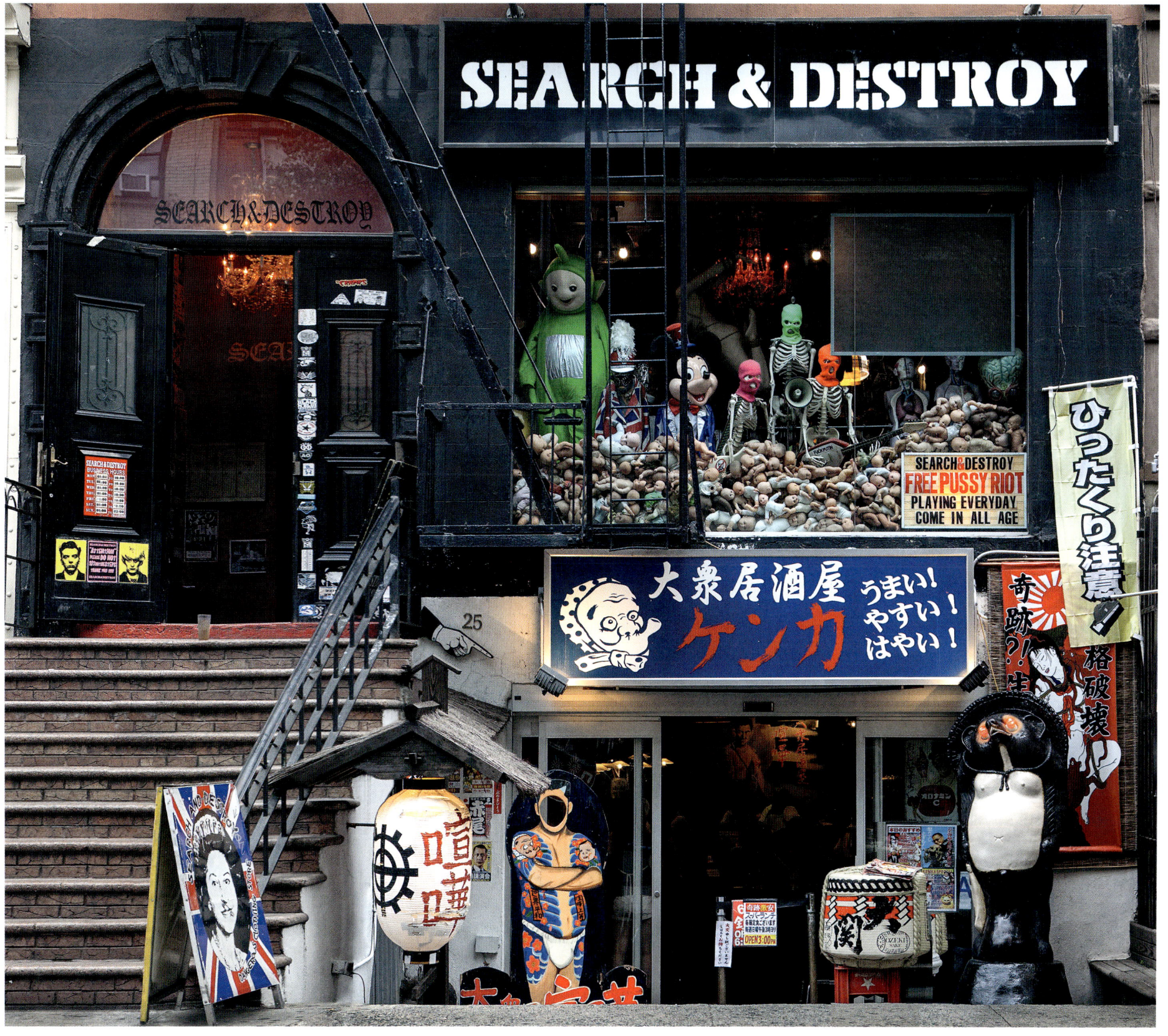

DE ROBERTIS CAFFÉ
1st Avenue near East 11th Street, East Village, 2010

SEARCH & DESTROY
St. Marks Place near 2nd Avenue, East Village, 2013

MANHATTAN

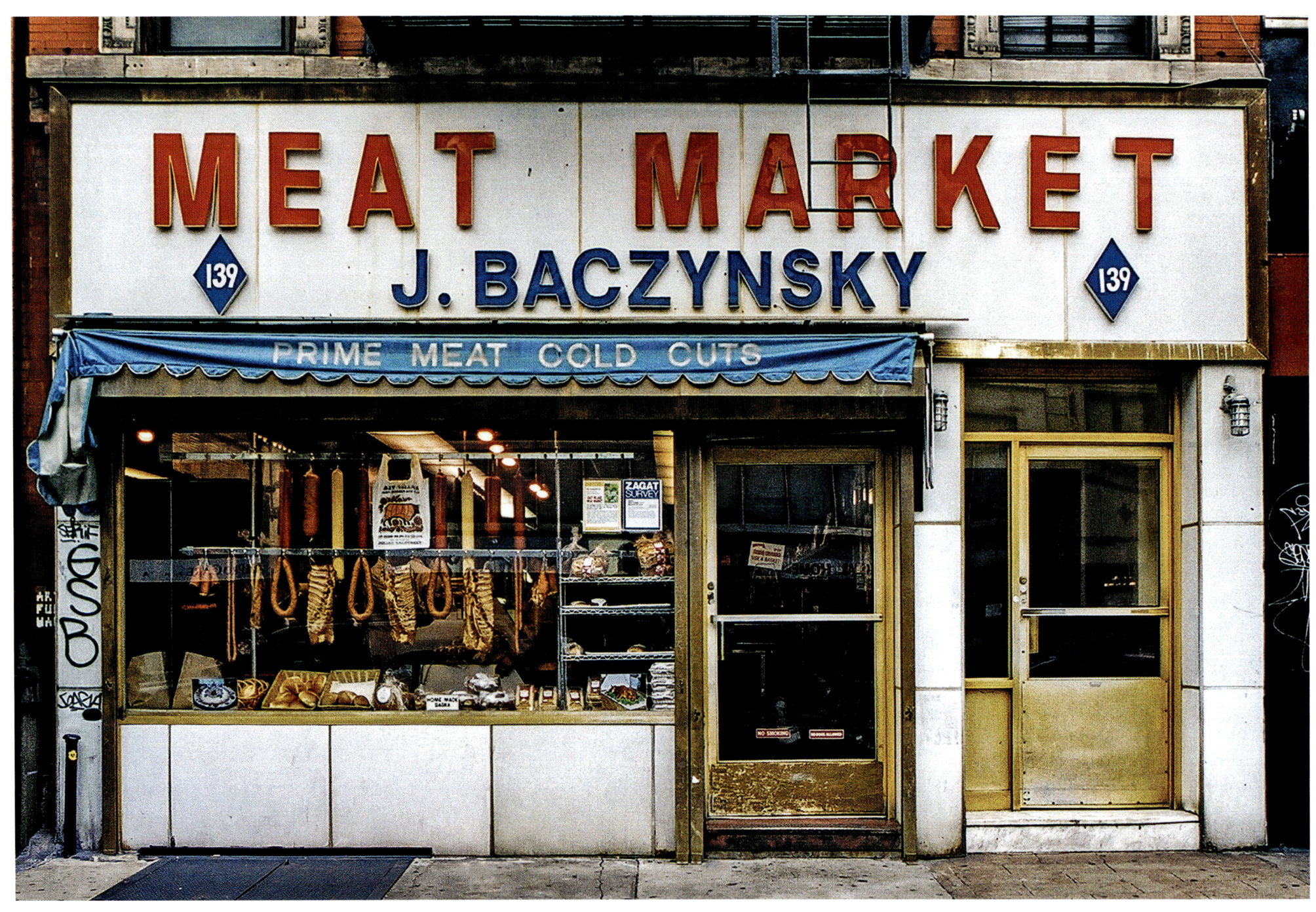

J. BACZYNSKY EAST VILLAGE MEAT MARKET
2nd Avenue near East 9th Street, East Village, 2003

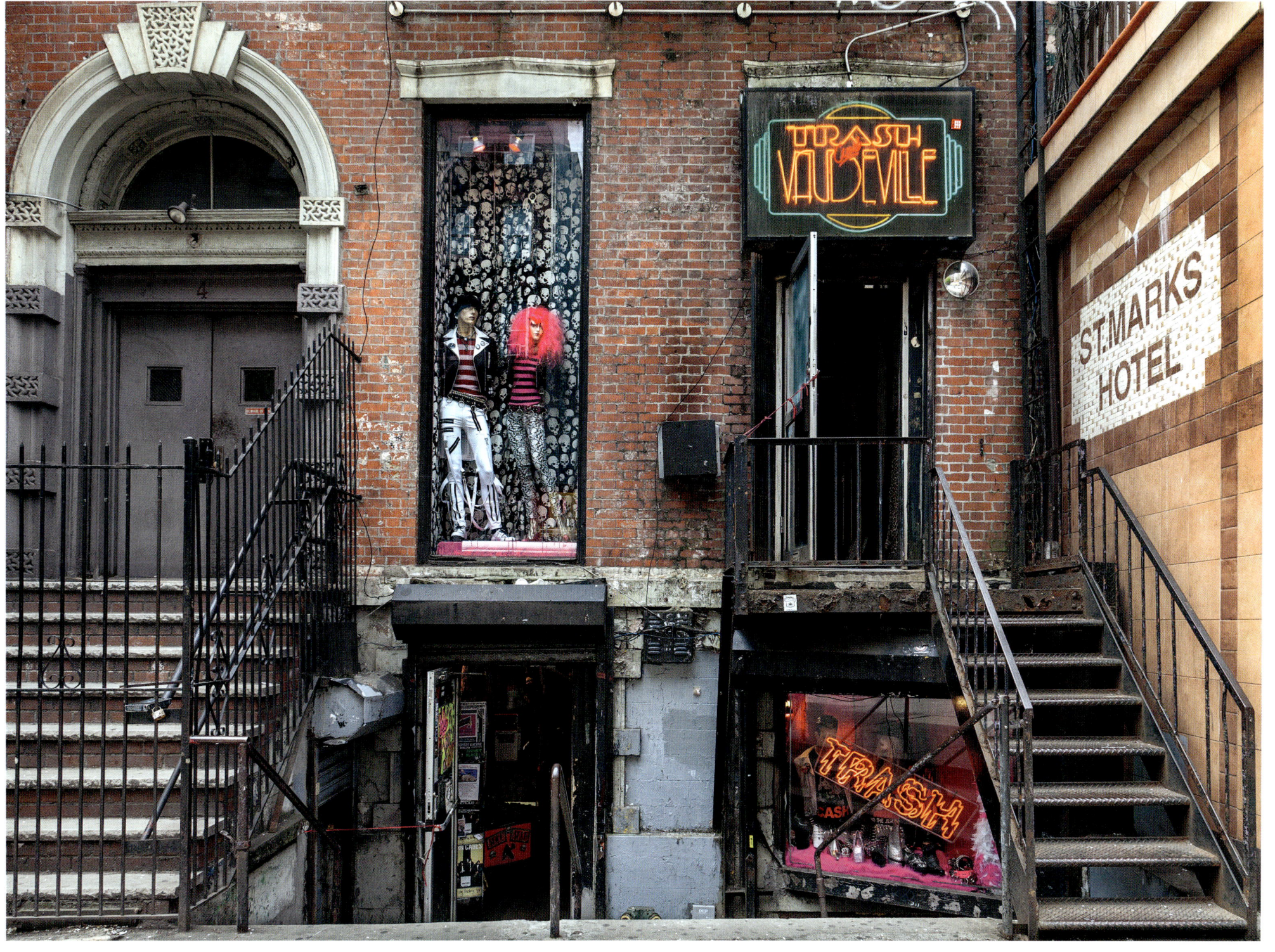

TRASH & VAUDEVILLE
St. Marks Place near 3rd Avenue, East Village, 2015

MANHATTAN

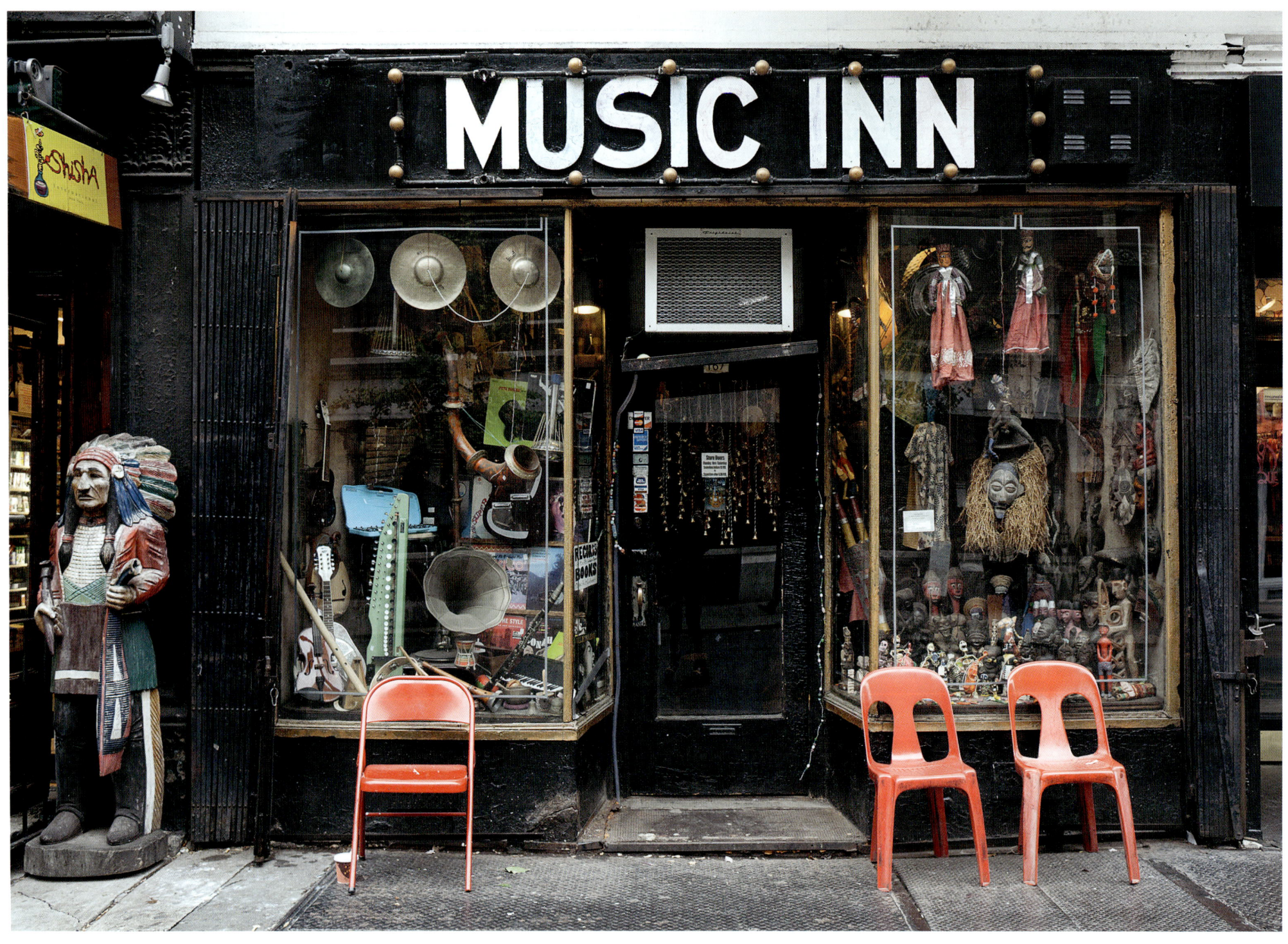

MUSIC INN
West 4th Street near Jones Street, Greenwich Village, 2009

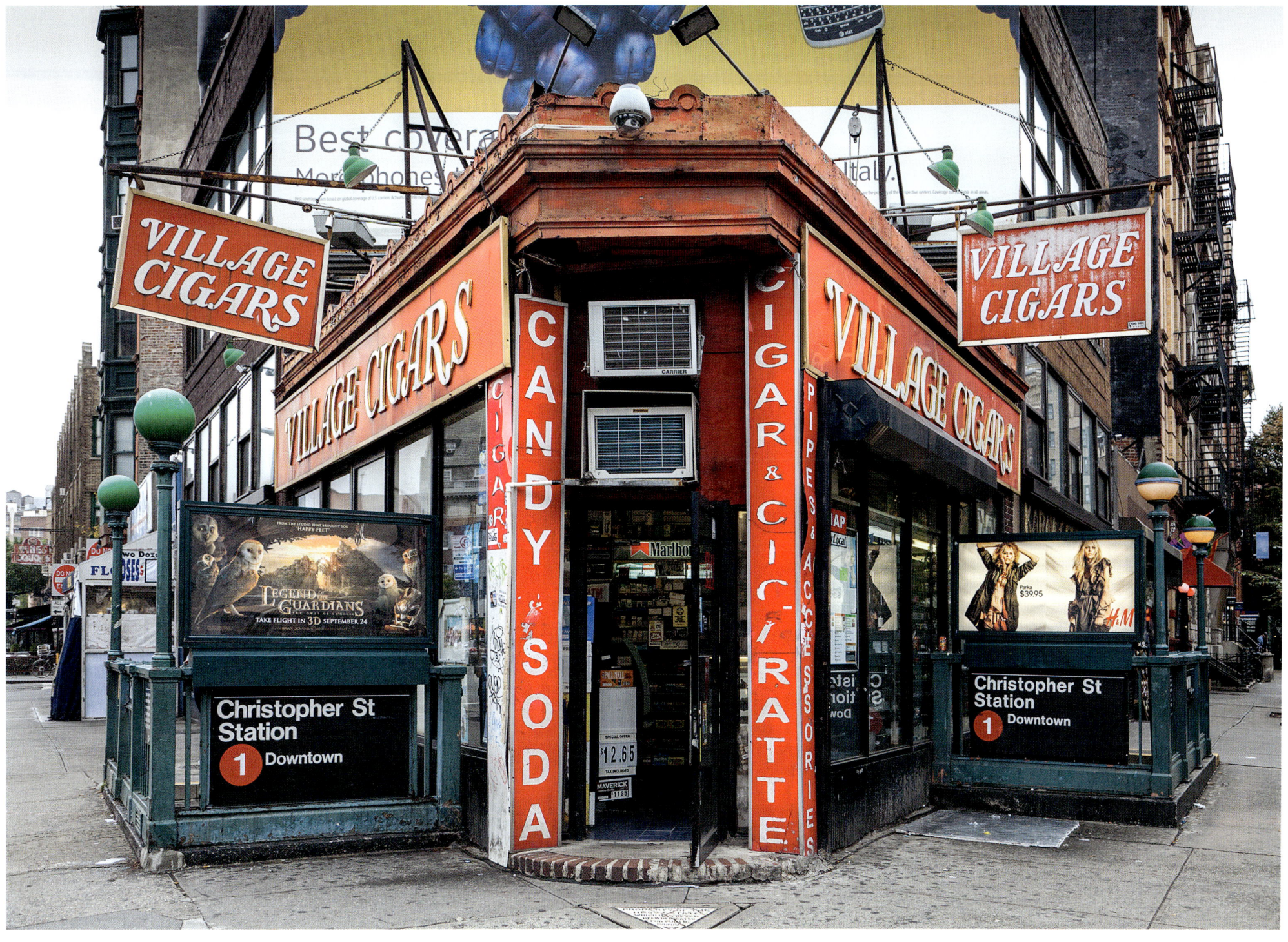

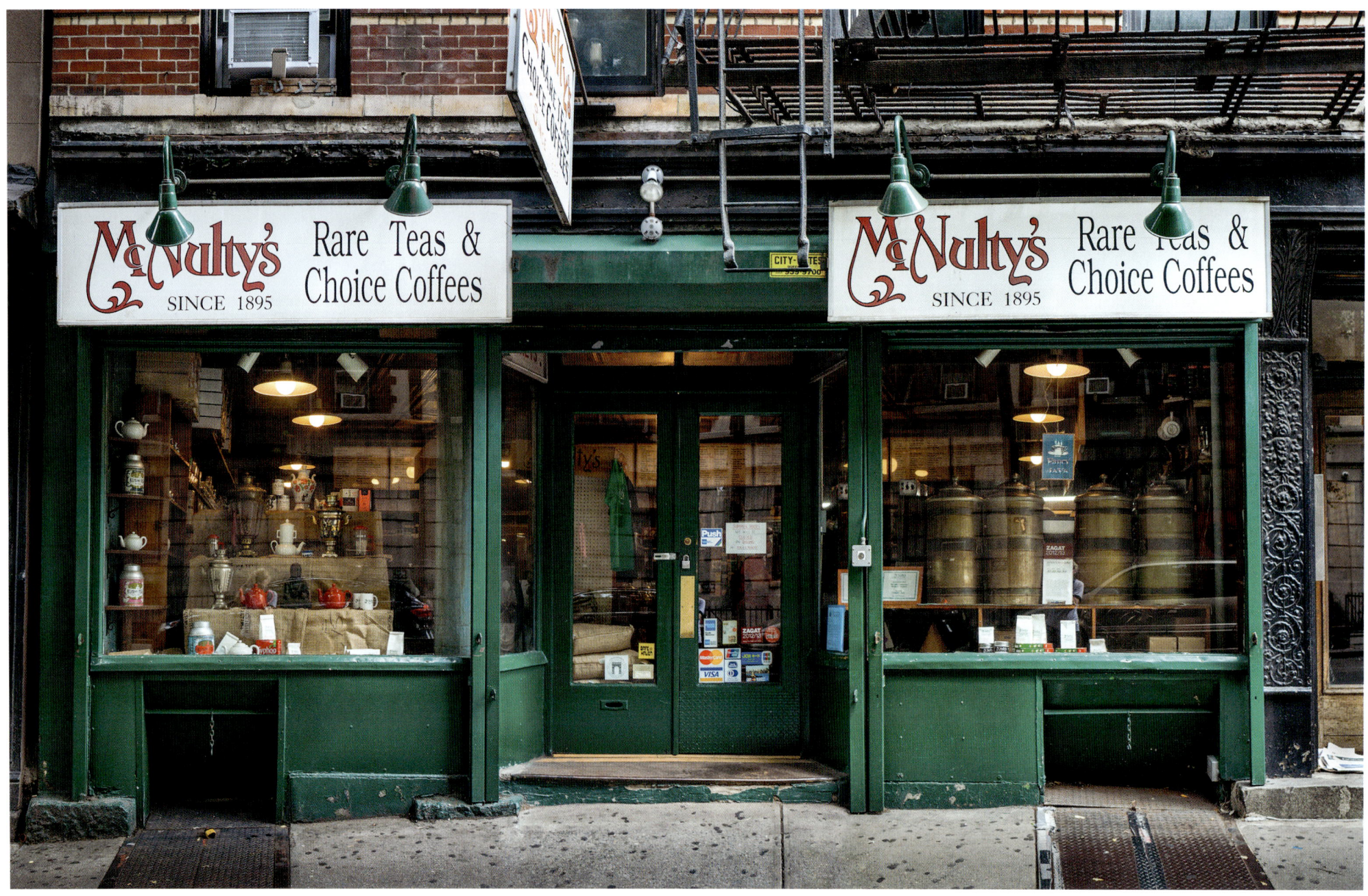

MCNULTY'S TEA & COFFEE
Christopher Street near Bleecker Street, Greenwich Village, 2014

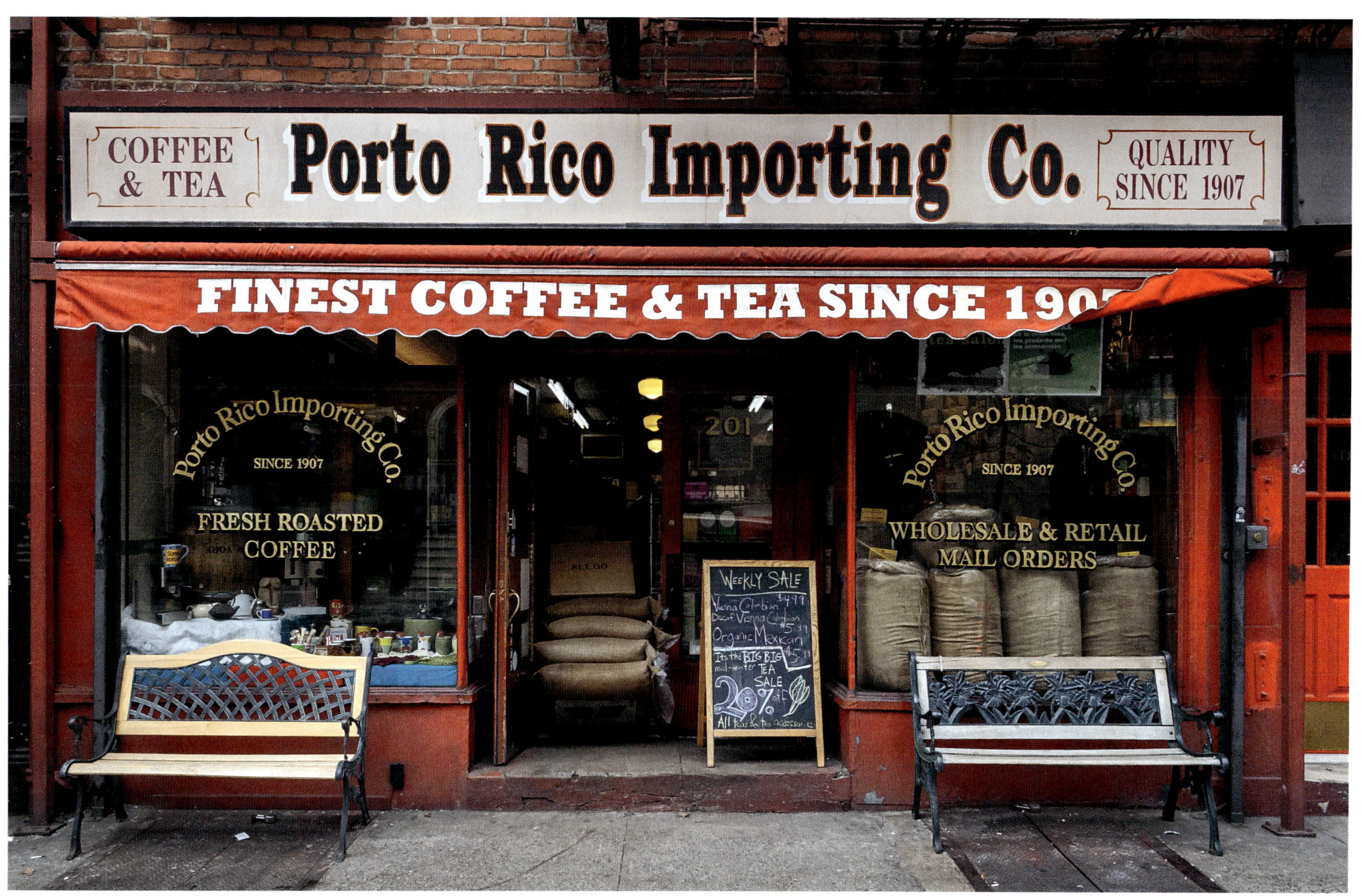

PORTO RICO IMPORTING CO.
Bleecker Street near 6th Avenue, Greenwich Village, 2007

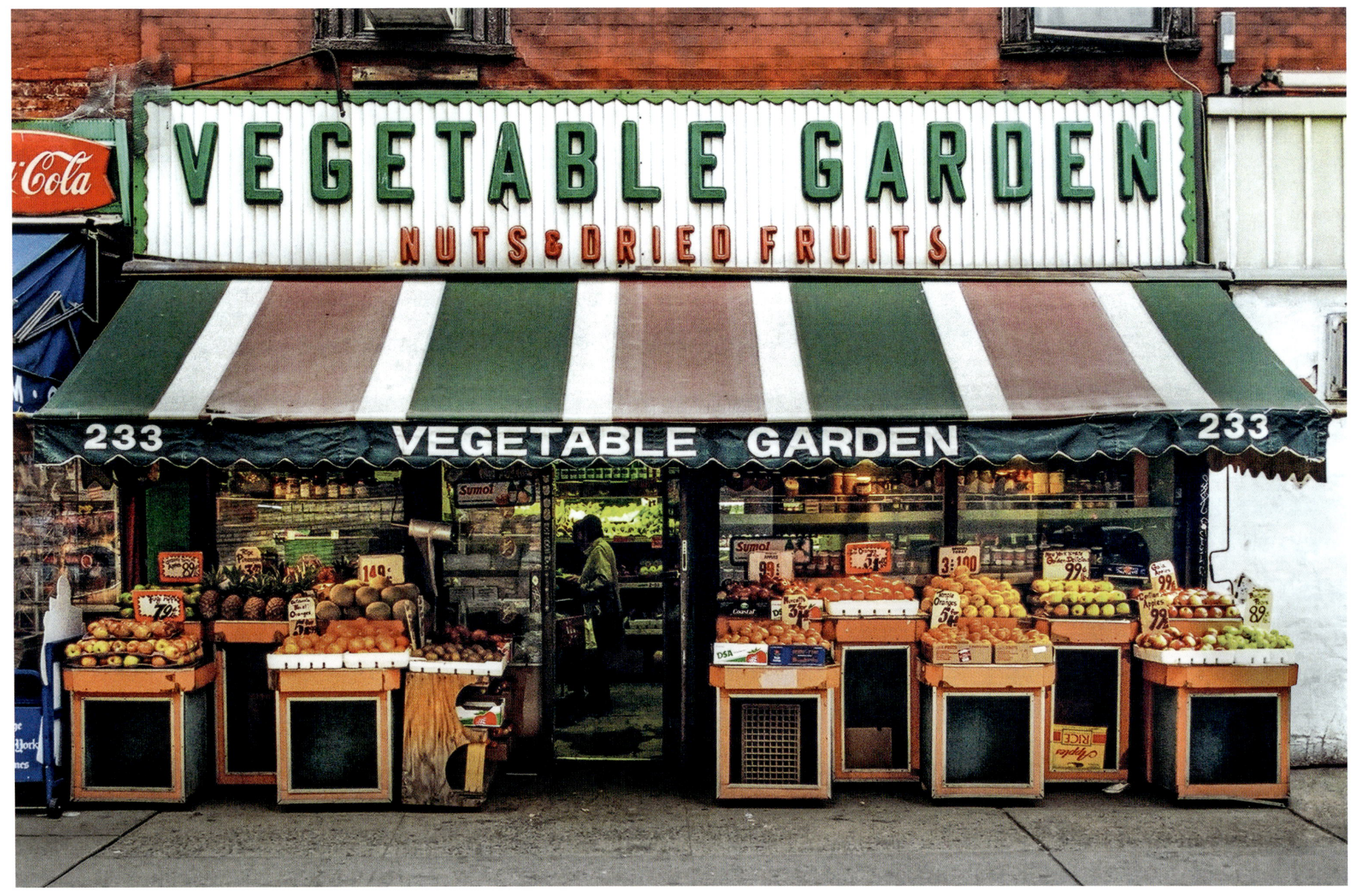

68 VEGETABLE GARDEN
Bleecker Street near Carmine Street, Greenwich Village, 2001

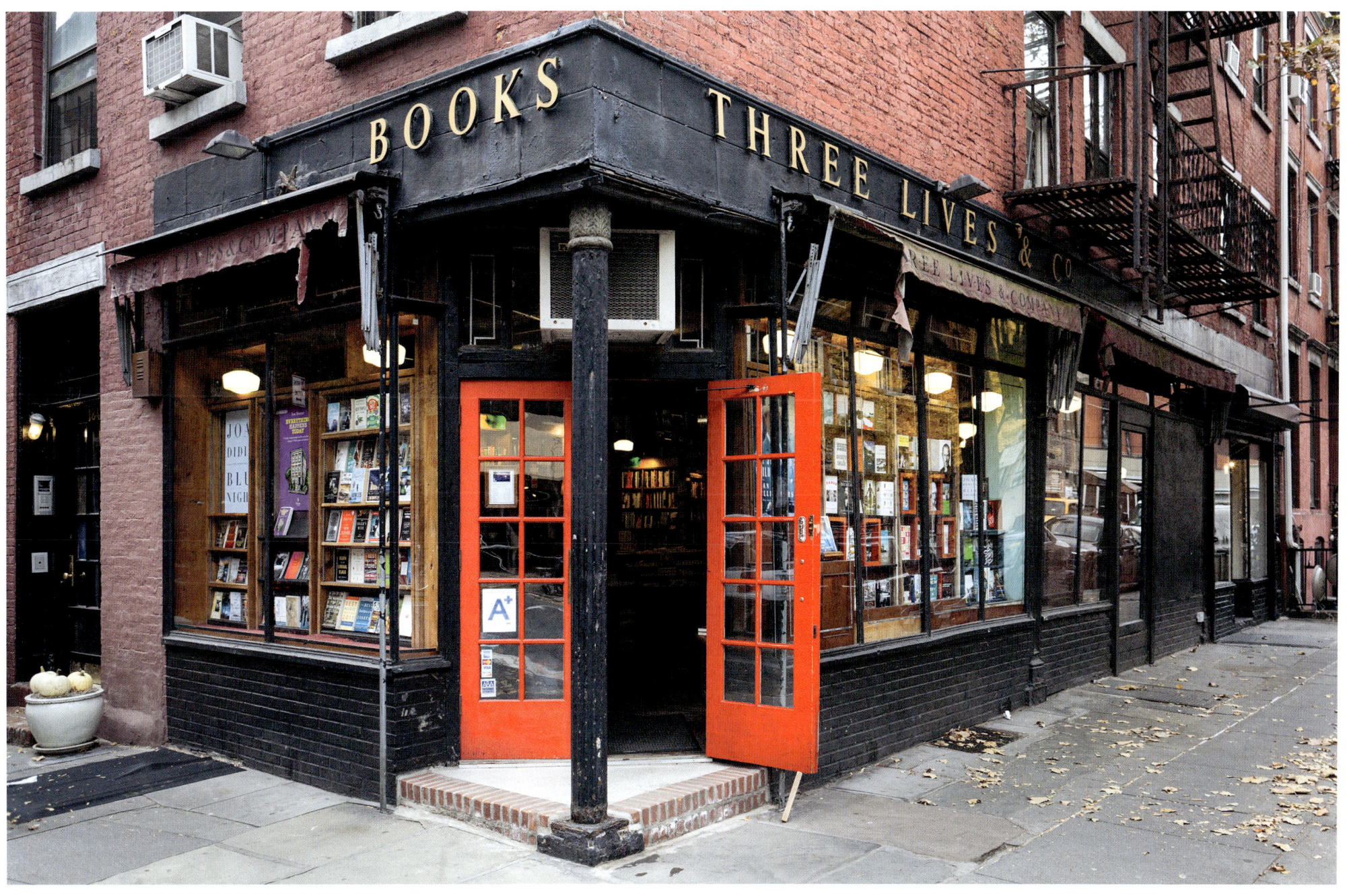

THREE LIVES & COMPANY
West 10th Street at Waverly Place, Greenwich Village, 2011

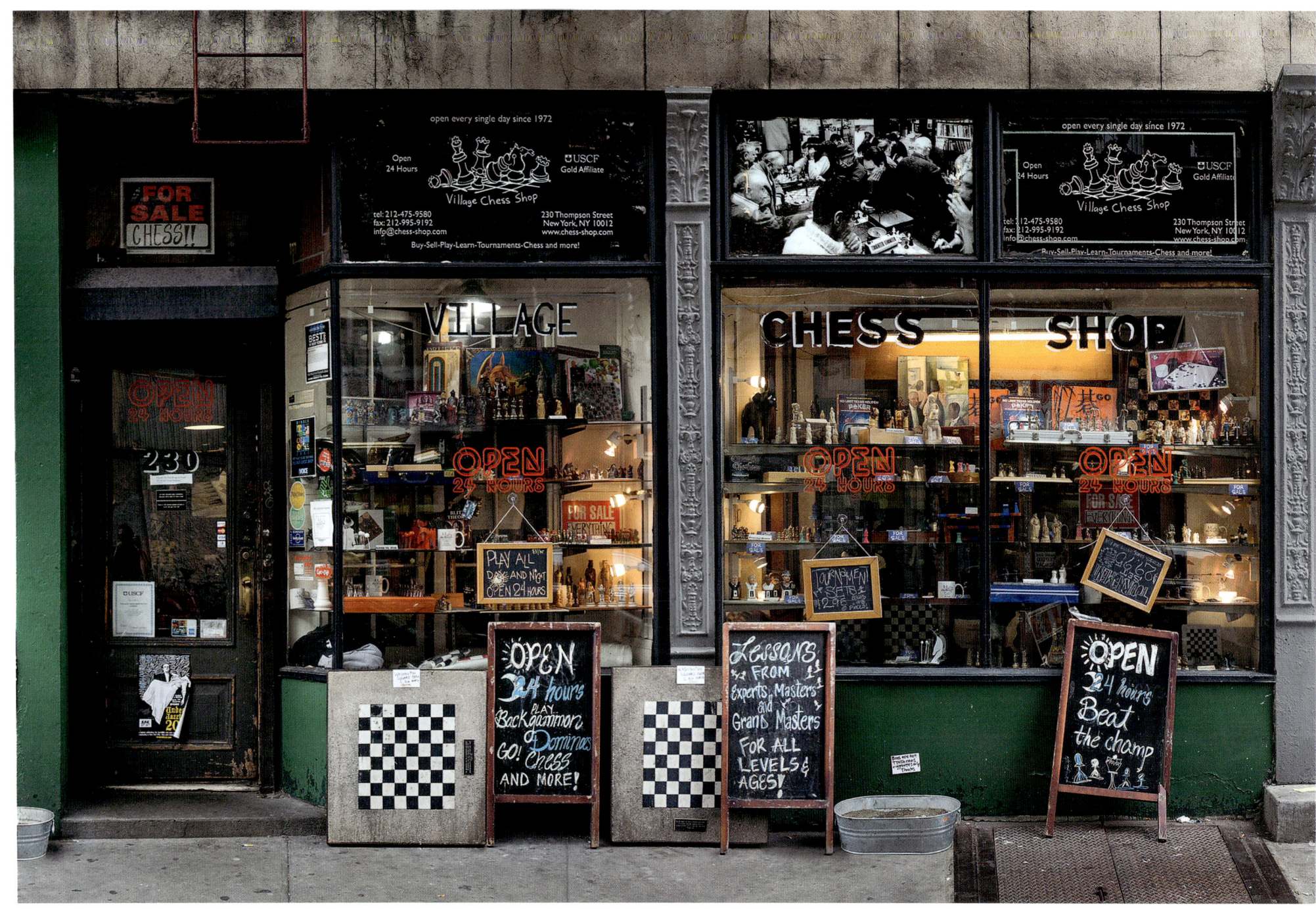

VILLAGE CHESS SHOP
Thompson Street near West 3rd Street, Greenwich Village, 2011

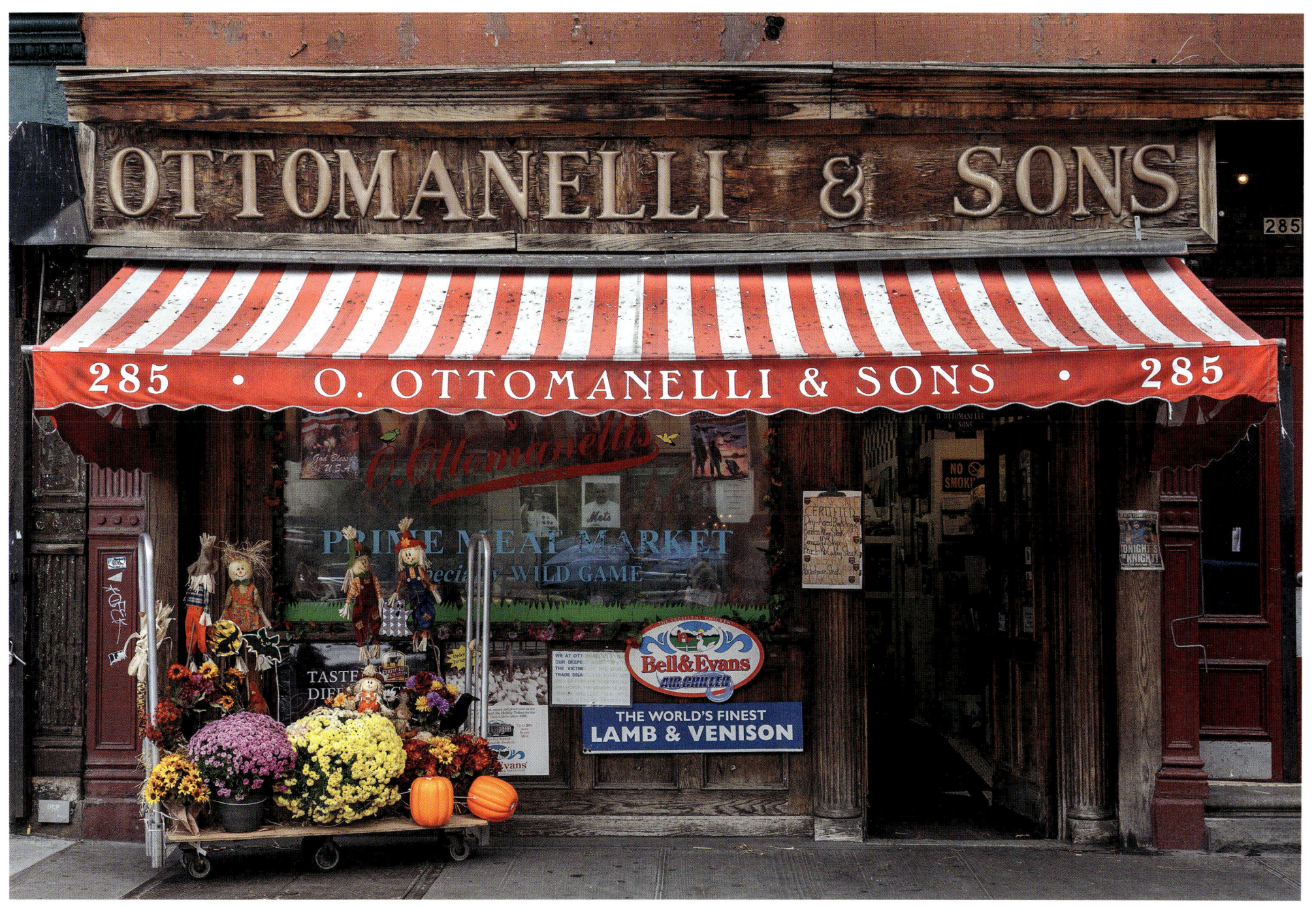

71 OTTOMANELLI & SONS
Bleecker Street near 7th Avenue South, Greenwich Village, 2015

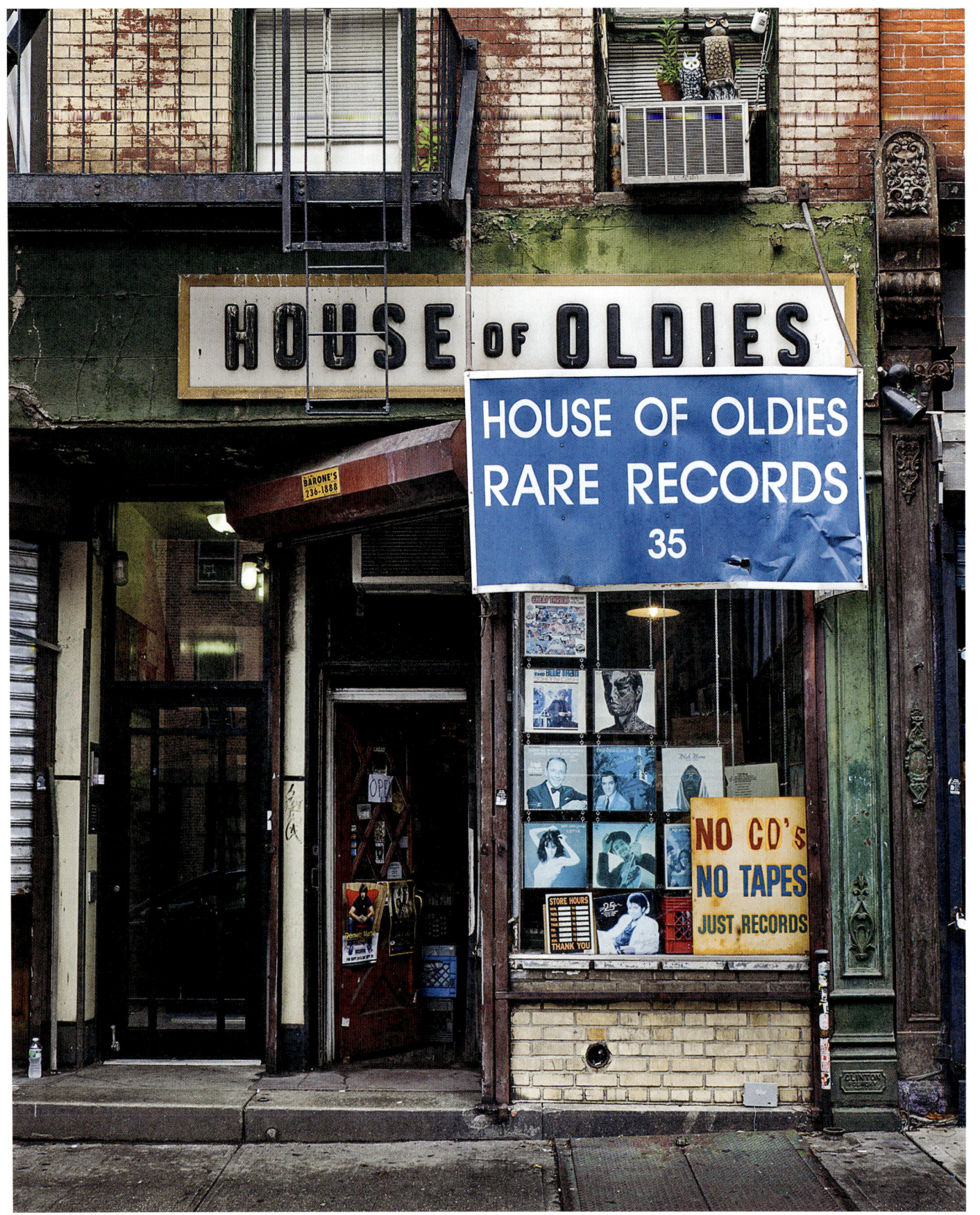

HOUSE OF OLDIES
Carmine Street near Bleecker Street,
Greenwich Village, 2010

→
ZITO'S BAKERY
Bleecker Street near Cornelia Street,
Greenwich Village, 2001

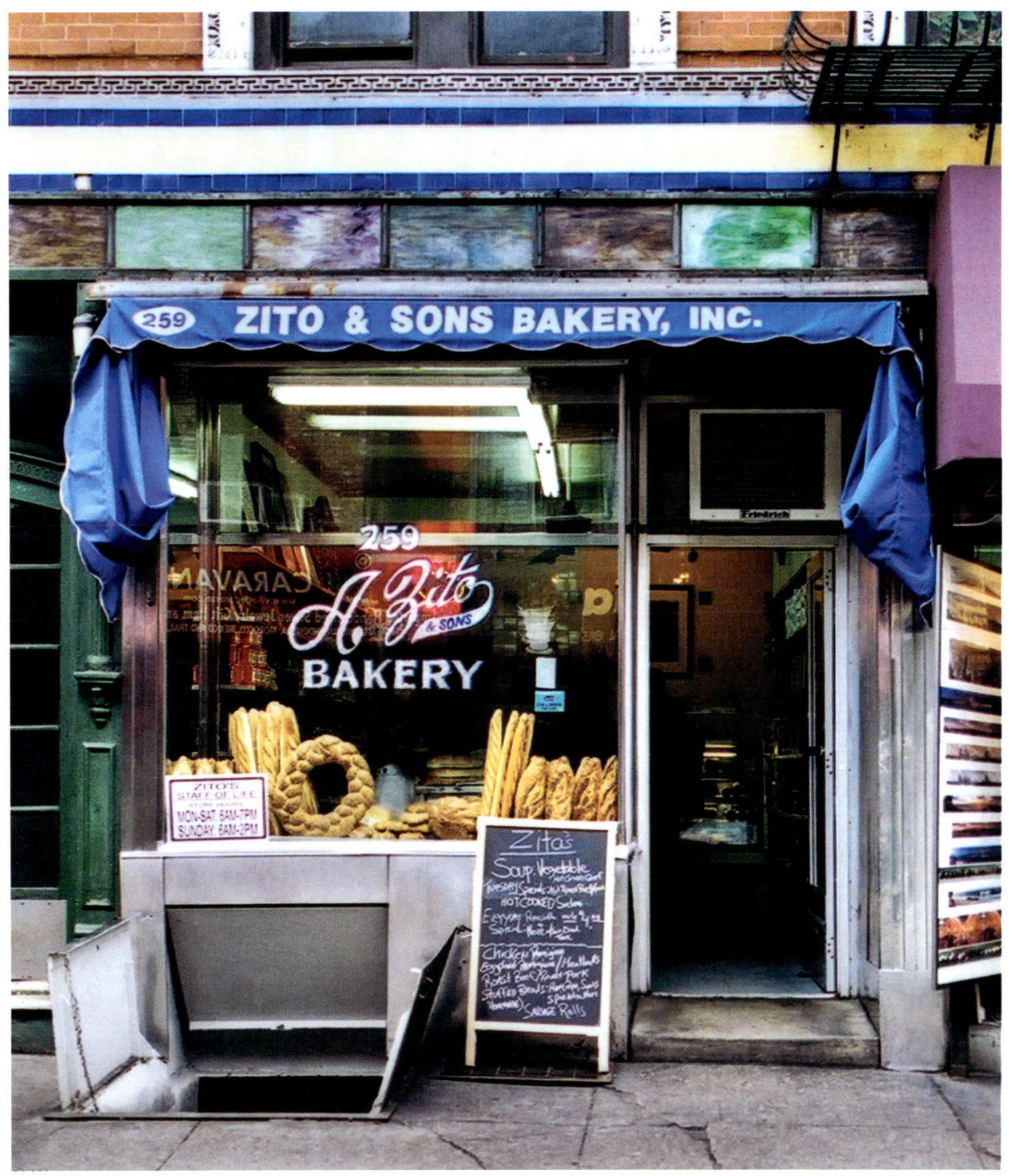

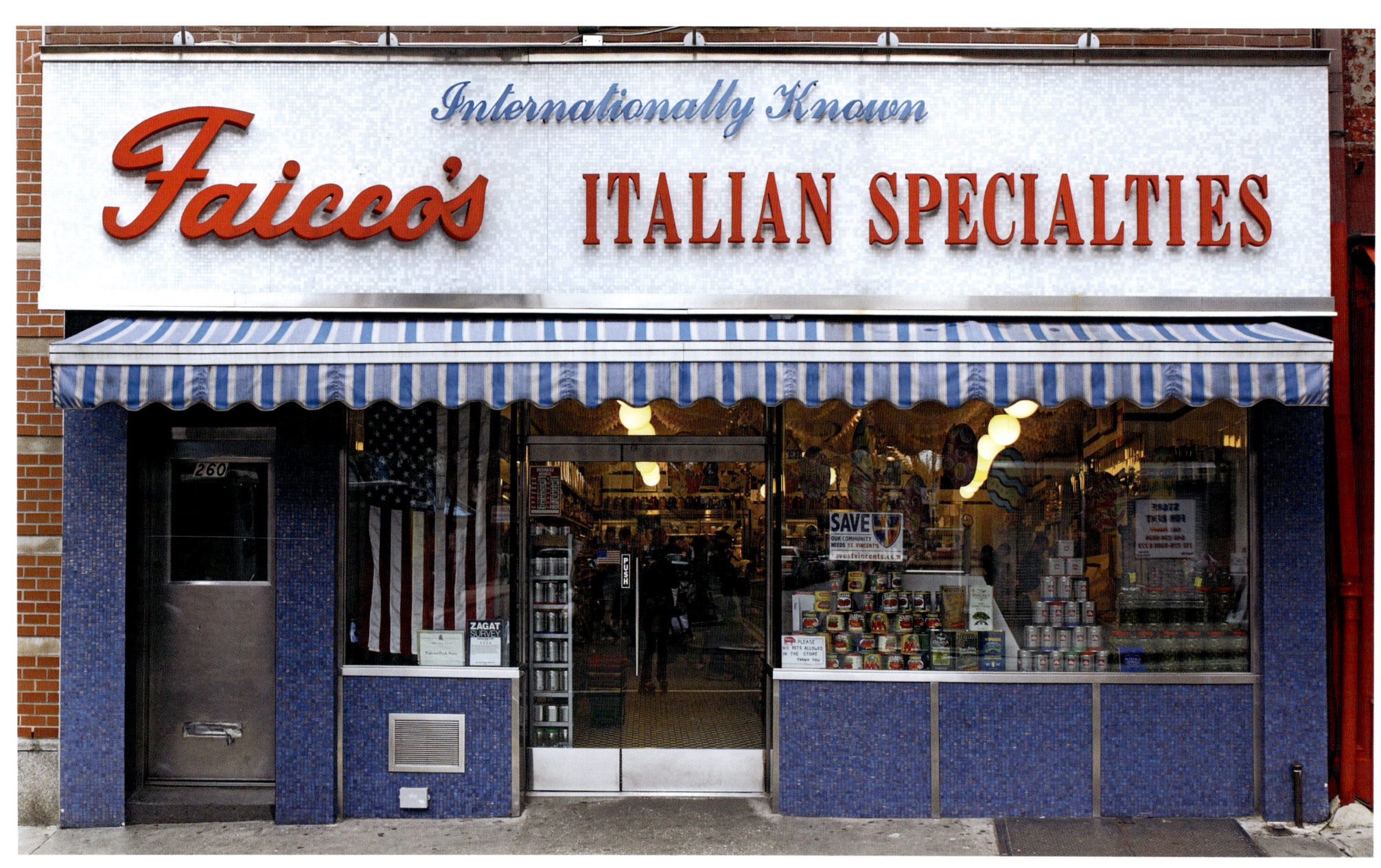

74 FAICCO'S ITALIAN SPECIALTIES
Bleecker Street at Cornelia Street, Greenwich Village, 2010

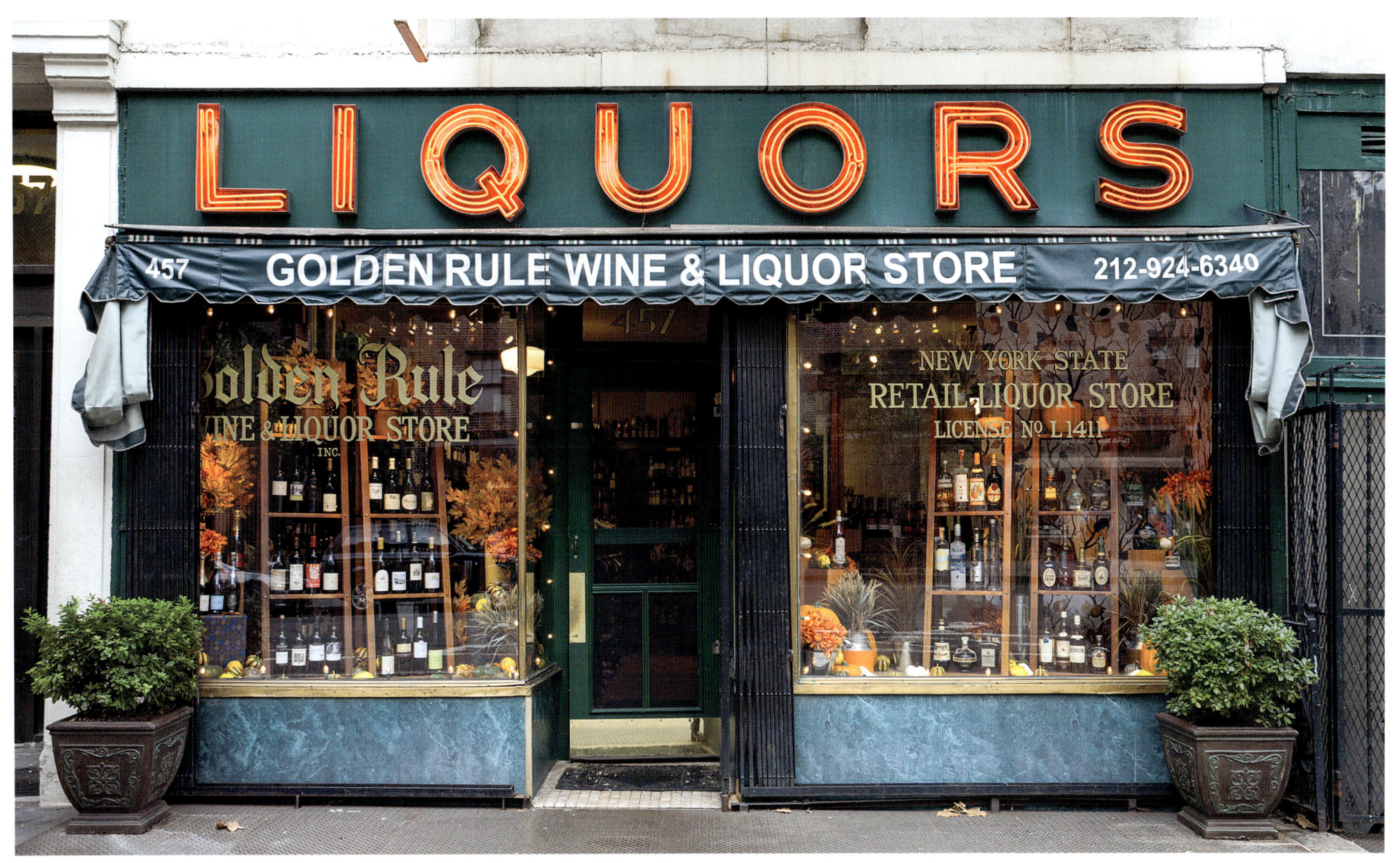

GOLDEN RULE WINE & LIQUOR STORE
Hudson Street near Barrow Street, Greenwich Village, 2010

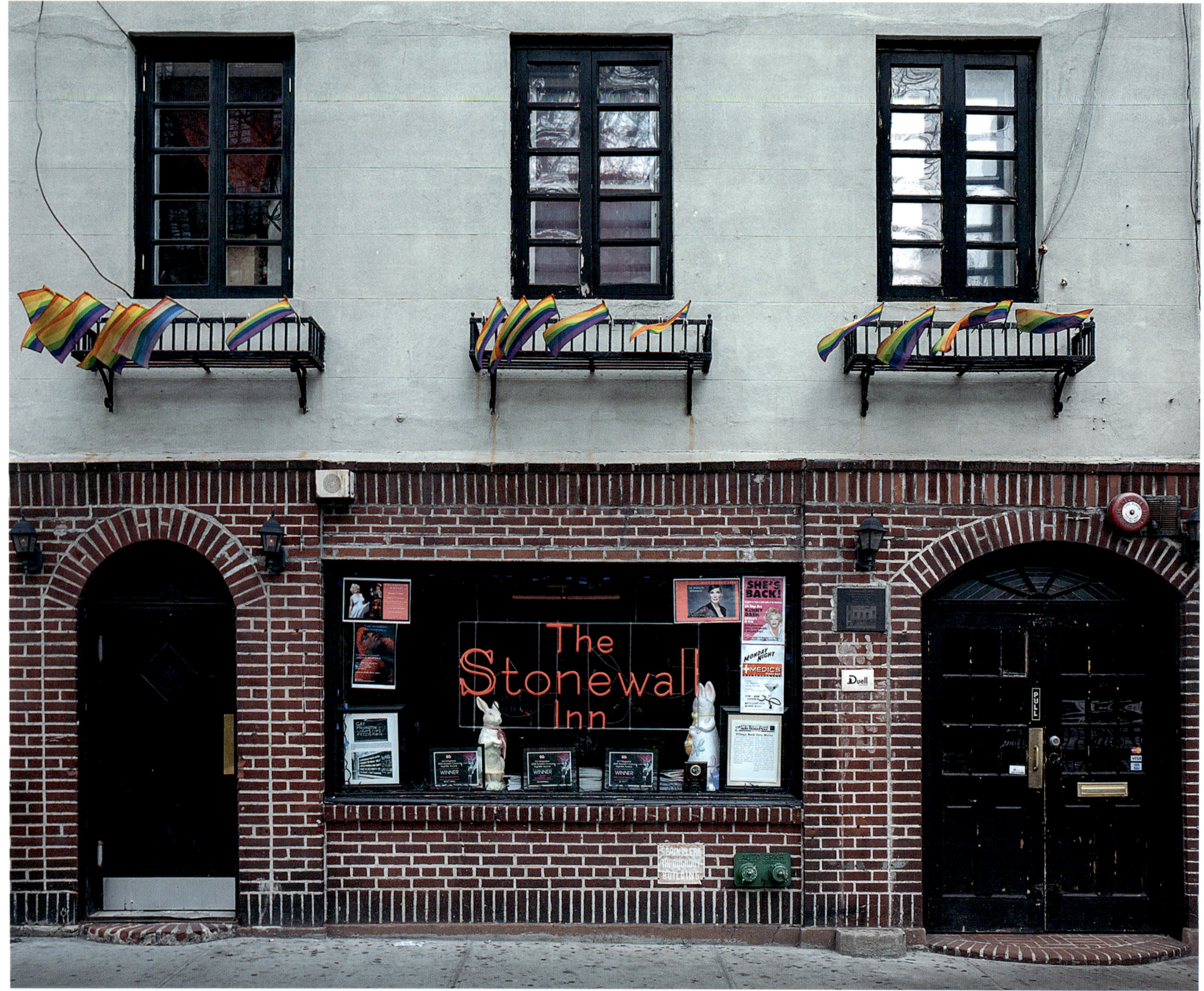

THE STONEWALL INN
Christopher Street near 7th Avenue South, Greenwich Village, 2009

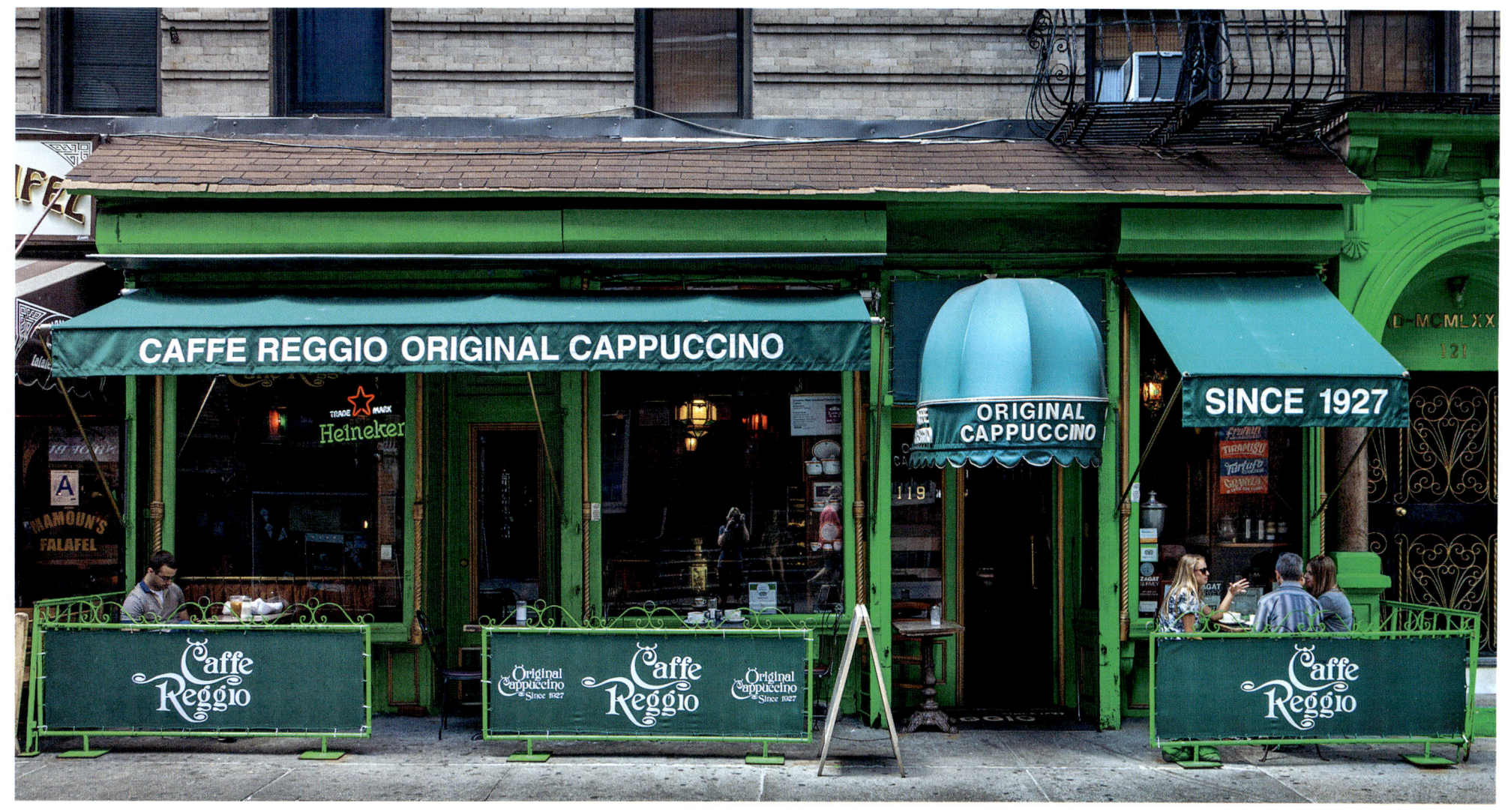

CAFFE REGGIO
MacDougal Street near West 3rd Street, Greenwich Village, 2015

MANHATTAN

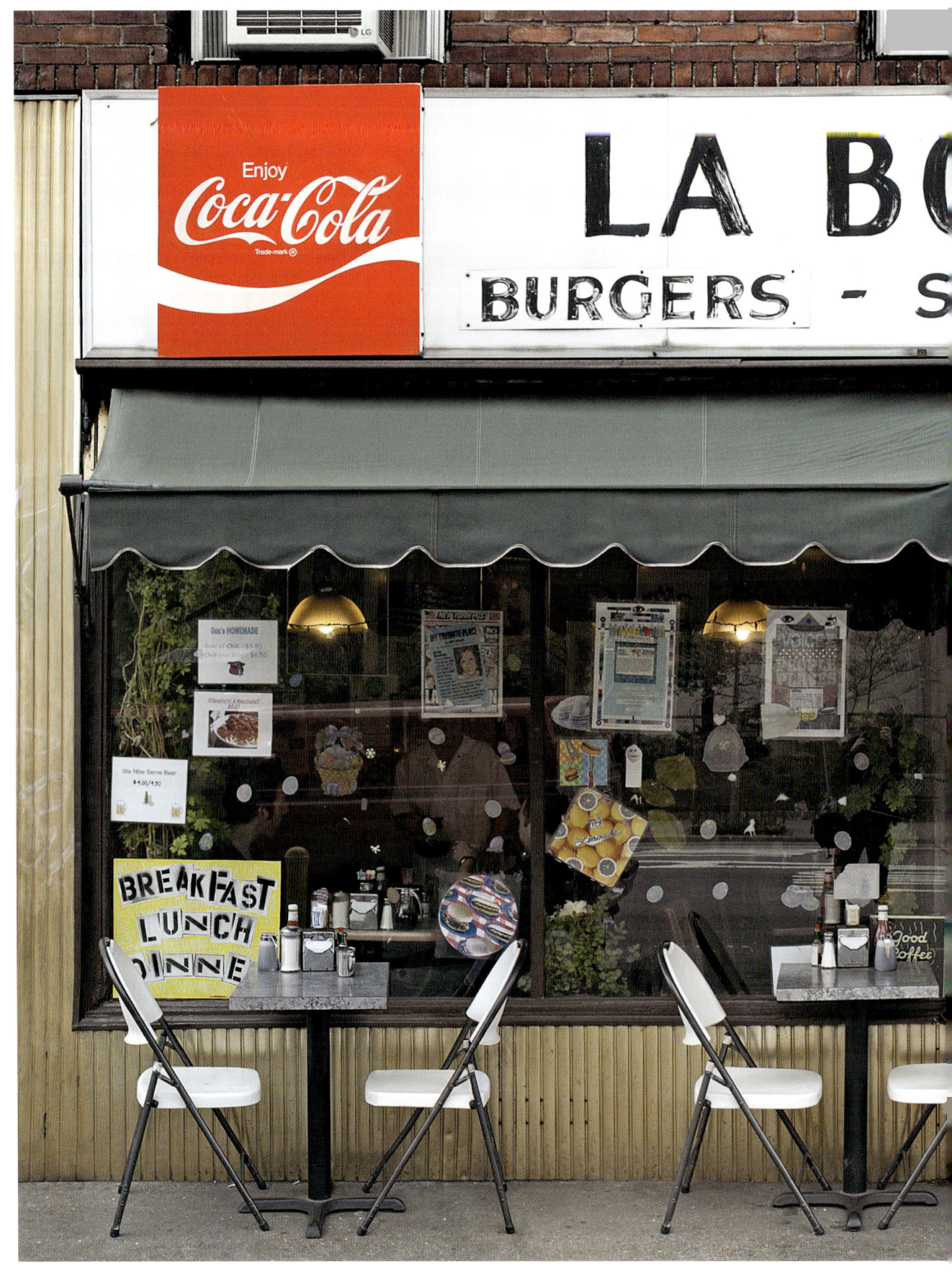

LA BONBONNIERE
8th Avenue near West 12th Street, Greenwich Village, 2010

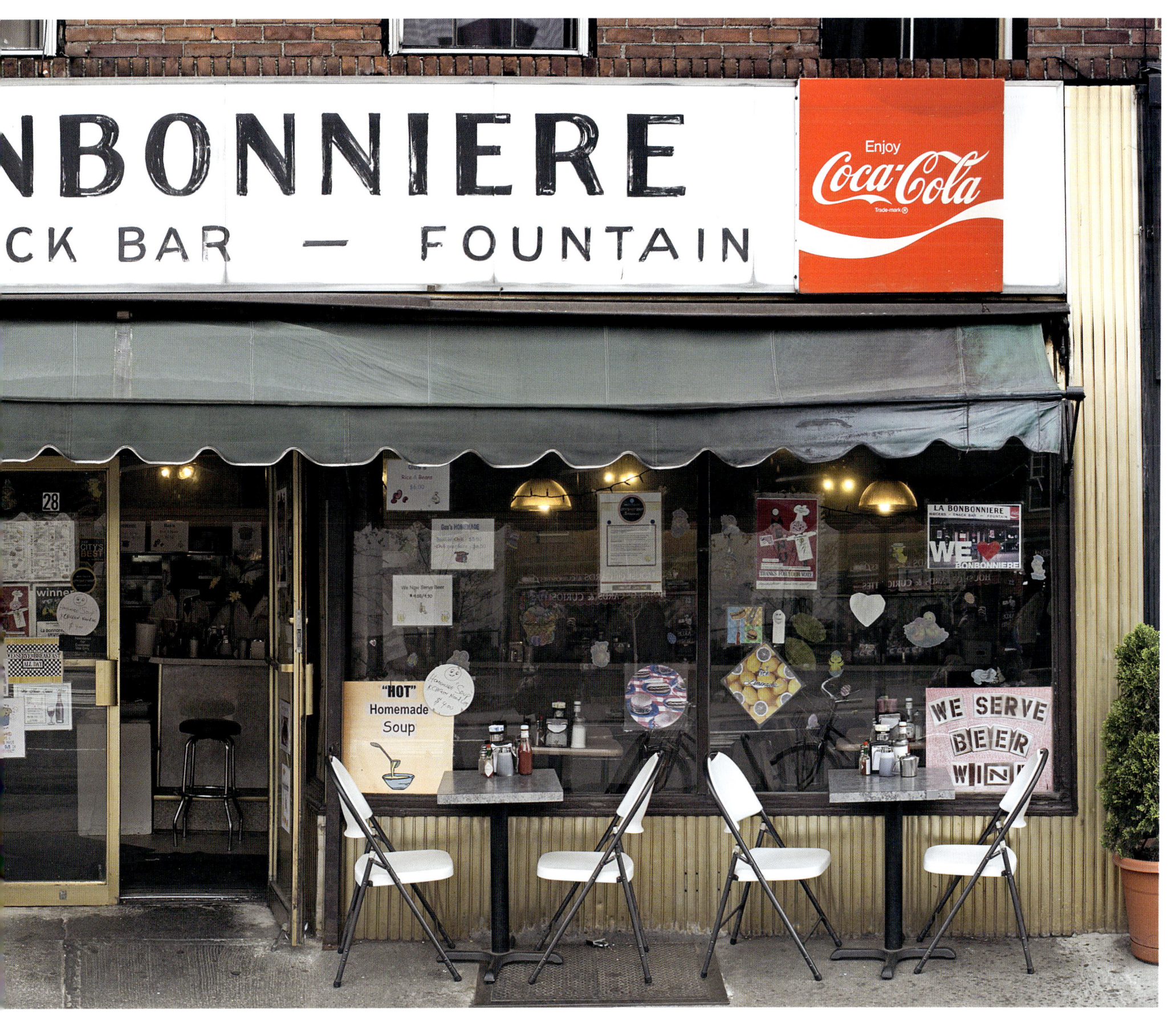

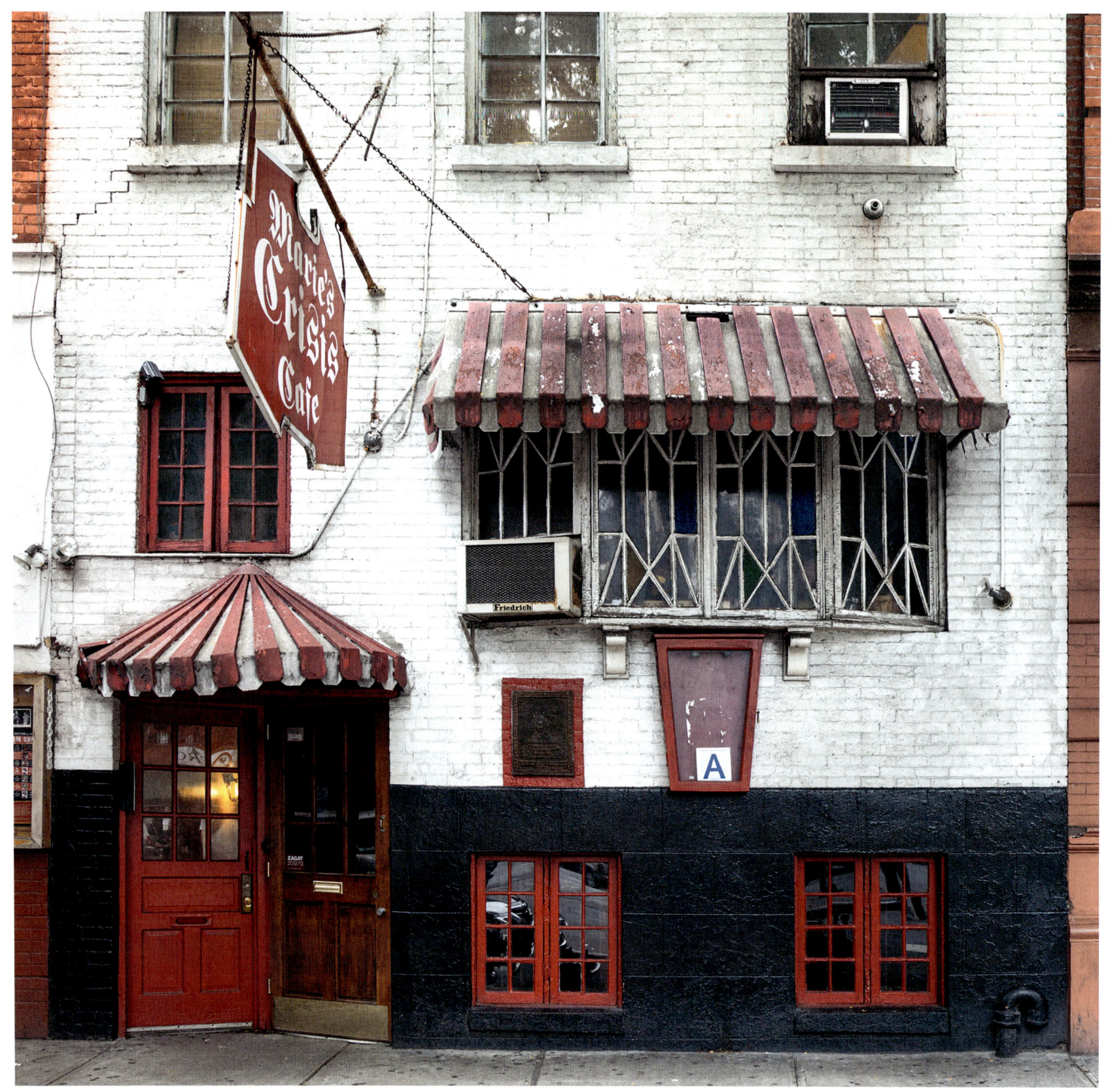

MARIE'S CRISIS CAFE
Grove Street near 7th Avenue South, Greenwich Village, 2014

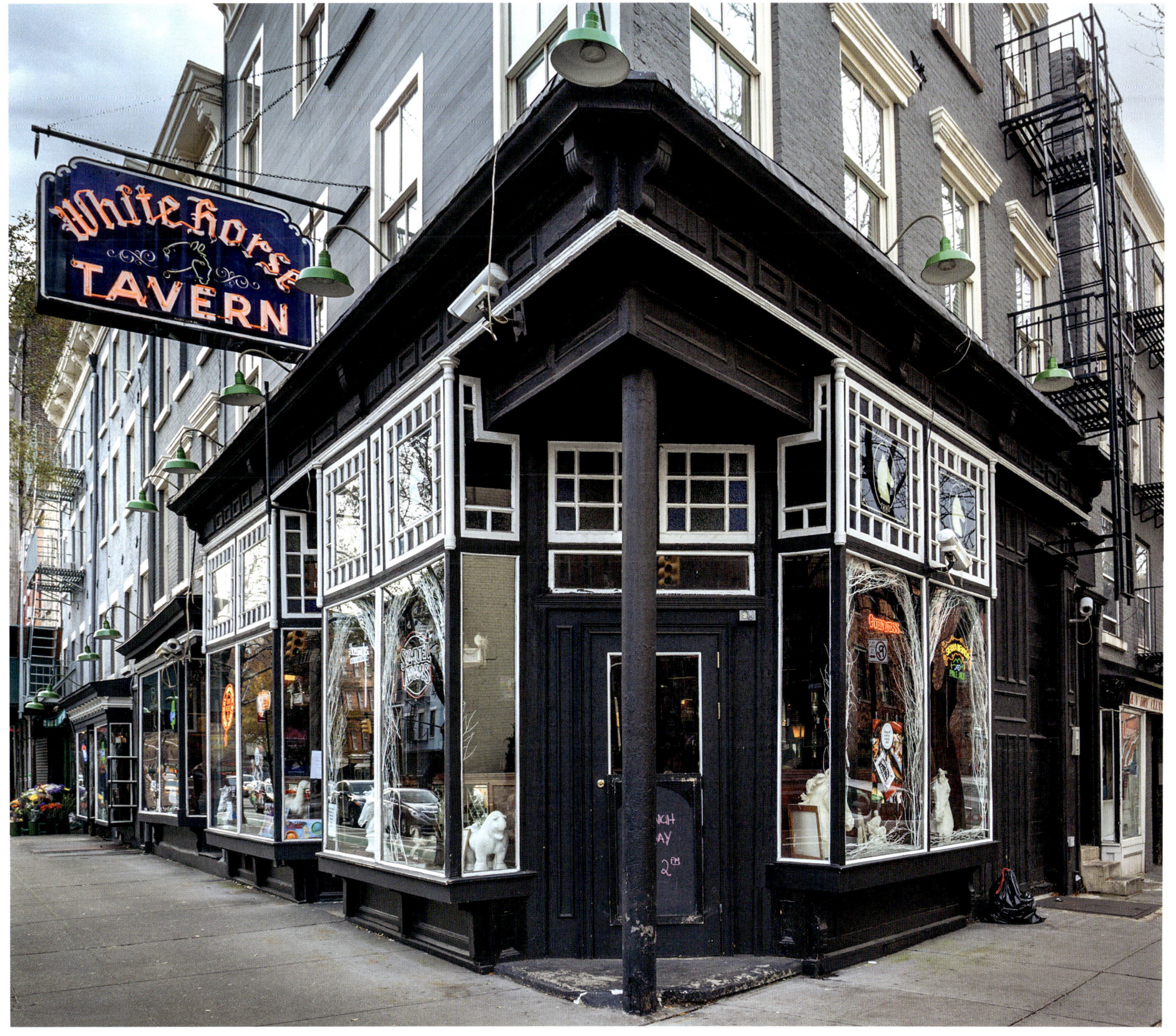

WHITE HORSE TAVERN
Hudson Street at West 11th Street, Greenwich Village, 2014

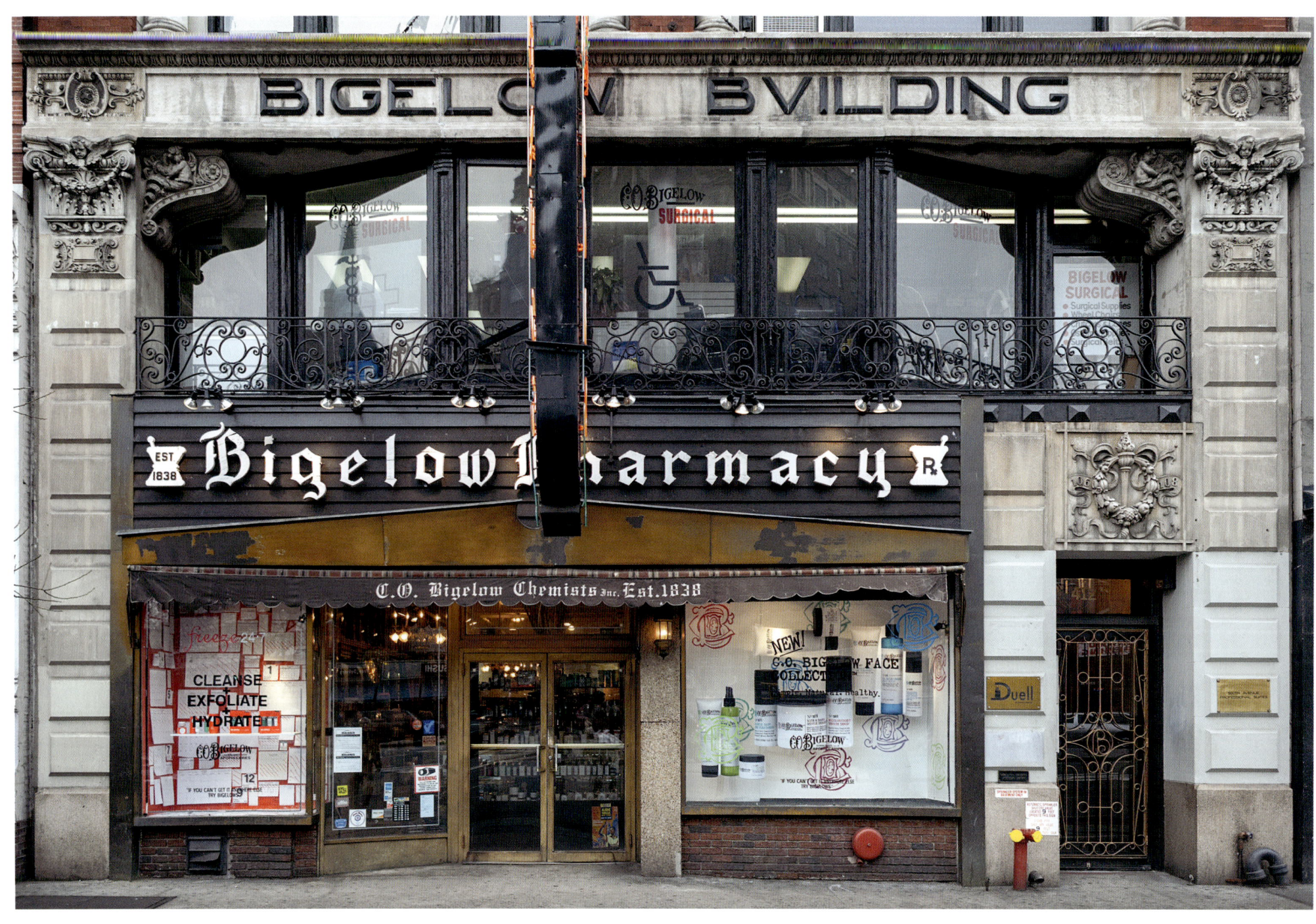

82 C.O. BIGELOW PHARMACY
6th Avenue near West 9th Street, Greenwich Village, 2009

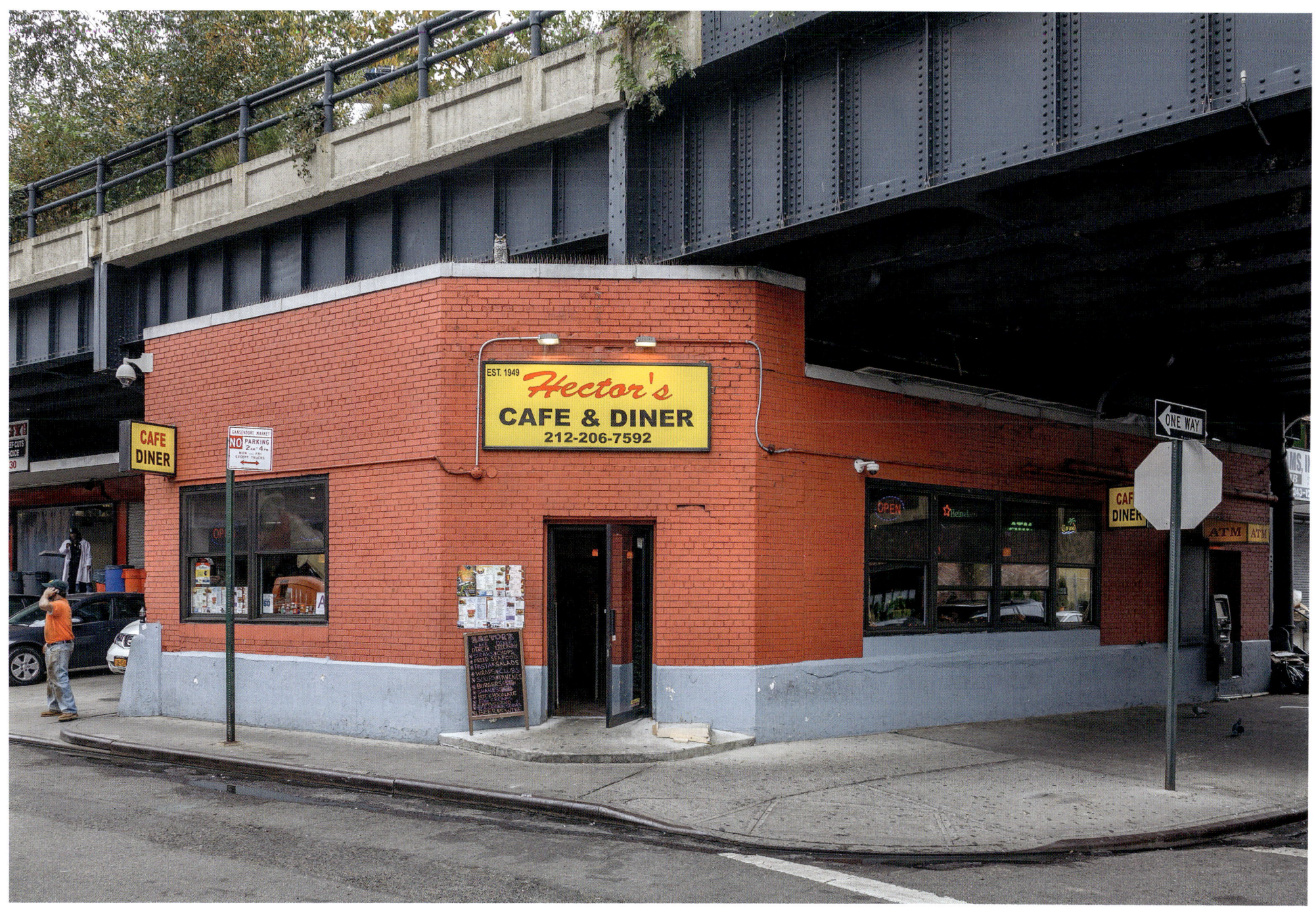

HECTOR'S CAFÉ & DINER
Little West 12th Street at Washington Street, Greenwich Village, 2012

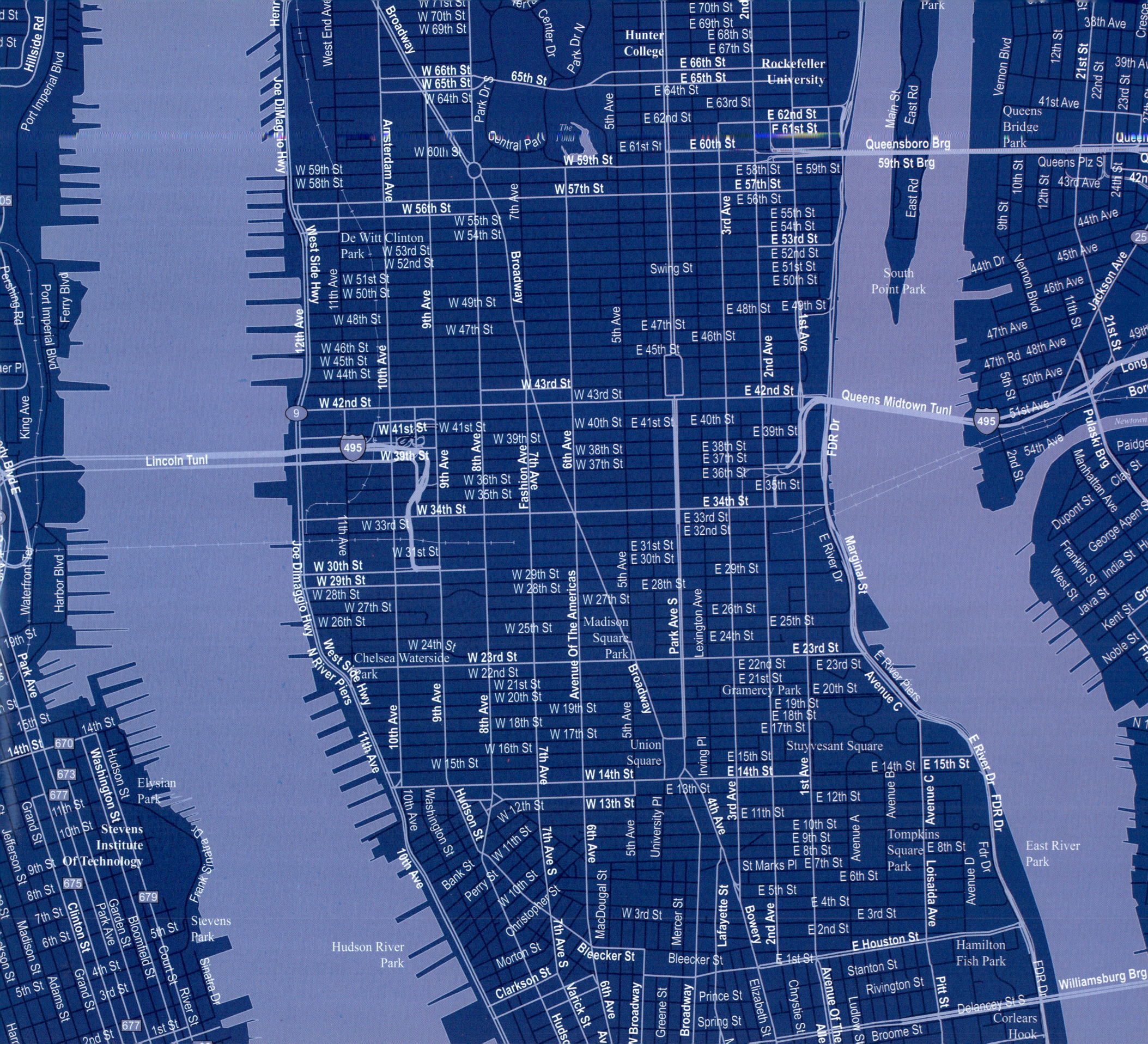

14TH TO 59TH STREETS

CHELSEA — FLATIRON DISTRICT — GRAMERCY — KIPS BAY — MIDTOWN — HELL'S KITCHEN — THEATER DISTRICT (including TIMES SQUARE)

The area from 14th Street to 59th Street encompasses many neighborhoods, each with their own fashionable shops, cafés, restaurants, and bars.

Chelsea is bounded to the south by West 14th Street and to the west by the Hudson River. Its northern and eastern boundaries are difficult to define, but correspond roughly to 34th Street and 6th Avenue. After a period of decline, much of Chelsea was revitalized in the 1980s and '90s, especially by the gay community. Now, it is home to some of New York City's most sought-after addresses, with a variety of housing options and many restaurants, bars, and nightclubs.

The **Flatiron District**, which lies between Chelsea and Gramercy, is bounded to the north by 23rd Street, by Park Avenue to the east, by 14th Street to the south, and by 6th Avenue to the west. By the mid-1800s, Broadway and 6th Avenue became known as Ladies' Mile, an elegant shopping district. Although Ladies' Mile was abandoned by department stores by the time of World War I for sites further north, the area experienced a commercial revival during the 1990s. Today, once again, it is one of New York City's popular shopping destinations.

Gramercy is bounded to the north by 23rd Street, to the east by 1st Avenue, to the south by 14th Street, and to the west by Park Avenue South. The land was once farmland owned by Peter Stuyvesant, the influential Dutch governor who helped develop the city in the mid-1600s, when it was known as New Amsterdam. The property was later bought by the developer Samuel Ruggles, who in 1831 built streets in an English style around a private park and offered lots for sale, which became luxury townhouses. Today, Gramercy Park is one of the only private parks in the city; keys to its wrought iron gates are reserved for people residing around the park who pay an annual fee.

Kips Bay is bounded to the north by 34th Street, to the east by the East River, to the south by 27th Street, and to the west by 3rd Avenue. It is named for Jacobus Kip, who owned a large farm in the area in the 1600s. By the early 1900s, elevated rail lines were built along 2nd and 3rd Avenues, and many estates were replaced by tenements. Starting in the 1960s, large apartment complexes were built there, including Kips Bay Plaza, which contained the first exposed concrete structures in the city.

Midtown comprises the center of Manhattan and is roughly bounded to the north by 59th Street, to the east by 3rd Avenue, to the south by 34th Street, and to the west by 8th Avenue. In the 1920s, Midtown became New York City's central business district due largely to the presence of Grand Central Terminal and the convergence of numerous subway lines. At the center of Midtown is Rockefeller Center, and to the west are the Theater and Garment Districts.

Hell's Kitchen is bounded to the north by 59th Street, to the east by 8th Avenue, to the south by 34th Street, and to the west by the Hudson River. The area's moniker is most likely based on the name of a notorious local gang. After two children were killed in gang violence in 1959, local organizations sought to improve the neighborhood's image by promoting the area using its other name, Clinton, after the DeWitt Clinton Park. Hell's Kitchen resisted gentrification until the mid-1990s, but is now a less touristy adjunct to the nearby Theater District, with many stylish restaurants and bars.

The **Theater District**, where most Broadway theaters can be found, is bounded to the north by West 56th Street, to the east by 6th Avenue, to the south by West 40th Street, and to the west by 8th Avenue. It includes **Times Square**, a section of Midtown centered at the intersection of Broadway and 7th Avenue. Beginning in the late 1980s and early '90s, the area was revitalized, and it is now a major tourist destination known as "the crossroads of the world."

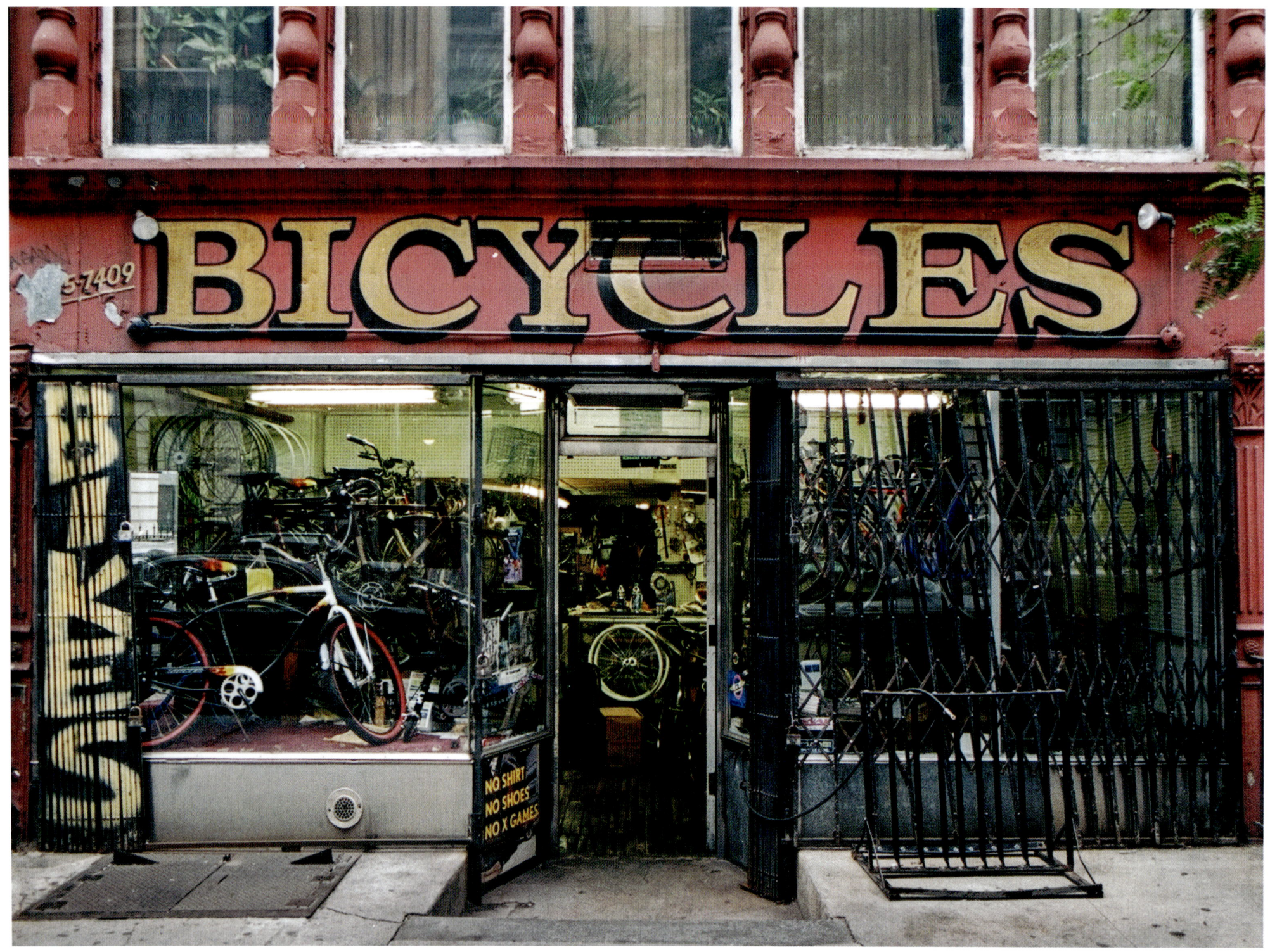

EMEY'S BIKE SHOP
East 17th Street near 3rd Avenue, Gramercy, 2003

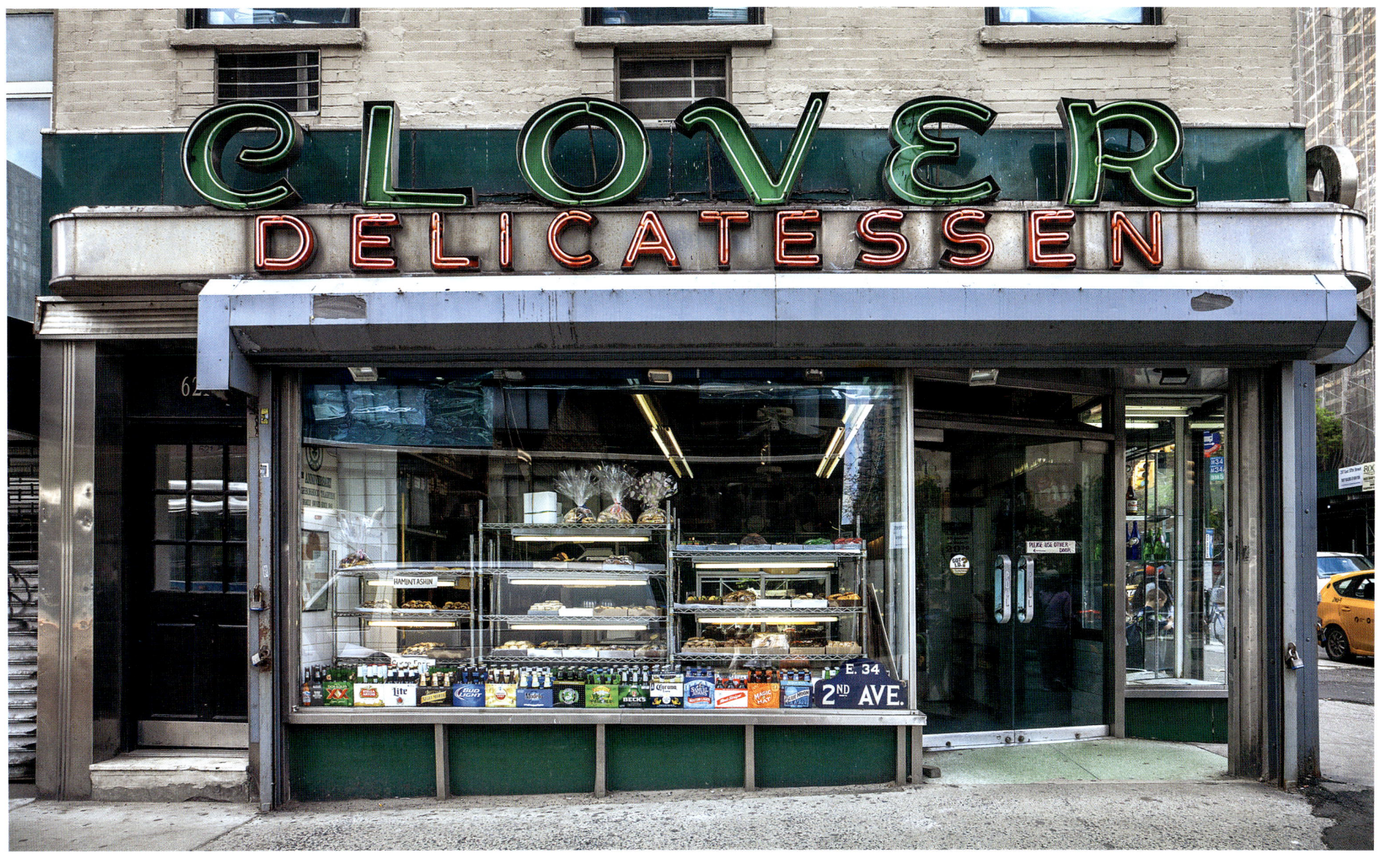

CLOVER DELICATESSEN
2nd Avenue at East 34th Street, Kips Bay, 2017

MANHATTAN

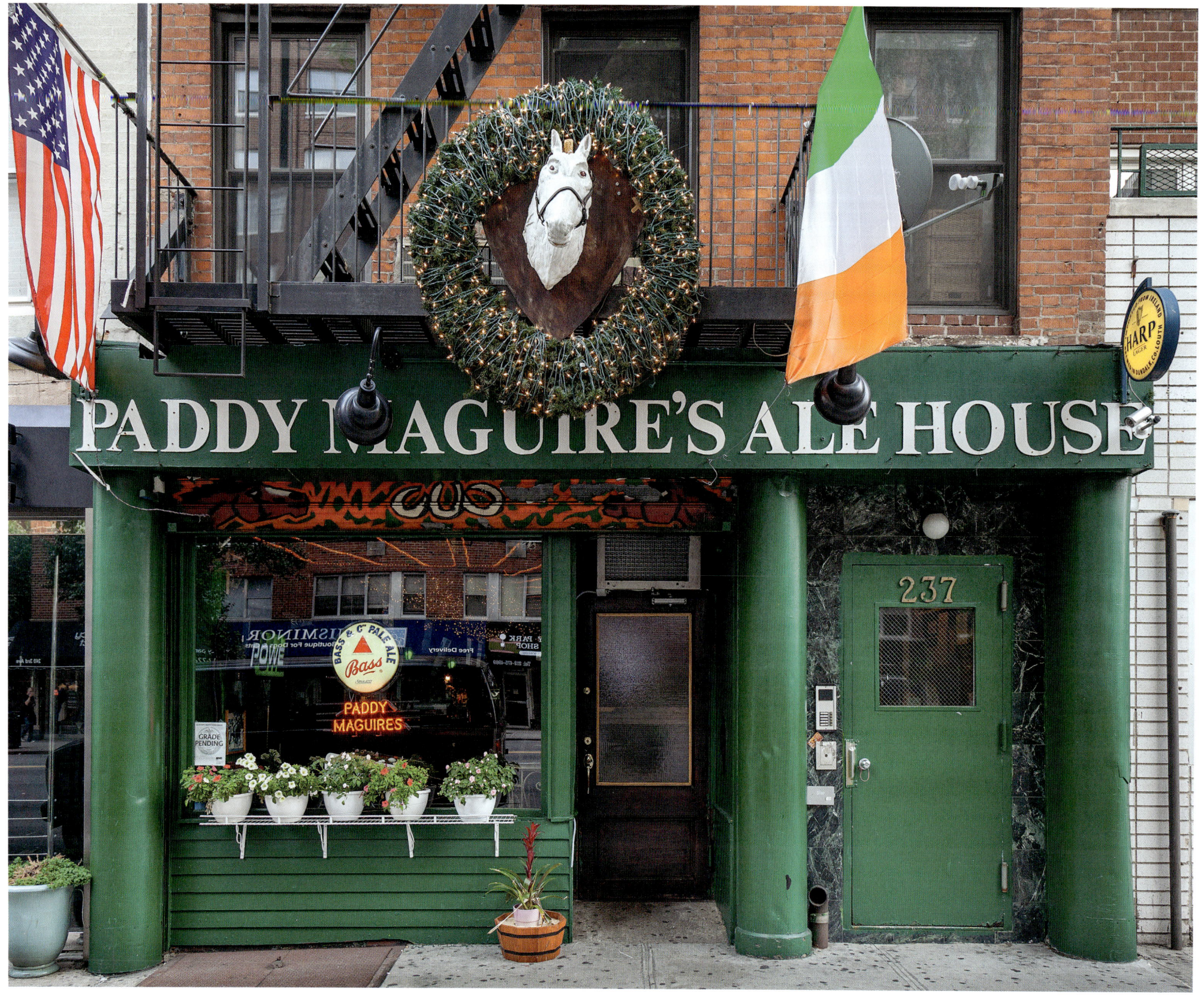

PADDY MAGUIRE'S ALE HOUSE
3rd Avenue near East 20th Street, Gramercy, 2011

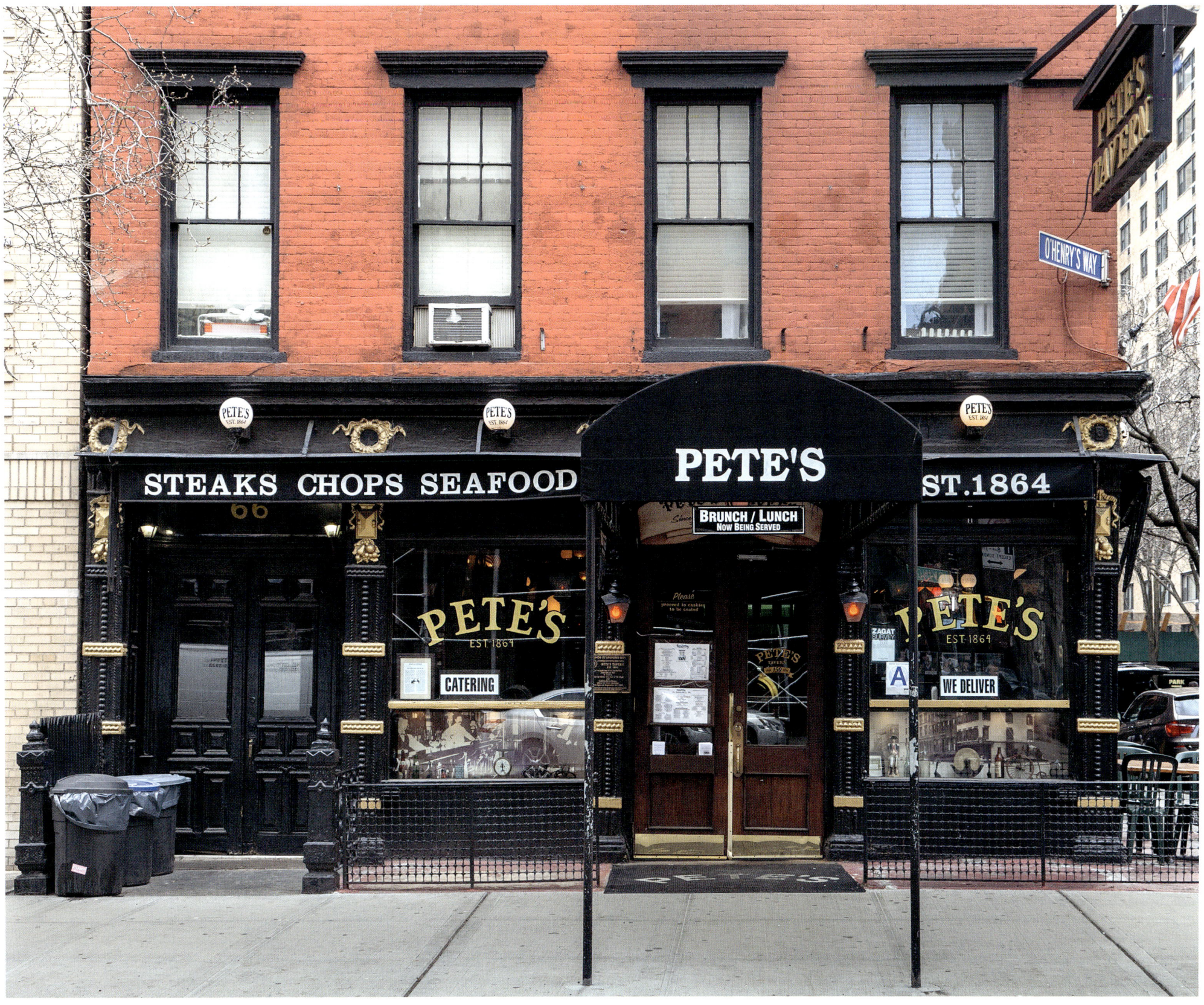

PETE'S TAVERN
East 18th Street at Irving Place, Gramercy, 2014

MANHATTAN

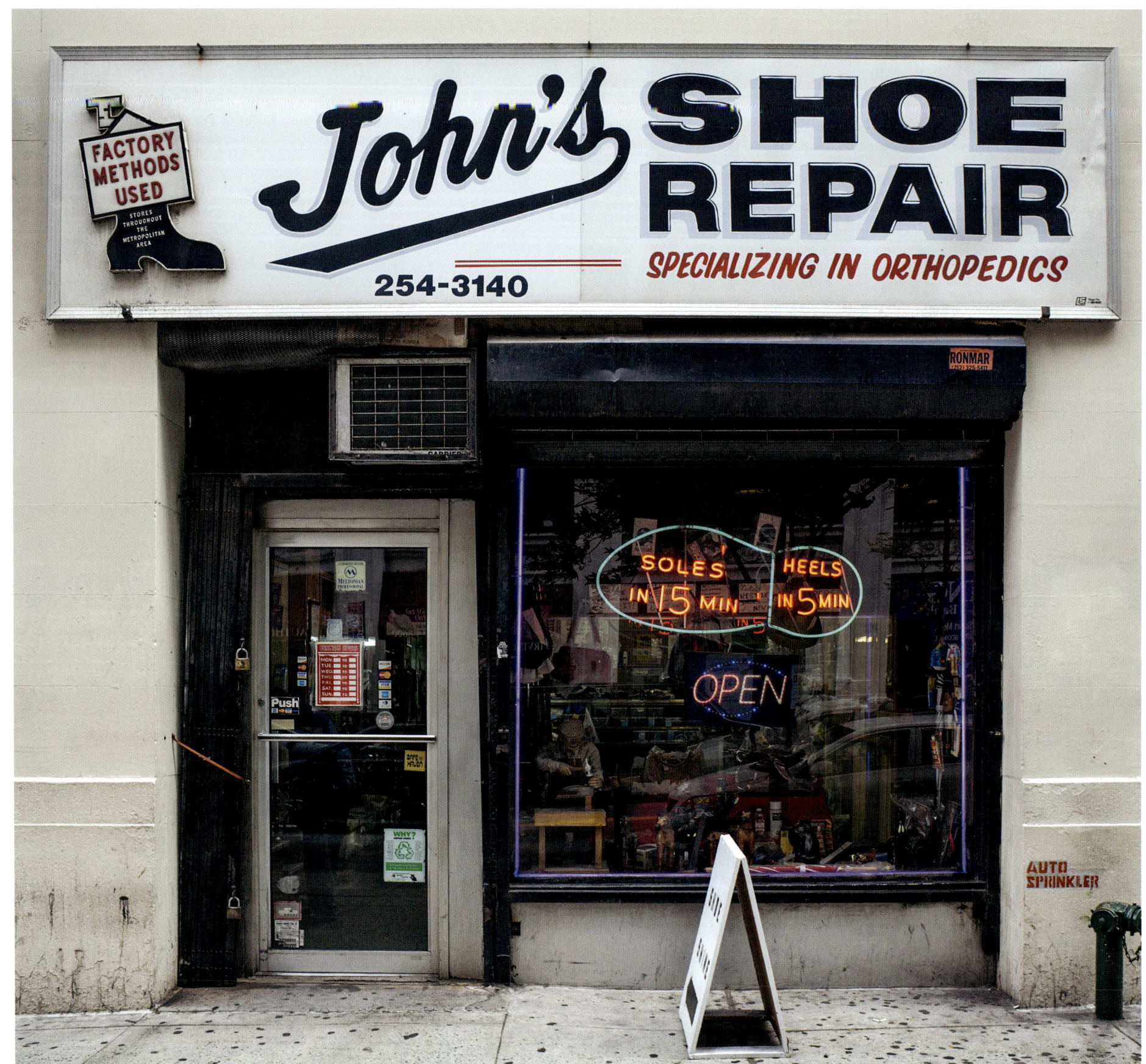

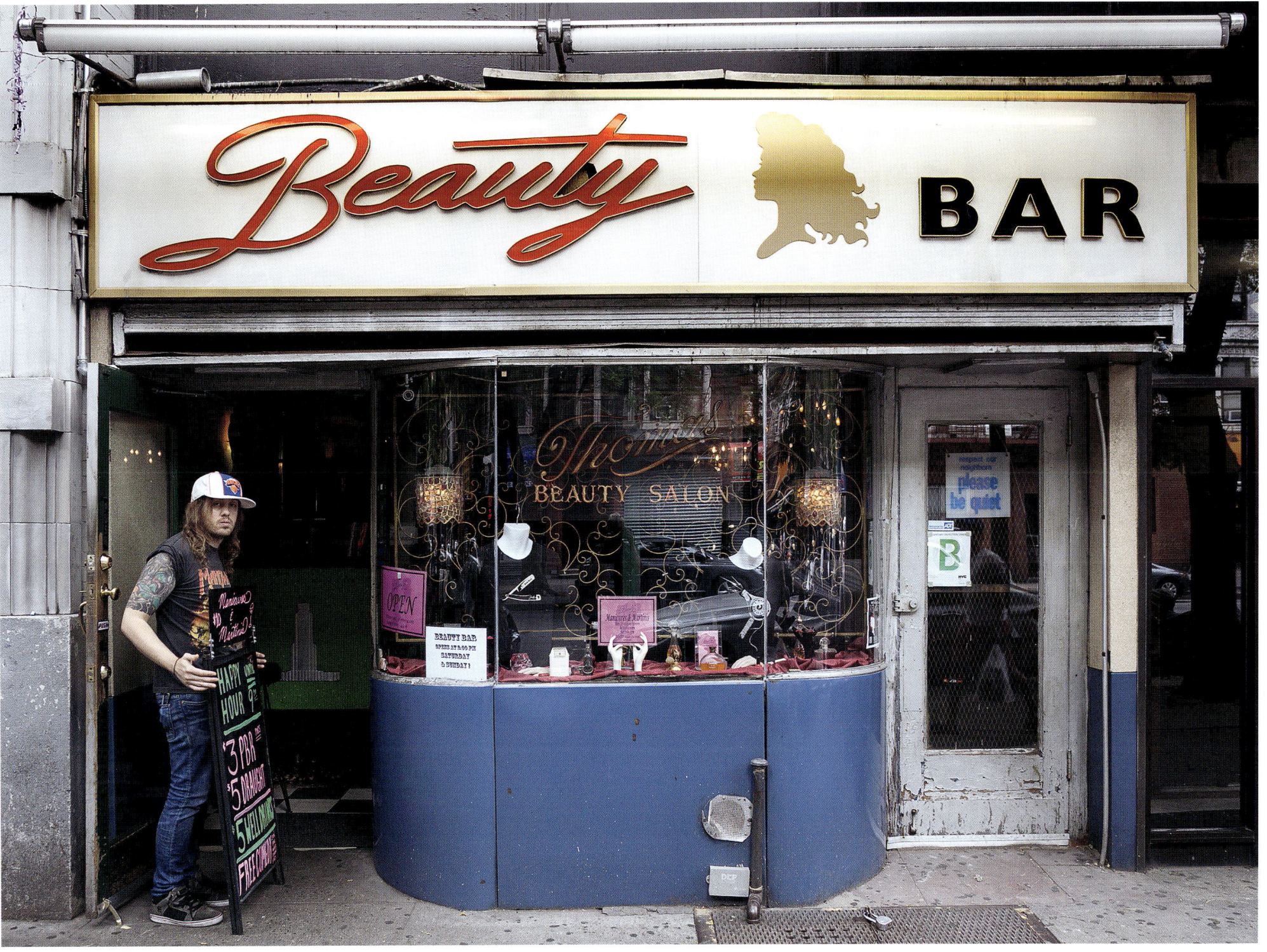

JOHN'S SHOE REPAIR
Irving Place near East 16th Street, Gramercy, 2010

BEAUTY BAR
East 14th Street near 2nd Avenue, Gramercy, 2013

MANHATTAN

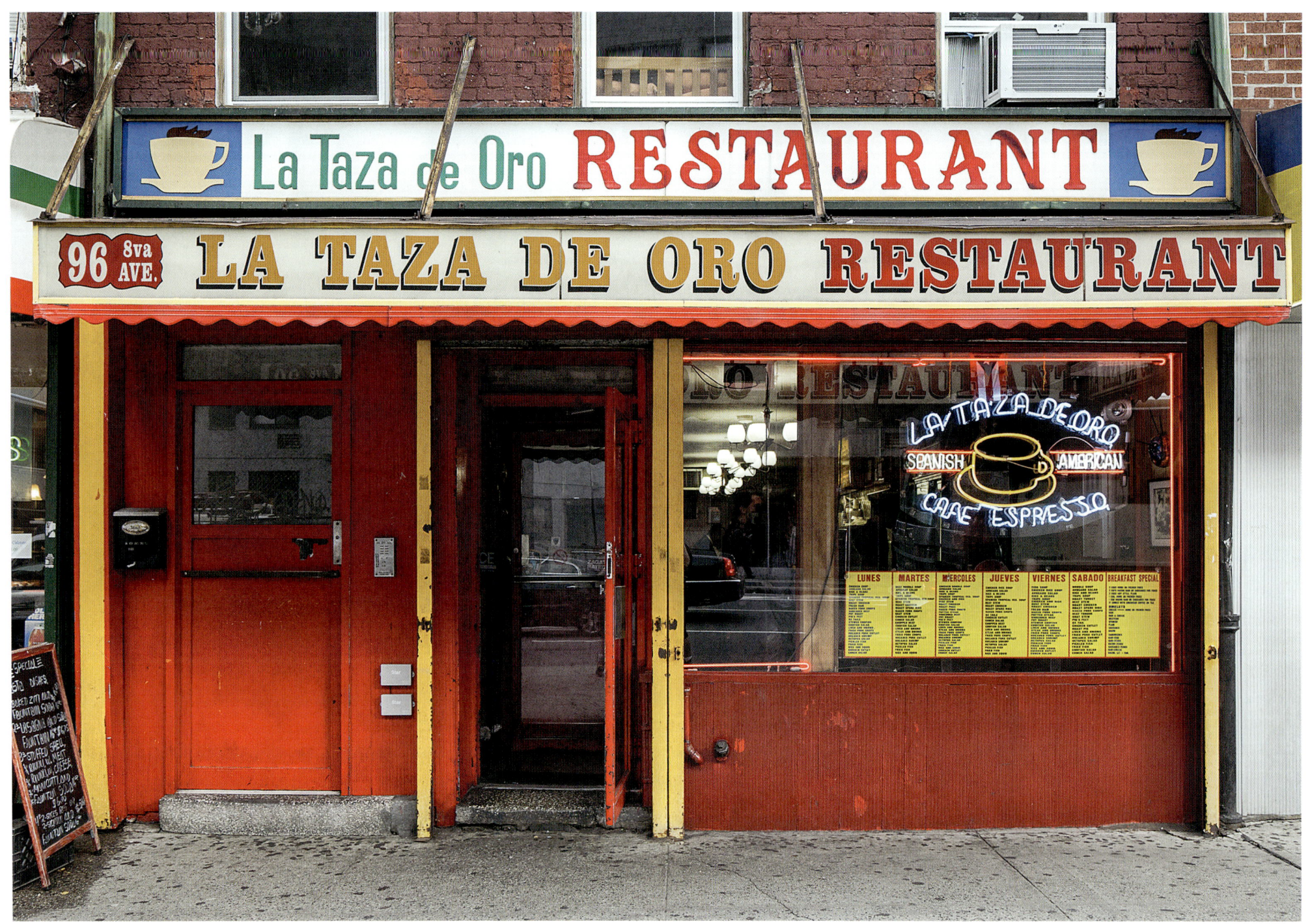

LA TAZA DE ORO
8th Avenue near West 15th Street, Chelsea, 2010

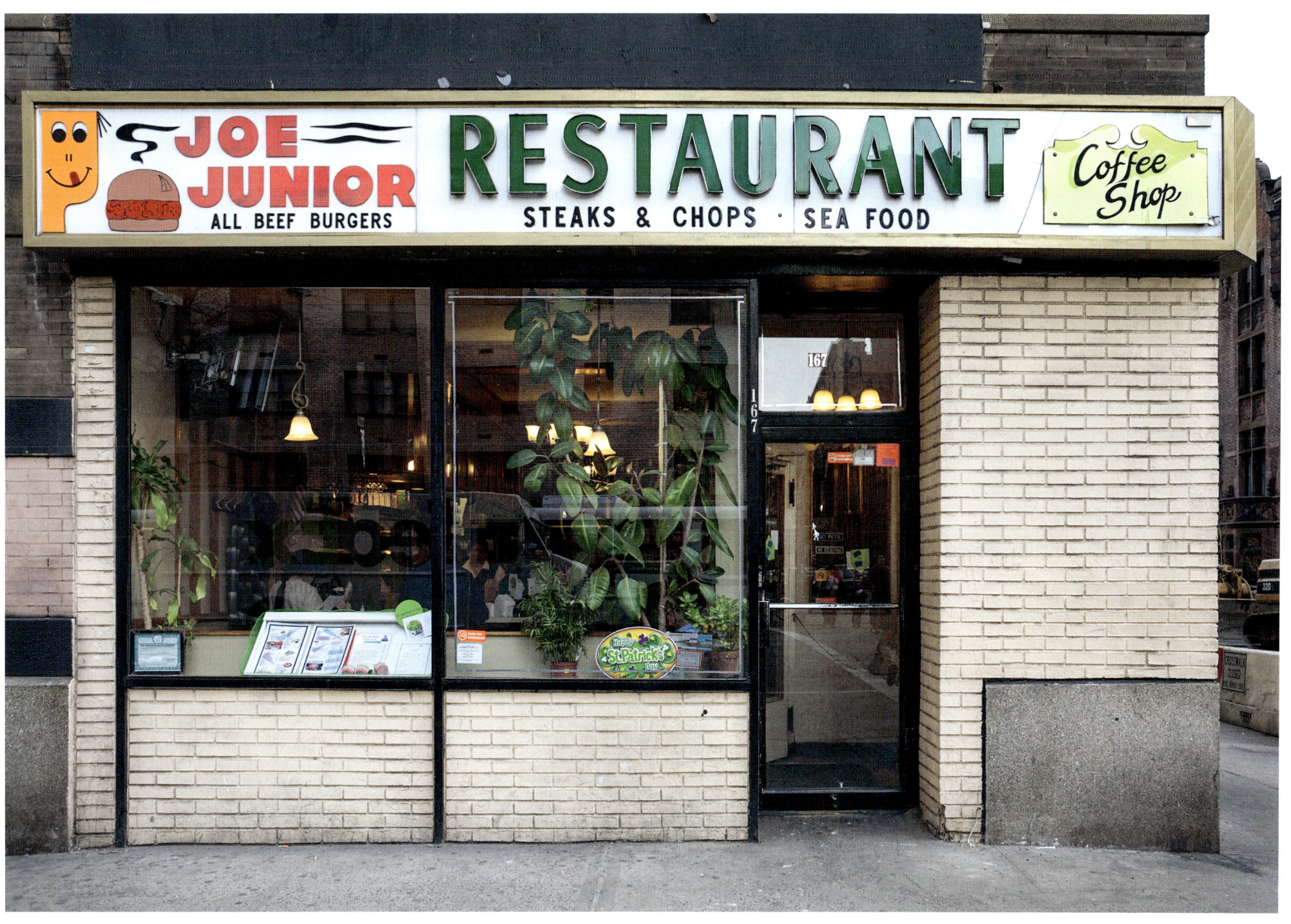

JOE JUNIOR RESTAURANT
3rd Avenue at East 16th Street, Gramercy, 2009

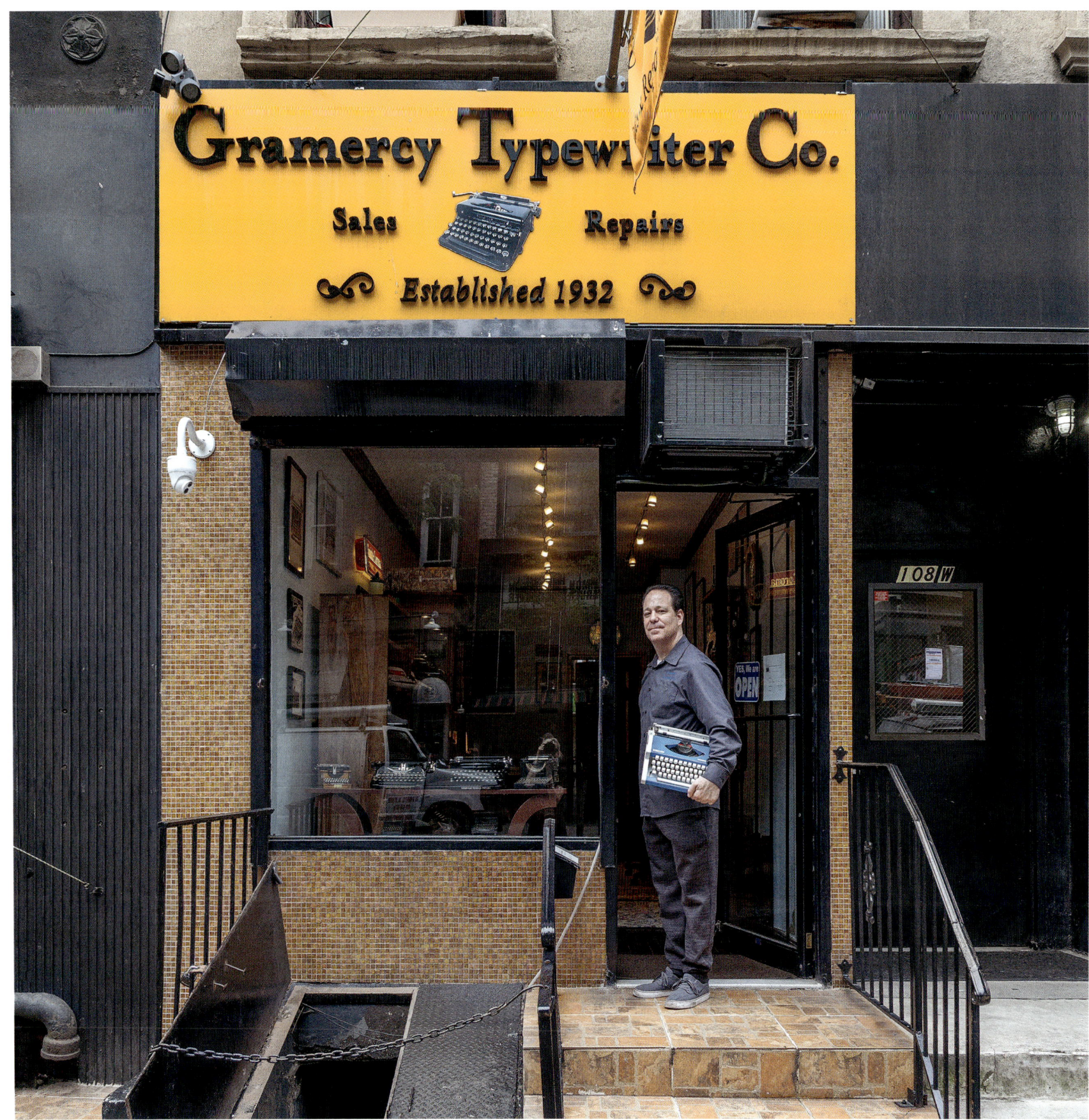

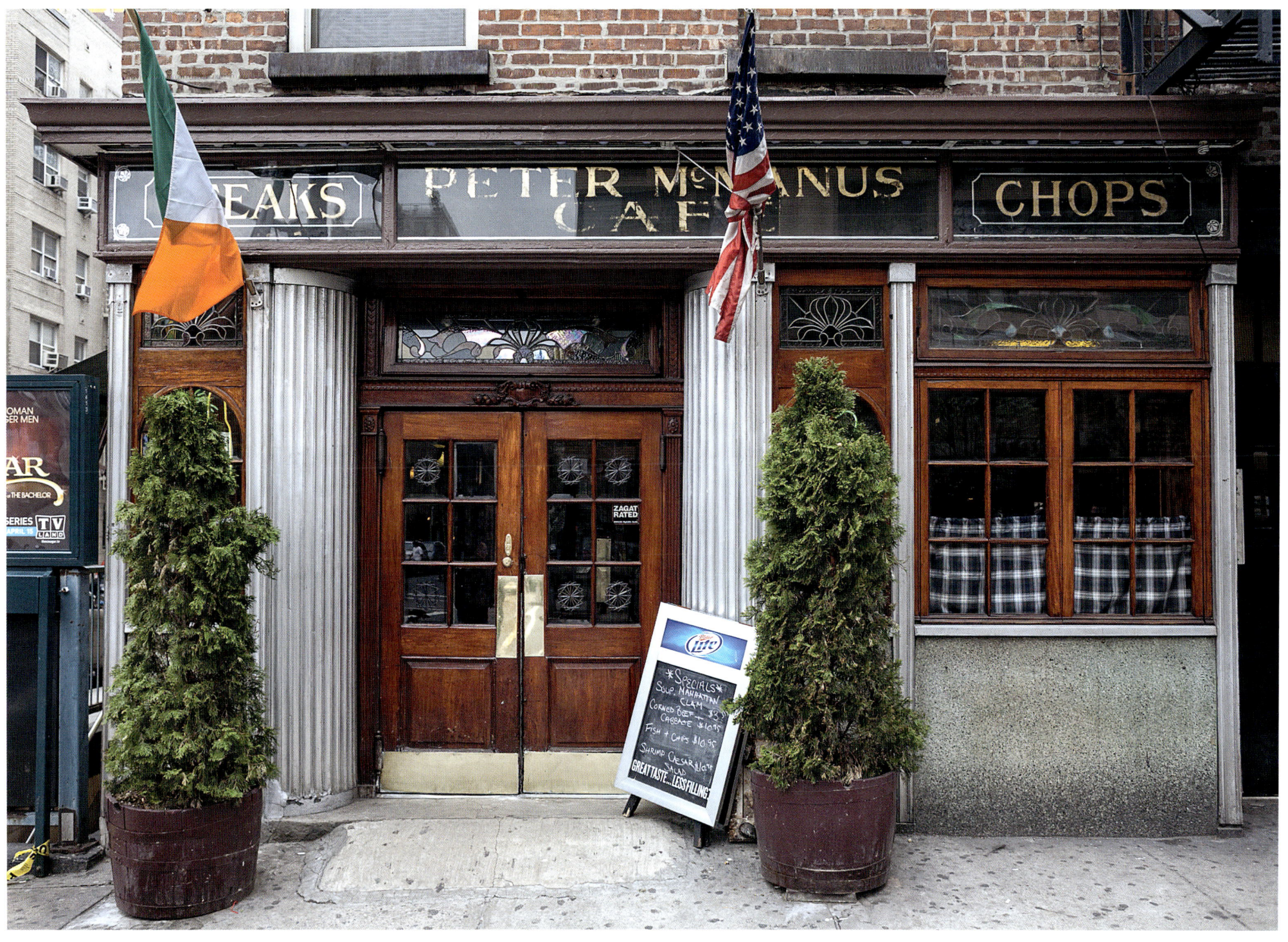

GRAMERCY TYPEWRITER CO.
West 17th Street near 6th Avenue, Chelsea, 2020

PETER MCMANUS CAFE
7th Avenue at West 19th Street, Chelsea, 2009

MANHATTAN

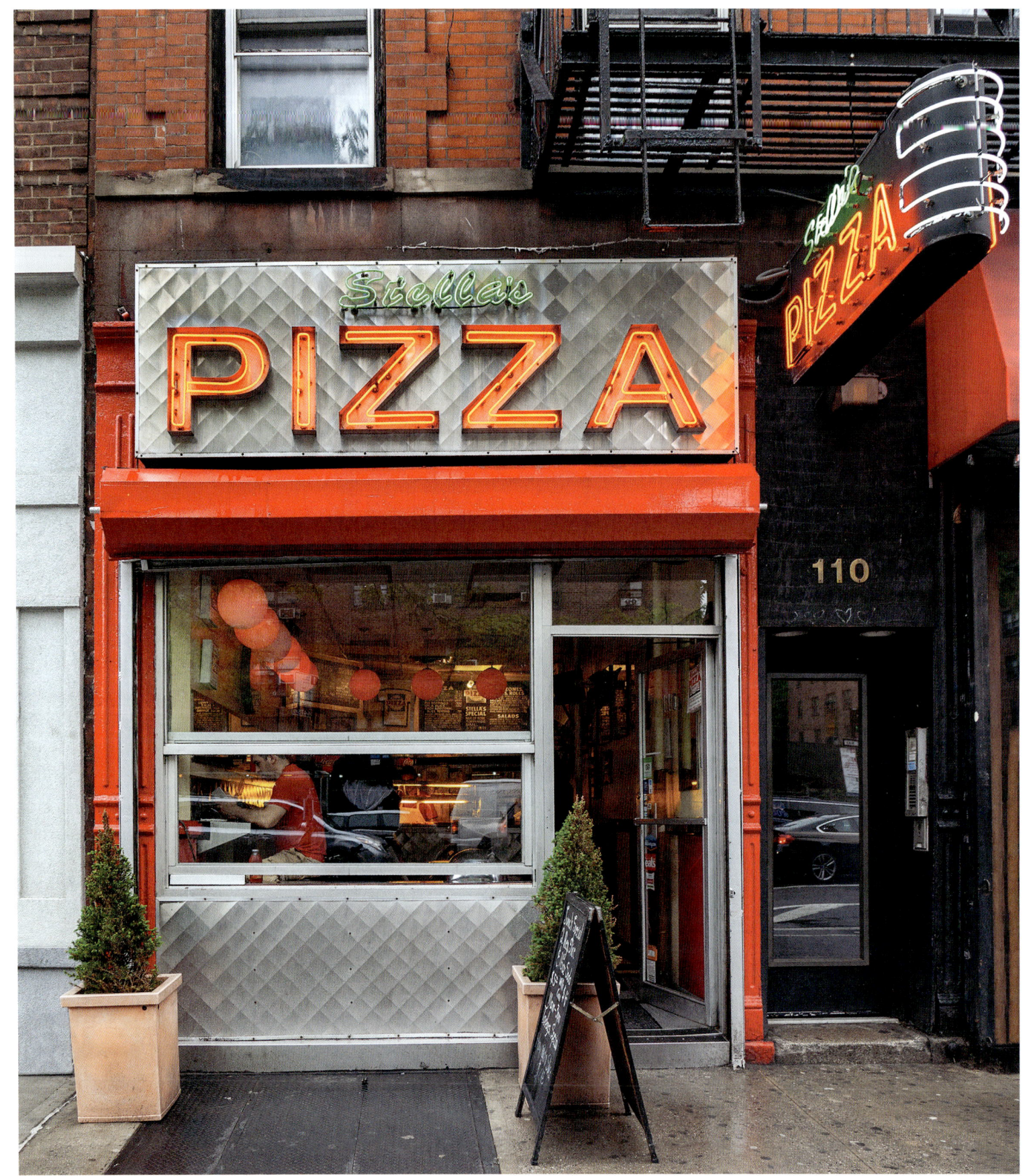

STELLA'S PIZZA
9th Avenue near West 17th
Street, Chelsea, 2020

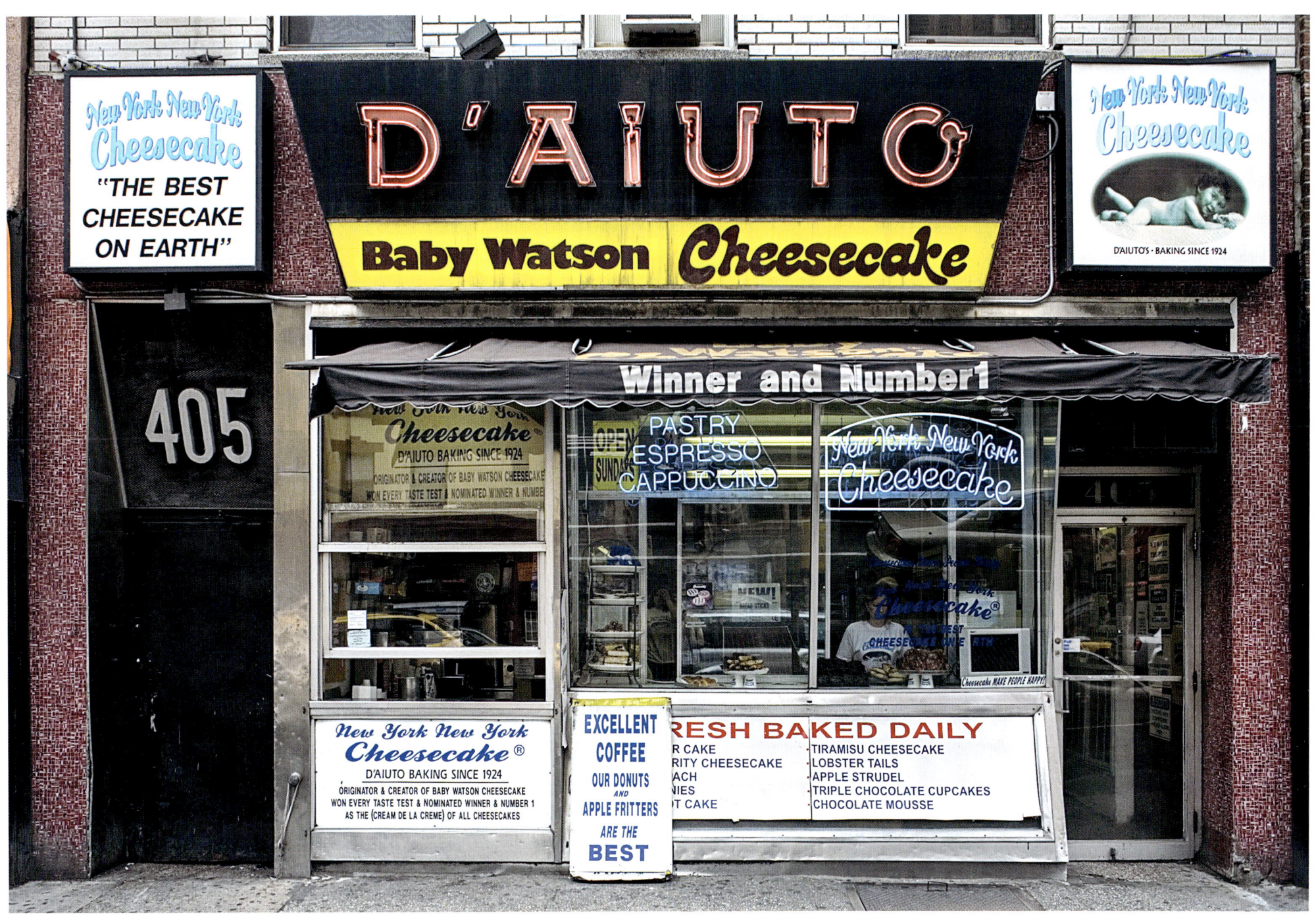

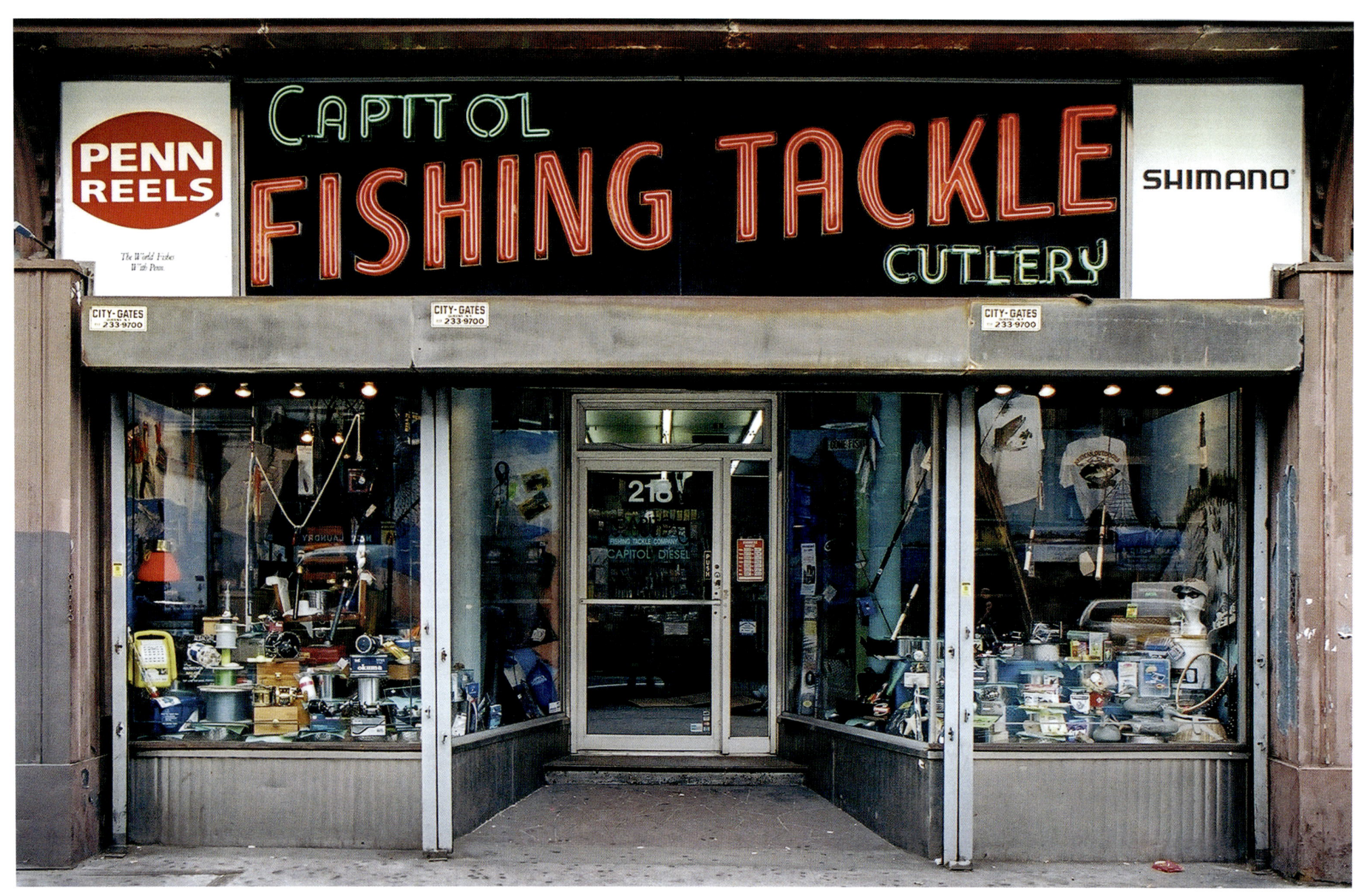

CAPITOL FISHING TACKLE COMPANY
West 23rd Street near 7th Avenue, Chelsea, 2004

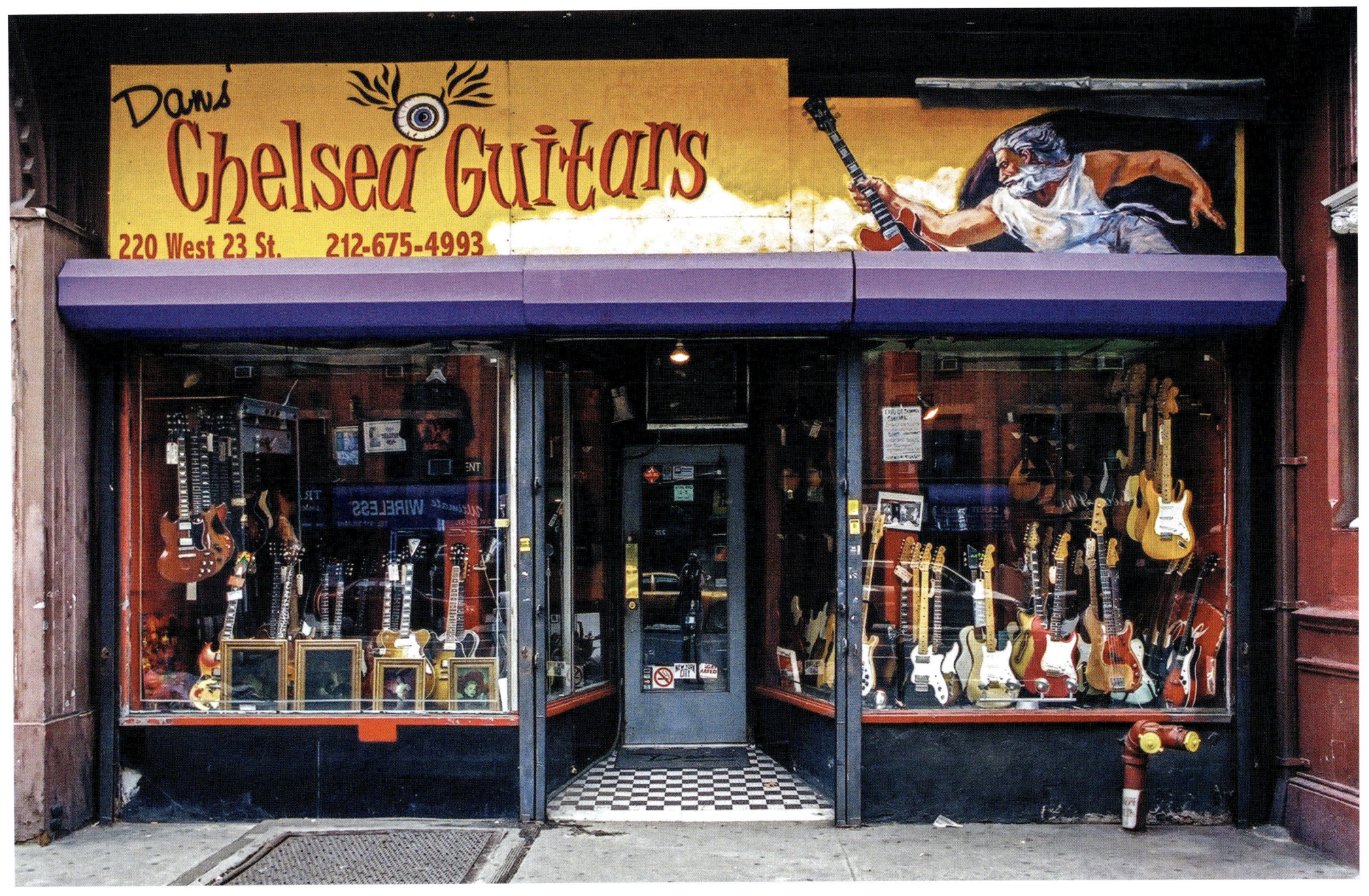

DAN'S CHELSEA GUITARS
West 23rd Street near 7th Avenue, Chelsea, 2004

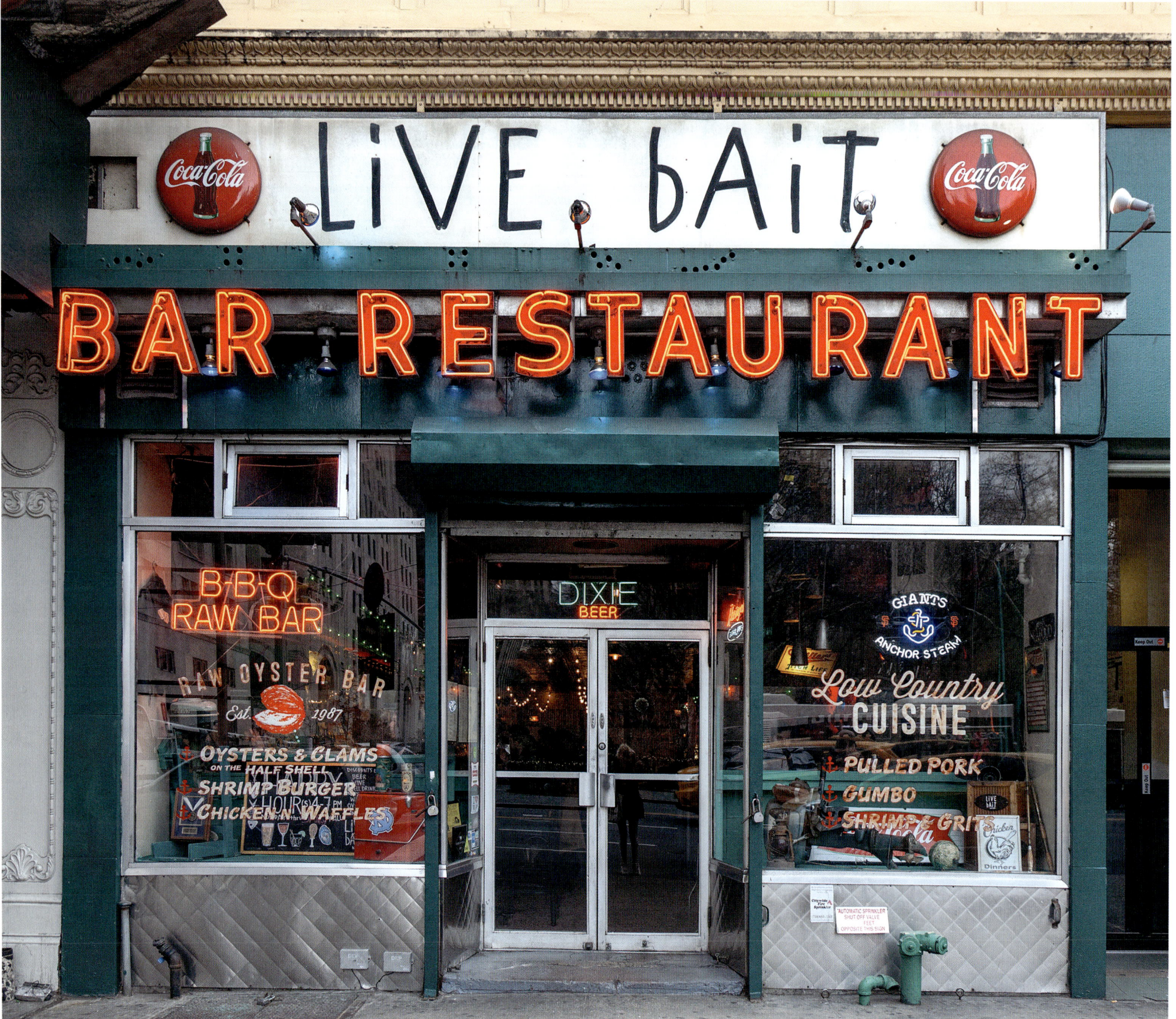

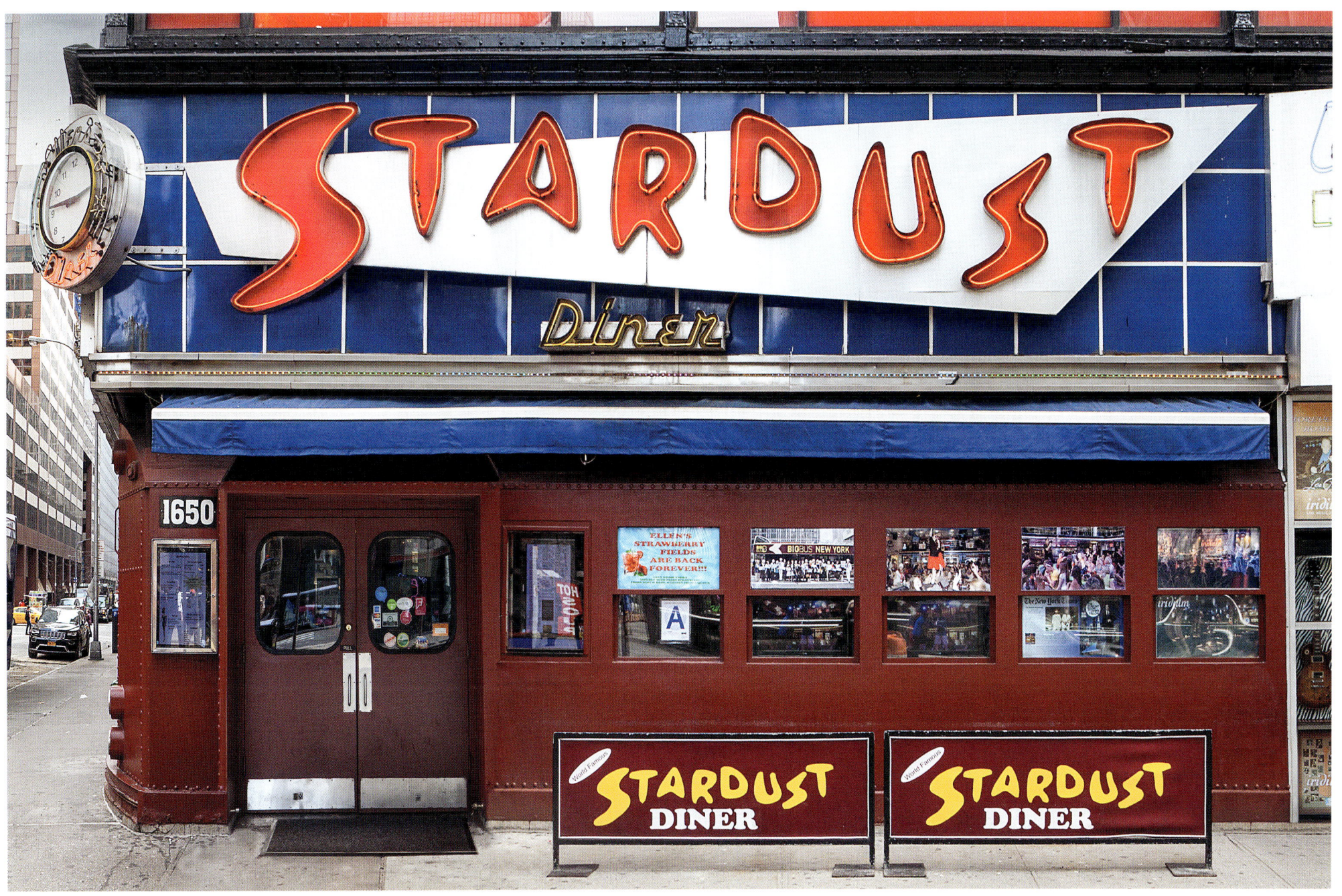

LIVE BAIT
West 23rd Street near Madison Avenue, Flatiron District, 2015

ELLEN'S STARDUST DINER
Broadway at West 51st Street, Midtown, 2015

MANHATTAN

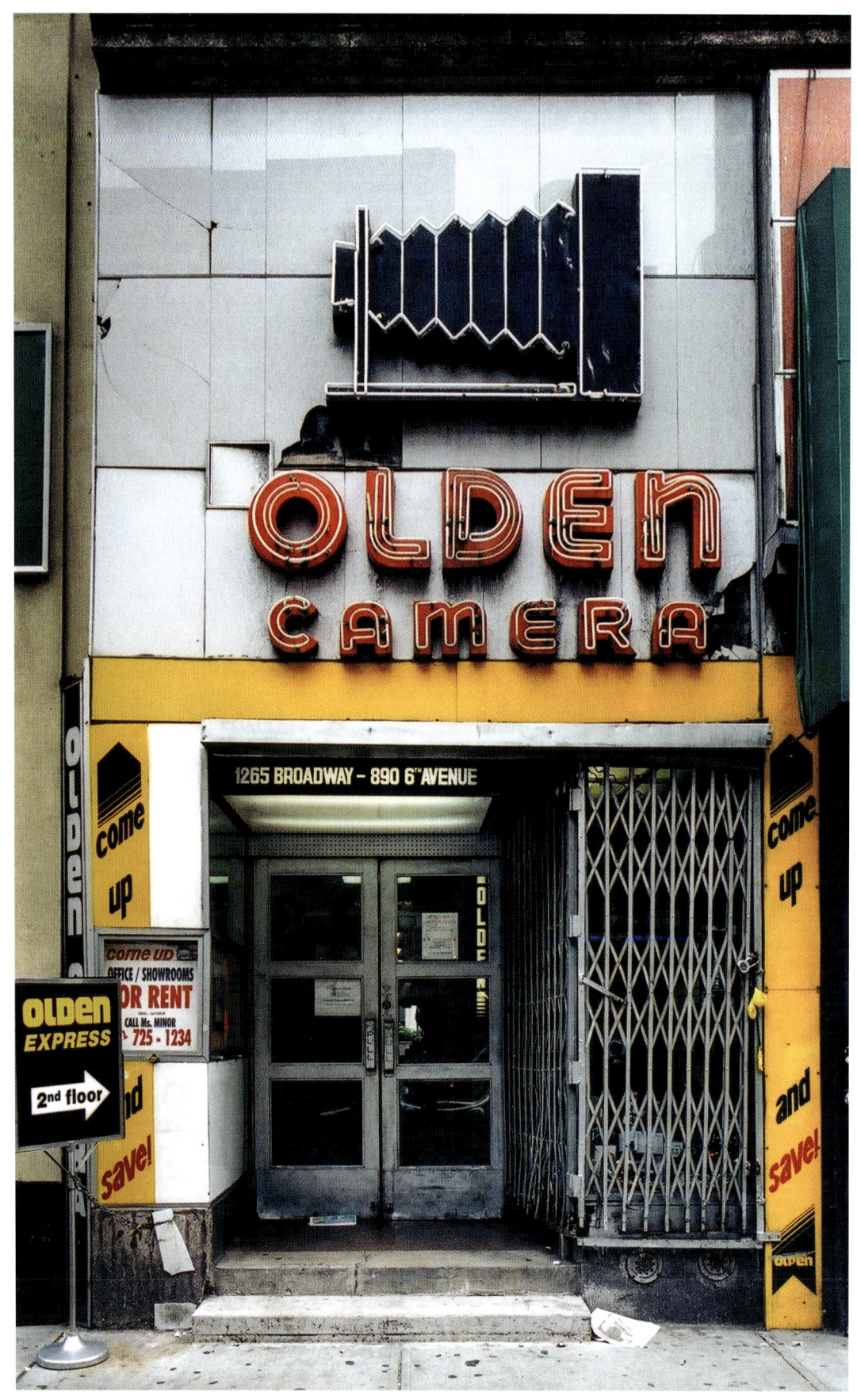

OLDEN CAMERA & LENS CO.
Broadway near West 32nd Street, Midtown, 2004

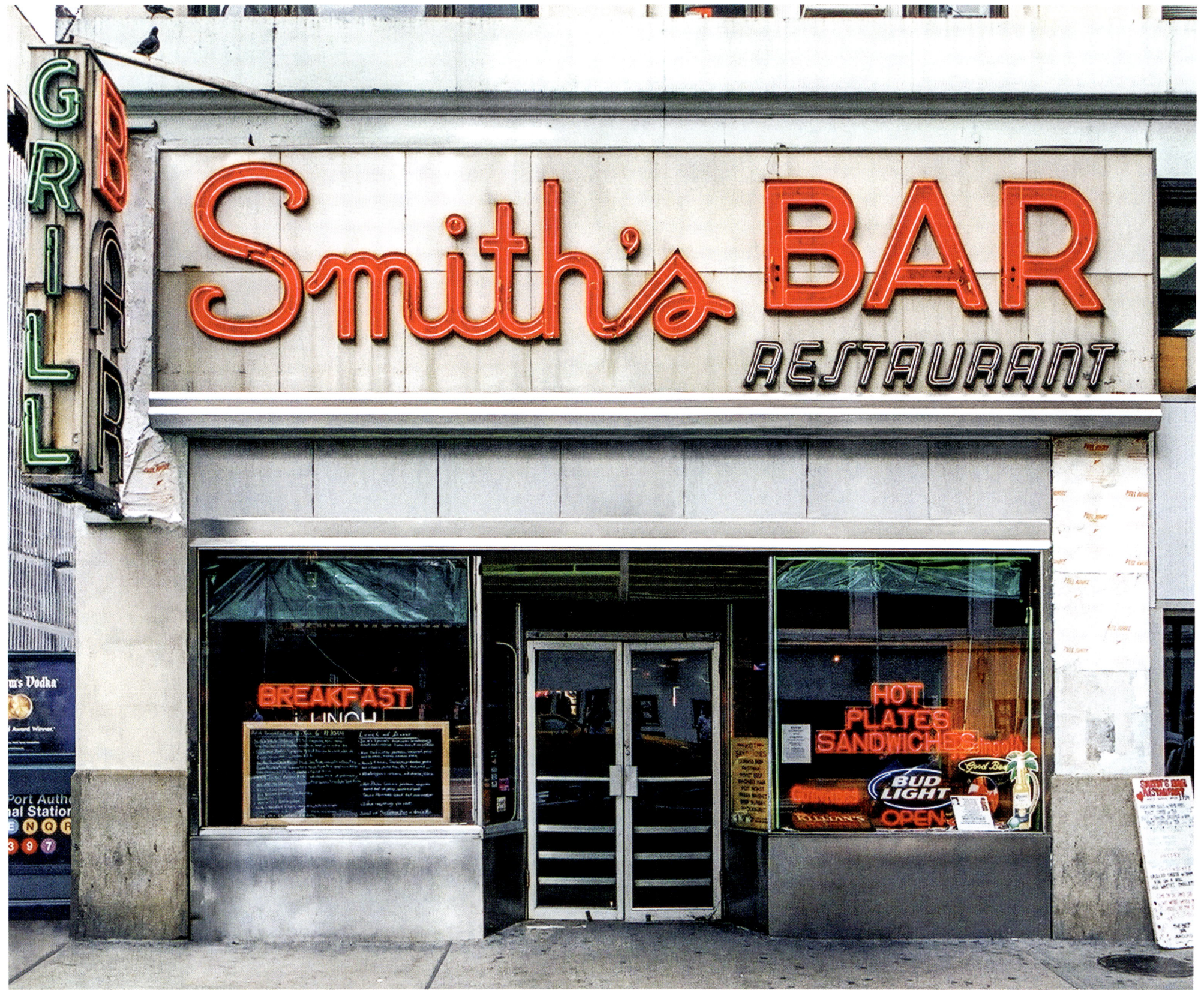

SMITH'S BAR & RESTAURANT
8th Avenue at West 44th Street, Theater District, 2004

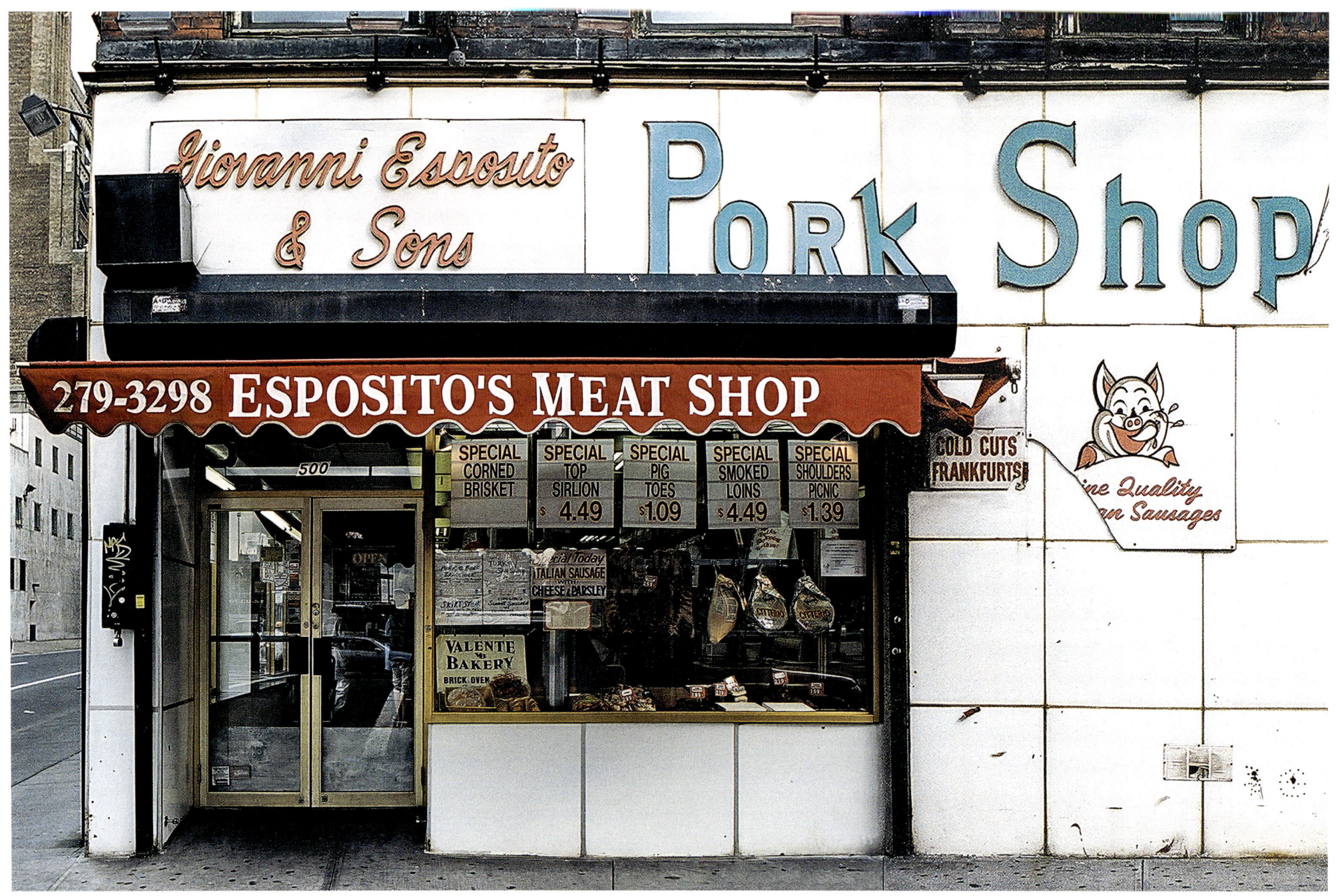

104 GIOVANNI ESPOSITO & SONS PORK SHOP
9th Avenue at West 38th Street, Hell's Kitchen, 2004

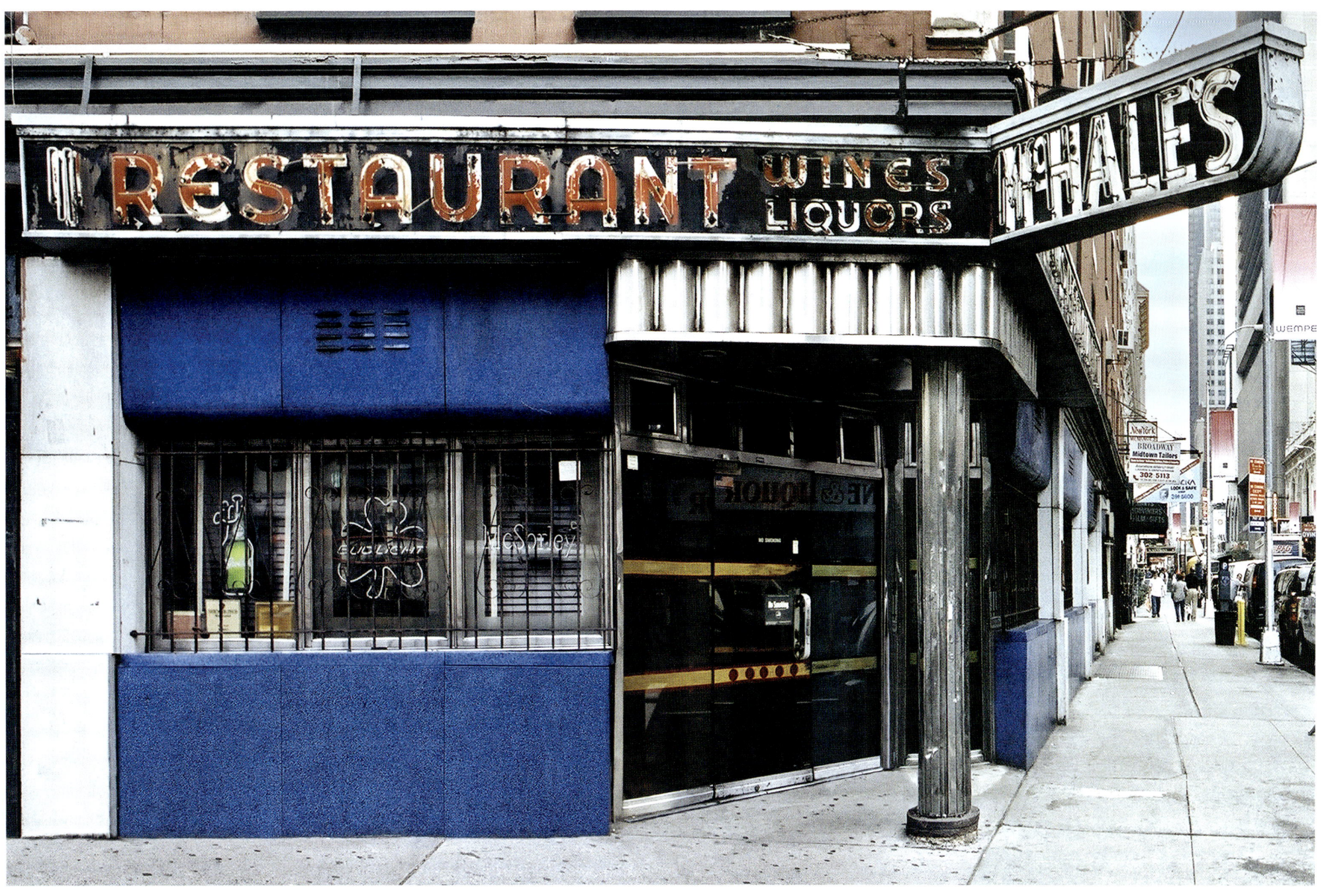

MCHALE'S BAR & GRILL
8th Avenue at West 46th Street, Theater District, 2004

MANHATTAN

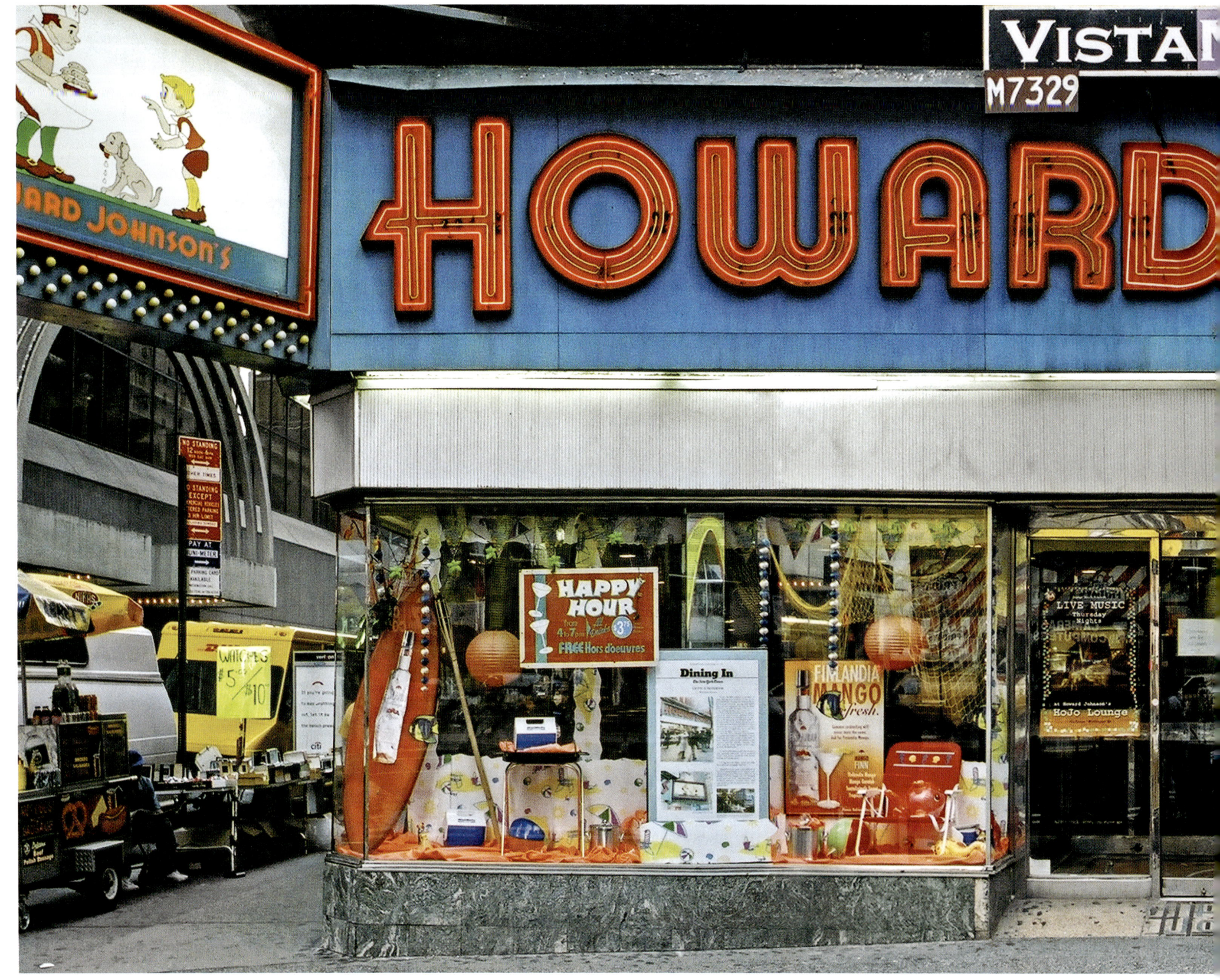

HOWARD JOHNSON'S
Broadway at West 46th Street, Times Square, 2004

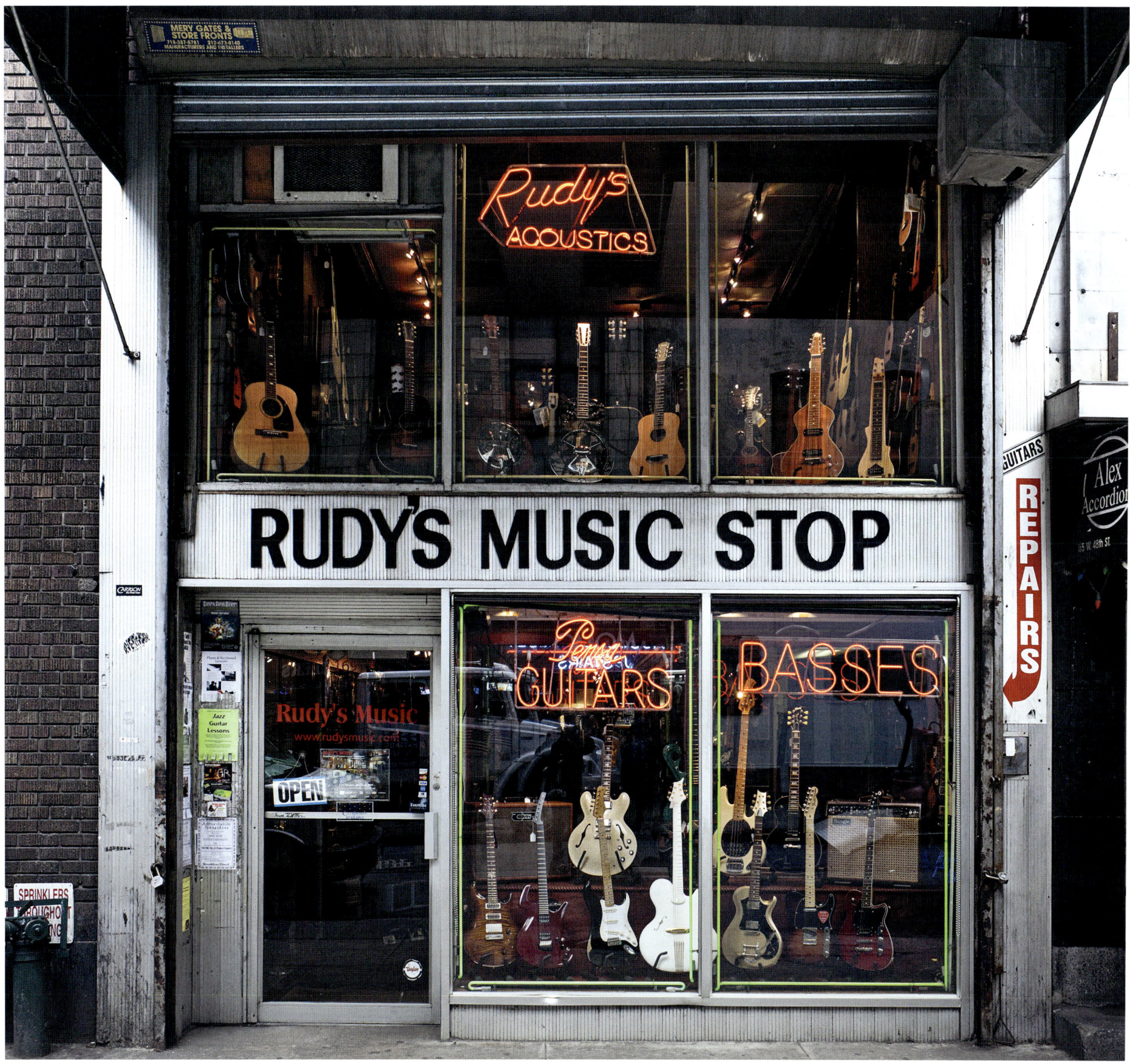

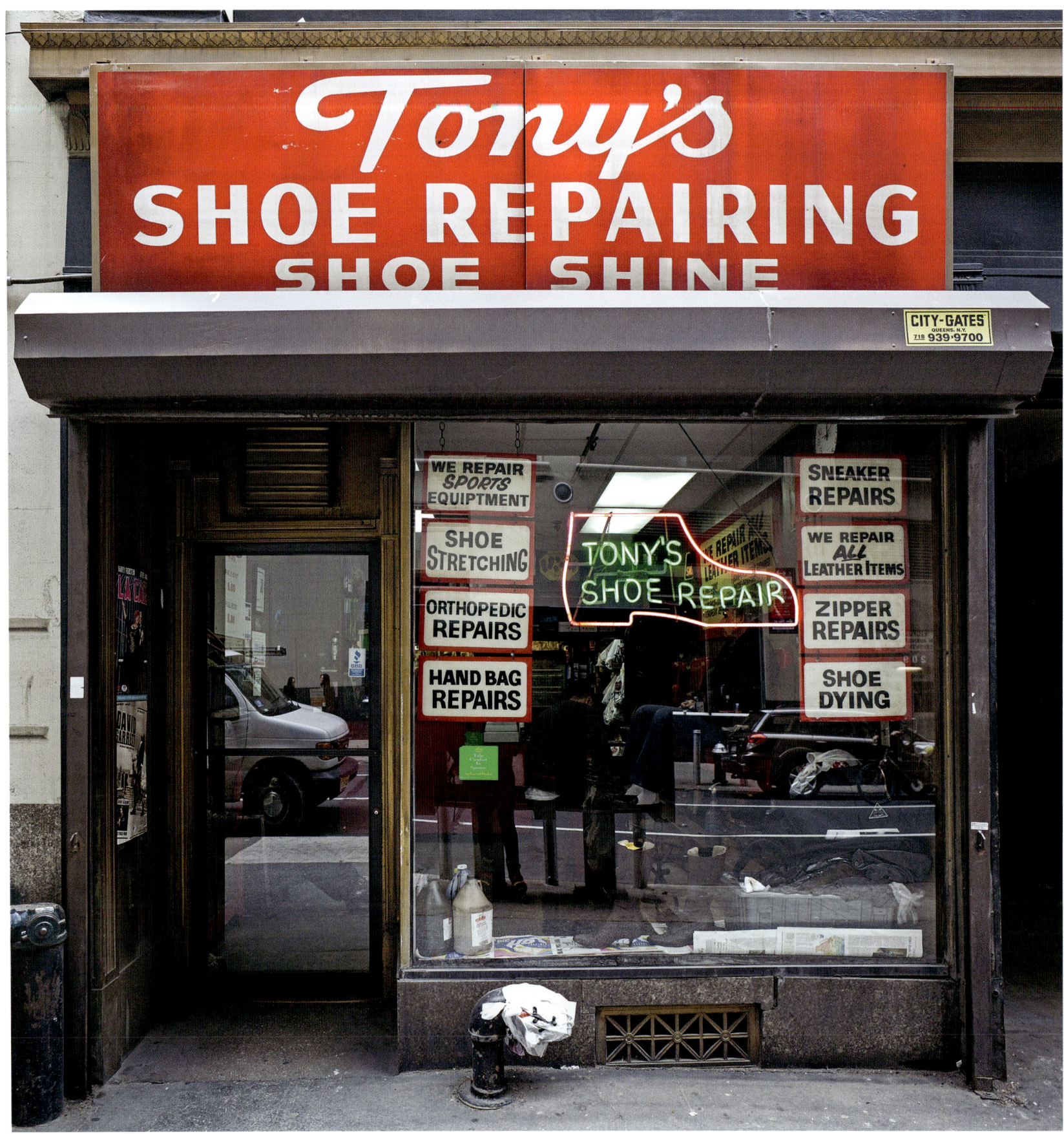

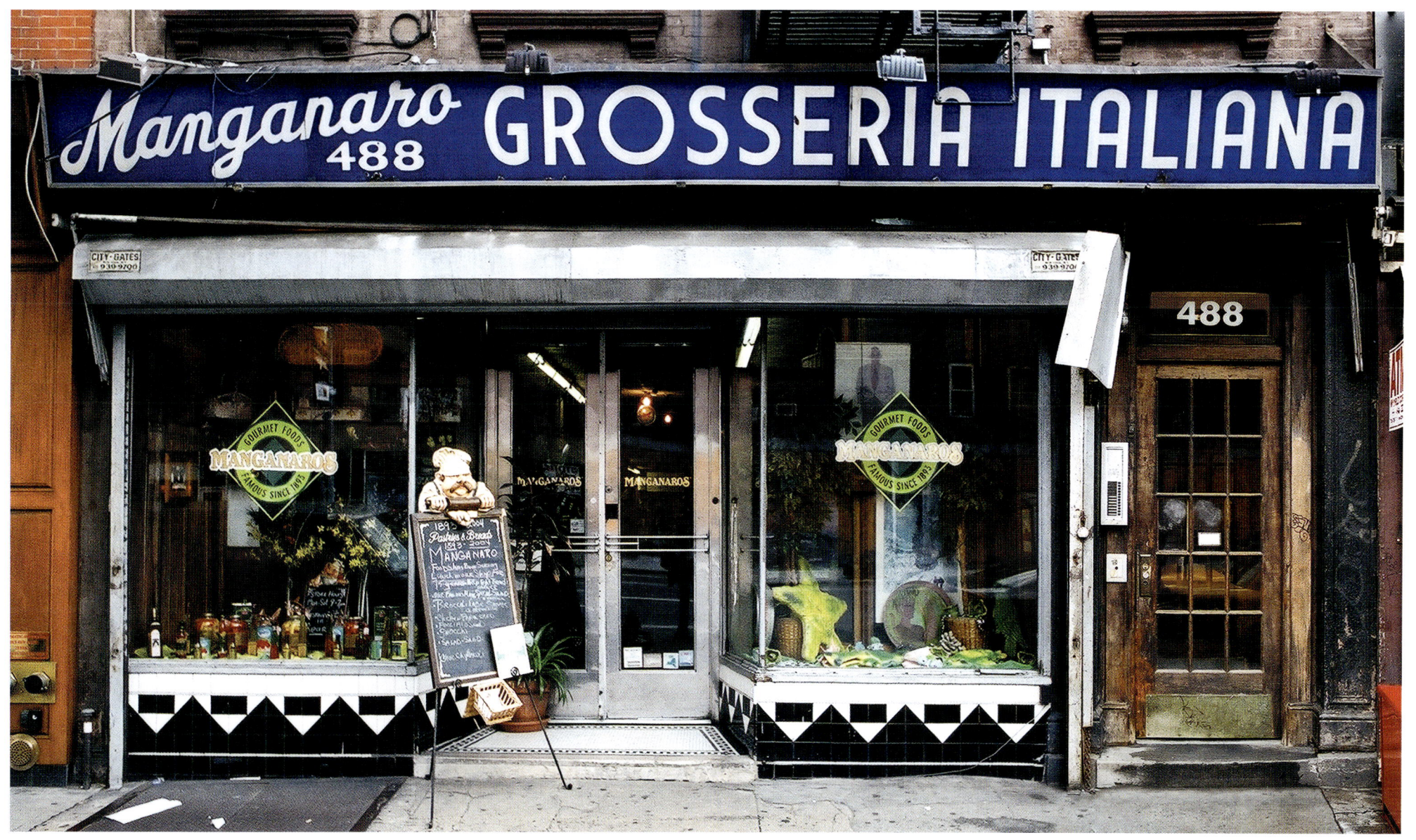

TONY'S SHOE REPAIR
West 35th Street near 7th Avenue, Midtown, 2011

MANGANARO'S GROSSERIA ITALIANO
9th Avenue near West 37th Street, Hell's Kitchen, 2004

MANHATTAN

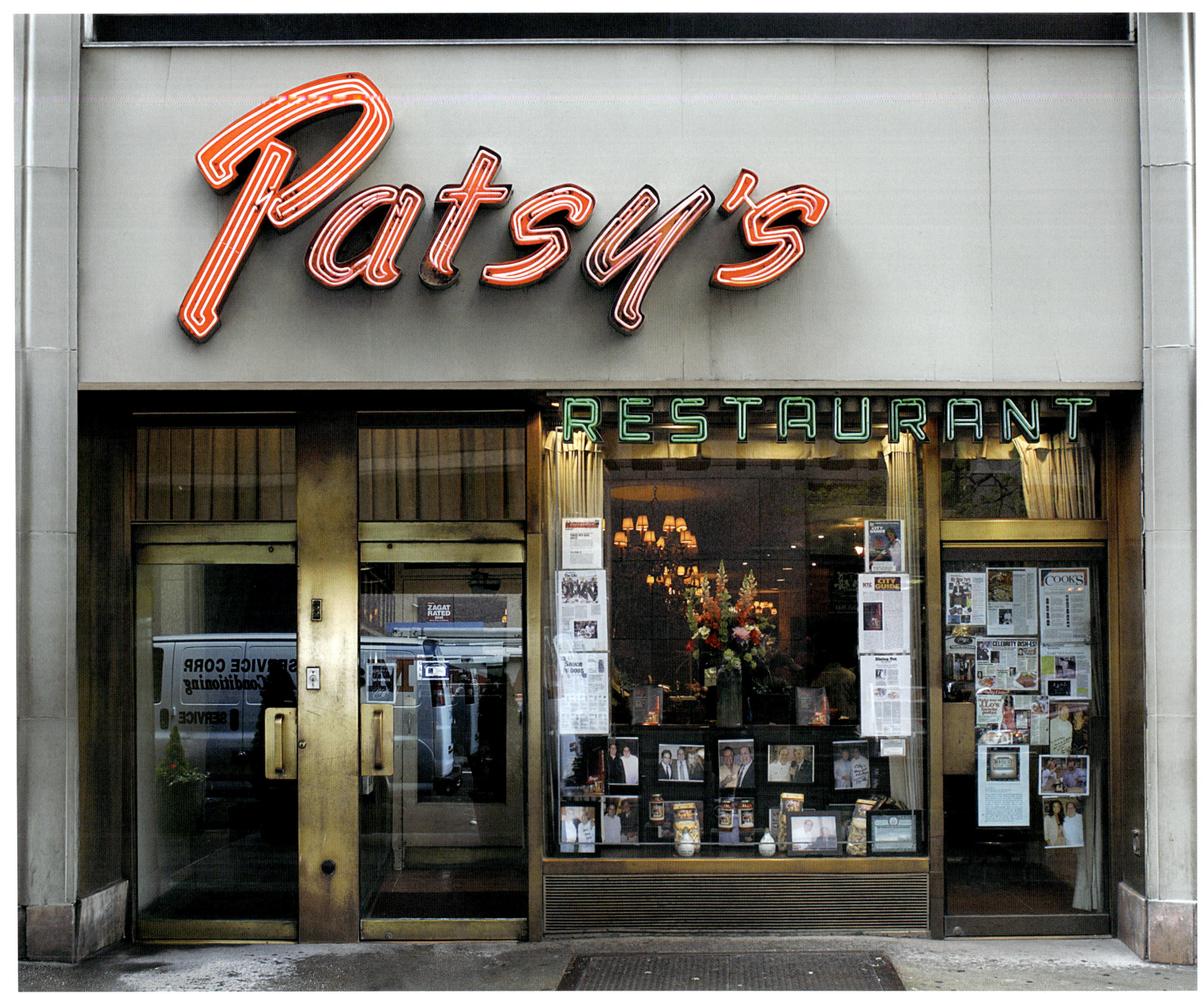

112   PATSY'S RESTAURANT
West 56th Street near Broadway, Theater District, 2010

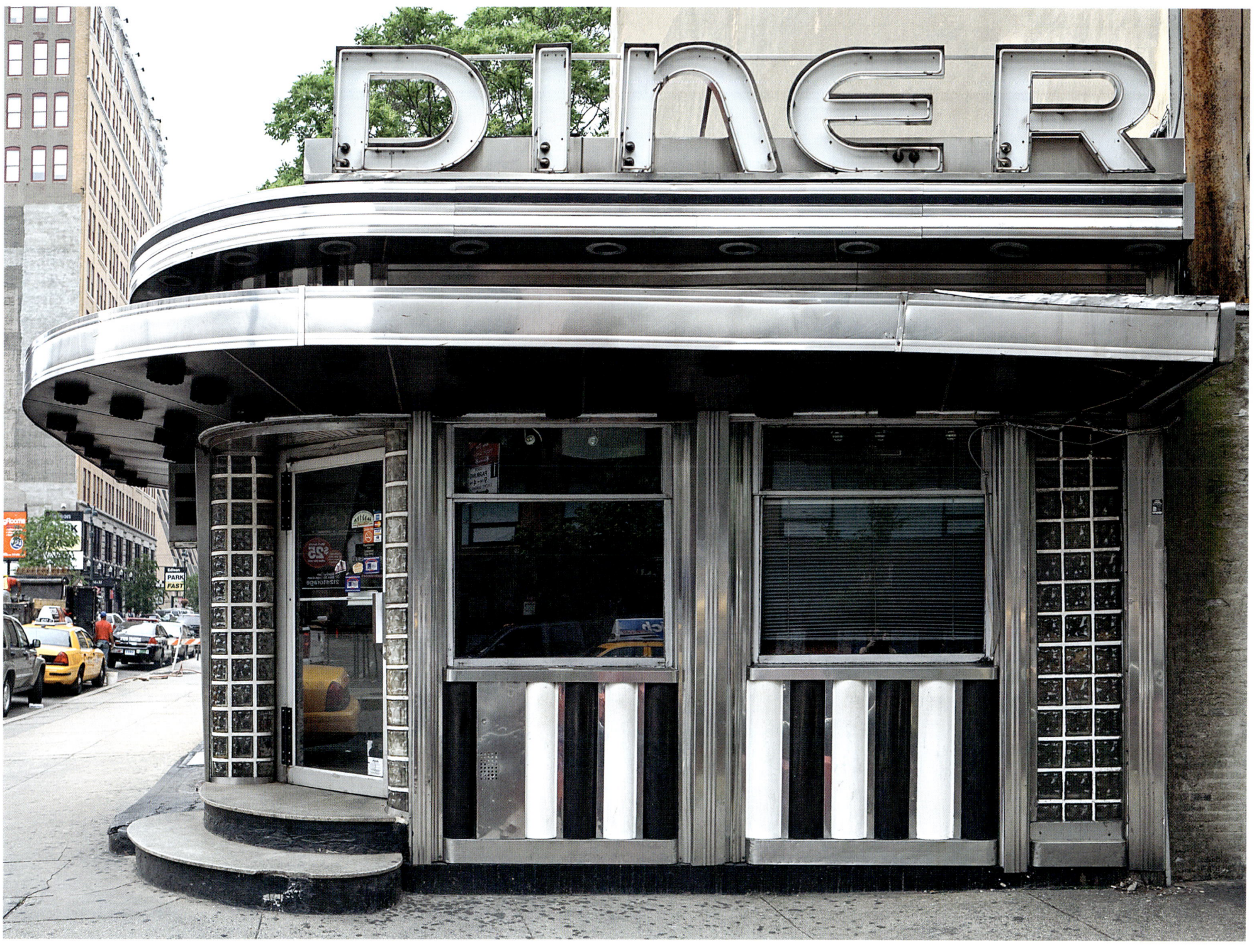

CHEYENNE DINER
9th Avenue at West 33rd Street, Chelsea, 2008

MANHATTAN

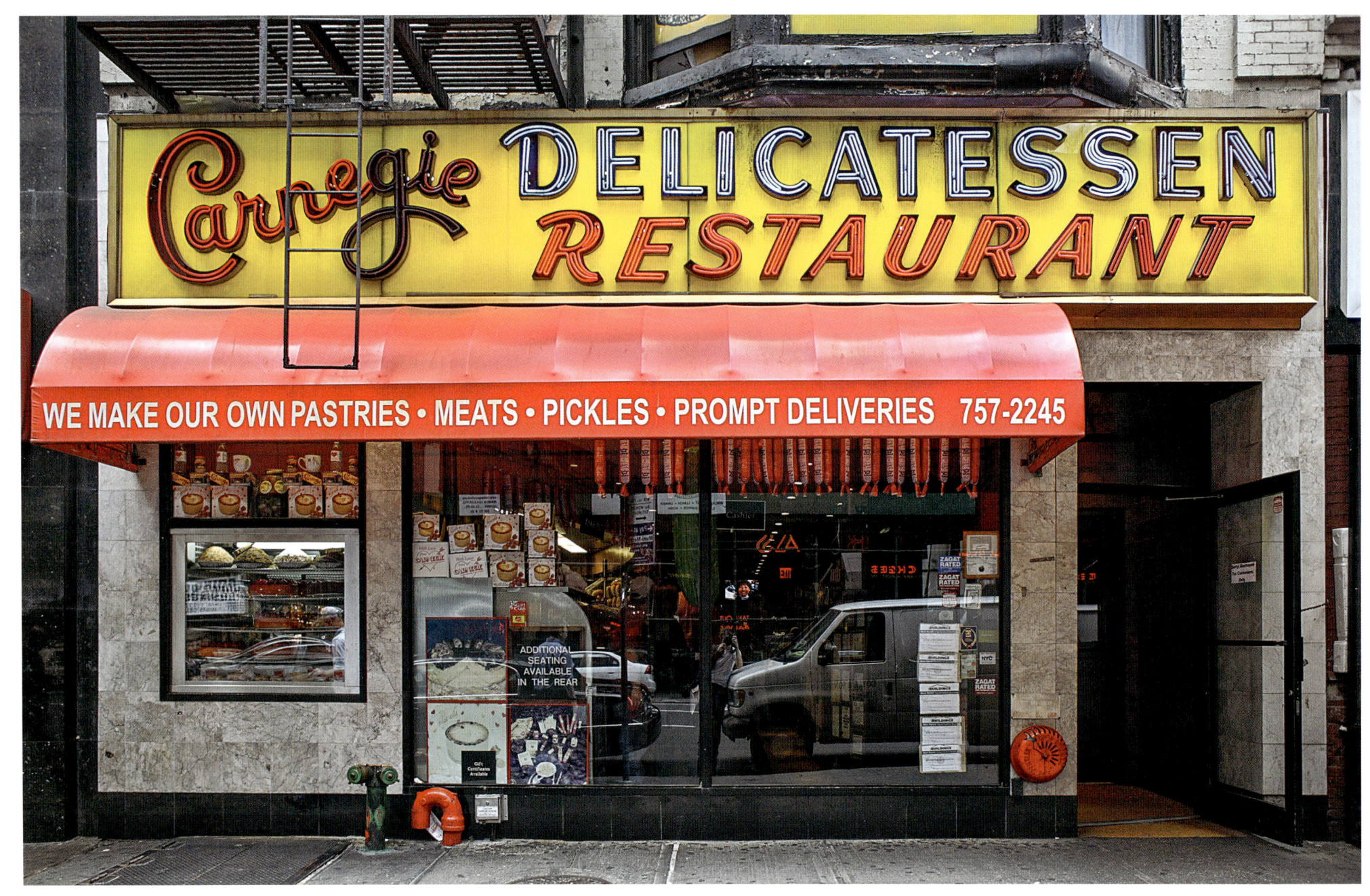

114 CARNEGIE DELICATESSEN
7th Avenue near West 55th Street, Theater District, 2009

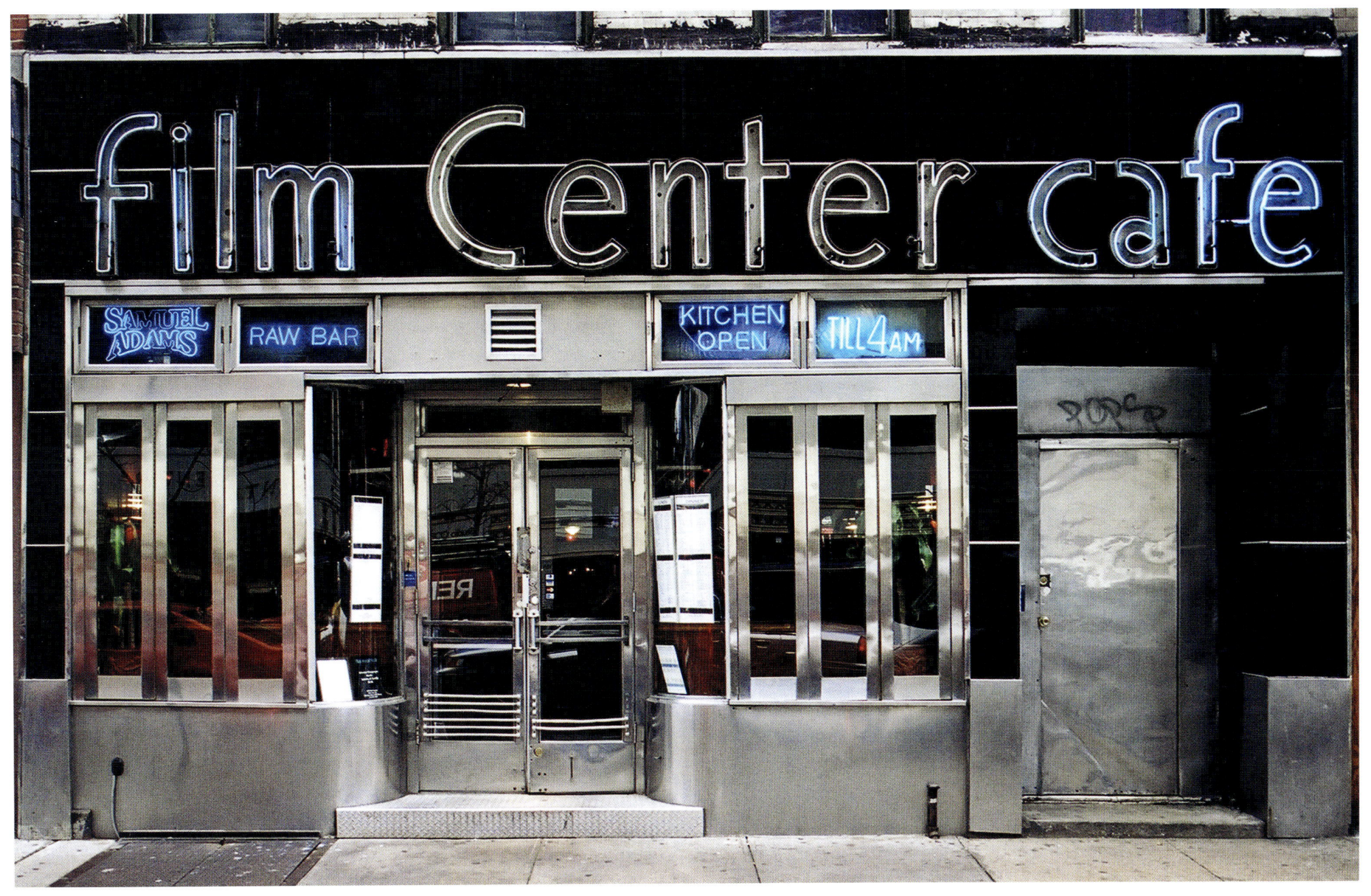

FILM CENTER CAFE
9th Avenue near West 45th Street, Hell's Kitchen, 2001

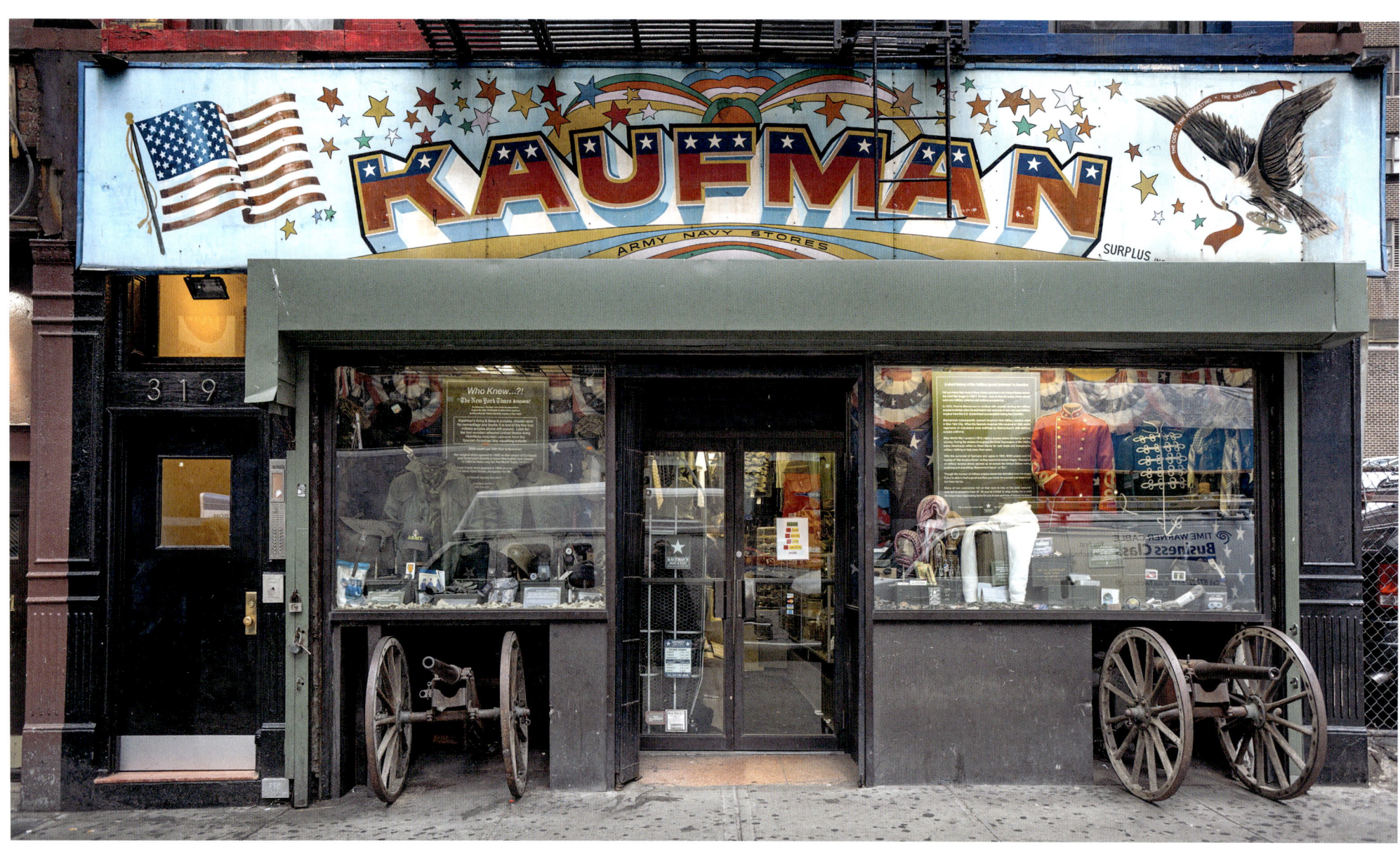

KAUFMAN'S ARMY & NAVY
West 42nd Street near 8th Avenue, Hell's Kitchen, 2012

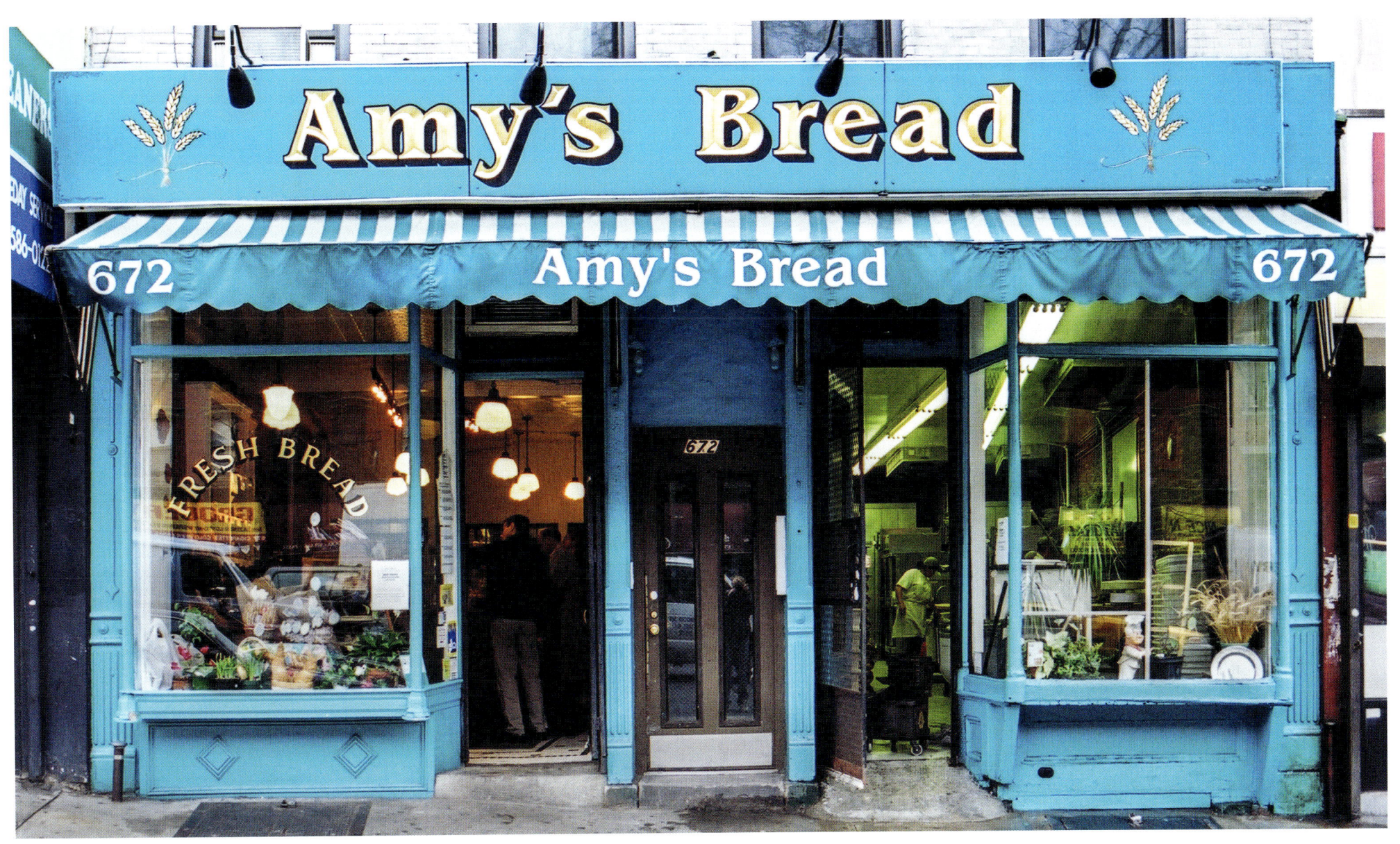

AMY'S BREAD
9th Avenue near West 47th Street, Hell's Kitchen, 2001

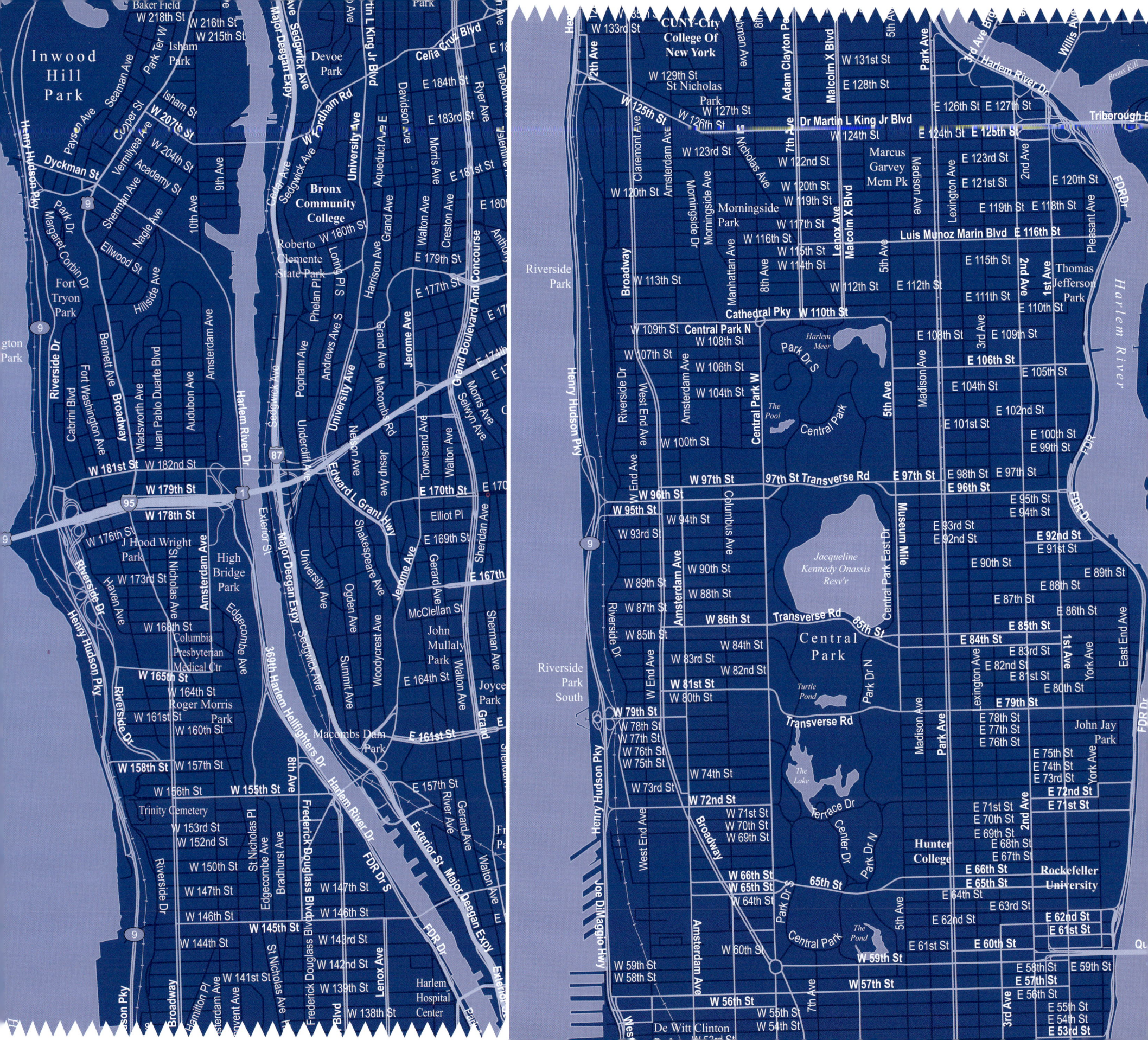

ABOVE 59TH STREET

UPPER EAST SIDE — UPPER WEST SIDE — HARLEM — WASHINGTON HEIGHTS — INWOOD

The northernmost area of Manhattan, which comprises all of the mainly residential neighborhoods above 59th Street, is commonly known as "uptown."

The **Upper East Side** is bounded to the north by East 96th Street, to the east by the East River, to the south by East 59th Street, and to the west by 5th Avenue. Within the neighborhood is Yorkville, an area which became predominantly German by 1850, after prosperous families left their overcrowded tenements downtown and settled in brownstones and mansions. After World War II, Yorkville began to lose its ethnic character. Today, the area north of 59th Street and east of Central Park contains some of the city's most expensive residential real estate, with a mix of opulent townhouses, brownstones, and luxury apartments.

The **Upper West Side** is bounded to the north by 125th Street, to the east by Central Park, to the south by 59th Street, and to the west by the Hudson River. In the 1880s, the numbered avenues there were given more romantic names to enhance the neighborhood's appeal. The opening of Lincoln Center for the Performing Arts helped establish the area as a center for the arts, and by the late 1980s, real estate prices started to rise as restaurants, bars, and shops opened along Broadway and Columbus and Amsterdam Avenues.

Harlem encompasses many neighborhoods, including East Harlem, Hamilton Heights, and Sugar Hill. When a railroad was built along Park Avenue in 1837, Harlem was divided into east and west sections. East Harlem has imprecise boundaries but roughly extends to the East River in the east, East 96th Street to the south, East 142nd Street to the north, and 5th Avenue to the west. West Harlem is bounded to the east by 5th Avenue, to the south by 110th Street (Central Park North), to the north by the Harlem River, and to the west by Morningside and St. Nicholas Avenues. In the early 1900s, African Americans from all over the country began to move to Harlem because of its economic opportunities and vibrant musical and cultural life, including the literary and artistic movement that became known as the Harlem Renaissance. The Great Depression, however, devastated the local economy and caused an end to the area's golden period. In recent years, Harlem has been revitalized, with new restaurants, clubs, and stores opening amid historic places related to a golden age of African American culture.

Washington Heights is bounded to the north by Dyckman Street, to the east by the Harlem River, to the south by 155th Street, and to the west by the Hudson River. In the first half of the 1900s, a large number of Greek, Irish, and Jewish people settled in the area, but by the early 1960s many of them left and African Americans, Puerto Ricans, and Cubans moved in. After the mid-1960s, Dominicans increased in number. In the mid-1990s poverty, overcrowding, and drug trafficking overtook the neighborhood, but businesses still flourished. Broadway has long divided the poor and working-class sections of Washington Heights to the east from the more affluent regions to the west. This division is still somewhat evident today, even though the racial and ethnic composition of the area has changed dramatically due to gentrification.

Inwood, located at the northern tip of Manhattan, is bounded to the north and east by the Harlem River, to the south by Fairview Avenue and Fort George Hill, and to the west by the Hudson River. In the early 1900s Jewish and Irish immigrants moved into Inwood, but over the years the demographics changed as many Latinos and African Americans settled in the area.

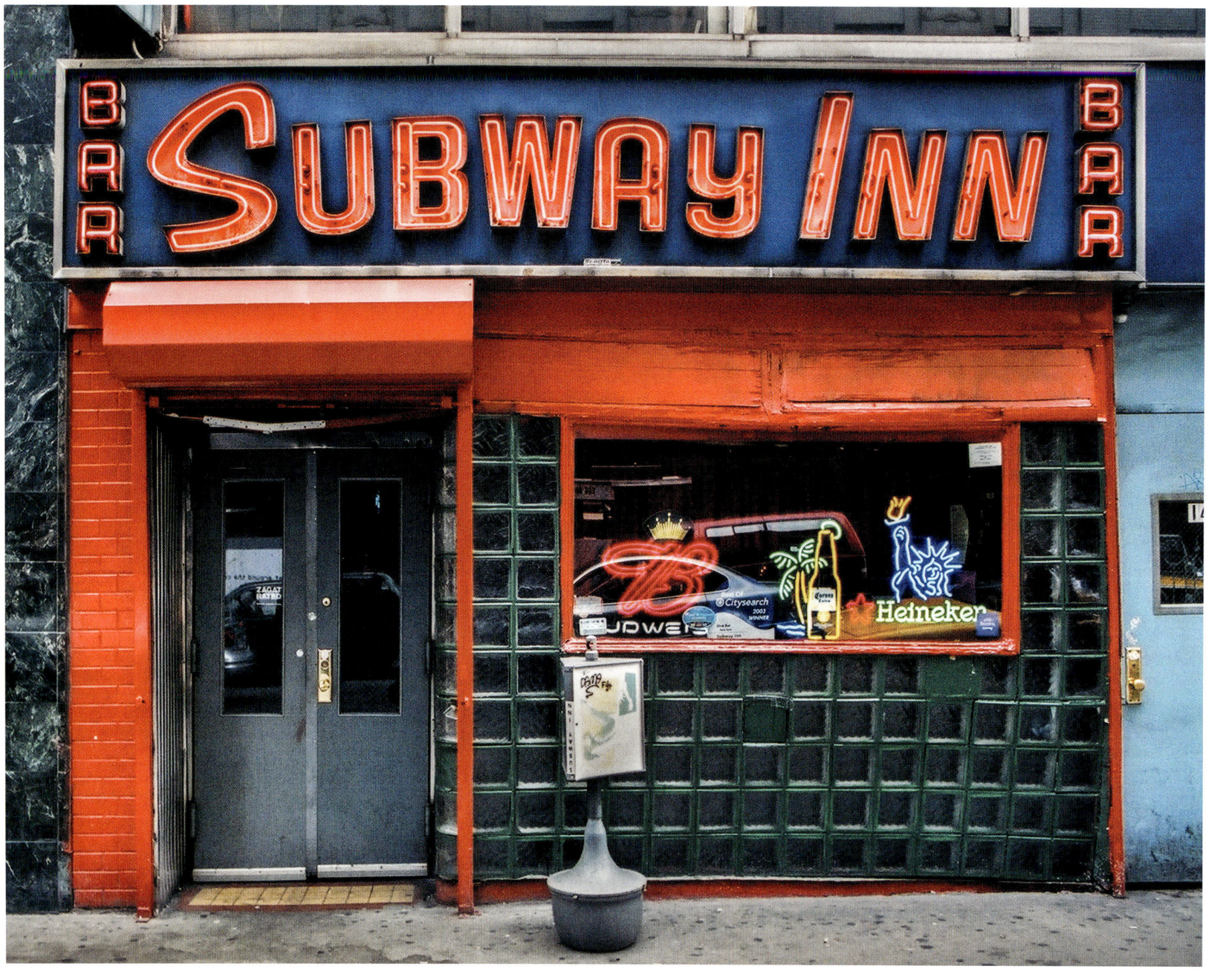

120 SUBWAY INN
East 60th Street near Lexington Avenue, Upper East Side, 2004

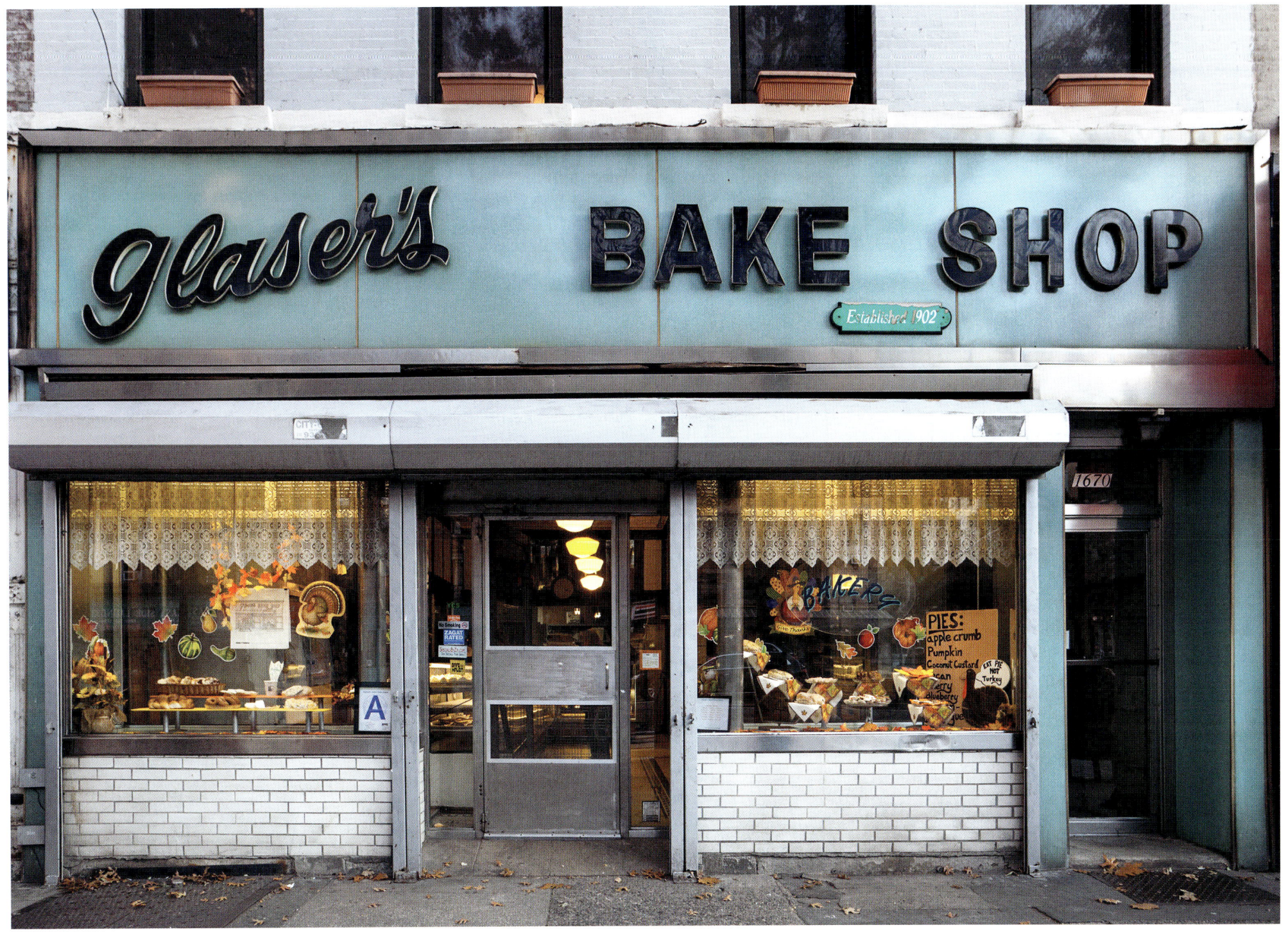

GLASER'S BAKE SHOP
1st Avenue near East 87th Street, Upper East Side, 2017

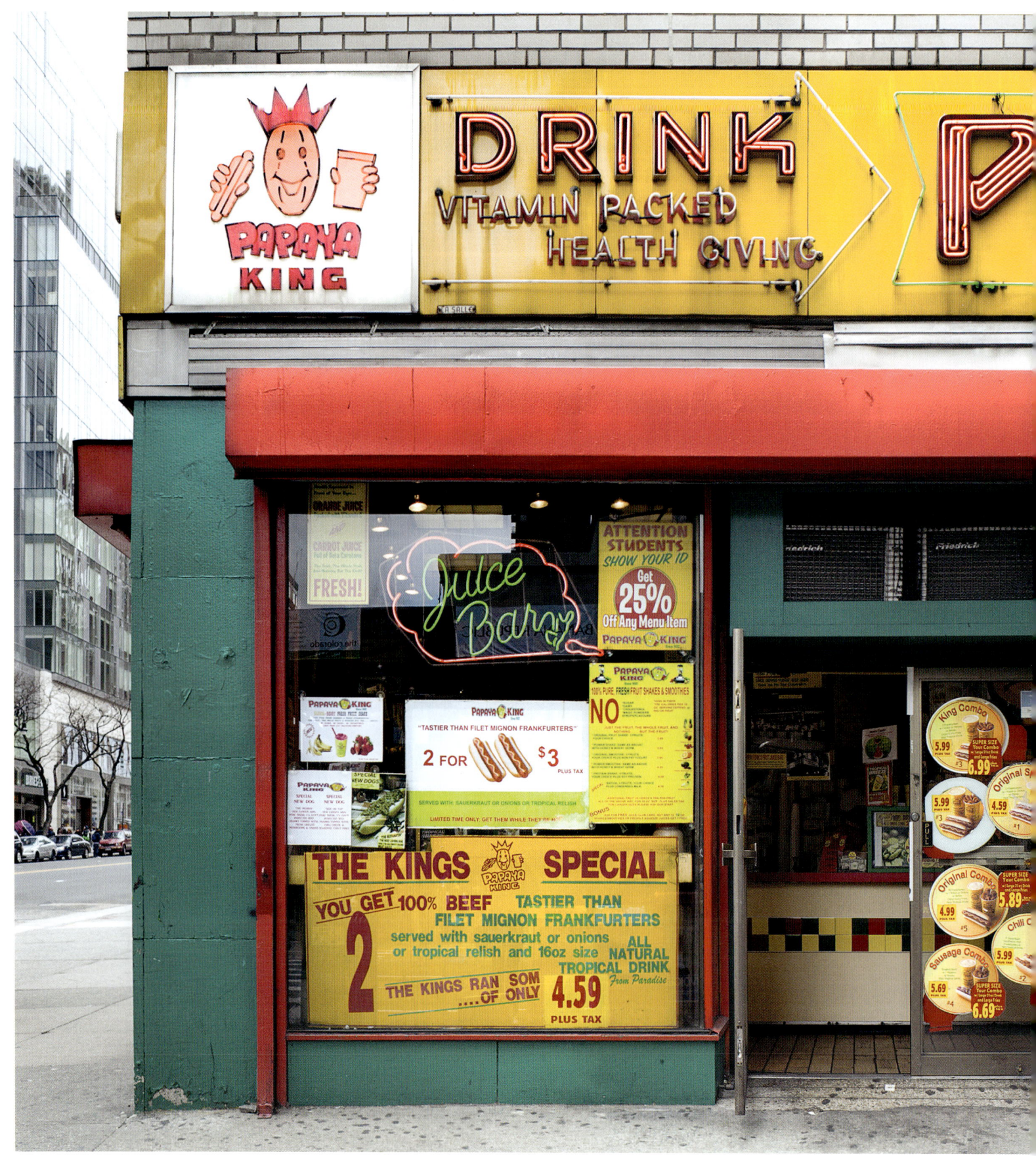

PAPAYA KING
East 86th Street at 3rd Avenue,
Upper East Side, 2010

122

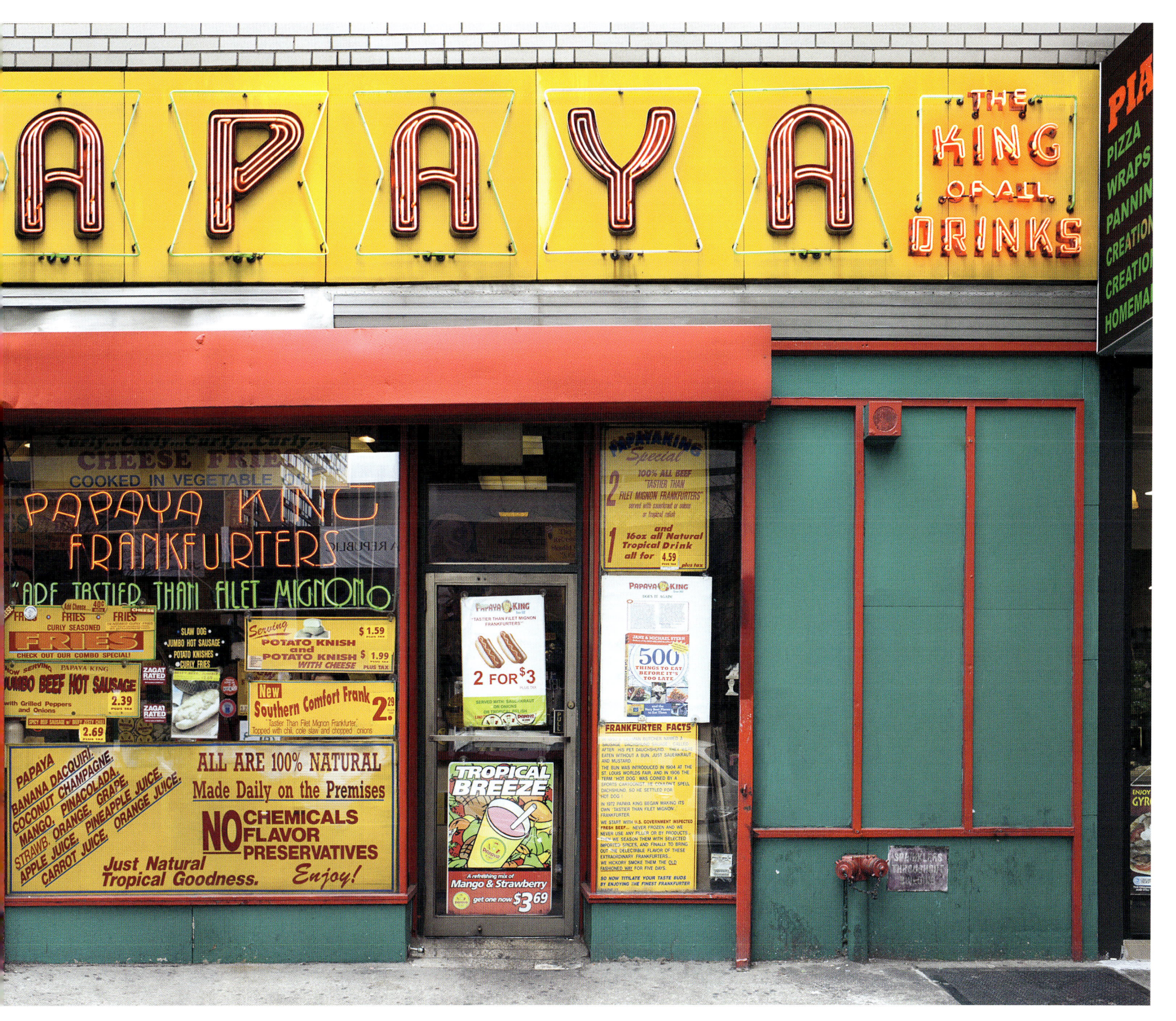

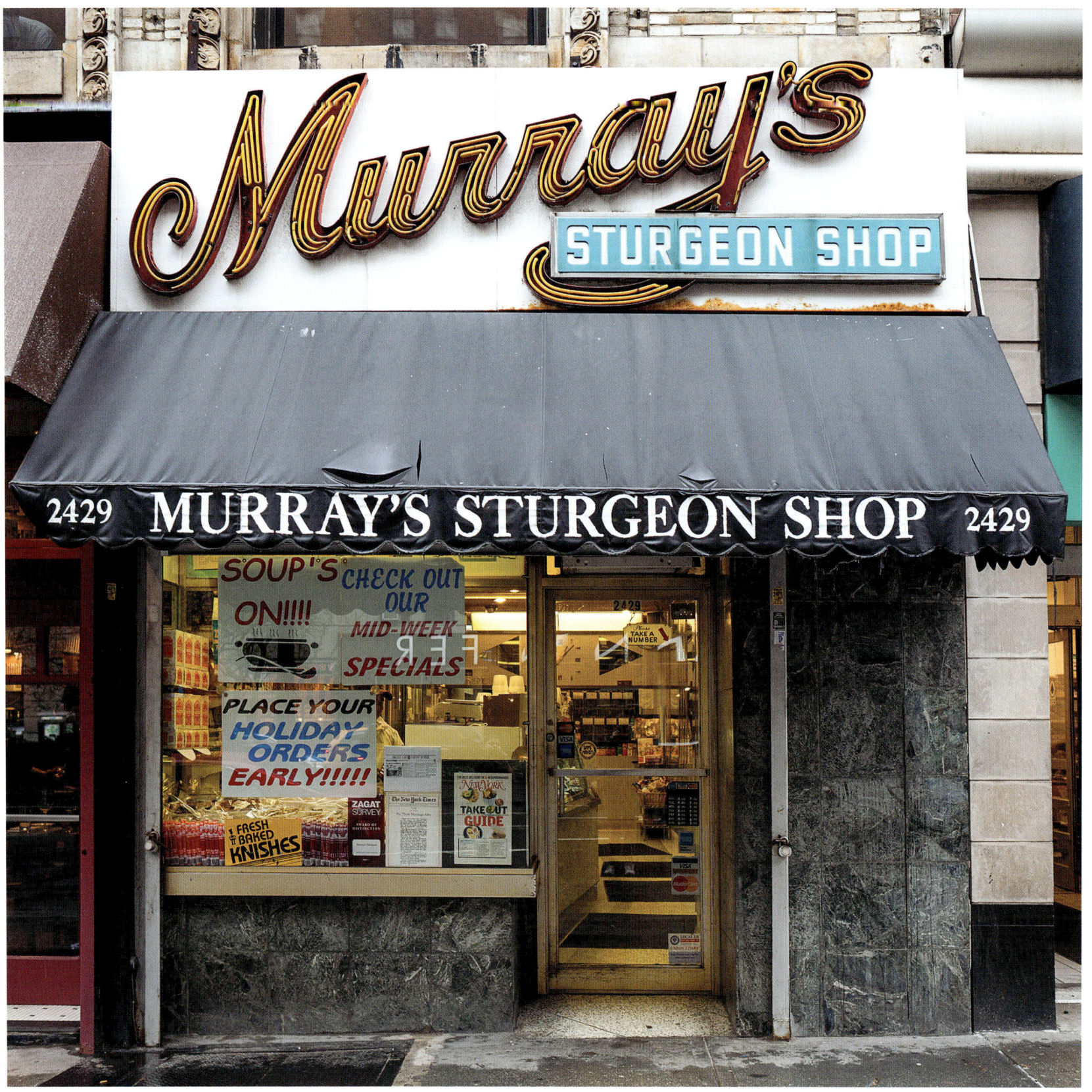

MURRAY'S STURGEON SHOP
Broadway near West 89th Street, Upper West Side, 2010

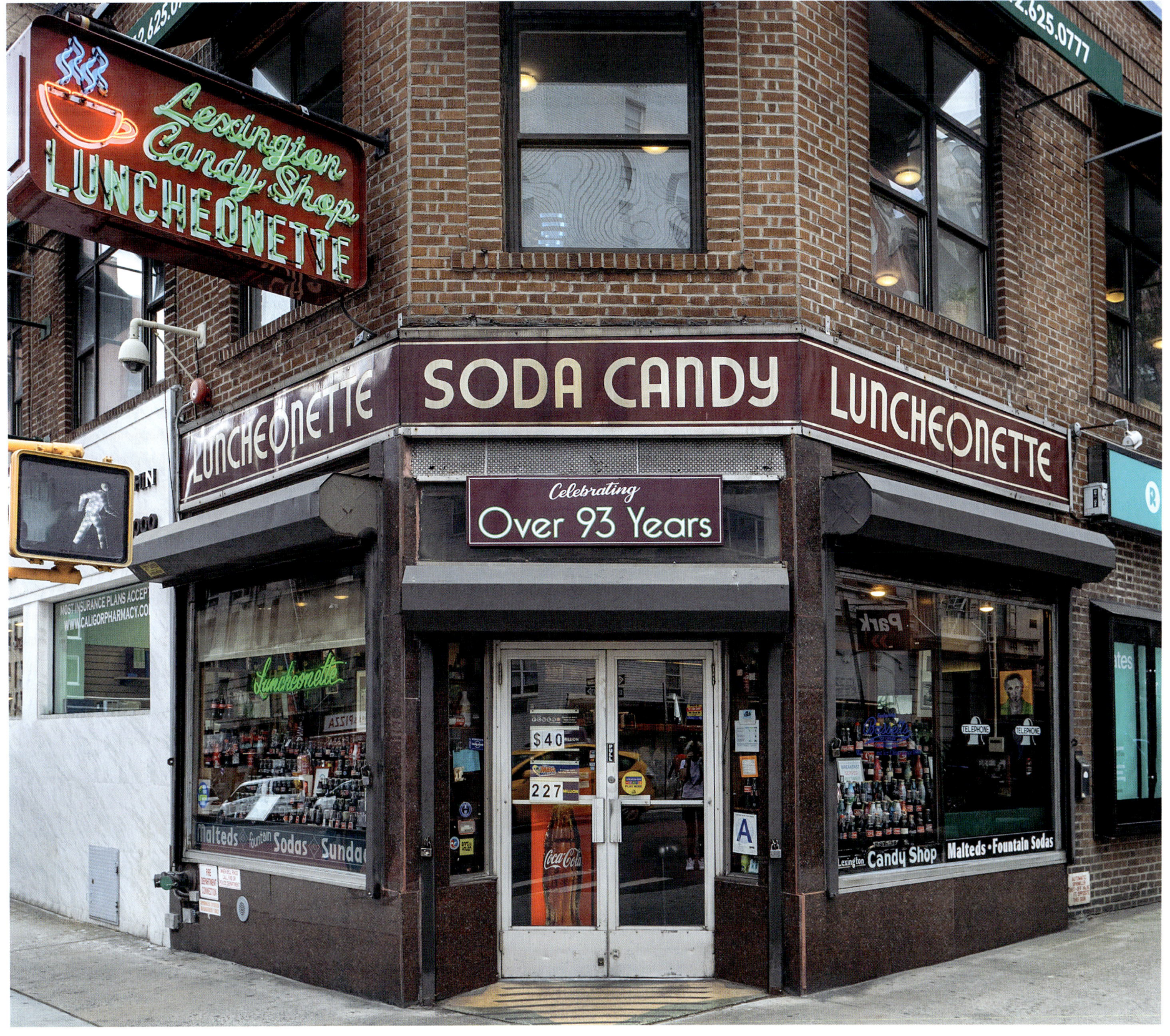

LEXINGTON CANDY SHOP
Lexington Avenue at East 83rd Street, Upper East Side, 2019

MANHATTAN

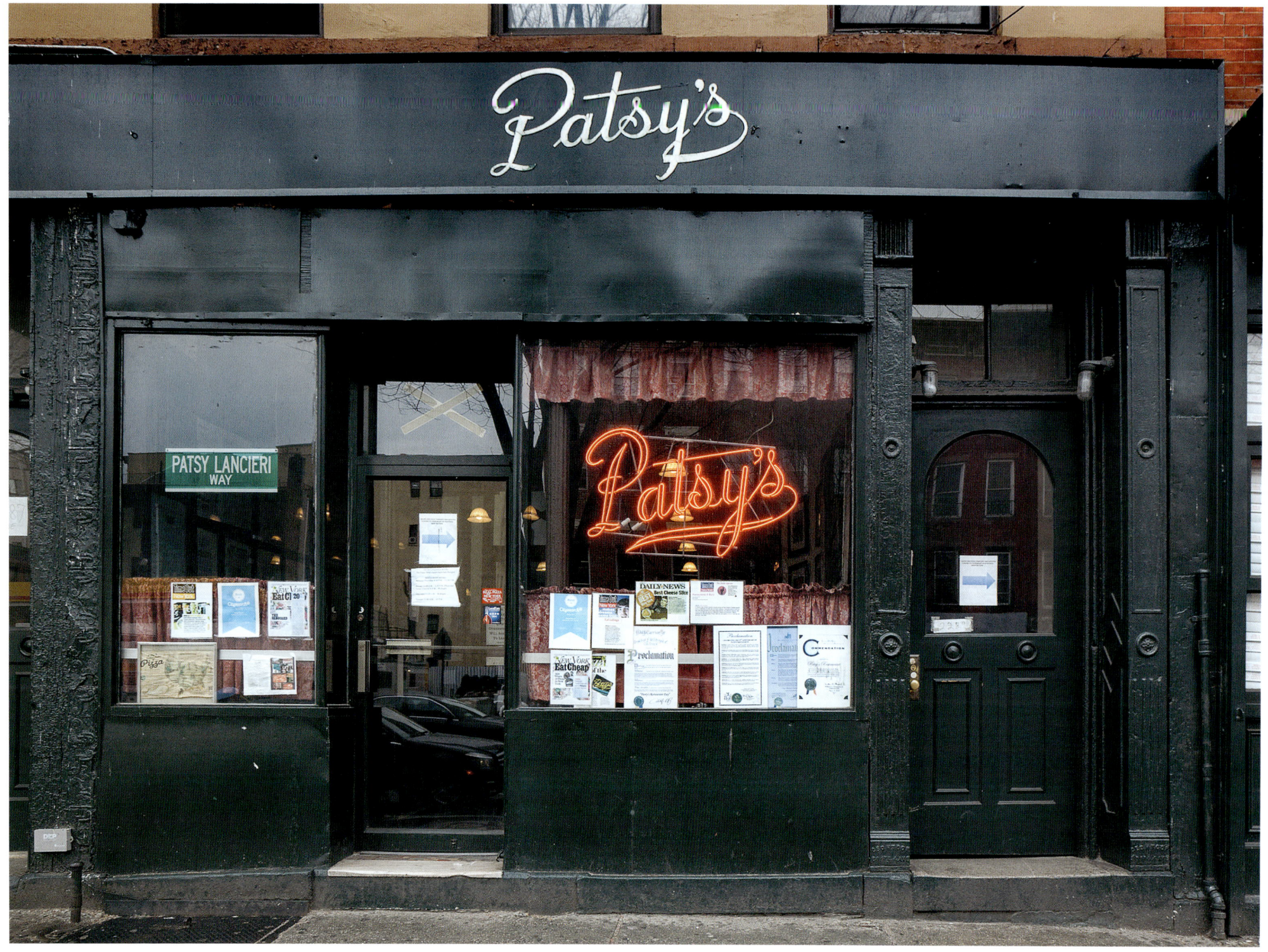

PATSY'S PIZZERIA
1st Avenue near East 118th Street, Harlem, 2014

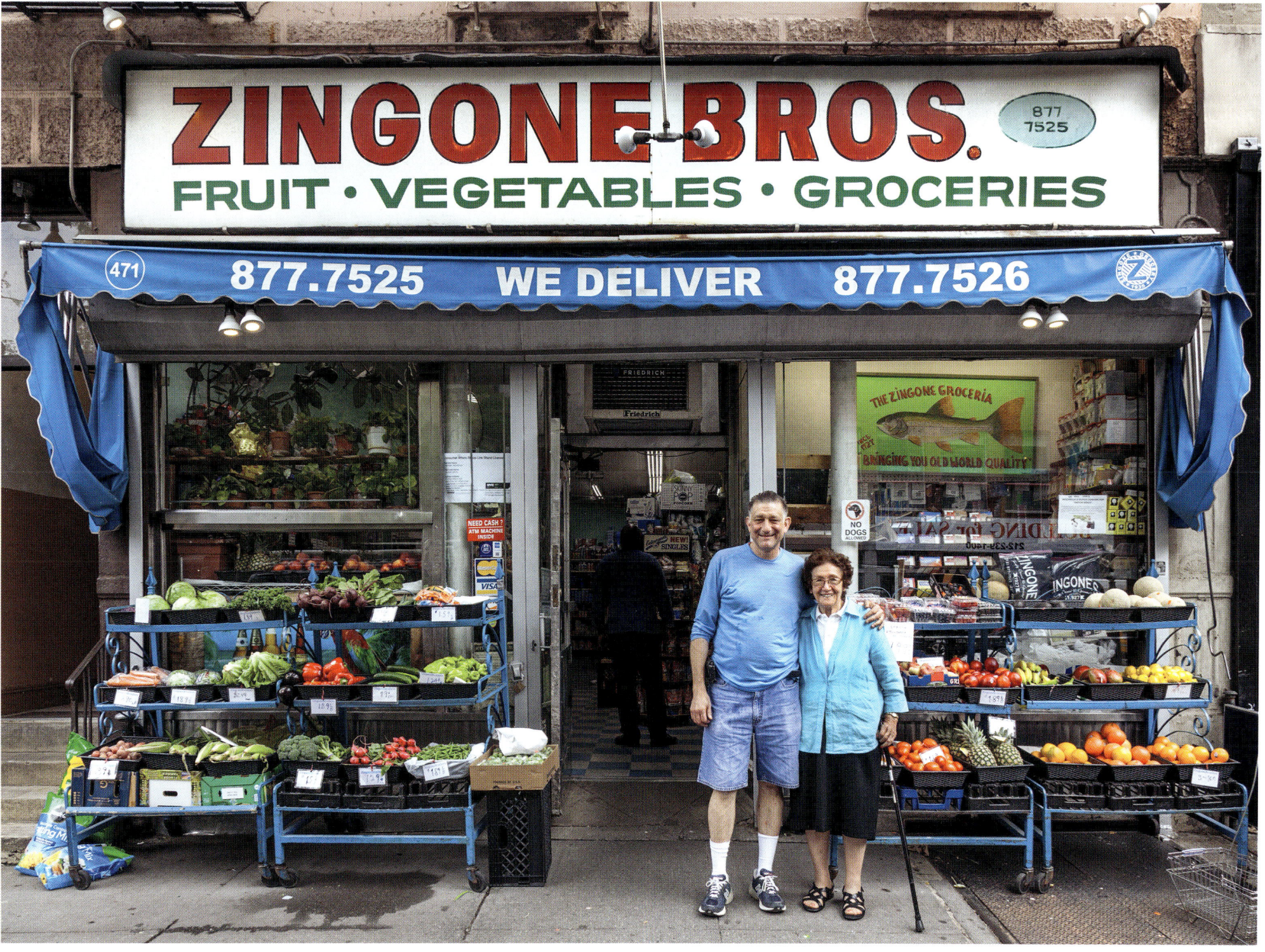

ZINGONE BROTHERS
Columbus Avenue near West 83rd Street, Upper West Side, 2016

MANHATTAN

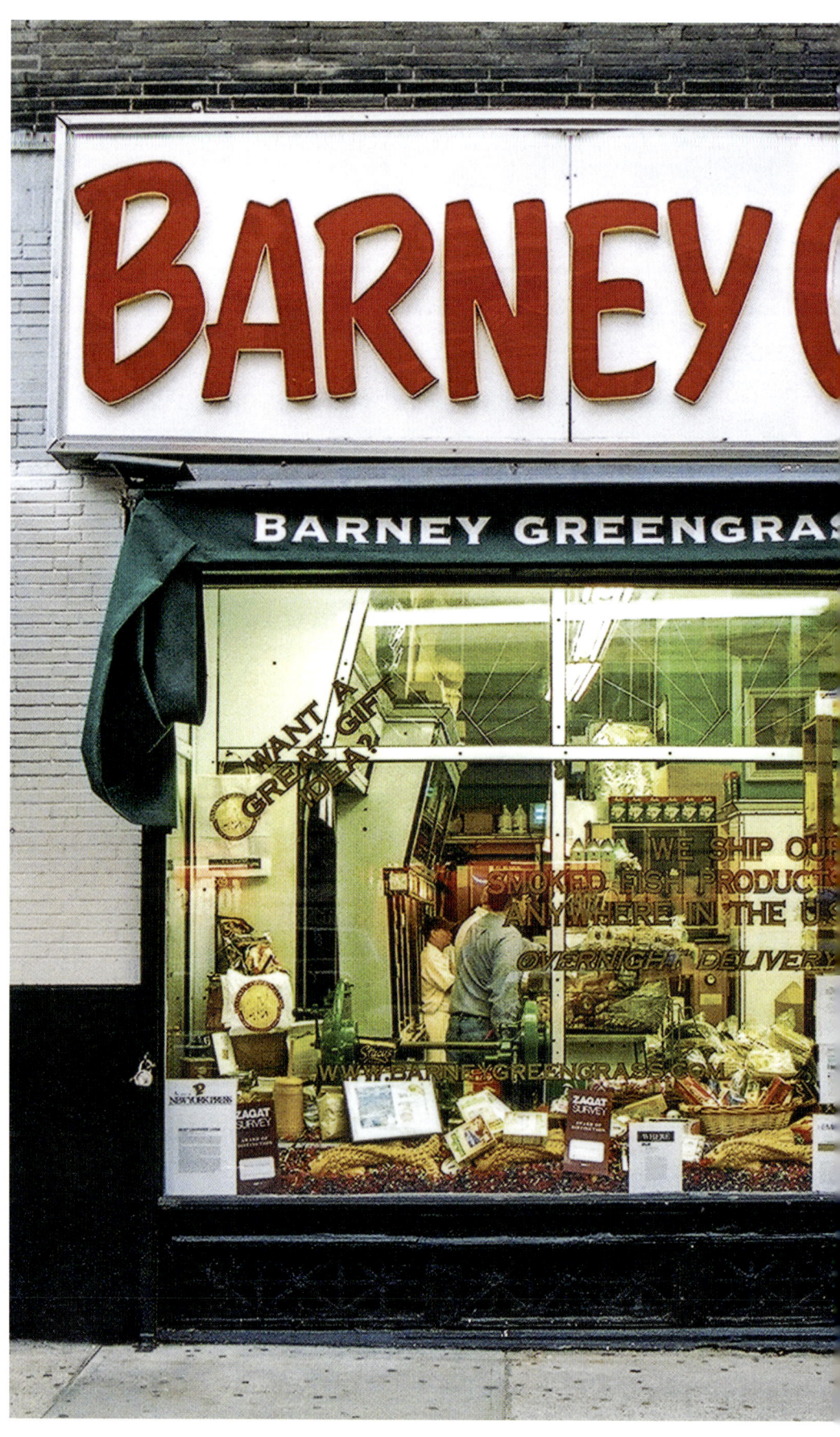

BARNEY GREENGRASS
Amsterdam Avenue near West 86th
Street, Upper West Side, 2004

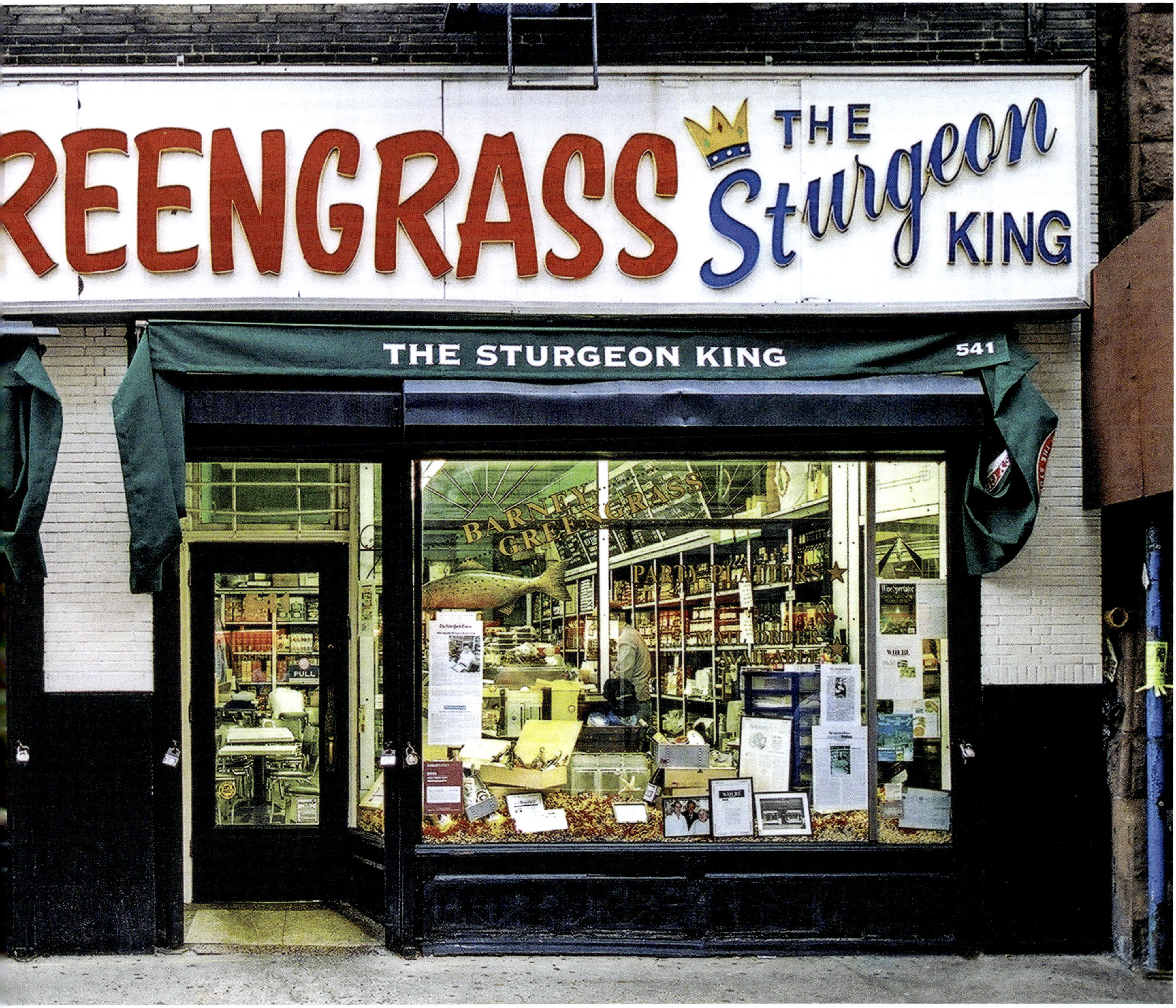
REENGRASS
THE Sturgeon KING
THE STURGEON KING
541
BARNEY GREENGRASS
PARTY PLATTERS
MAIL ORDER AVAILABLE
PULL

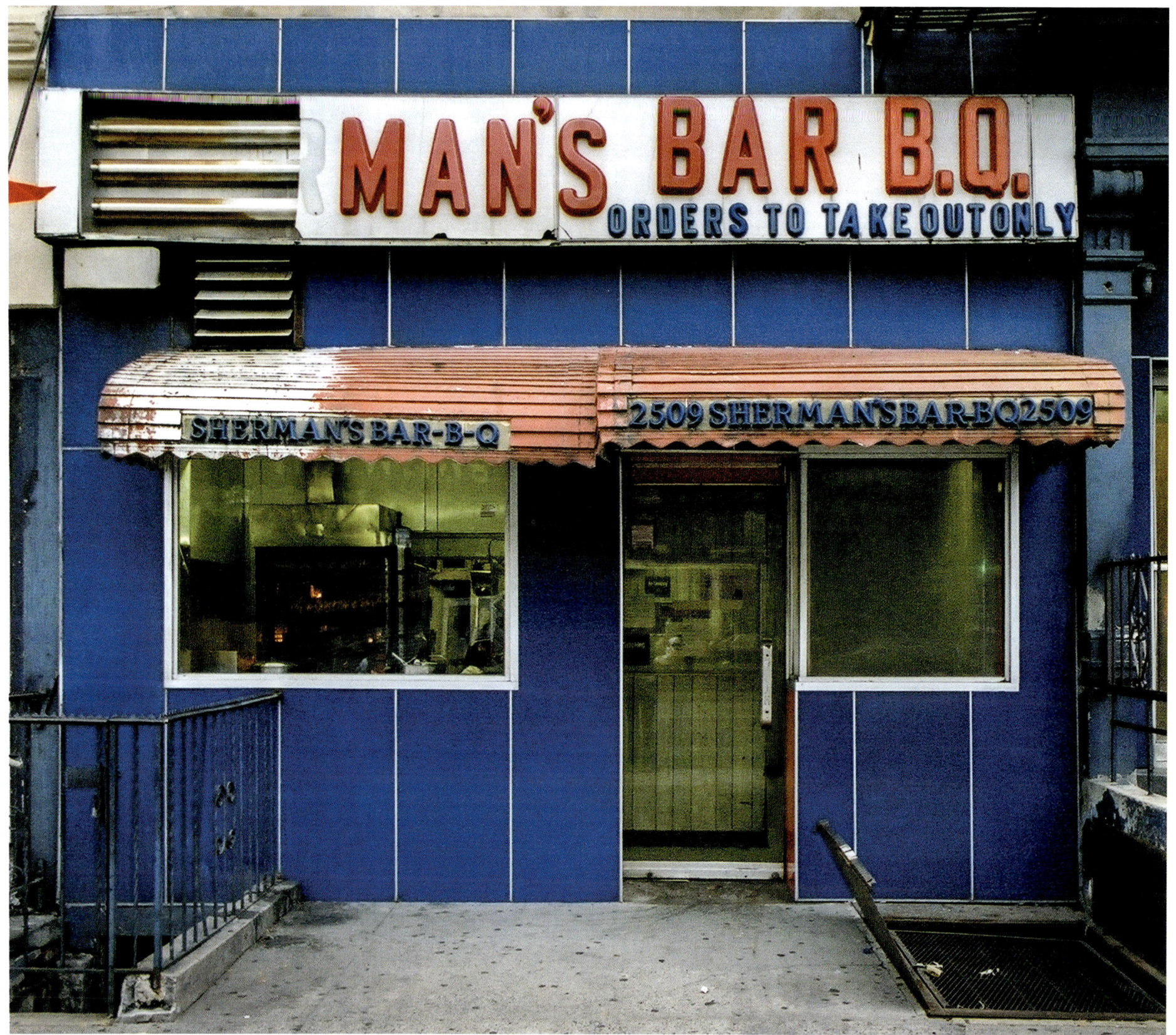

SHERMAN'S BAR-B-Q
Adam Clayton Powell Jr. Boulevard near West 145th Street, Harlem, 2004

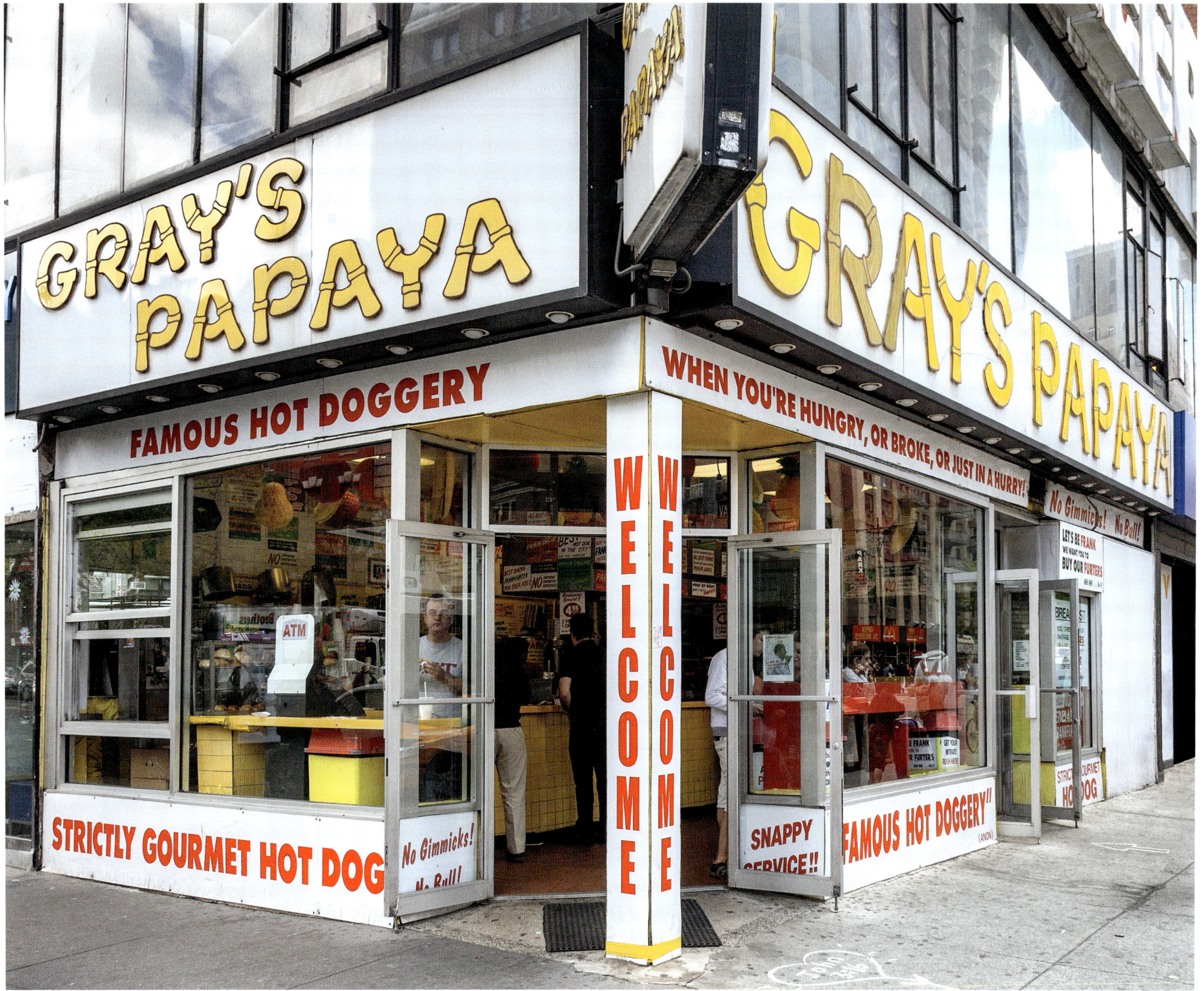

131 GRAY'S PAPAYA
Broadway at West 72nd Street, Upper West Side, 2015

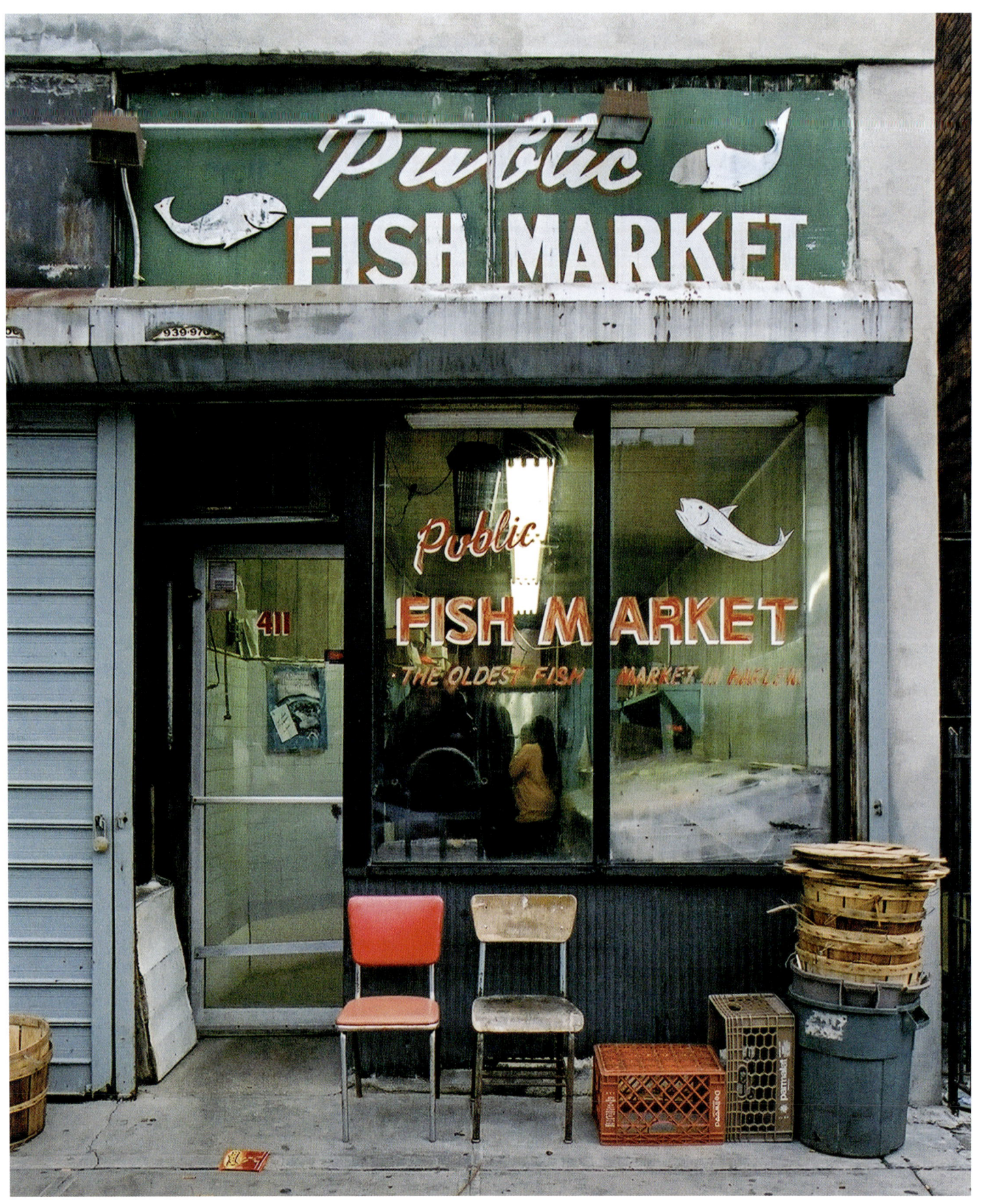

PUBLIC FISH MARKET
Malcolm X Boulevard near West 131st
Street, Harlem, 2004

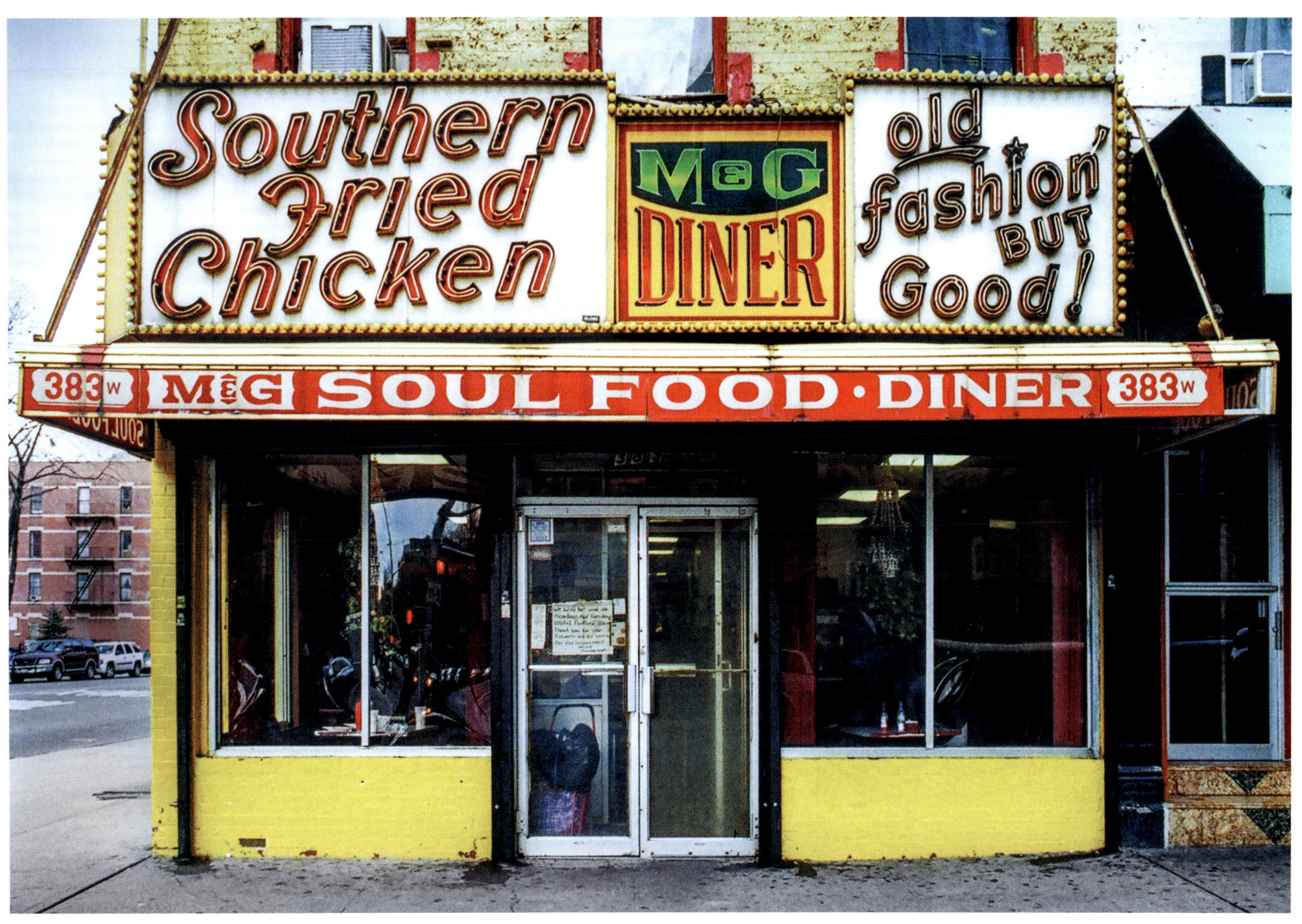

M&G DINER
West 125th Street at Morningside Avenue, Harlem, 2007

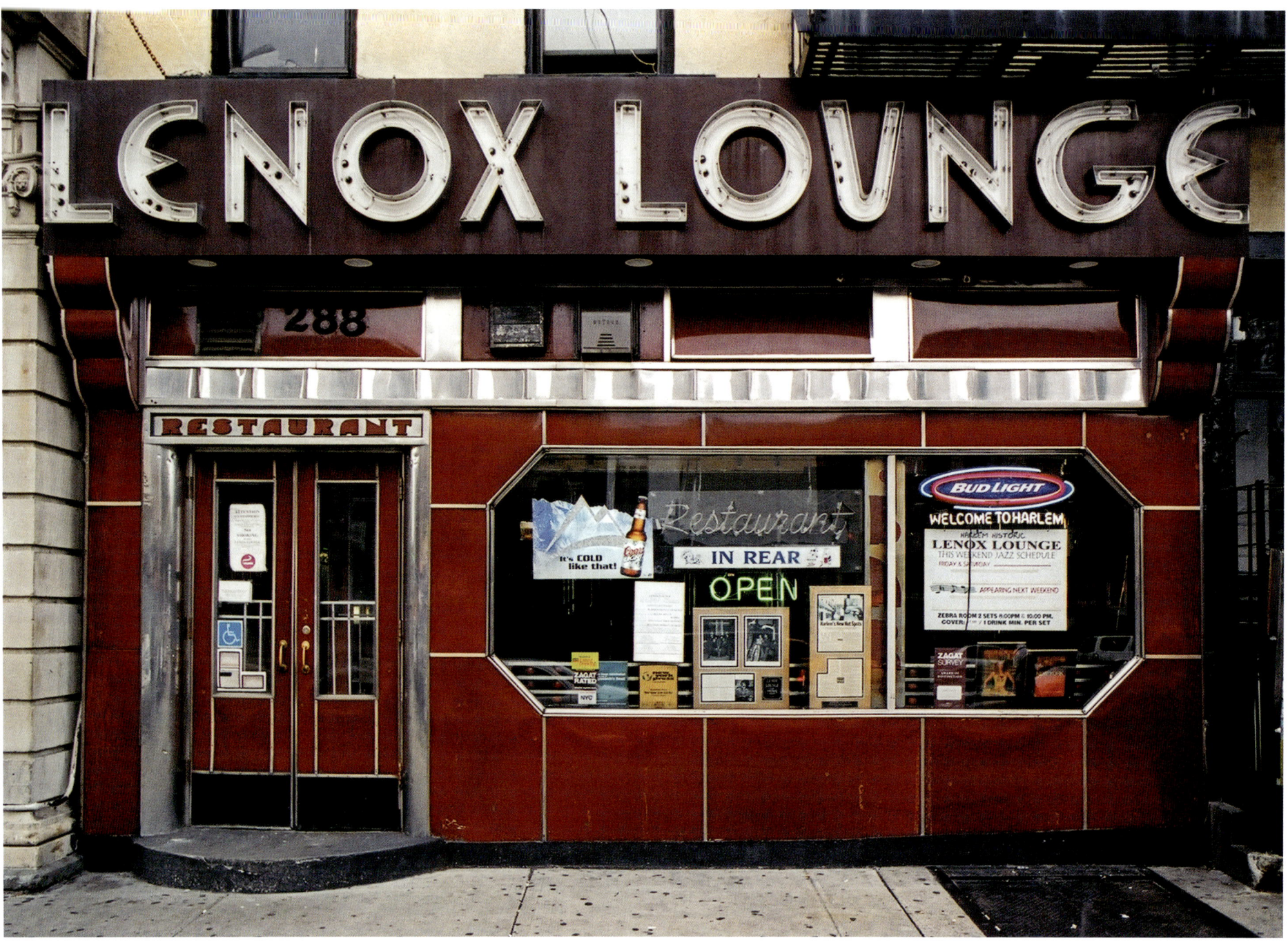

134 LENOX LOUNGE
Malcolm X Boulevard near West 124th Street, Harlem, 2004

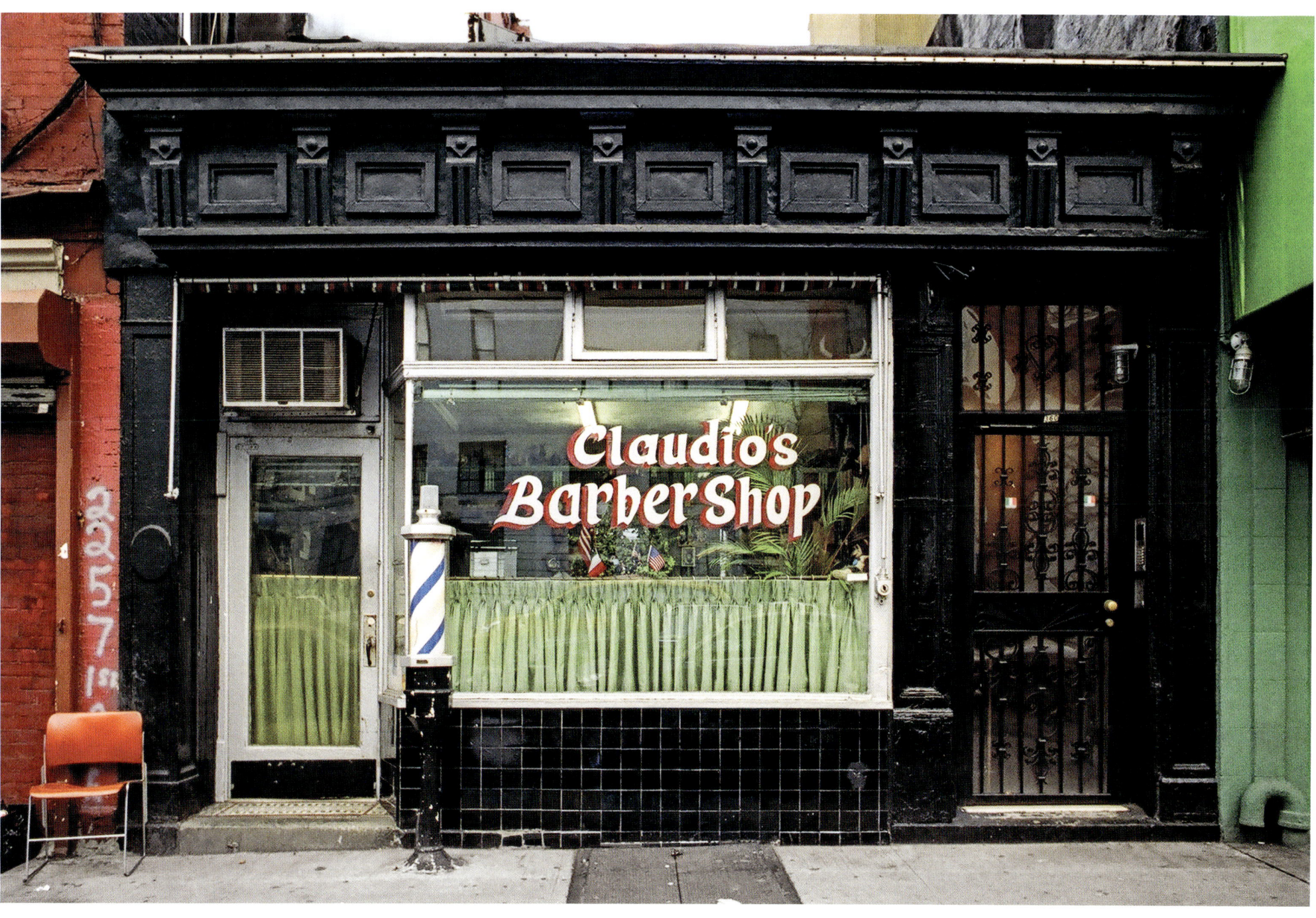

CLAUDIO'S BARBER SHOP
East 116th Street near 1st Avenue, Harlem, 2007

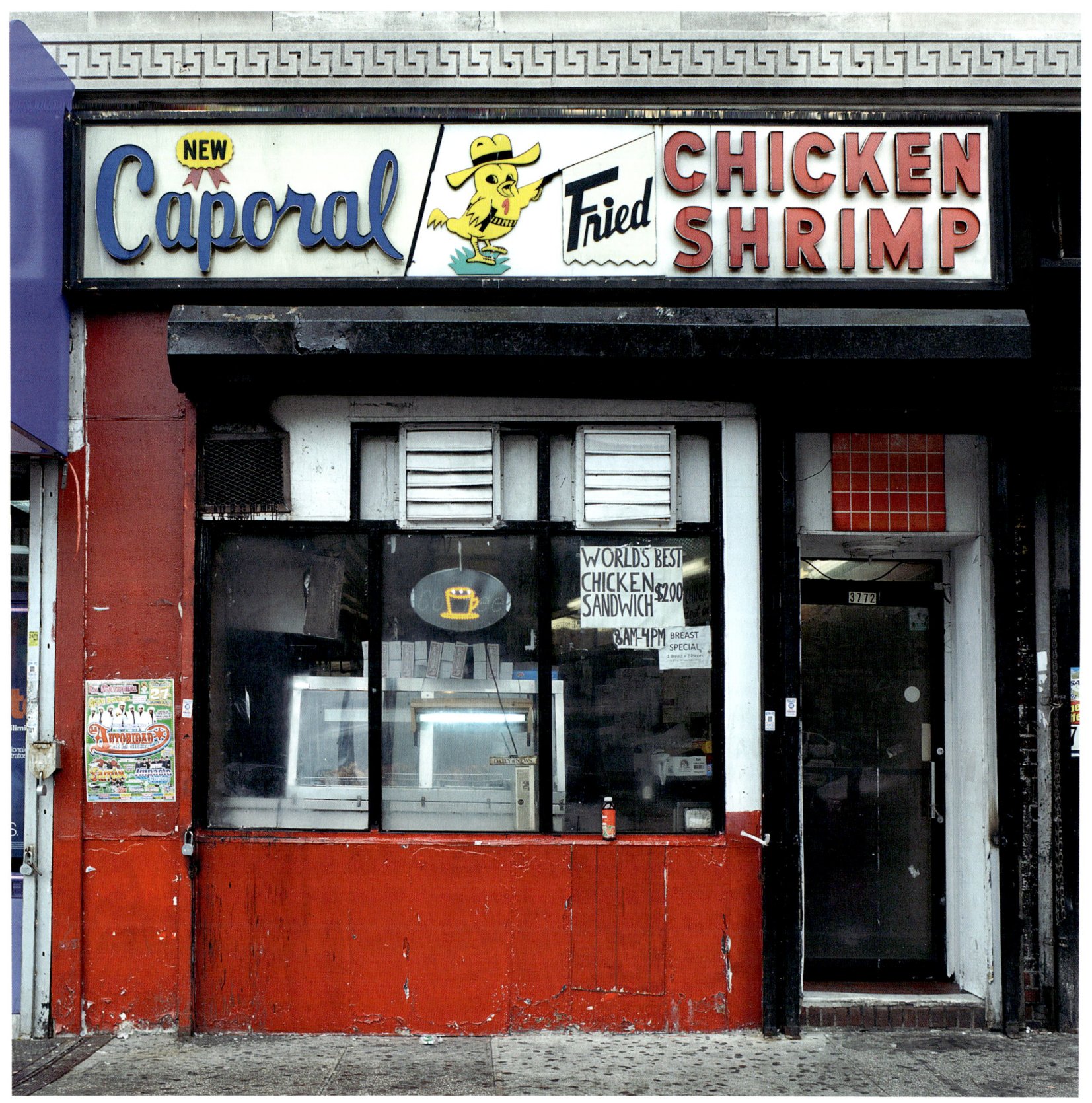

136 NEW CAPORAL FRIED CHICKEN & SHRIMP
Broadway near West 157th Street, Washington Heights, 2010

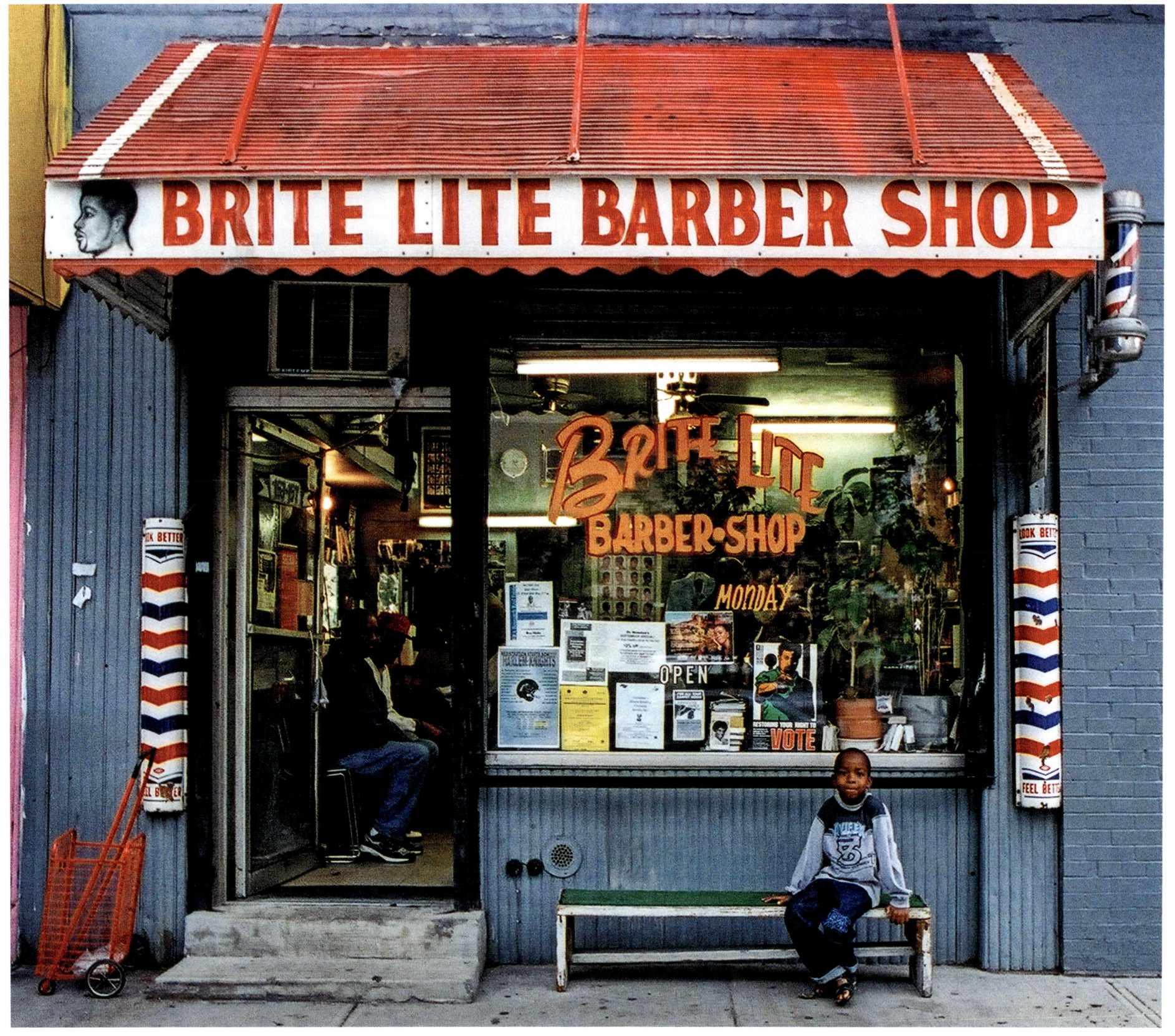

BRITE LITE BARBER SHOP
Malcolm X Boulevard near West 118th Street, Harlem, 2004

MANHATTAN

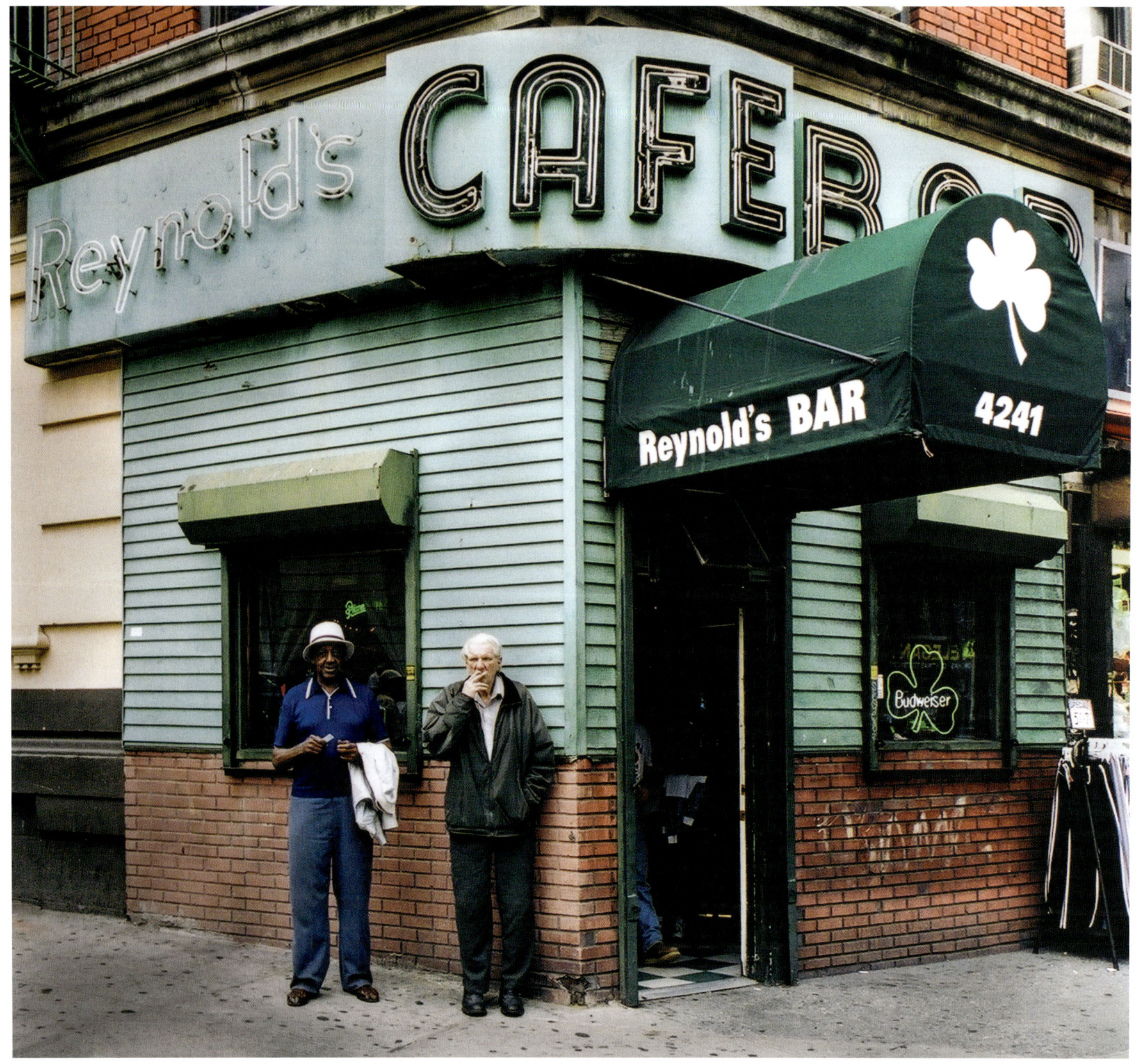

138 REYNOLD'S CAFE
Broadway at West 180th Street, Washington Heights, 2004

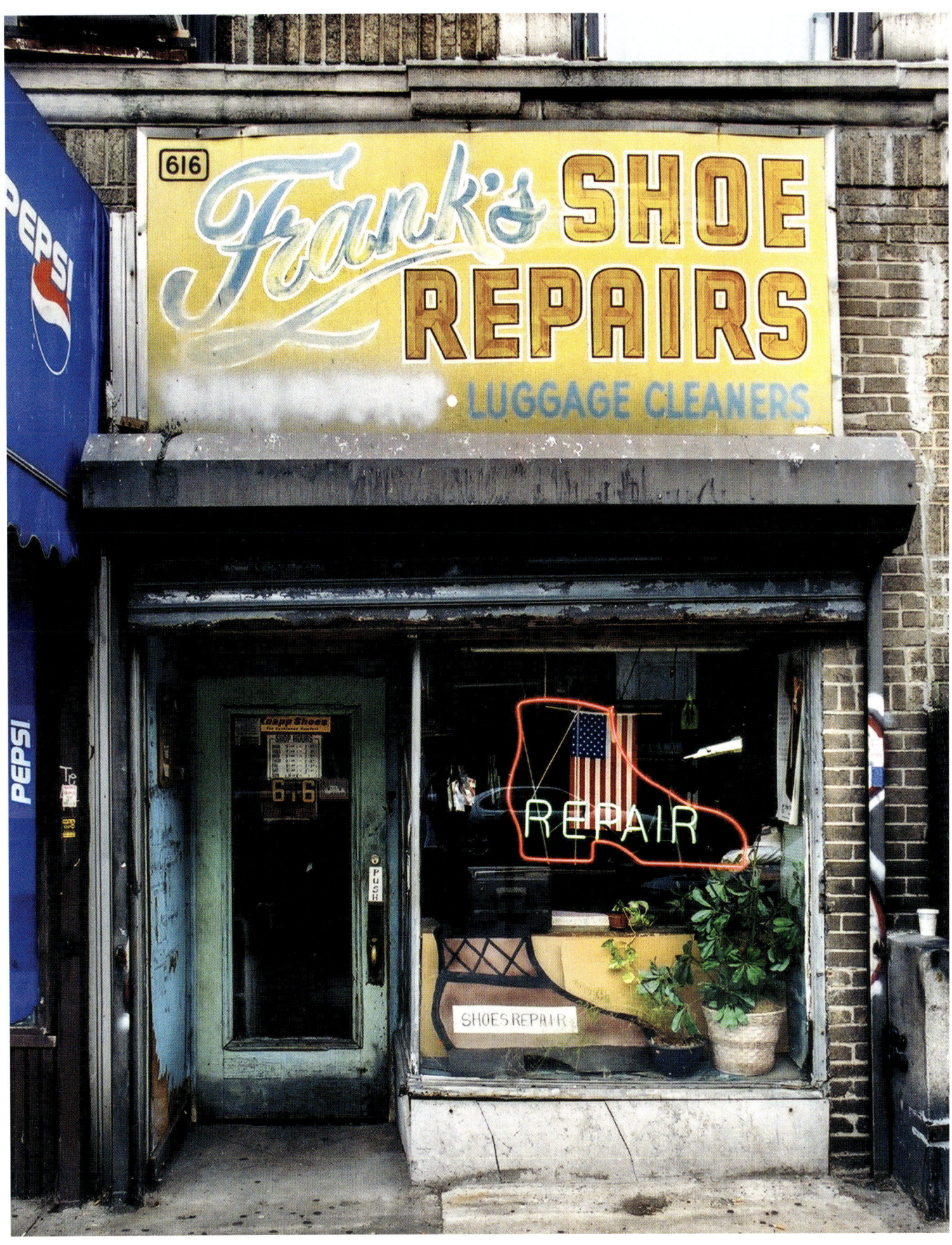

139 FRANK'S SHOE REPAIRS
West 207th Street near Broadway, Inwood, 2004

THE BRONX

The Bronx is the northernmost borough of New York City, and was annexed by the city in the late 1800s. It is the only borough that belongs to the North American mainland. During the early part of the 1900s, after the first subway connecting the Bronx to Manhattan was built, thousands of Irish, German, Italian, and Jewish immigrants moved from overcrowded tenements in Manhattan to spacious new apartments in the Bronx.

After World War II, many longtime residents moved from older housing in the southern neighborhoods into privately built housing in the northern Bronx, or to other boroughs and suburbs. At the same time, about 170,000 people displaced by slum clearance in Manhattan (mostly African Americans and Puerto Ricans) moved to areas in the southern Bronx including Mott Haven, Melrose, and Tremont. Despite becoming a symbol of urban blight in the late 1970s, a number of devastated neighborhoods in the Bronx were rebuilt during the 1980s and '90s, and businesses began to flourish again.

The Bronx is made up of roughly 25 percent parkland, more than in any other borough. Famous landmarks include the Bronx Zoo and the New York Botanical Garden. Yankee Stadium, the home of the New York Yankees baseball team, is also located there.

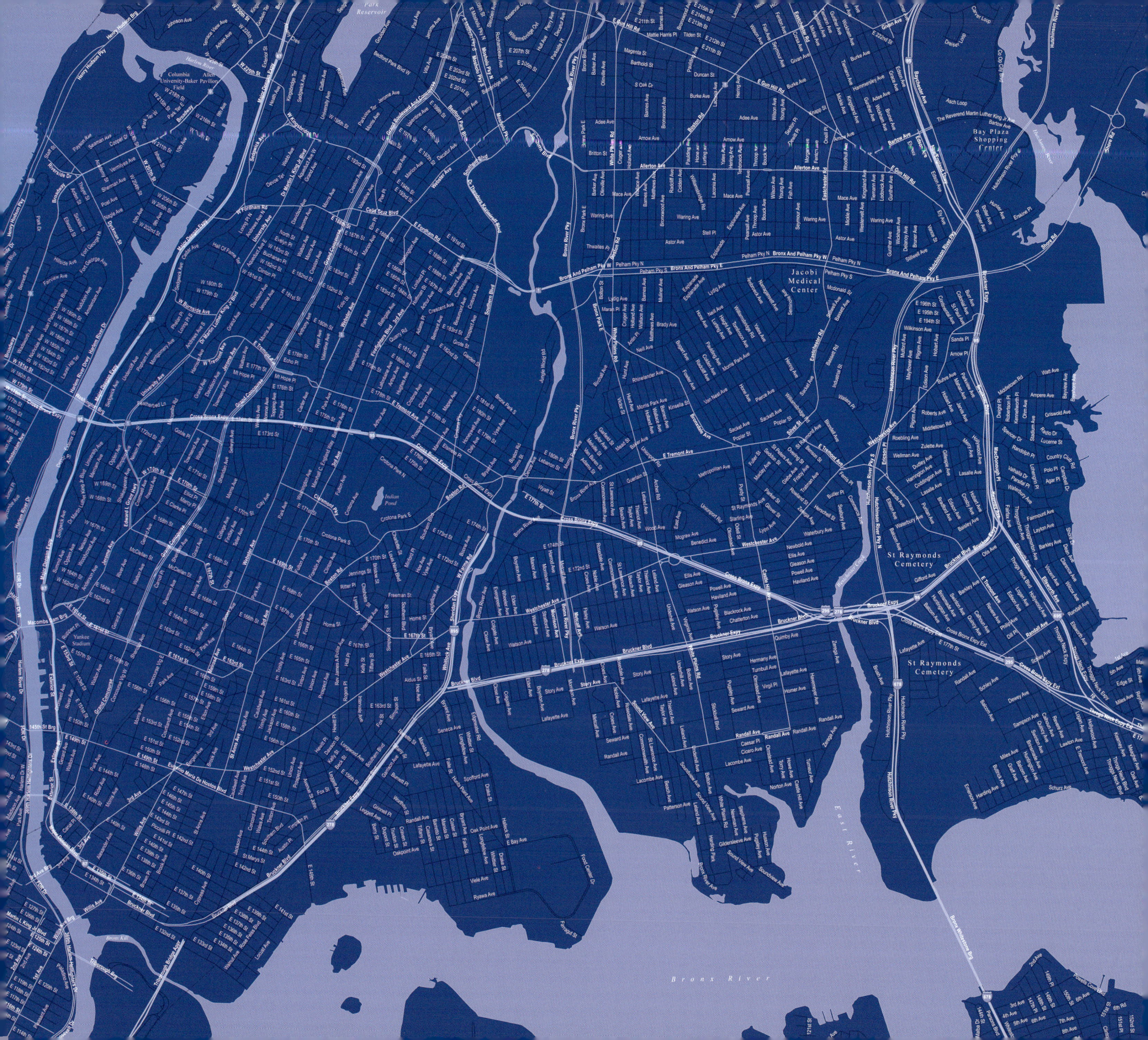

THE BRONX

UNIVERSITY HEIGHTS — FORDHAM — BELMONT — VAN NEST — MOTT HAVEN

University Heights is bounded to the north by West Fordham Road, to the east by Jerome Avenue, to the south by West Burnside Avenue, and to the west by the Harlem River. The neighborhood was given its name after New York University moved most of its operations there from Greenwich Village in 1894. NYU sold its campus to the city in 1973 to be used by Bronx Community College. The ethnic makeup of the neighborhood gradually changed, becoming predominantly Latino and African American.

Fordham is bounded to the north by Kingsbridge Road and East 194th Street, to the east by Fordham University and Webster Avenue, to the south by 183rd Street, and to the west by the Harlem River. In the early to mid-1900s, the large shopping district on Fordham Road became known throughout the Bronx. Most residents of Fordham were working-class Jewish, Irish, and Italian people. After the 1950s, the demographic shifted as older residents relocated to the suburbs, and by 1980, much of the population was African American and Latino, including Puerto Ricans and Dominicans. In the early 2000s there was also an influx of Mexican people.

Belmont, known as the Little Italy of the Bronx, is bounded to the north by East Fordham Road, to the east by Southern Boulevard, to the south by East 181st Street, and to the west by Webster Avenue. When construction began on the Bronx Zoo and the New York Botanical Garden in the late 1890s, real estate developers encouraged Italians—who made up a large part of the construction industry—to settle in the area. It is one of the few Bronx neighborhoods that has retained its original ethnic character. It is home to Arthur Avenue, known for its numerous Italian restaurants.

Van Nest is bounded to the north by Park Avenue and the Esplanade, to the east by Bronxdale Avenue, to the south by East Tremont Avenue, and to the west by the Bronx River Parkway. After apartment buildings were constructed in the 1920s, the neighborhood attracted a large Italian and Irish population. By the 1980s, the area became more diverse, and included many Latino and Asian immigrants.

Mott Haven is bounded to the north by East 149th Street and St. Mary's Park, to the east by the southerly continuation of East 149th Street and the East River, to the south by the Bronx Kill, and to the west by the Harlem River. The neighborhood was initially developed in the 1850s as an industrial village and residential suburb for people working in Manhattan. After the 3rd Avenue elevated subway line was extended to the area in 1886, elegant row houses were built, and many Germans, Jews, Irish, and Italians settled there. Mott Haven became predominately Puerto Rican after the 1950s, and despite more recent attempts at residential redevelopment in the 2000s, the neighborhood remains largely ungentrified.

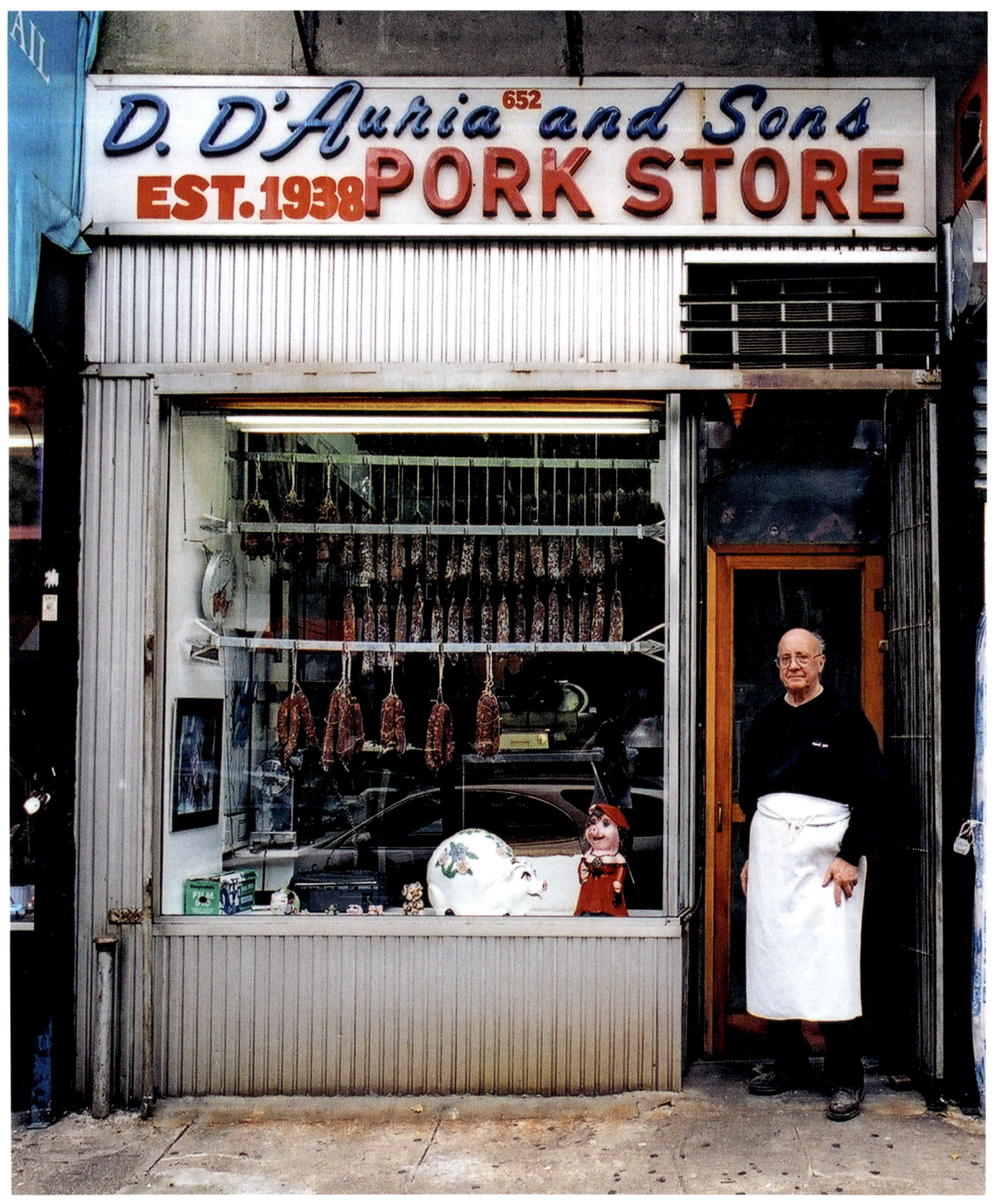

D. D'AURIA & SONS PORK STORE
East 187th Street near Cambreleng Avenue, Belmont, 2004

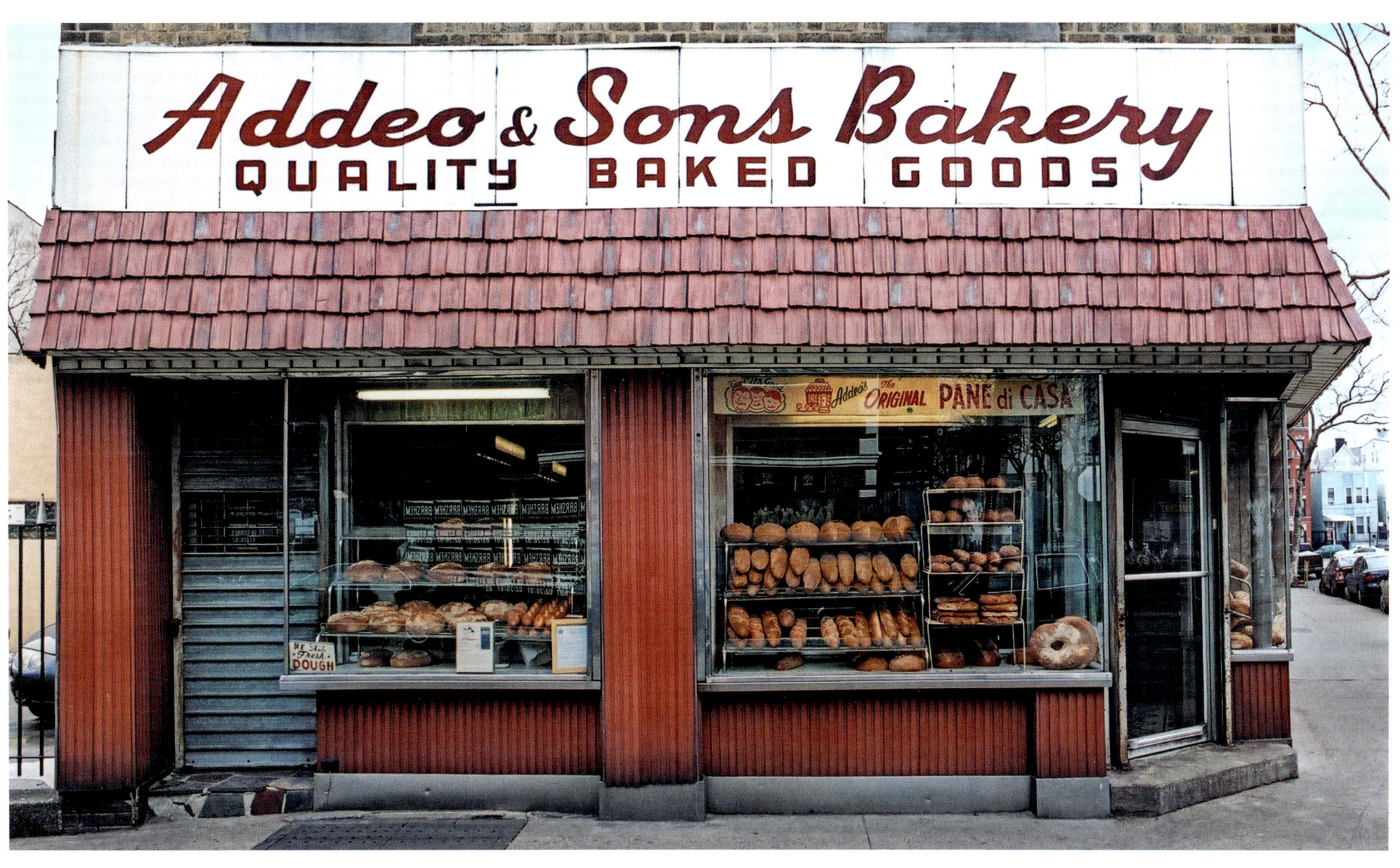

ADDEO & SONS BAKERY
Hughes Avenue at East 186th Street, Belmont, 2006

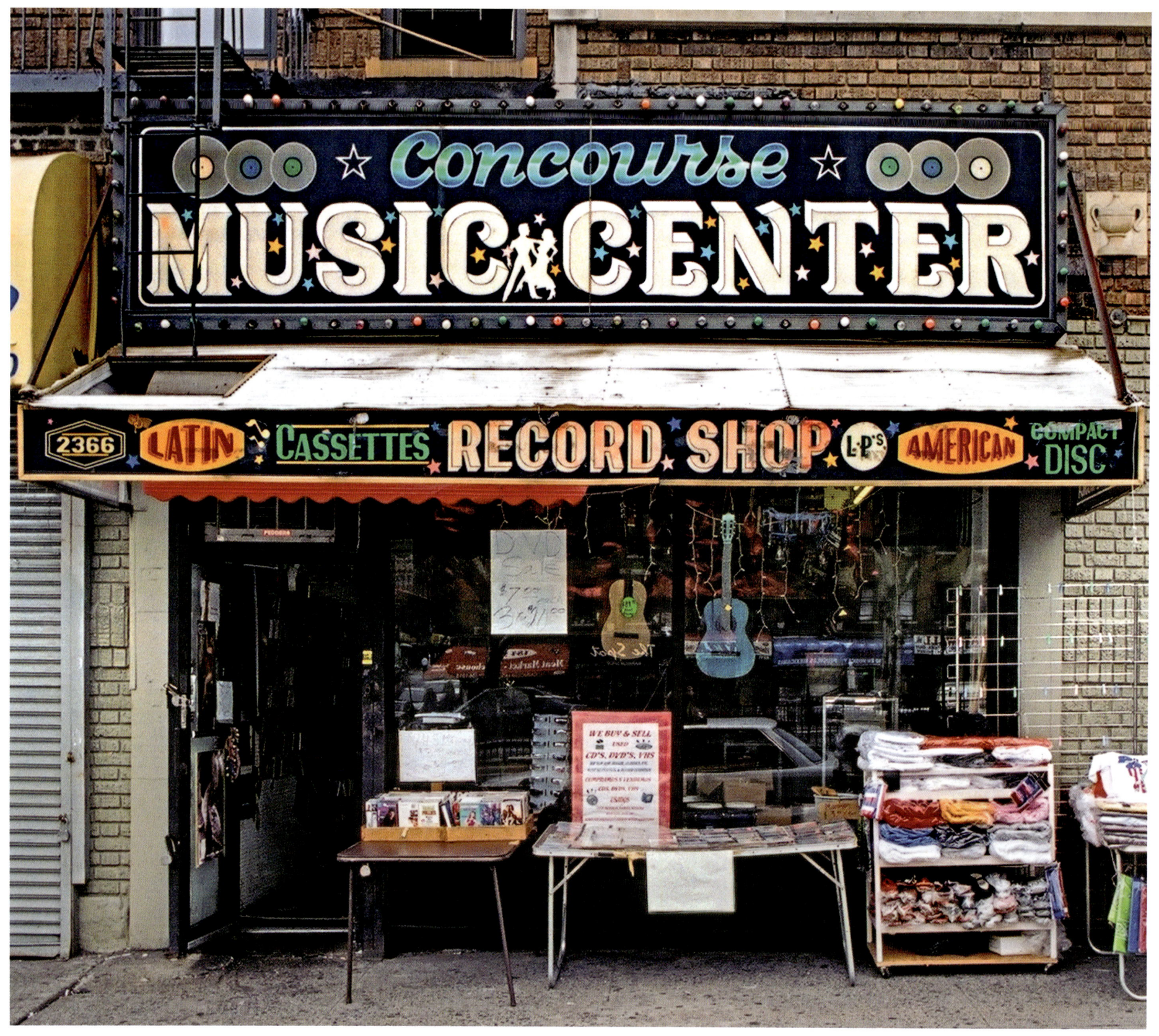

CONCOURSE MUSIC CENTER
Grand Concourse near East 184th Street, University Heights, 2004

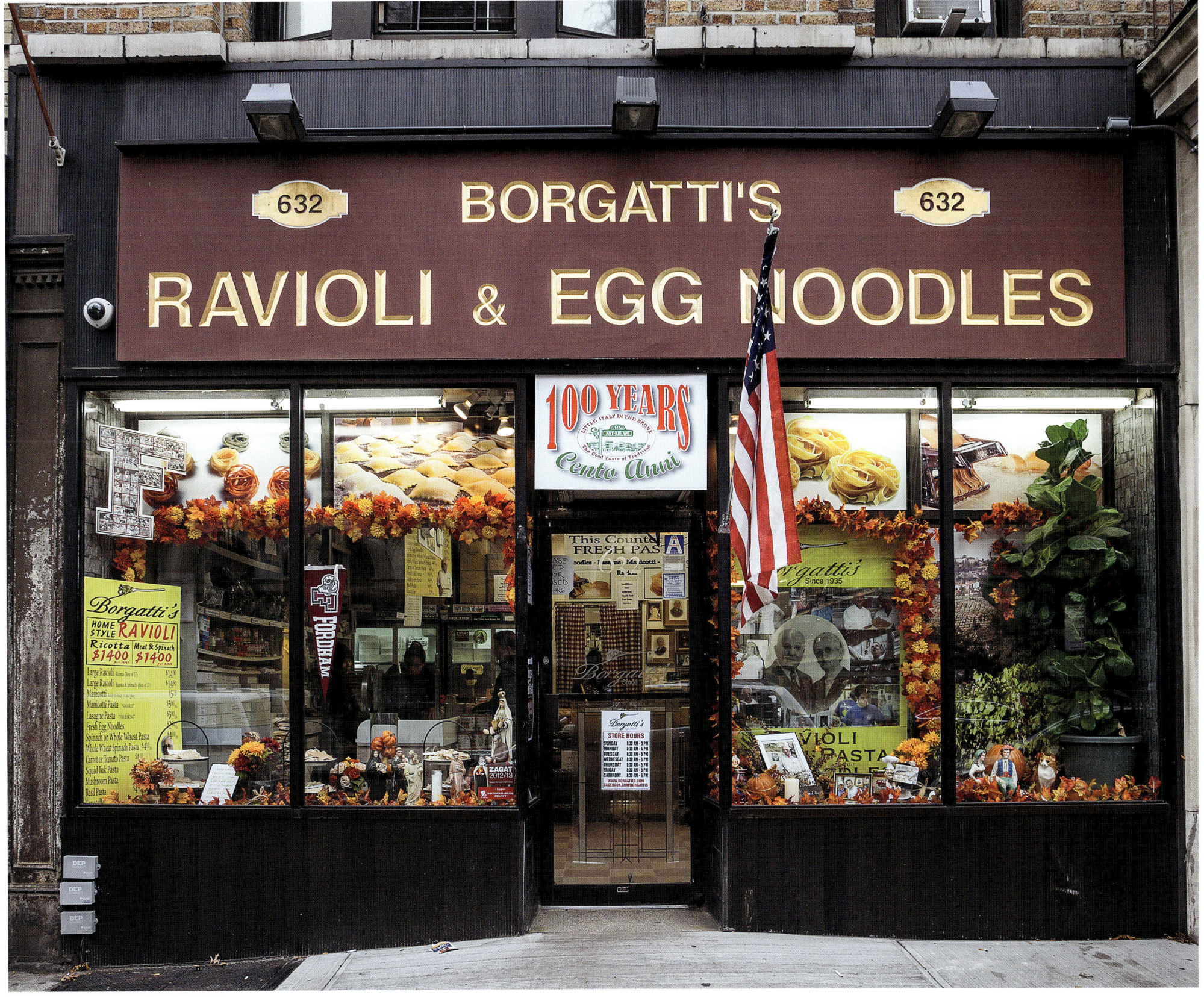

BORGATTI'S RAVIOLI & EGG NOODLES
East 187th Street near Belmont Avenue, Belmont, 2014

THE BRONX

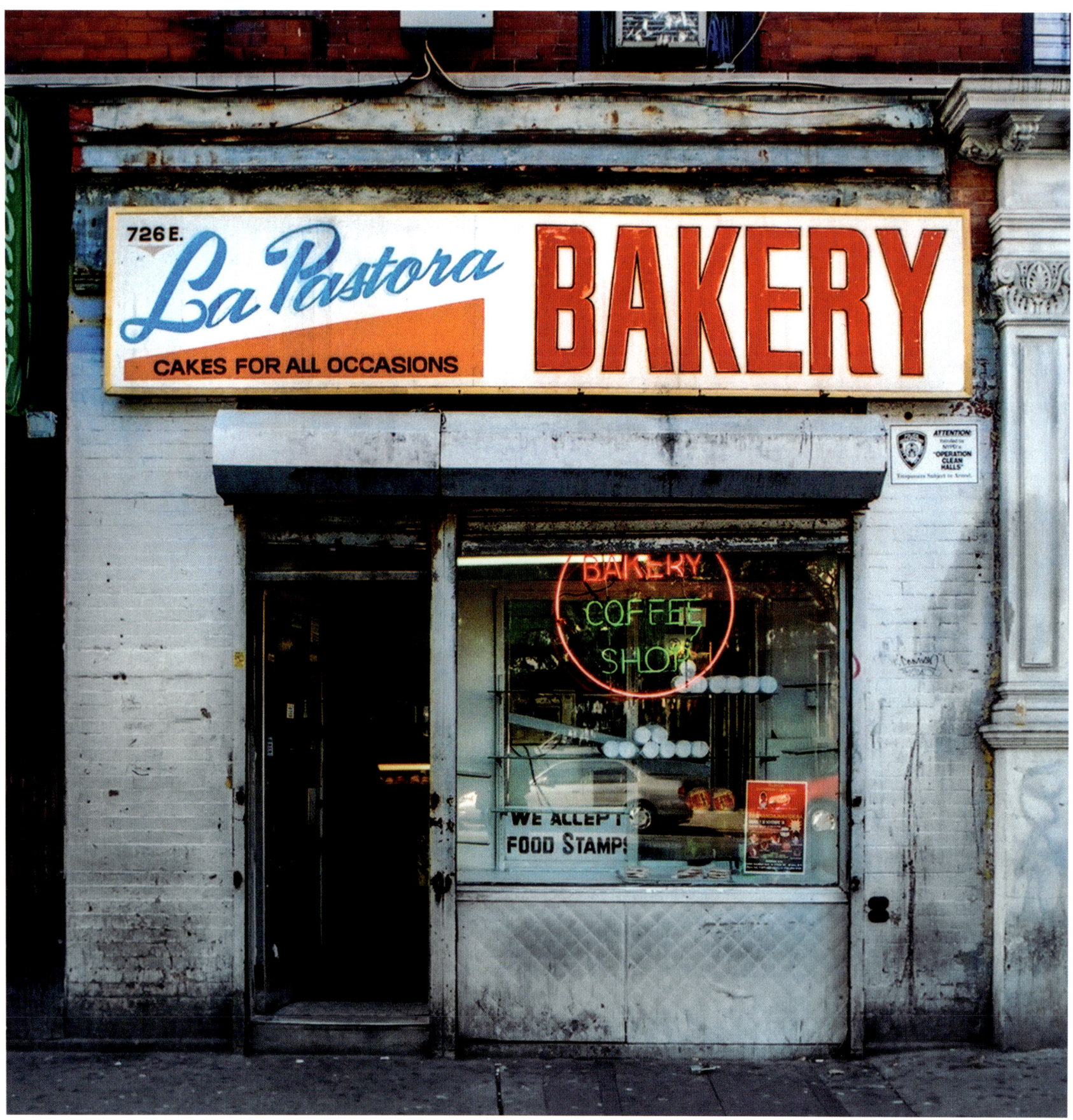

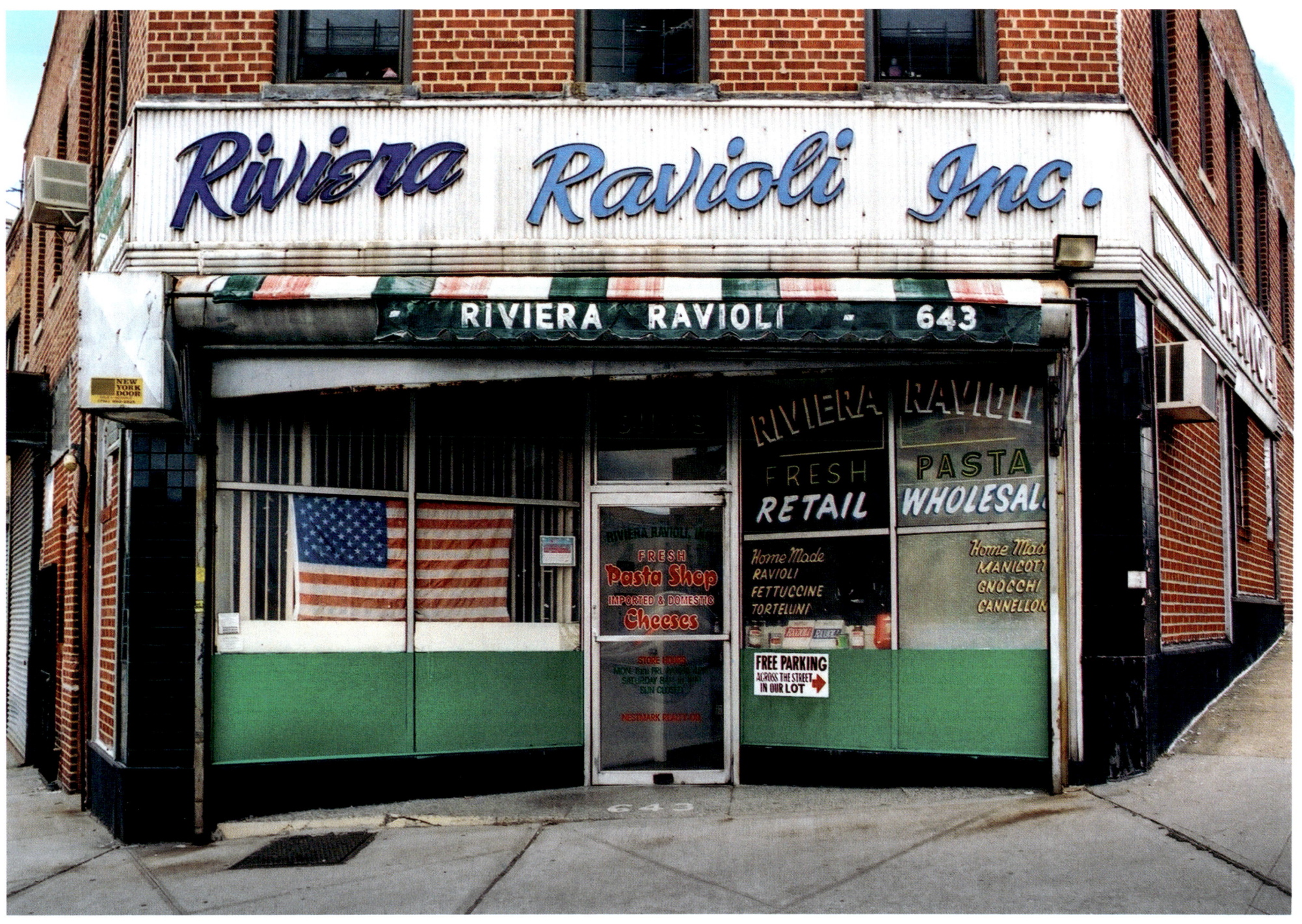

149   LA PASTORA BAKERY
East 152nd Street near Concord Avenue, Mott Haven, 2006

RIVIERA RAVIOLI INC.
Morris Park Avenue at Unionport Road, Van Nest, 2005

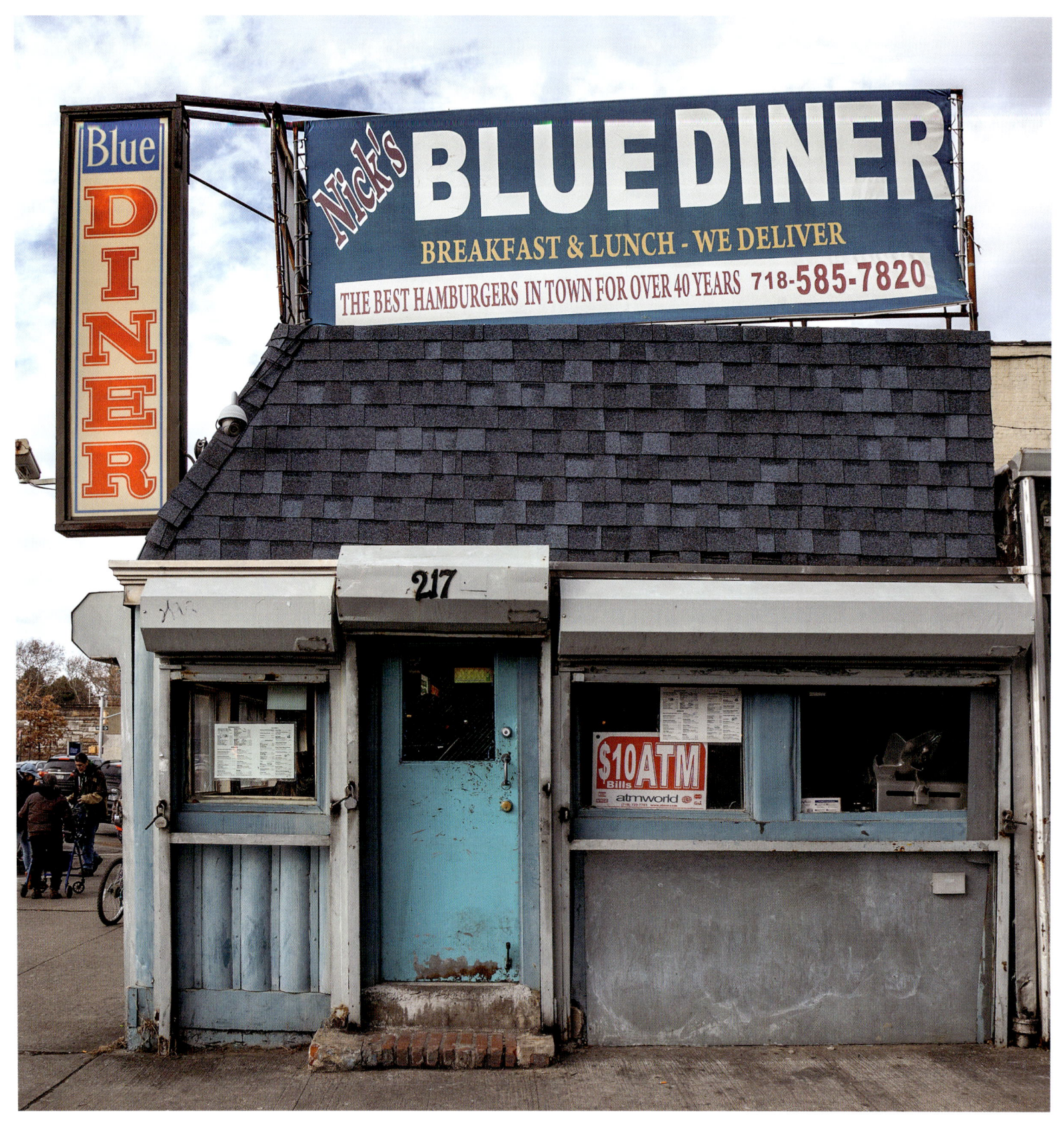

150 NICK'S BLUE DINER
East 138th Street at Canal Place, Mott Haven, 2017

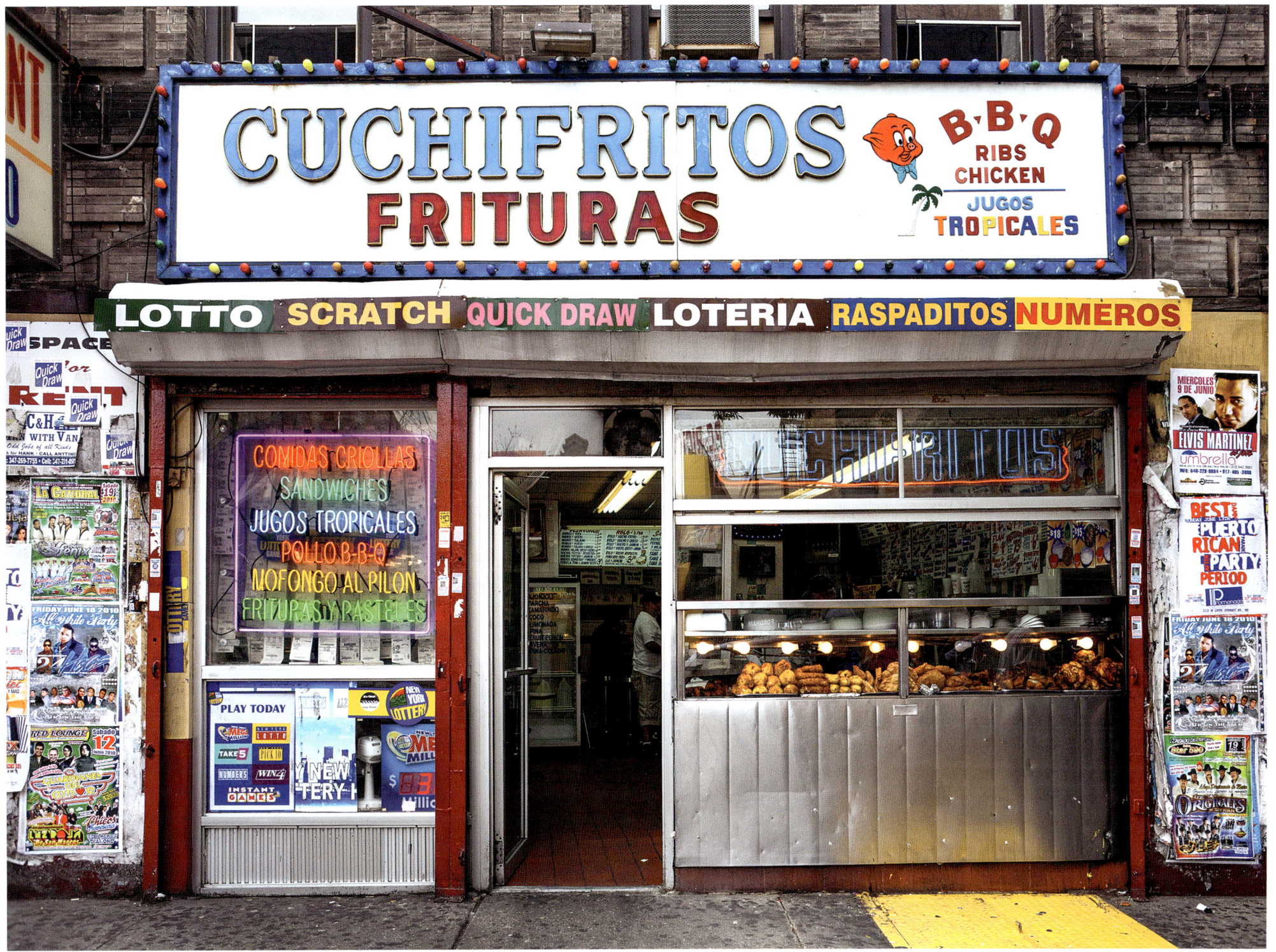

188 CUCHIFRITOS
East 188th Street near Grand Concourse, Fordham, 2010

BROOKLYN

Brooklyn is the most populous borough in New York City and has many distinct neighborhoods. Before it became a borough in 1898, it was an independent municipality and had been the nation's third-largest city for nearly half a century.

Brooklyn is located on the southwestern tip of Long Island and is situated on New York Harbor, across the East River from Manhattan. It was initially developed along its East River waterfront, where a major shipping port faced Manhattan. When the Brooklyn Bridge opened in 1883, the population grew tremendously, because transportation to Manhattan was no longer limited to boats. Development in Brooklyn intensified with the opening of the Williamsburg Bridge in 1903, the Manhattan Bridge in 1909, and several subway tunnels in the early 1900s.

Before the passage of national immigration laws in 1924, Brooklyn attracted huge numbers of immigrants, many of them from eastern and southern Europe. In the late 1950s and '60s, thousands of white, middle-class residents abandoned the borough and moved to Long Island, Staten Island, and New Jersey, and other racially and ethnically diverse groups came to populate the area. During the 1970s, a number of local working-class immigrant communities were plagued with abandonment, despite the city's attempts to revive these troubled regions. Other historic Brooklyn neighborhoods, through the efforts of longtime residents and new arrivals, were able to revitalize and flourish.

Despite recent gentrification, many Brooklyn neighborhoods still maintain distinct ethnic cultures, each with their own shopping, dining, and nightlife offerings.

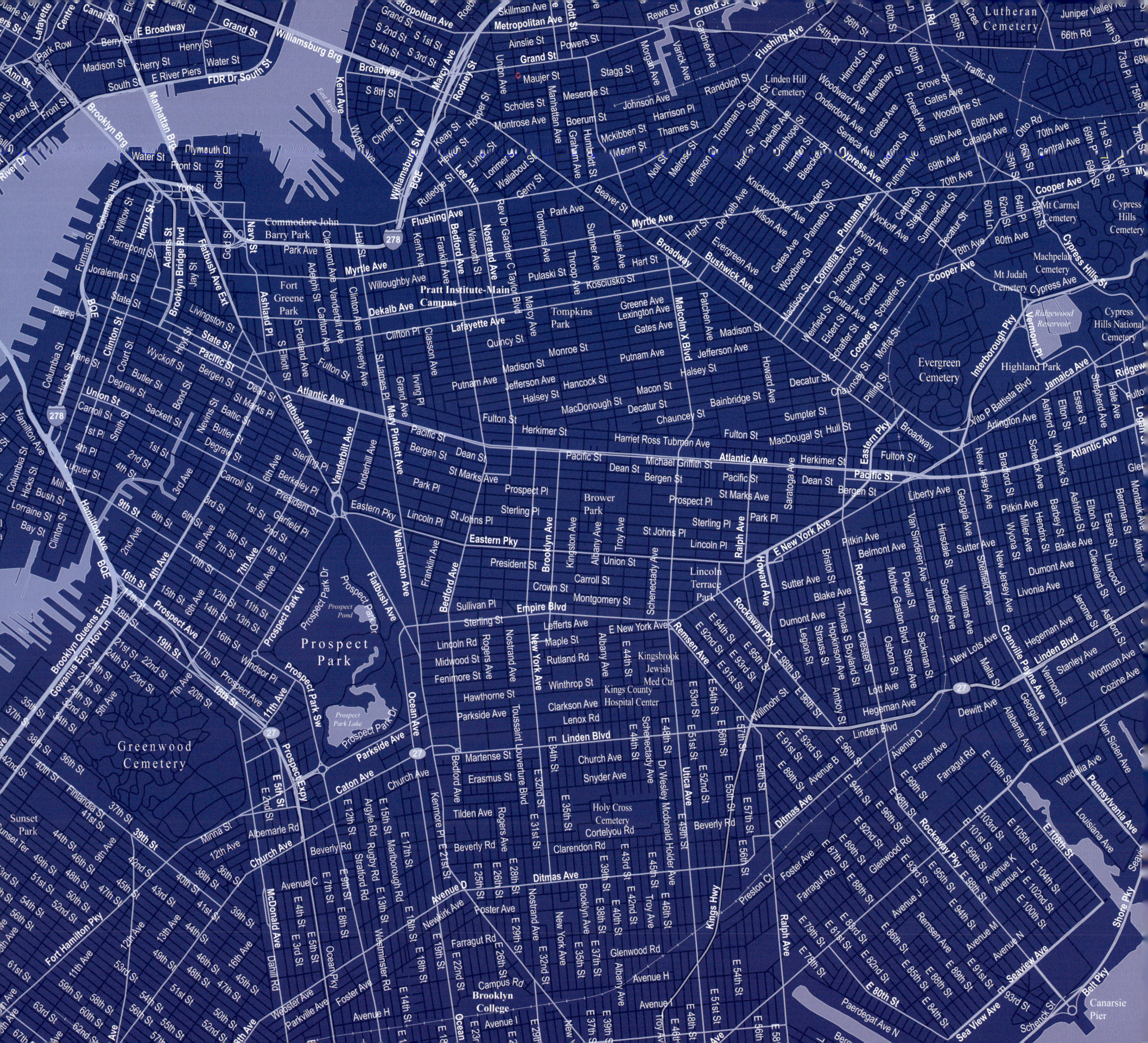

NORTHEASTERN AND CENTRAL BROOKLYN

BUSHWICK — BEDFORD-STUYVESANT — CROWN HEIGHTS — FLATBUSH (including PROSPECT LEFFERTS GARDENS) — BROWNSVILLE

Bushwick is bounded to the north by Flushing Avenue, to the east by Queens County, to the south by the Evergreens Cemetery and Conway Street, and to the west by Broadway. A large population of Germans lived in the area until the 1930s, and then it became heavily populated by Italians. After World War II, most of the Italians moved to Queens and the suburbs, while African Americans and Puerto Ricans settled in Bushwick. The neighborhood underwent a period of decline in the 1960s, and widespread arson and looting during the blackout of 1977 damaged it even further. In the 1980s, some sections began to be revitalized. Bushwick's population today is primarily Latino and African American with some Italians and Asians. Many young artists and students seeking affordable housing have created new cultural, shopping, and dining options.

Bedford-Stuyvesant, often abbreviated as Bed-Stuy, is bounded to the north by Flushing Avenue, to the east by Broadway and Saratoga Avenue, to the south by Atlantic Avenue, and to the west by Classon Avenue. As early as 1790, more than a quarter of its residents were African American (mostly enslaved people). After the Brooklyn Bridge opened in 1883 and subway service was brought to the neighborhood in 1936, the population increased. During and after World War II, African Americans from the South and Caribbean immigrants settled there. In the 1960s and '70s, race rioting connected to larger civil unrest in the city led to the destruction and looting of businesses. However, crime decreased significantly after the 1980s, and the area became economically sounder, attracting new immigrants. Since the late 1990s, Bed-Stuy has been the largest African American neighborhood in New York City.

Crown Heights is bounded to the north by Atlantic Avenue, to the east by Ralph Avenue, to the south by Empire Boulevard, and to the west by Washington Avenue. Caribbean immigrants settled there in the early 1900s, and German, Scandinavian, Irish, Italian, and Jewish immigrants moved in in the 1920s. Crown Heights attracted large numbers of the Hasidic sect of Lubavitchers, and by 1950 its population was half Jewish. Beginning in the 1960s, the neighborhood underwent significant decay, but efforts were made in the 1970s and '80s to improve the area and preserve its distinctive brownstones. Today, the population of Crown Heights is predominantly Black, including many Caribbean immigrants.

Flatbush consists of several smaller neighborhoods. It is bounded to the north by Parkside Avenue, to the east by Nostrand Avenue, to the south by Avenue H, and to the west by Coney Island Avenue. When the Brighton Beach subway line opened in 1920, large numbers of Jewish people settled in the area. However, after World War II, many of them moved out to the suburbs, and were replaced by people from other parts of the globe. The influx of Caribbean immigrants continued throughout the 1970s and '80s, with Flatbush becoming the predominately African American and West Indian (Haitian especially) community it remains today. **Prospect Lefferts Gardens** lies within northern Flatbush. The neighborhood was designated a historic district in 1979, and today is regarded as a racially integrated, professional, middle-class area.

Brownsville is bounded to the north by Eastern Parkway, to the east by Van Sinderen Avenue, to the south by Linden Boulevard, and to the west by Rockaway Parkway. The area remained mostly undeveloped until the late 1880s, when tenements were built and Jewish garment makers from the Lower East Side moved in. The neighborhood gradually grew more prosperous, but after World War II, many of its Jewish residents moved to the suburbs. Brownsville underwent a period of decay, abandonment, vandalism, and arson. During the 1980s, immigrants from the Caribbean moved there. Today, Brownsville's population remains largely Black, and it has one of the highest densities of public housing projects in New York City.

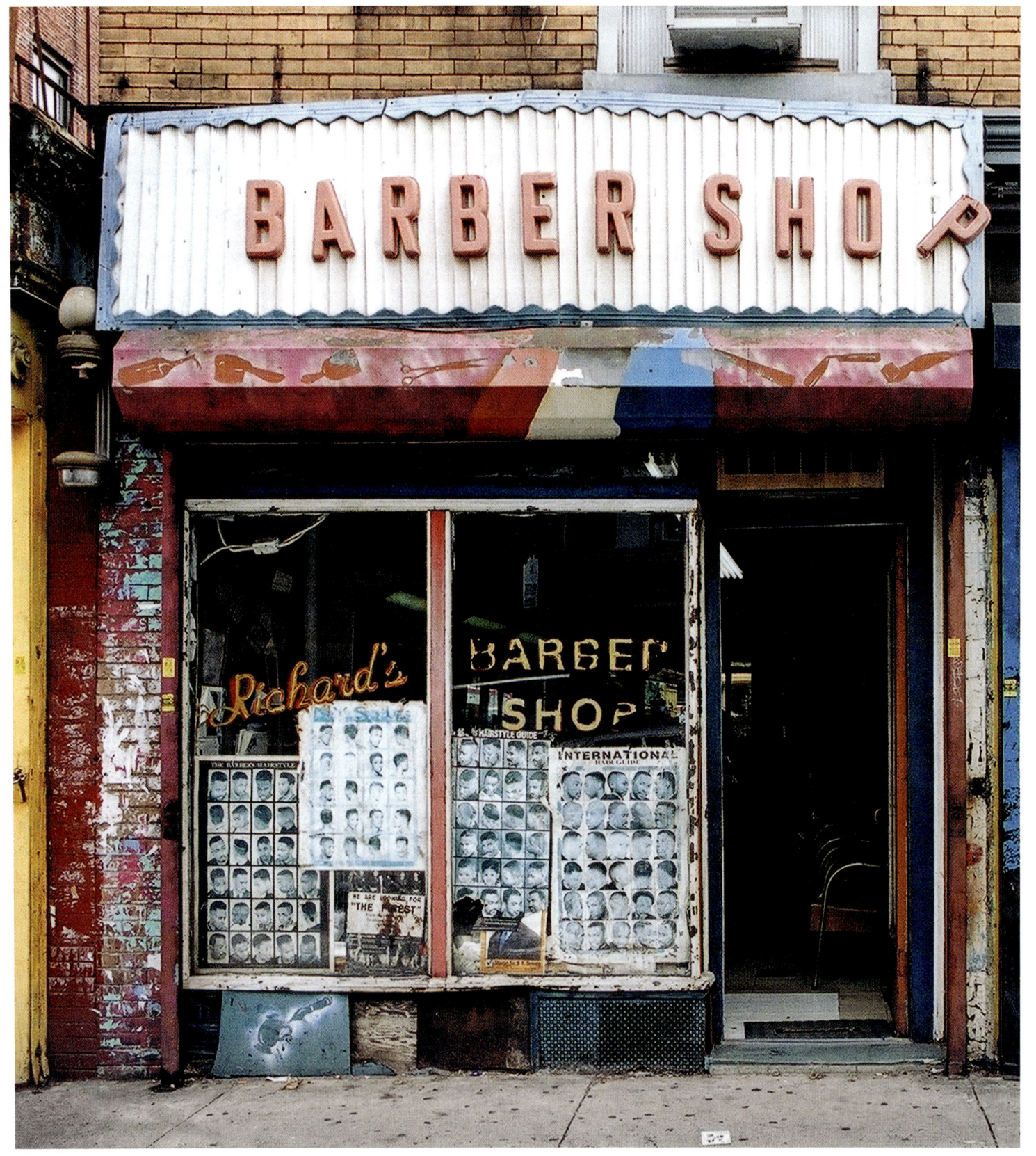

156   RICHARD'S BARBER SHOP
Nostrand Avenue near Park Place, Crown Heights, 2004

KATY'S CANDY STORE
Tompkins Avenue near Vernon Avenue, Bedford-Stuyvesant, 2004

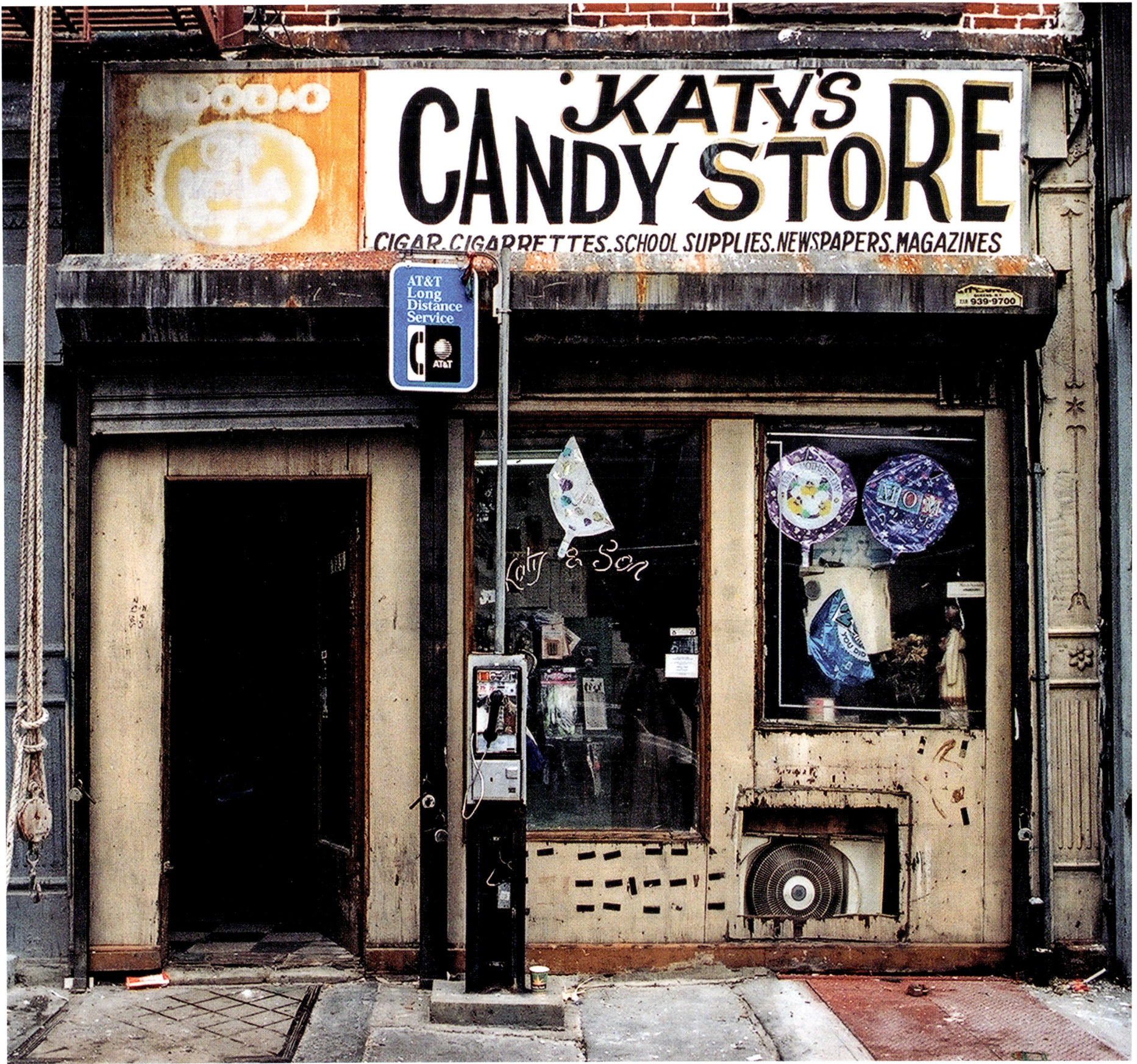

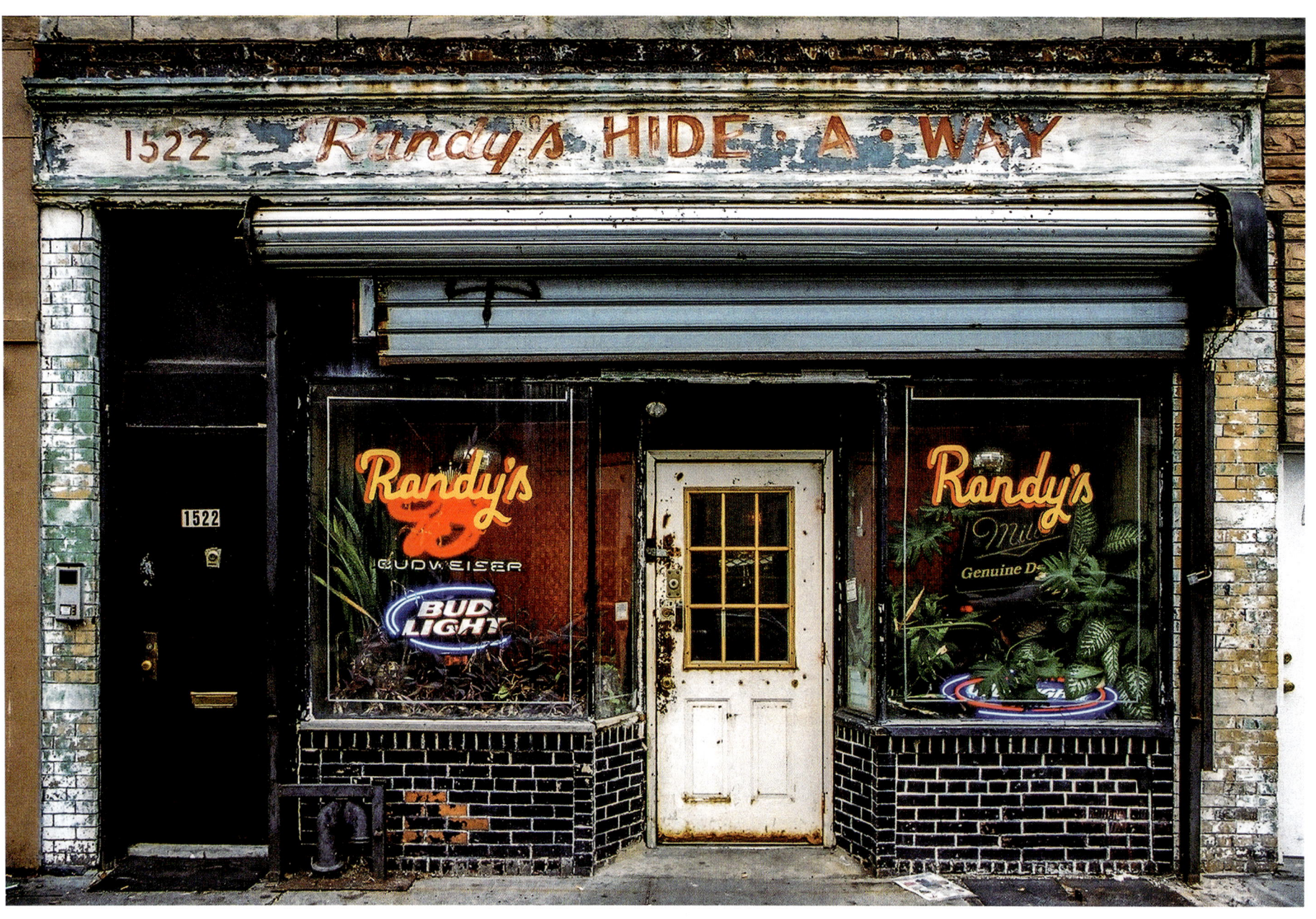

158 RANDY'S HIDE-A-WAY
Bergen Avenue near Schenectady Avenue, Crown Heights, 2006

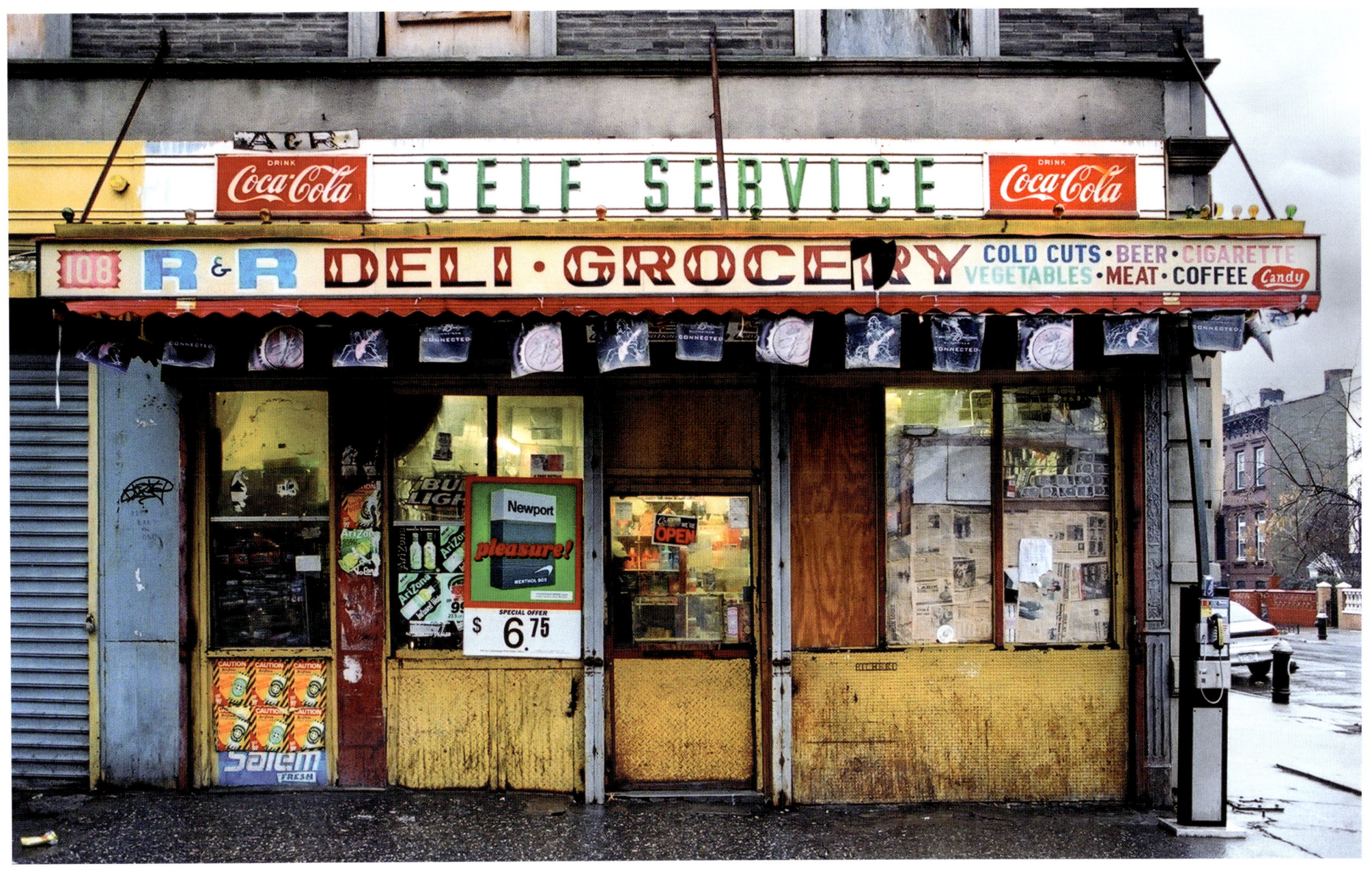

R&R SELF SERVICE
Albany Avenue at Pacific Street, Crown Heights, 2006

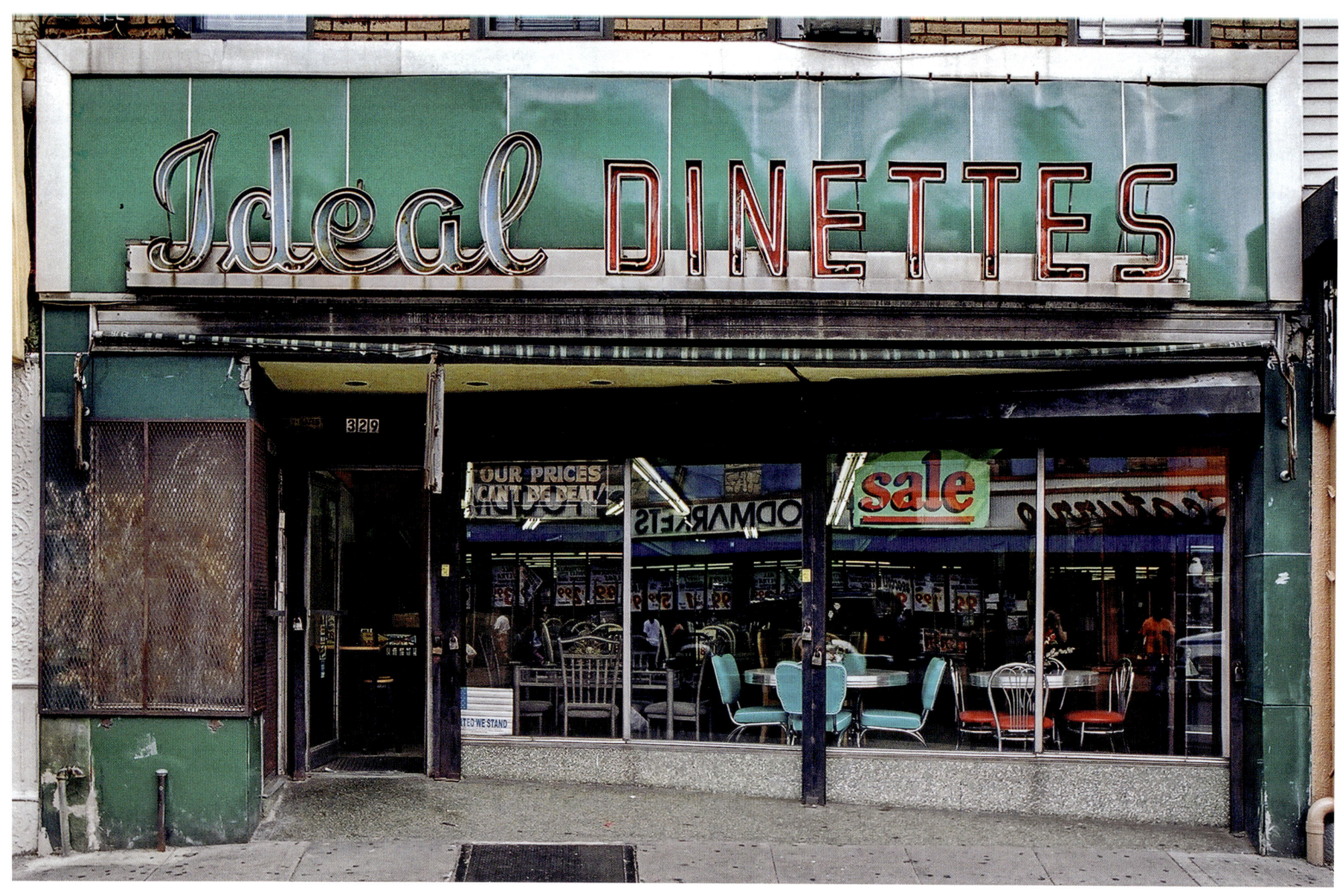

160   IDEAL DINETTES
Knickerbocker Avenue near DeKalb Avenue, Bushwick, 2004

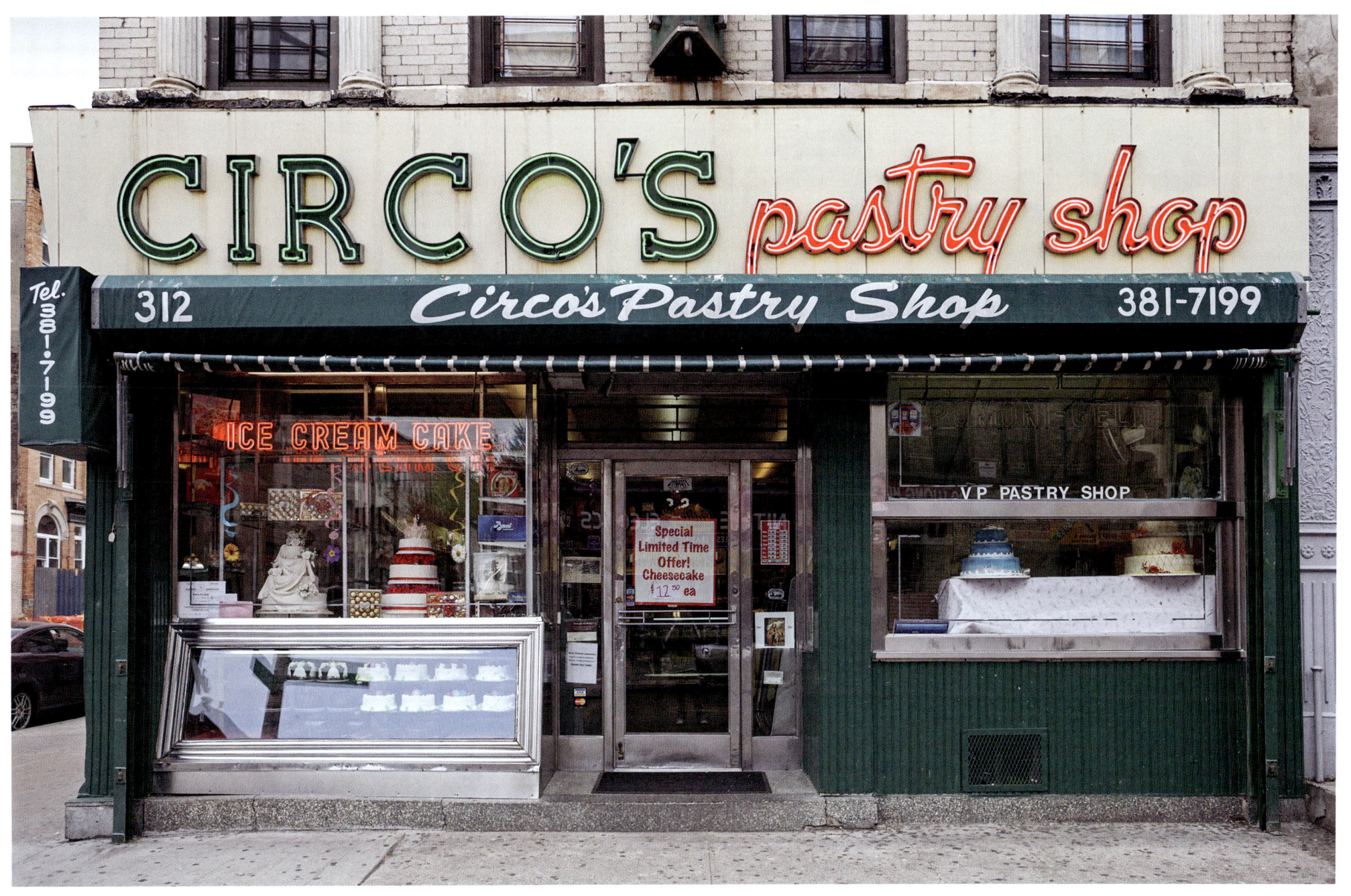

161   CIRCO'S PASTRY SHOP
Knickerbocker Avenue at Hart Street, Bushwick, 2017

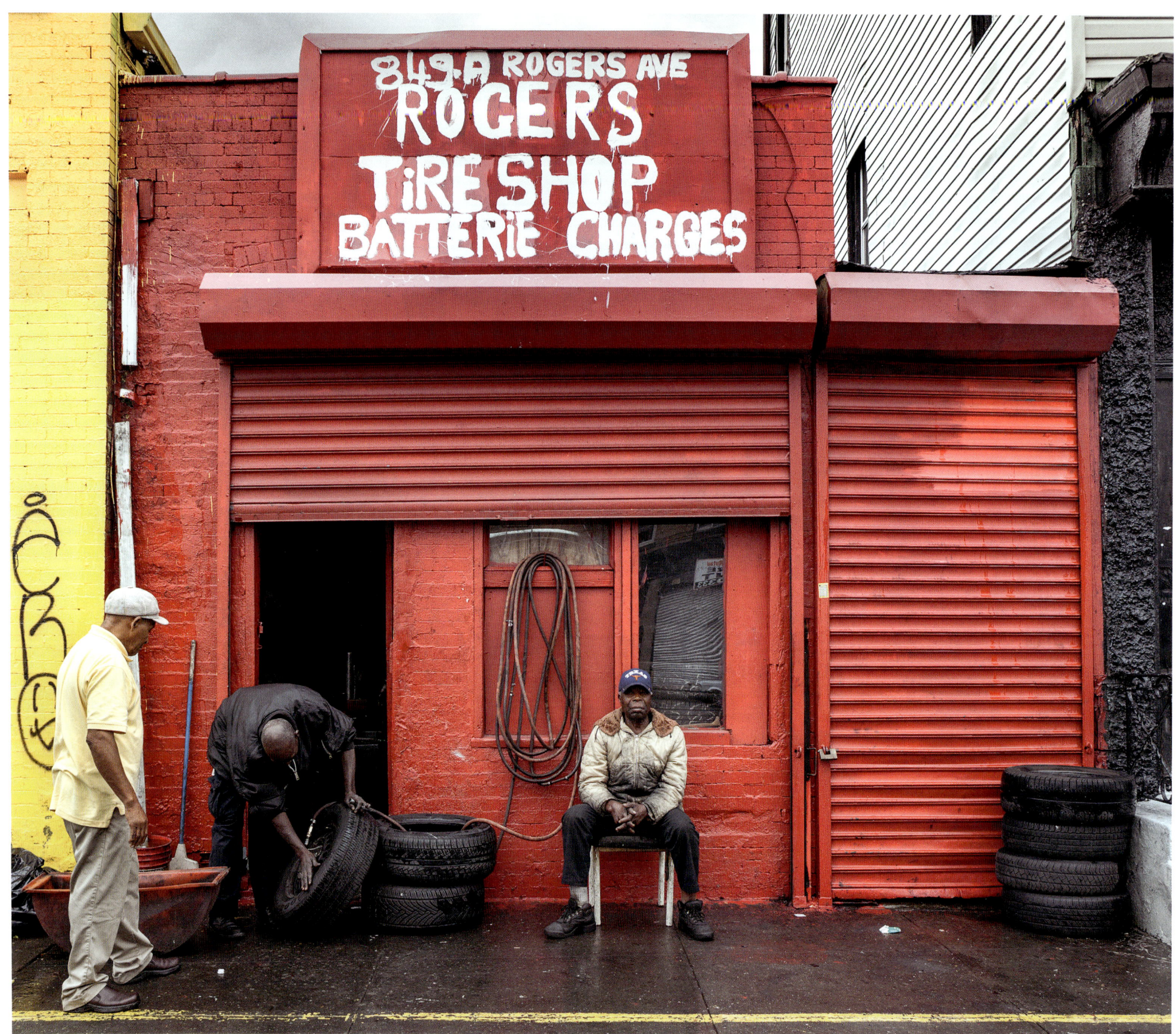

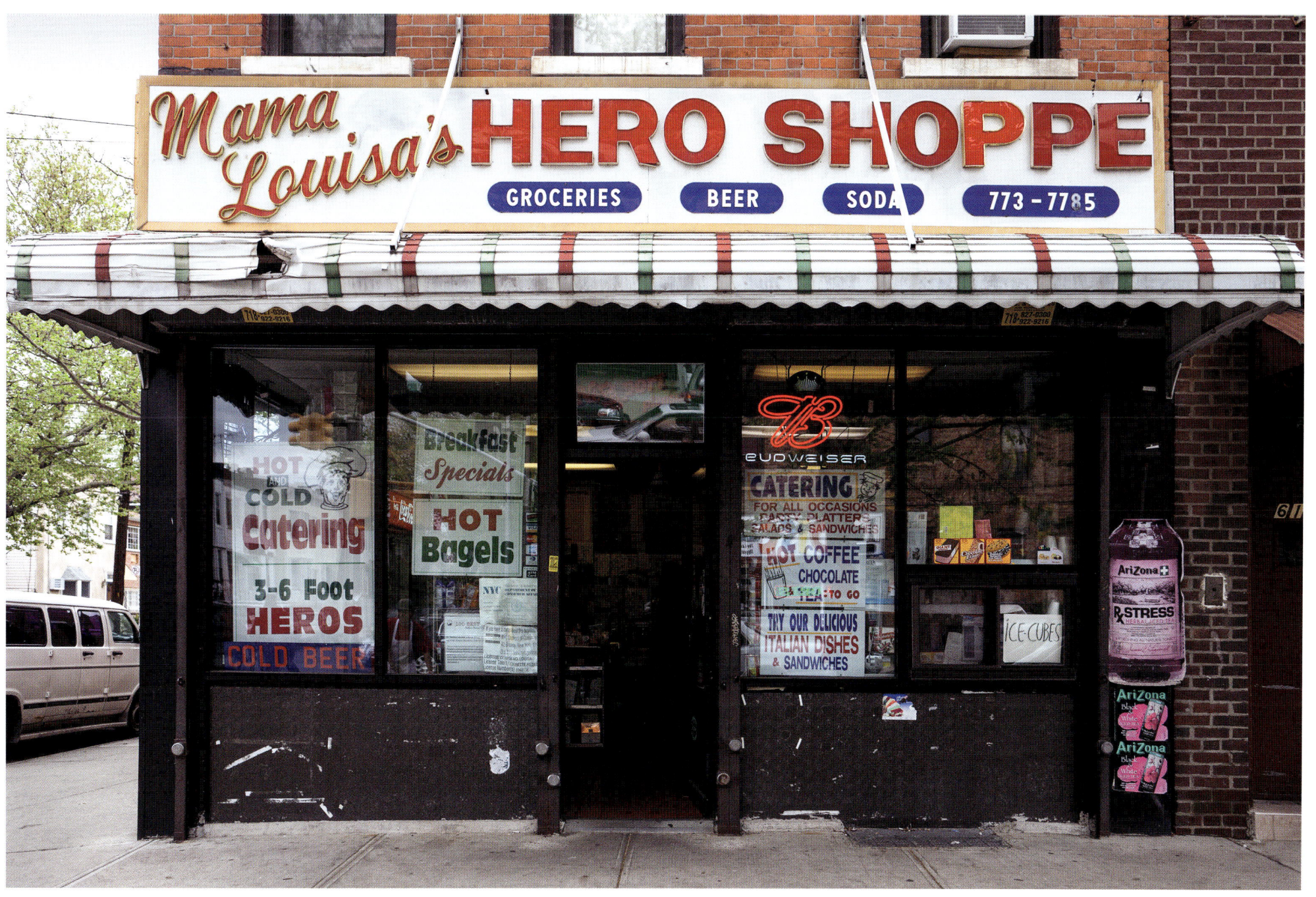

ROGERS TIRE SHOP
Rogers Avenue near Erasmus Street, Flatbush, 2009

MAMA LOUISA'S HERO SHOPPE
New York Avenue at Rutland Road, Prospect Lefferts Gardens, 2010

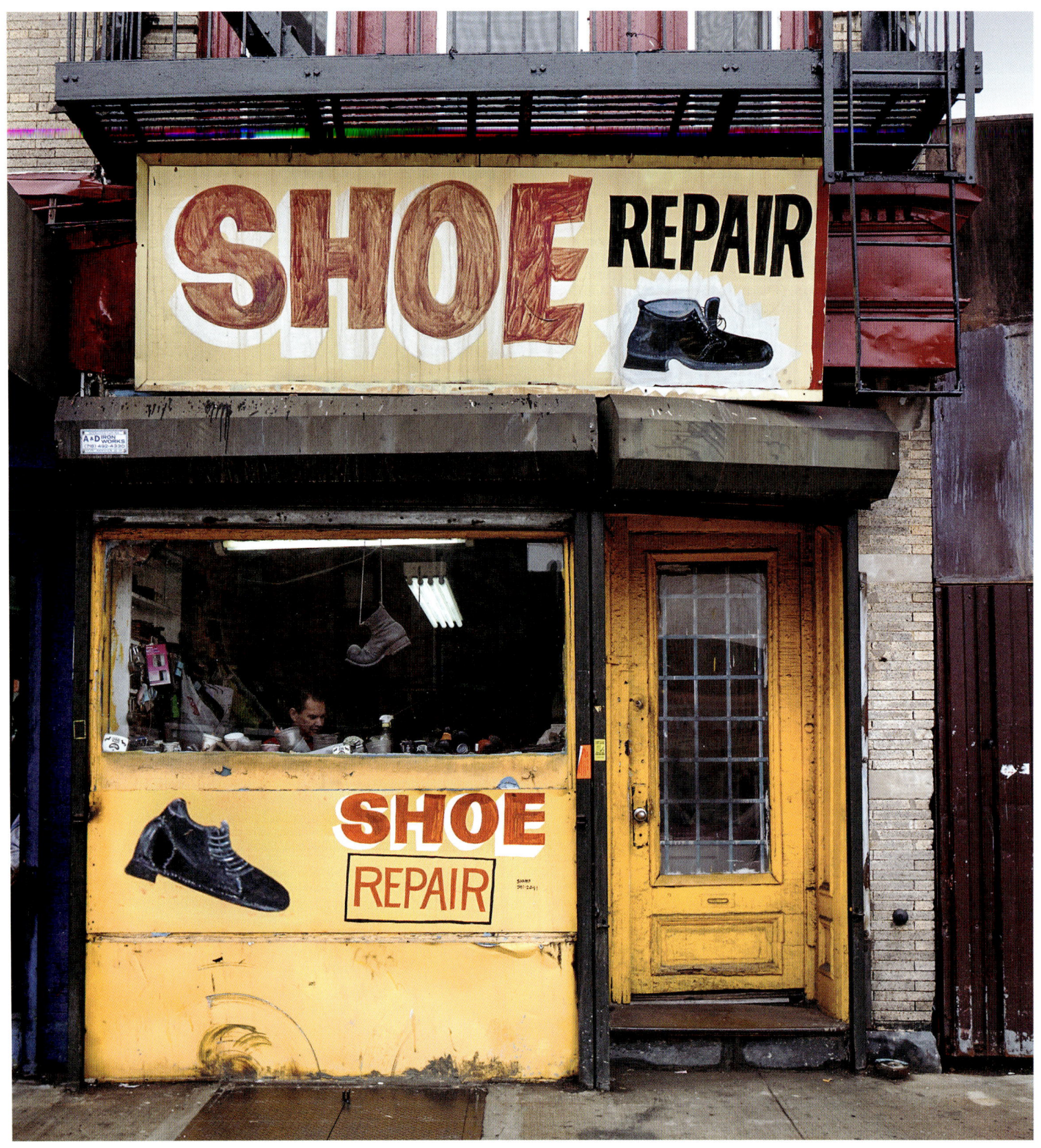

164   CARLOS SHOE REPAIR
Clarendon Road near Flatbush Avenue, Flatbush, 2009

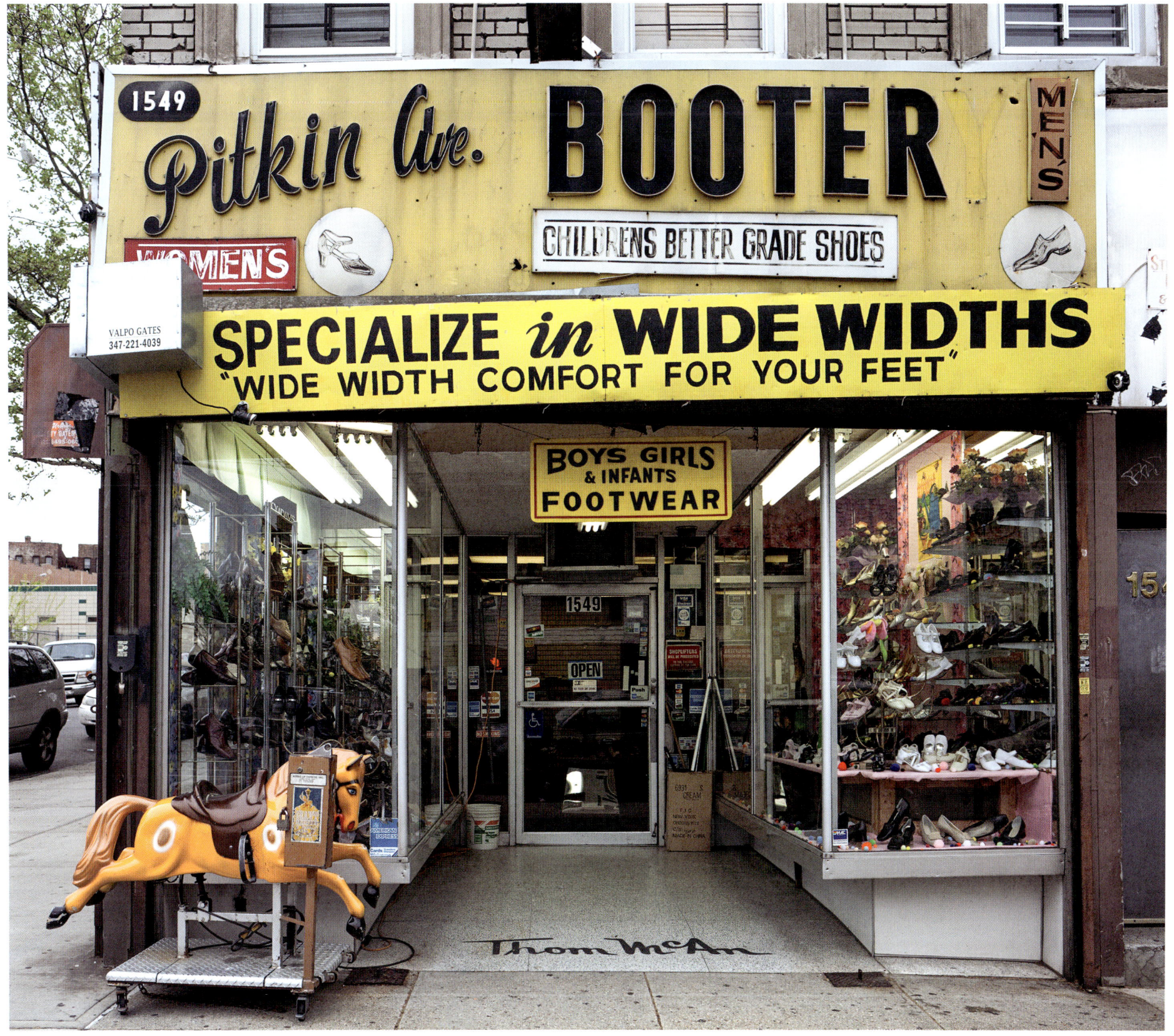

PITKIN AVE. BOOTERY
Pitkin Avenue at Strauss Street, Brownsville, 2009

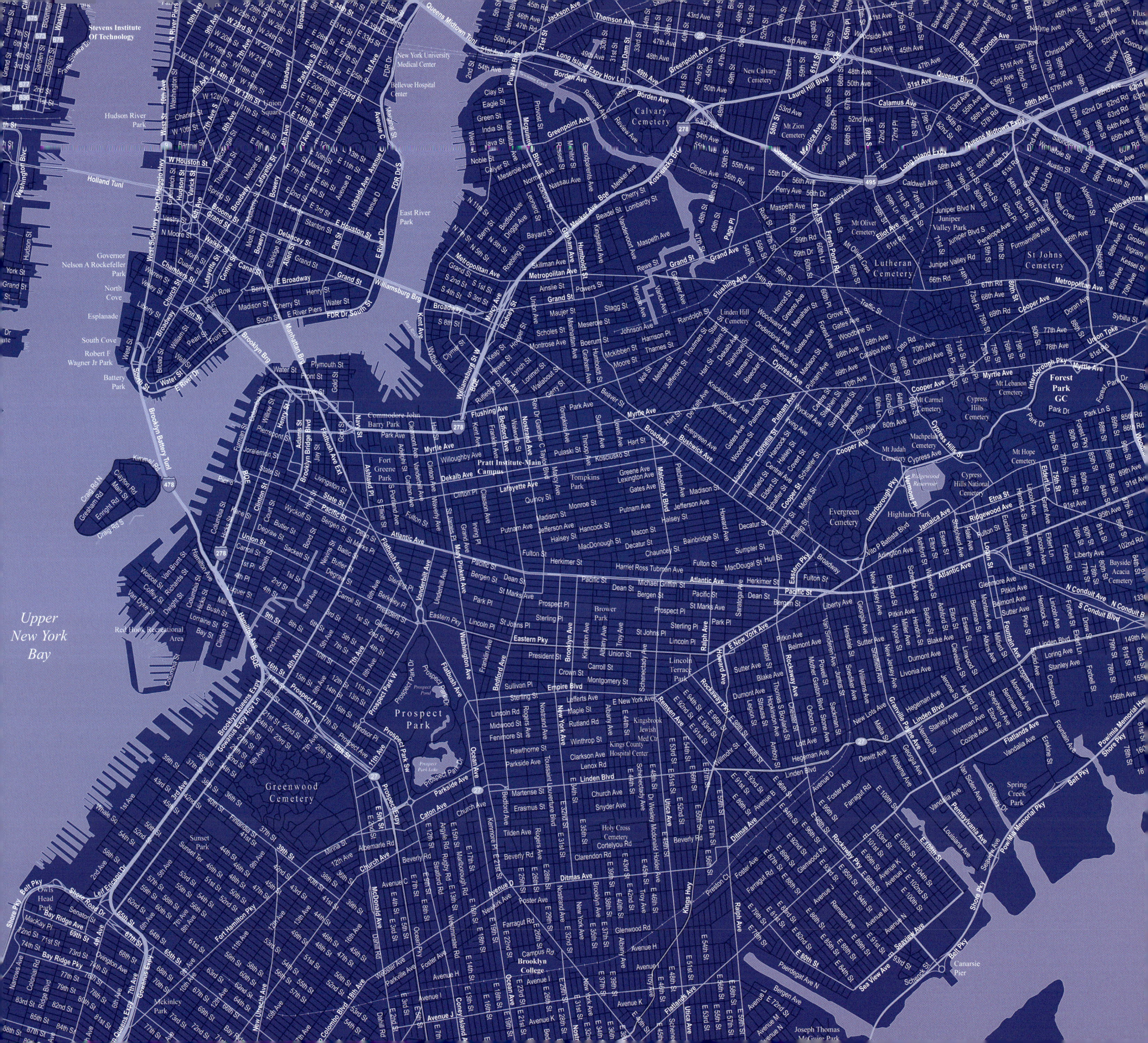

NORTHWESTERN AND WESTERN BROOKLYN

GREENPOINT — WILLIAMSBURG — COBBLE HILL — CARROLL GARDENS — PARK SLOPE (including SOUTH SLOPE) — SUNSET PARK

Greenpoint is bounded to the north and east by Newtown Creek, to the south by the Brooklyn-Queens Expressway and North 15th Street, and to the west by the East River. The population was mainly Dutch, English, and Irish until the 1880s, when immigrants from Poland, Russia, and, later, Italy settled in the area. After World War II there was an influx of Polish immigrants, making the neighborhood the center of the city's Polish community. Beginning in the late 1980s, many industrial buildings were converted into residential buildings. In 2005, the waterfront was rezoned, generating even more residential development.

Williamsburg is bounded to the north by North 15th Street and the Brooklyn-Queens Expressway, to the east by the Queens County line, to the south by Flushing Avenue, and to the west by the East River. After completion of the Williamsburg Bridge in 1903, thousands of Eastern European Jews moved there from the Lower East Side. Lithuanian, Polish, Russian Orthodox, and Italian immigrants also moved in. During the early 1930s, many businesses in the neighborhood declared bankruptcy and prosperous residents left. The Jewish community, however, continued to grow, and a large, distinct Hasidic district formed. Throughout the 1950s, there was an influx of Puerto Ricans. In 1957, the construction of the Brooklyn-Queens Expressway bisected Williamsburg and destroyed businesses and homes; decades of neglect and abandonment followed. Throughout the 1980s and early '90s, the blocks north of the base of the Williamsburg Bridge became an enclave for artists, designers, and musicians. In 2005, the city's rezoning plan reclassified some industrial areas as residential, spurring new high-rise construction and leading to increasing rents that displaced some longtime residents and small businesses.

Cobble Hill is bounded to the north by Atlantic Avenue, to the east by Court Street, to the south by Degraw Street, and to the west by the Brooklyn-Queens Expressway. Initially a working- and middle-class area, brownstone enthusiasts began moving in starting in the late 1950s and

were instrumental in having Cobble Hill designated a historic district. Today, it is one of Brooklyn's most sought-after residential neighborhoods.

Carroll Gardens is bounded to the north by Degraw Street, to the east by Hoyt Street, to the south by 9th Street, and to the west by the Brooklyn-Queens Expressway. The area was initially settled by the Irish, but in the early to mid-1900s, many Italians moved in. Beginning in the 1960s, young, middle-class professionals began to move to the area. The neighborhood is distinguished by its historic brownstones.

Park Slope is bounded to the north by 4th and Flatbush Avenues, to the east by Flatbush Avenue and Prospect Park West, to the south by Prospect Park West and 15th Street (where **South Slope** begins), and to the west by 4th Avenue. The neighborhood was developed after the park was completed and street railways reached the area in the 1870s. Mansions and brownstones were built, as well as apartments and row homes to house workers from nearby factories. After World War II, wealthy residents moved to the suburbs—but despite widespread abandonment, many of the historic homes were bought cheaply and restored. By the early 2000s, Park Slope was fully revitalized.

Sunset Park is bounded to the north by Greenwood Cemetery and the Prospect Expressway, to the east by 9th Avenue, to the south by 65th Street and the Gowanus Expressway, and to the west by the Brooklyn Army Terminal. From the 1800s through the early 1900s, its population grew rapidly due to large numbers of Irish, Polish, and Norwegian immigrants who settled there. After World War II, it went into a decline with the closing of the Army Terminal and the rise of truck-based shipping and ports in New Jersey. By 1990, Latinos comprised 50 percent of Sunset Park's population and helped rebuild the community. Since the 1980s, the neighborhood's East Asian population has grown steadily and today represents roughly a third of all residents. Sunset Park is home to Brooklyn's first and largest Chinatown.

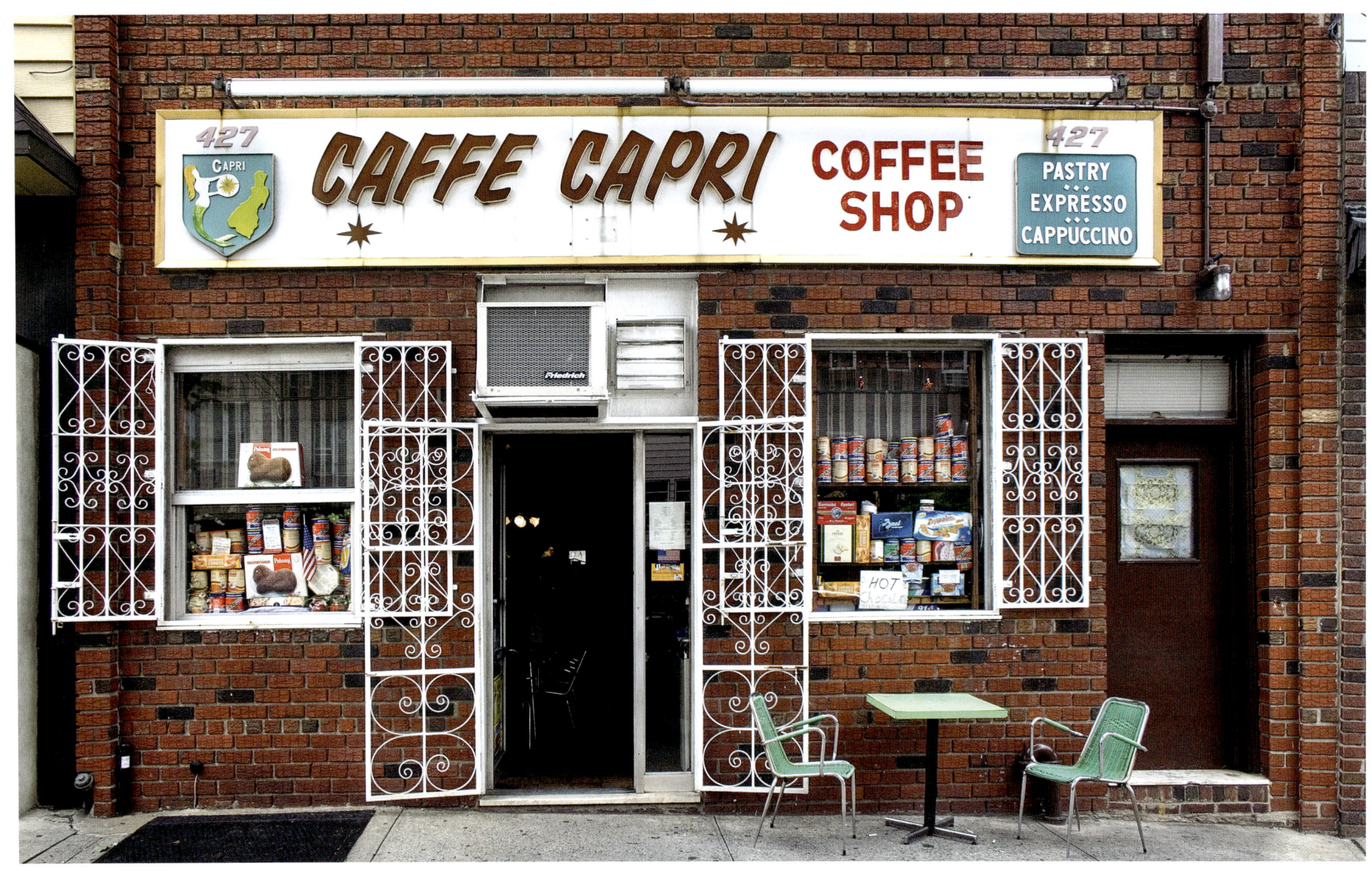

168   CAFFE CAPRI
Graham Avenue near Withers Street, Williamsburg, 2008

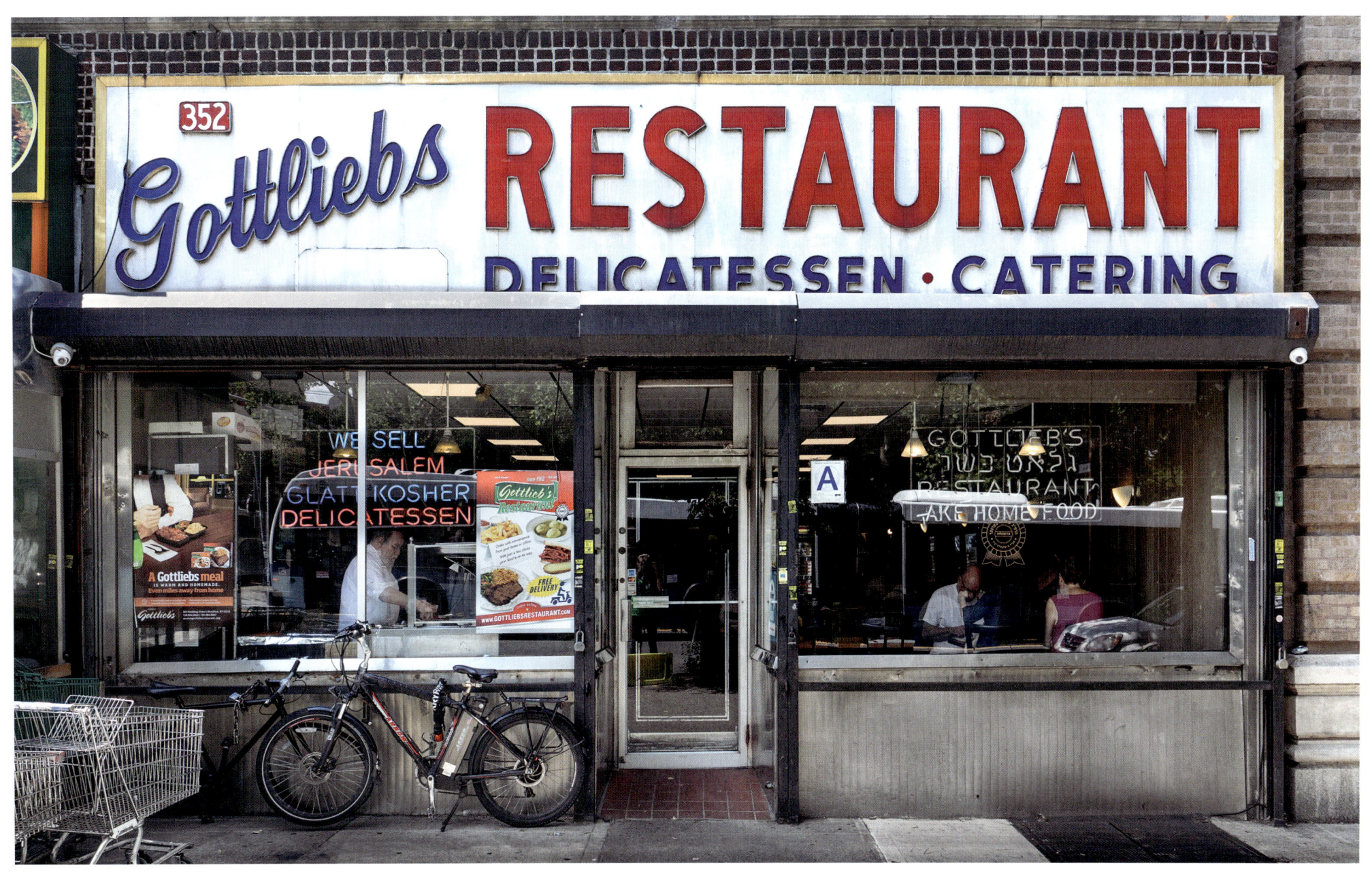

GOTTLIEB'S RESTAURANT
Roebling Street near Division Avenue, Williamsburg, 2018

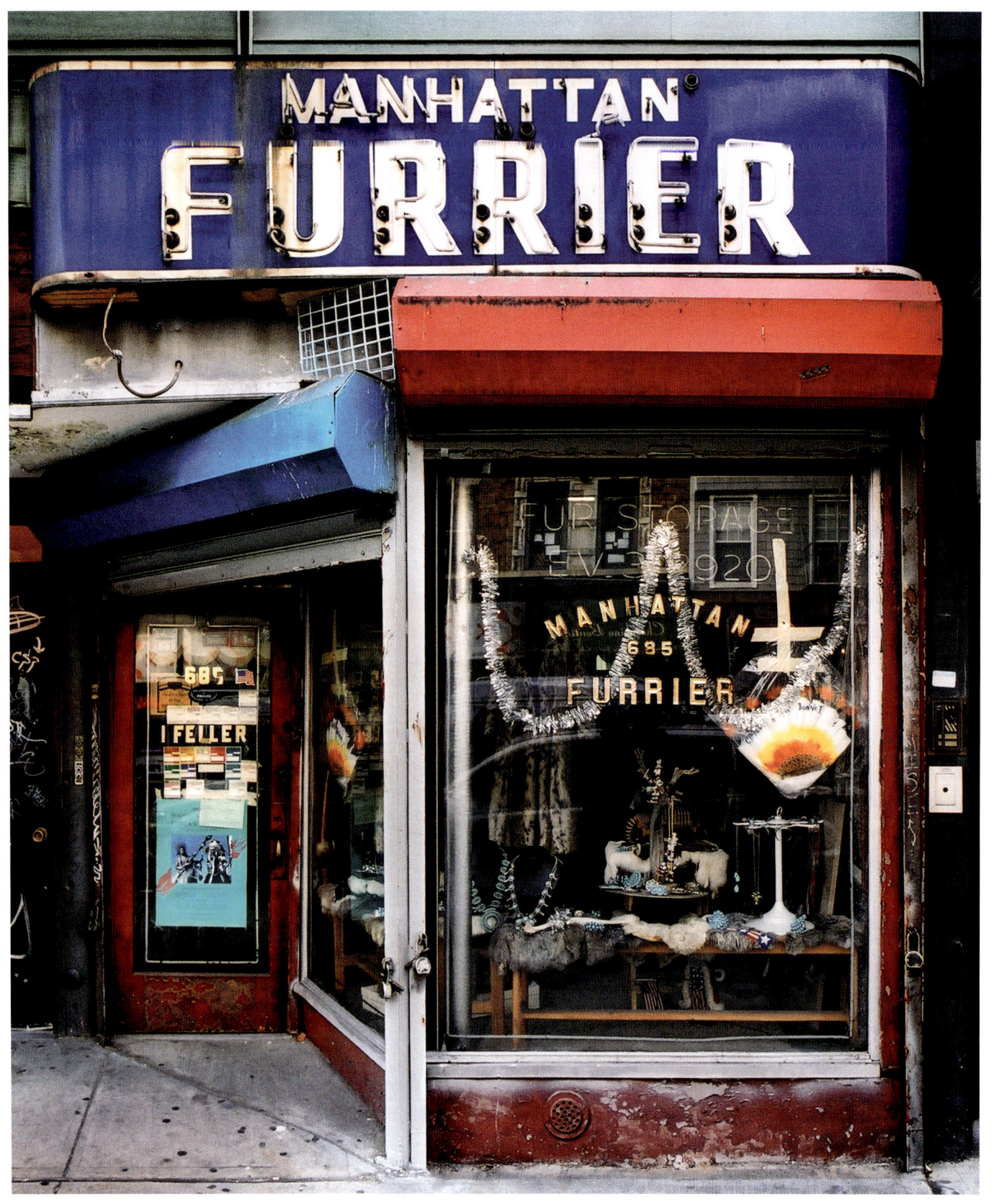

170 MANHATTAN FURRIER
Manhattan Avenue near Norman Avenue, Greenpoint, 2006

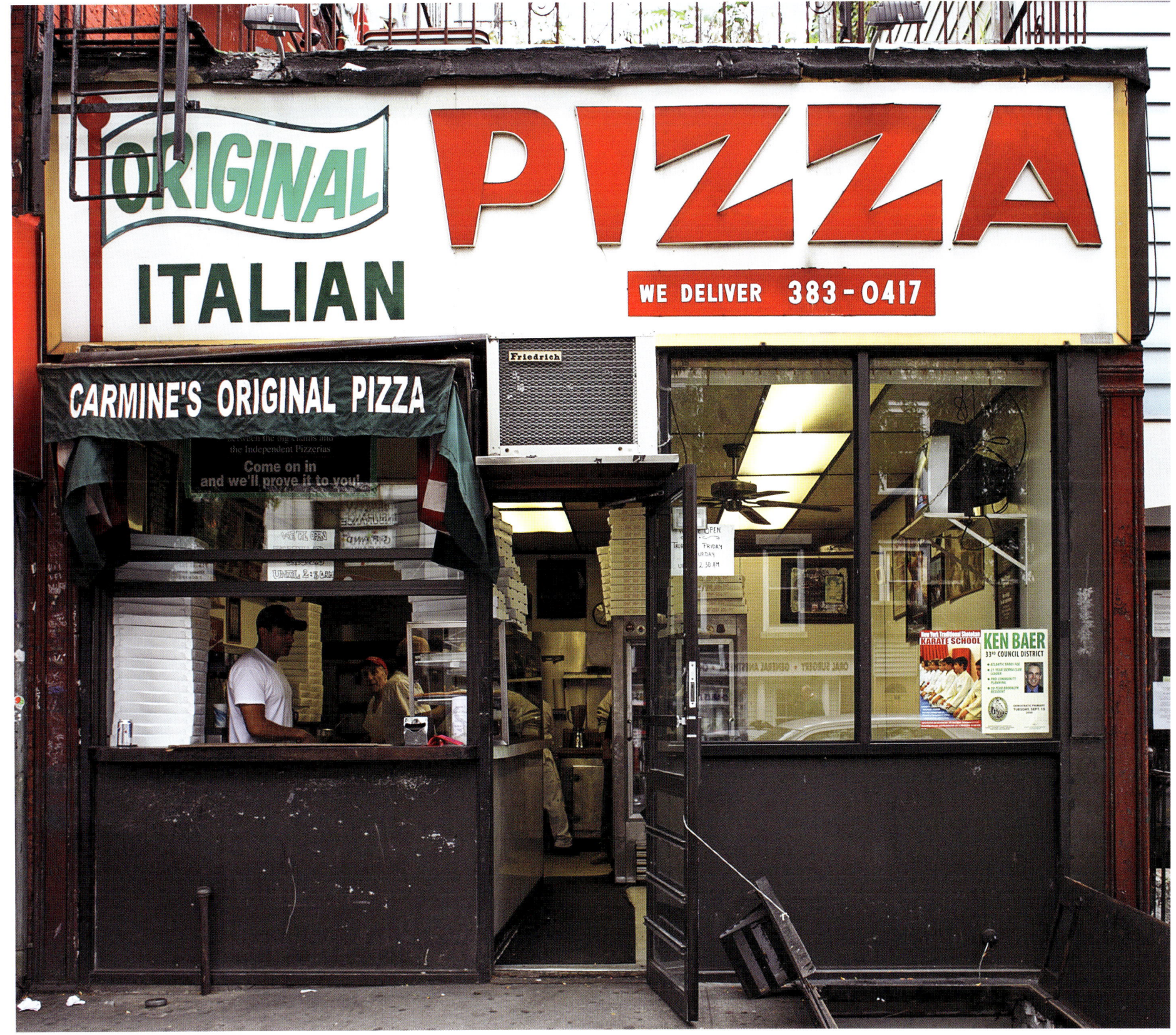

CARMINE'S ORIGINAL PIZZA
Norman Avenue near Manhattan Avenue, Greenpoint, 2009

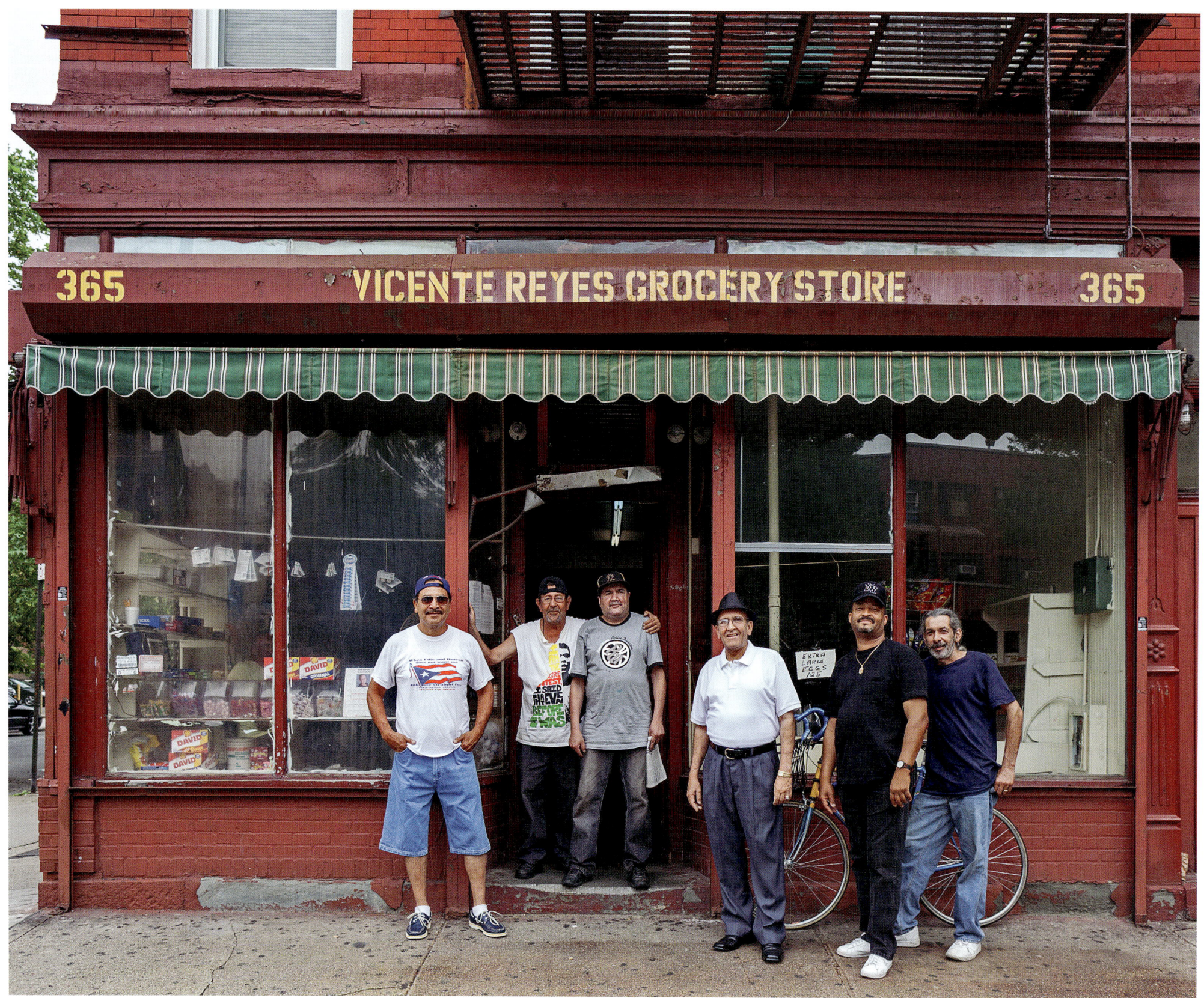

VICENTE REYES GROCERY STORE
Marcy Avenue at Lynch Street, Williamsburg, 2011

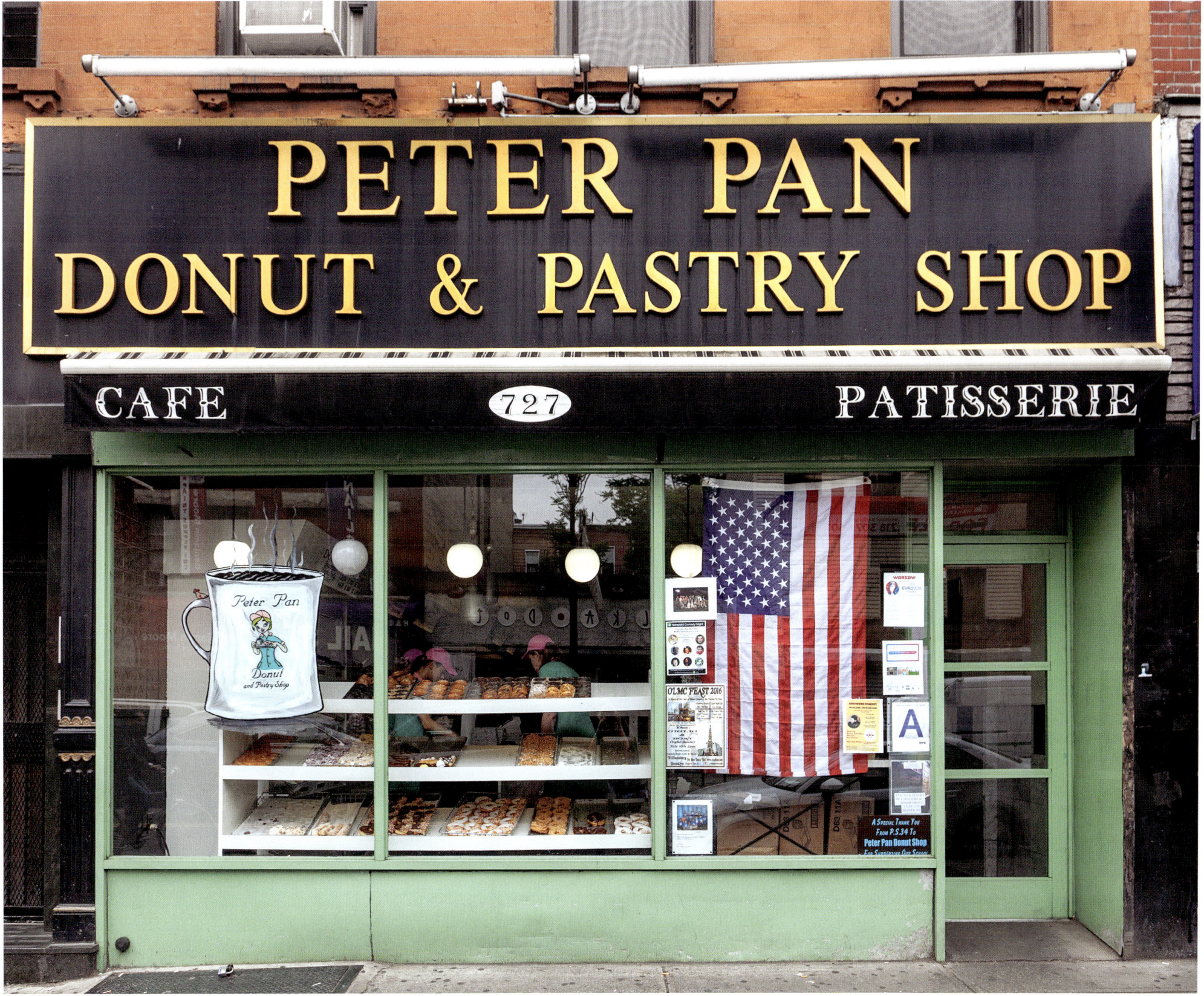

PETER PAN DONUT & PASTRY SHOP
Manhattan Avenue near Norman Avenue, Greenpoint, 2016

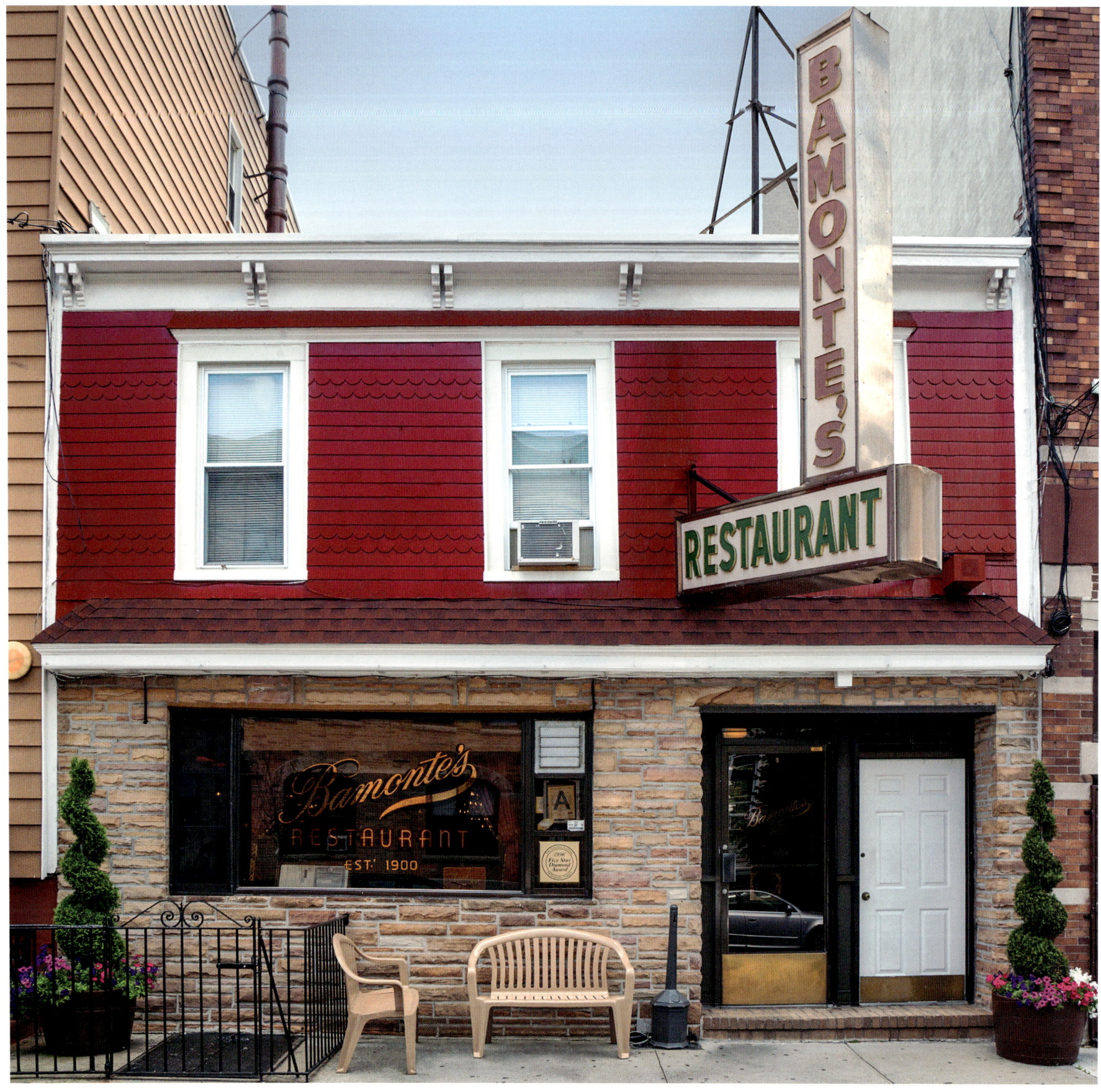

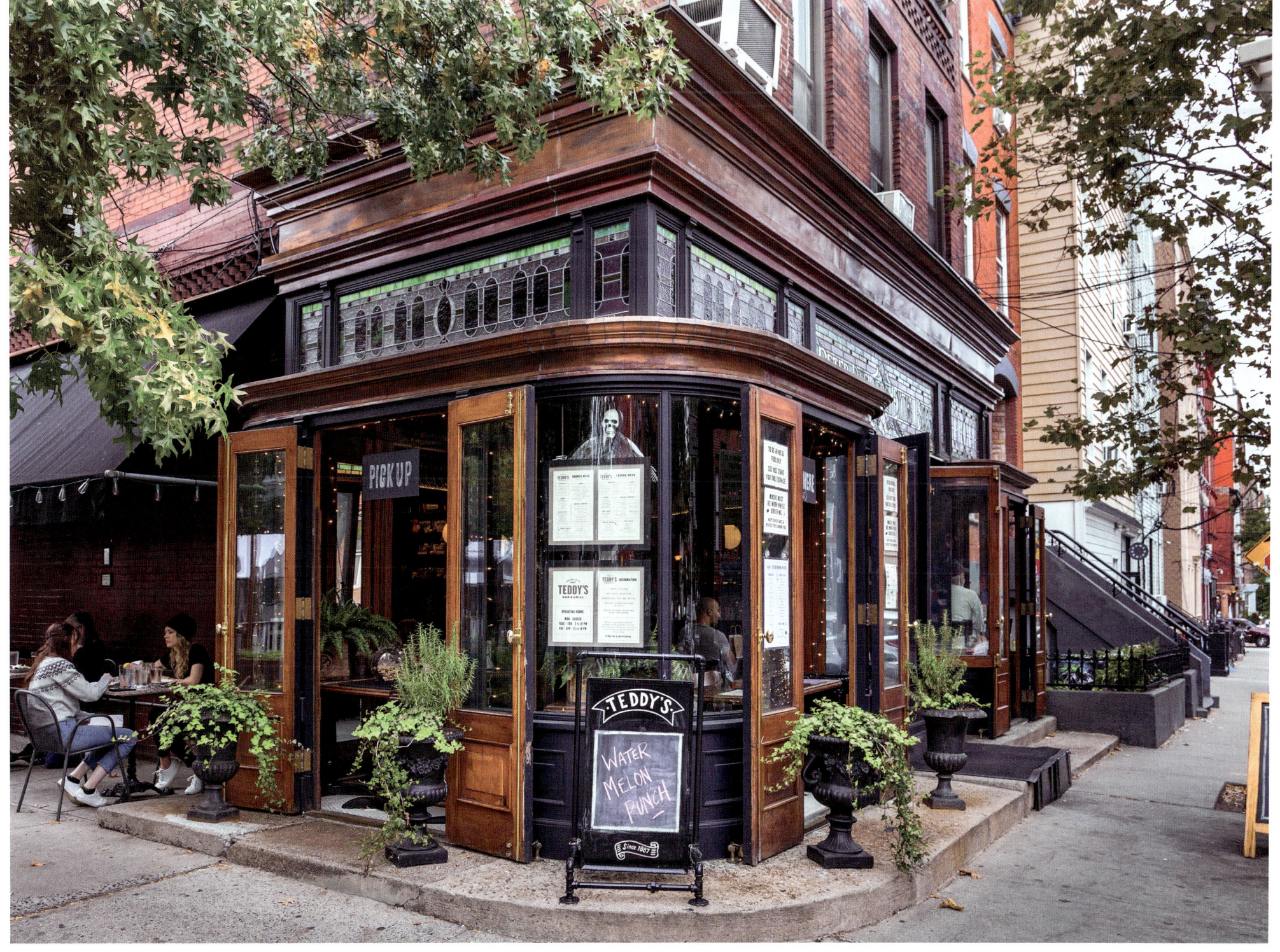

BAMONTE'S RESTAURANT
Withers Street near Union Avenue, Williamsburg, 2016

TEDDY'S BAR & GRILL
Berry Street at North 8th Street, Williamsburg, 2020

BROOKLYN

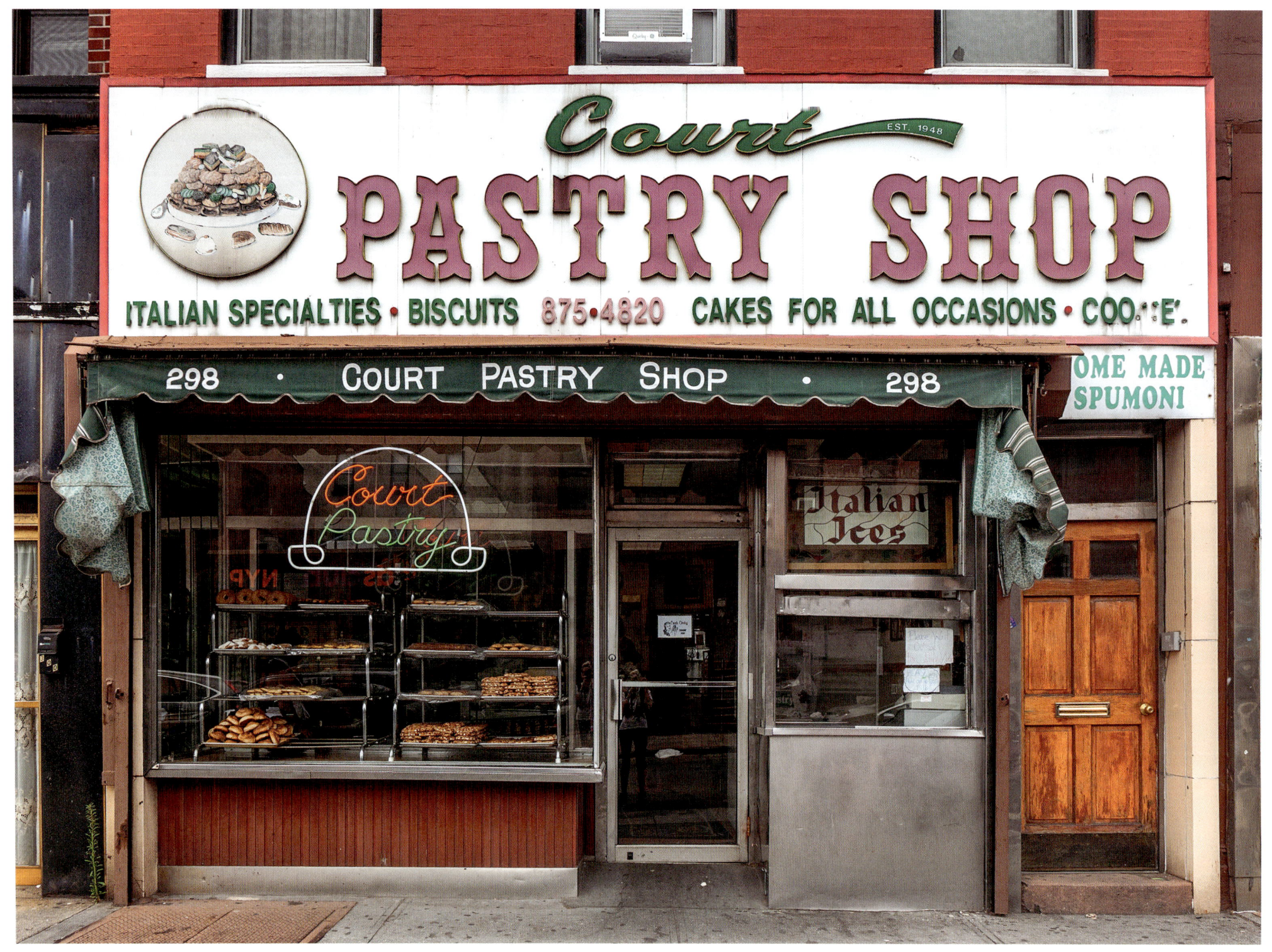

COURT PASTRY SHOP
Court Street near Degraw Street, Carroll Gardens, 2018

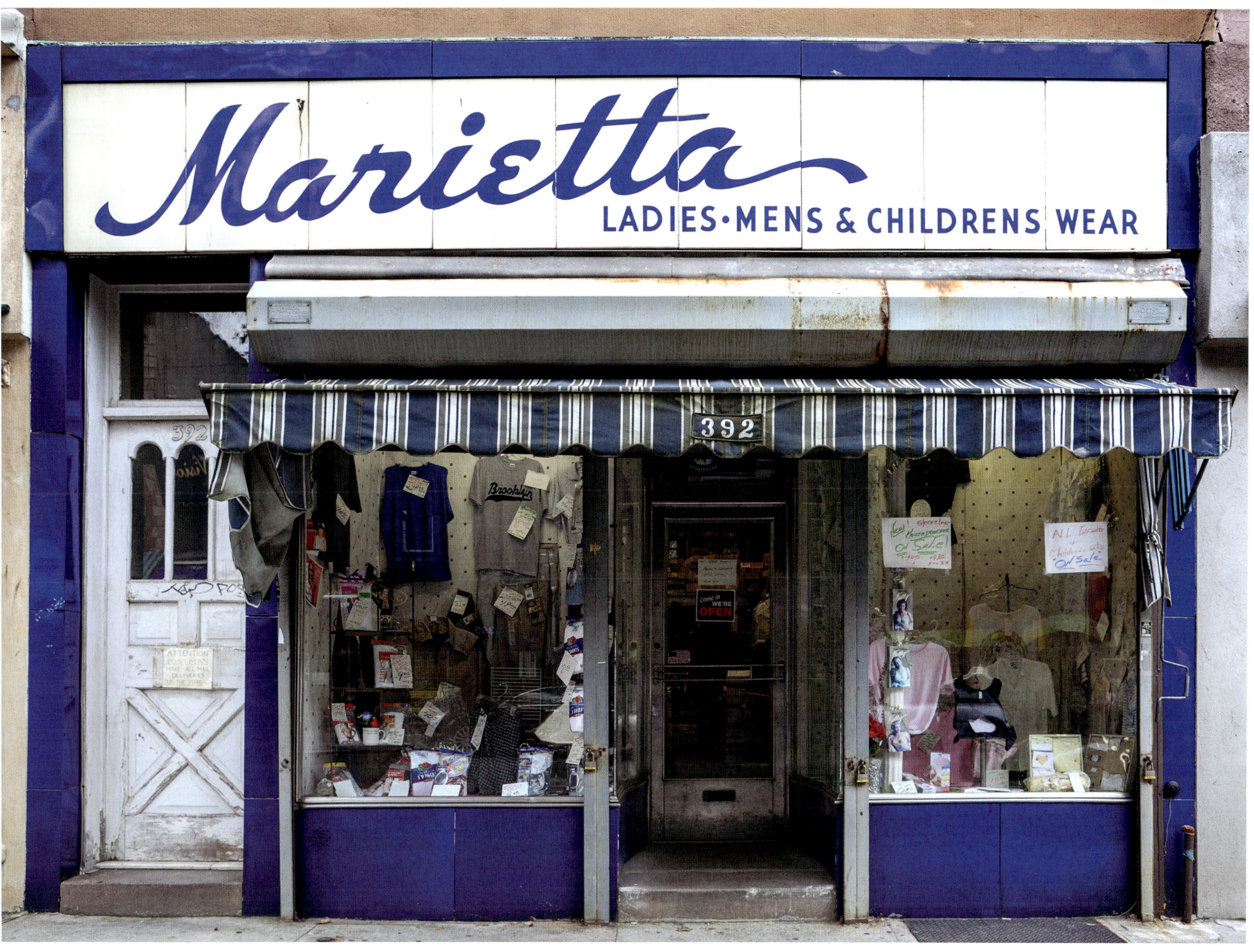

MARIETTA
Court Street near Carroll Street, Carroll Gardens, 2009

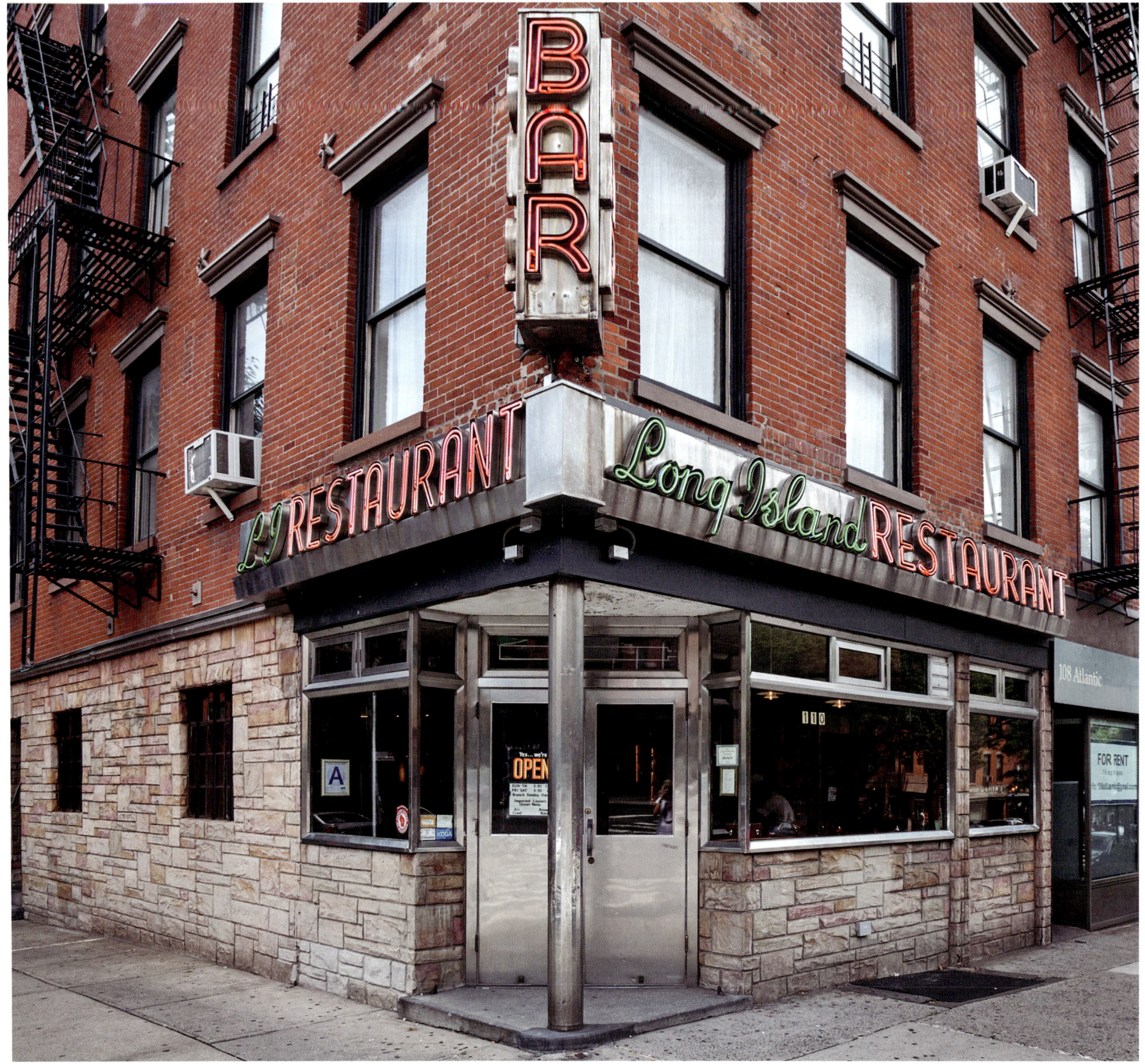

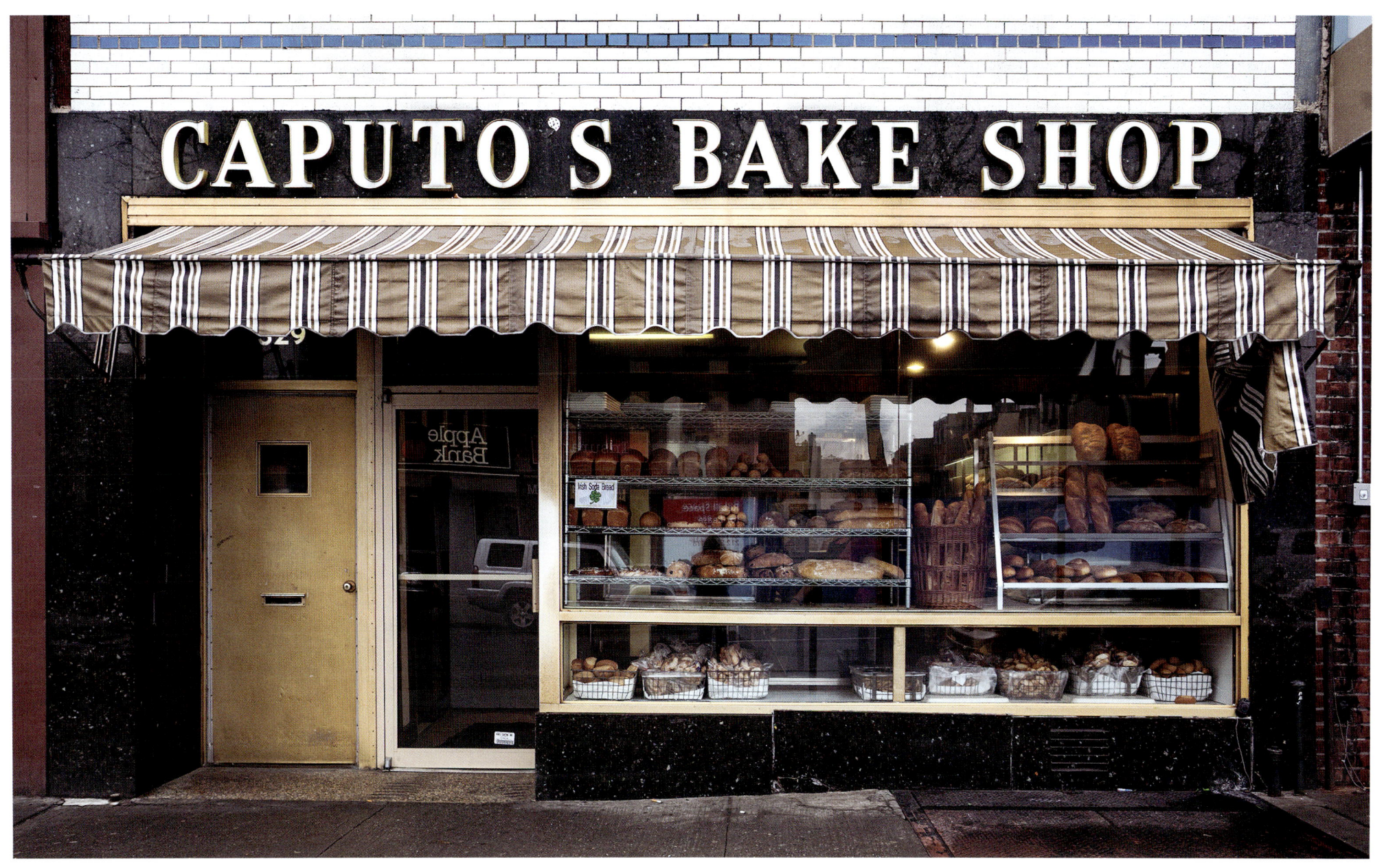

THE LONG ISLAND BAR & RESTAURANT
Atlantic Avenue at Henry Street, Cobble Hill, 2016

CAPUTO'S BAKE SHOP
Court Street near Sackett Street, Carroll Gardens, 2009

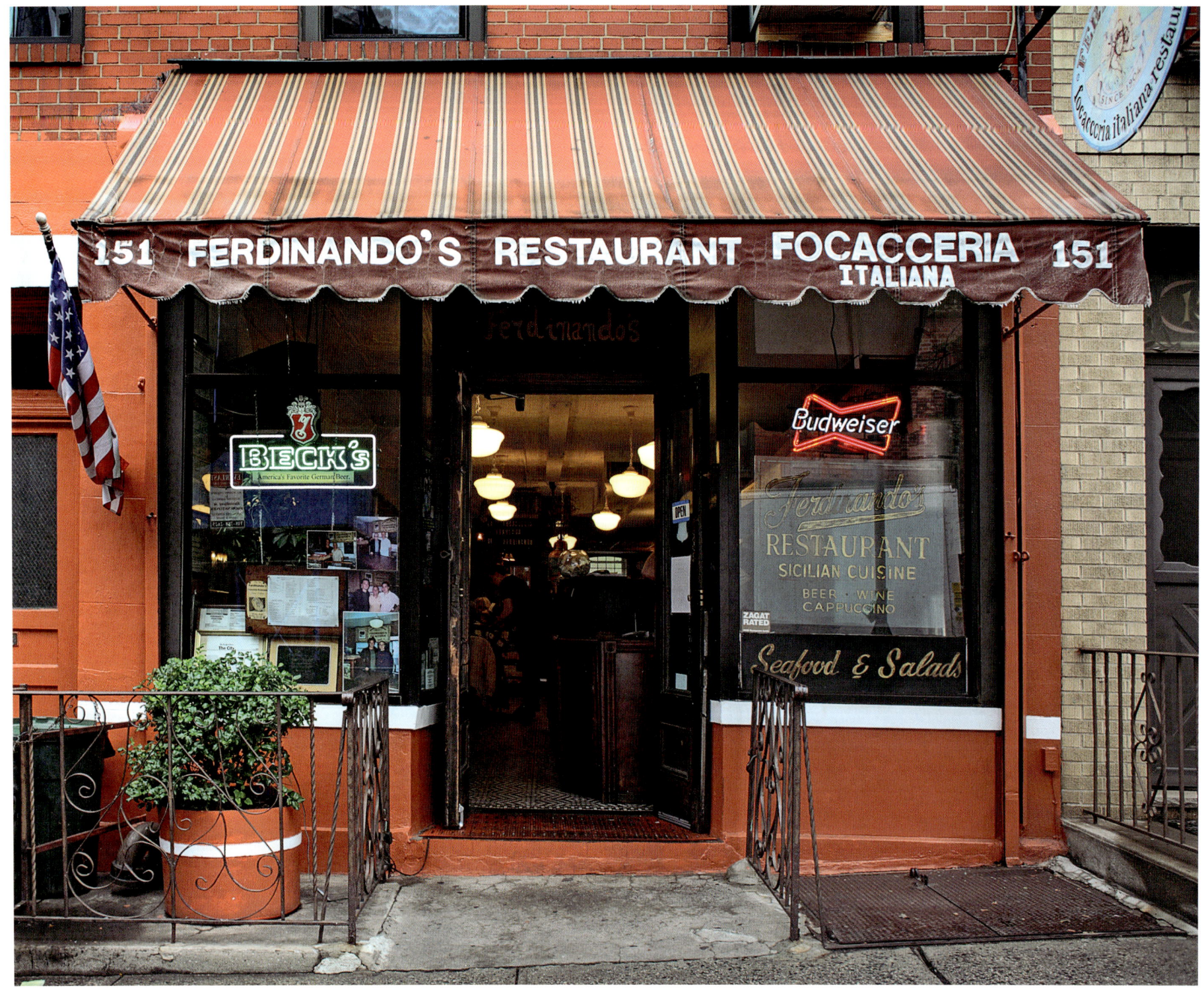

180 FERDINANDO'S FOCACCERIA
Union Street near Hicks Street, Carroll Gardens, 2009

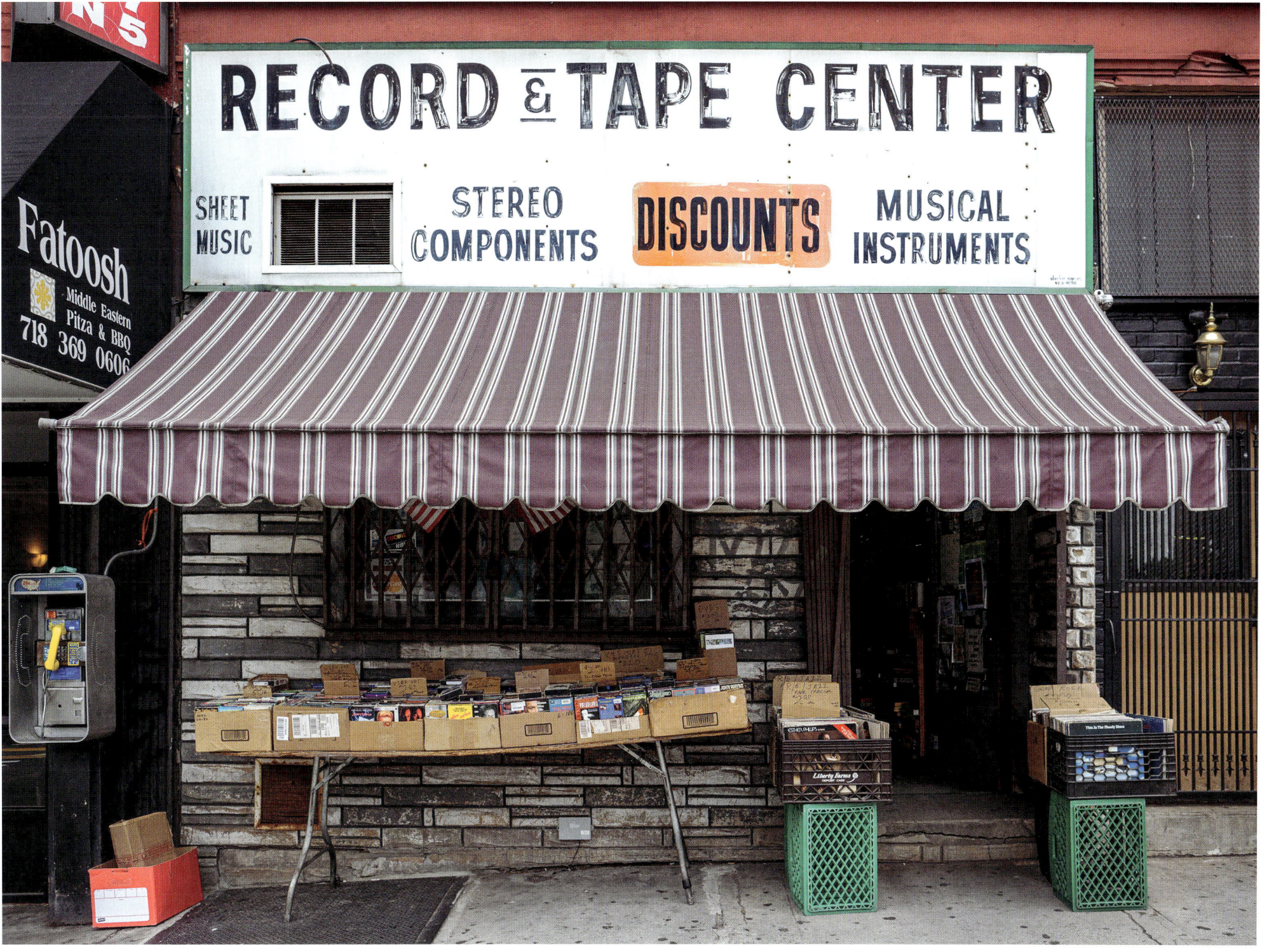

RECORD & TAPE CENTER
5th Avenue near 9th Street, Park Slope, 2009

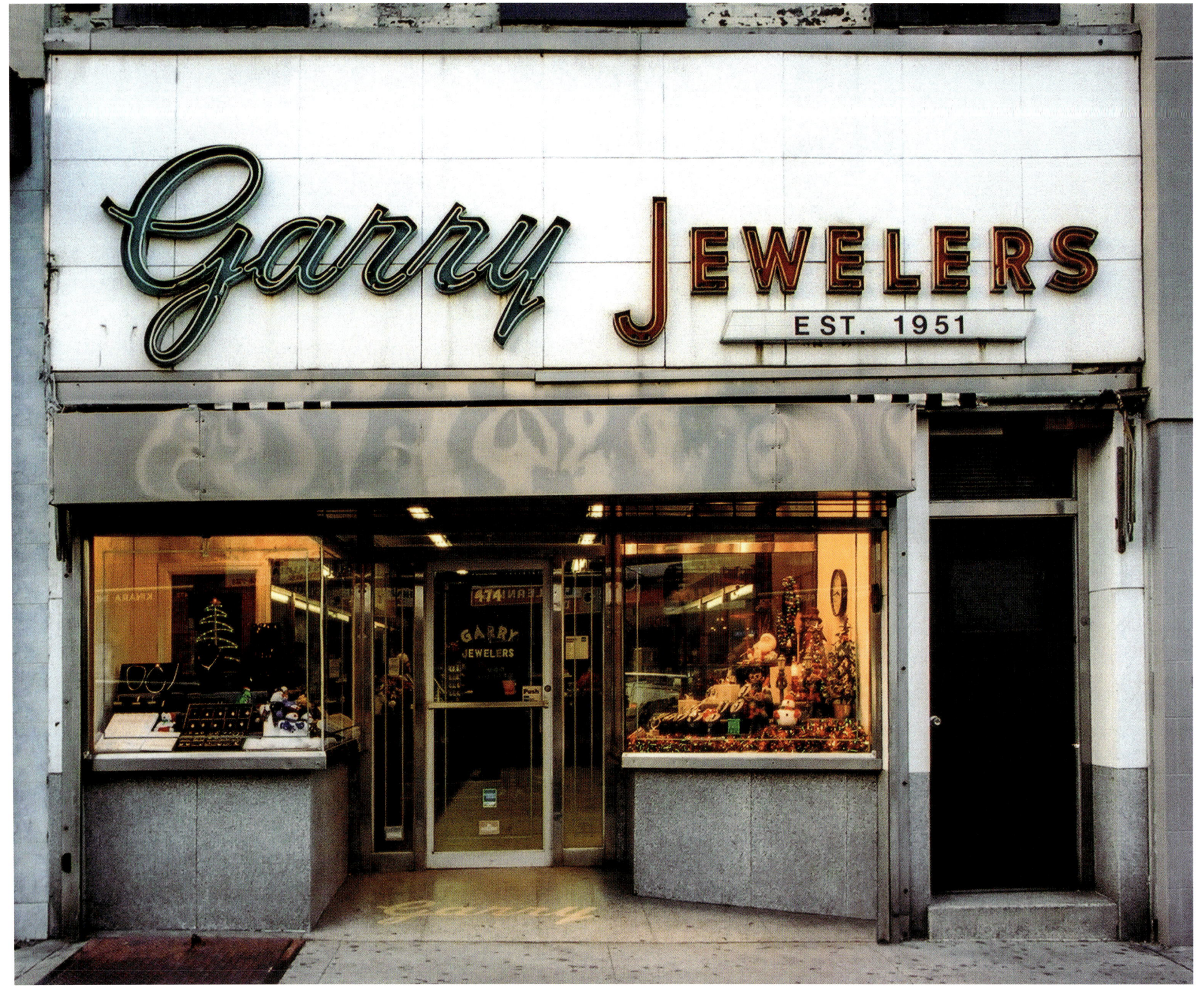

GARRY JEWELERS
5th Avenue near 10th Street, Park Slope, 2006

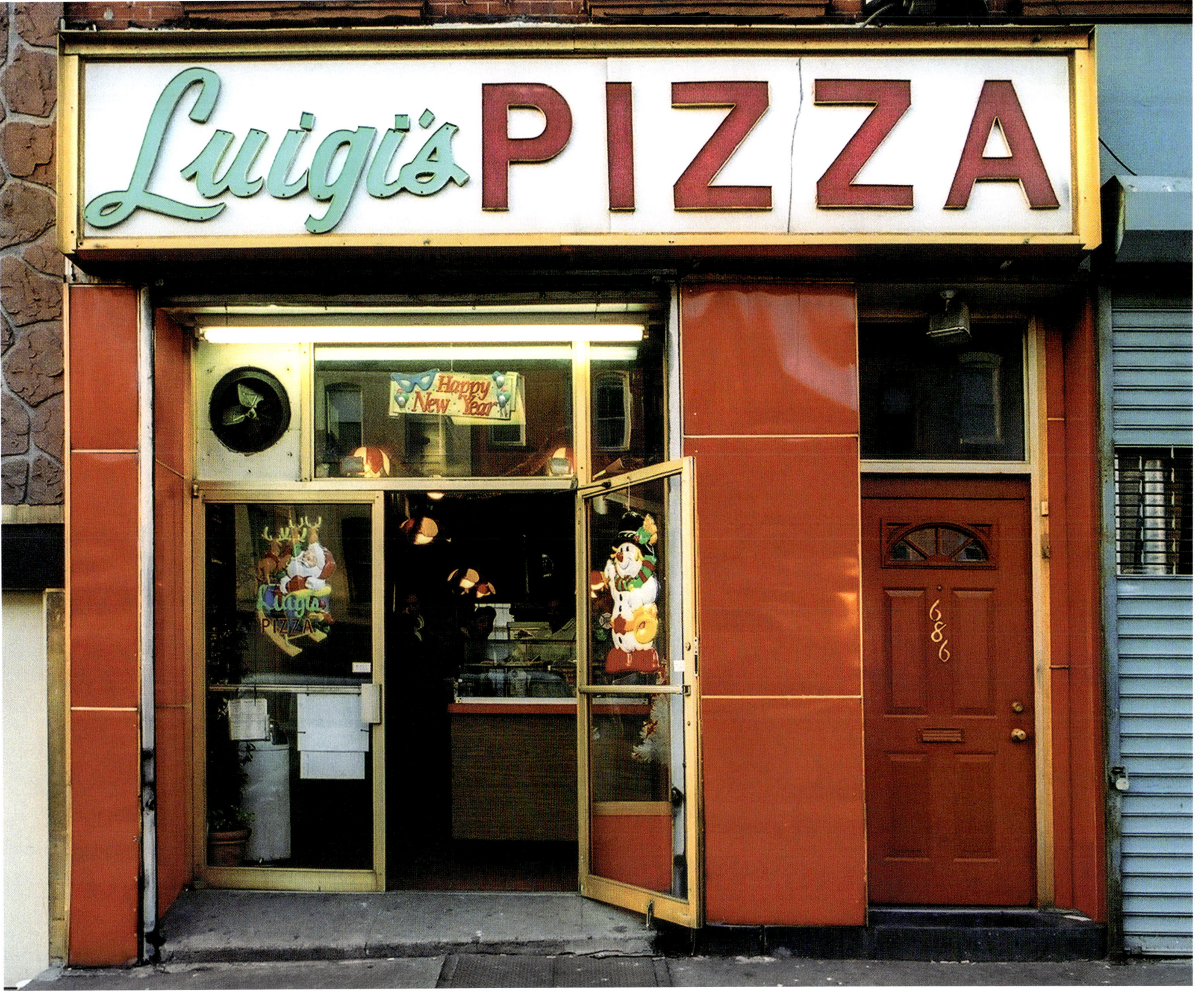

LUIGI'S PIZZA
5th Avenue near 21st Street, South Slope, 2006

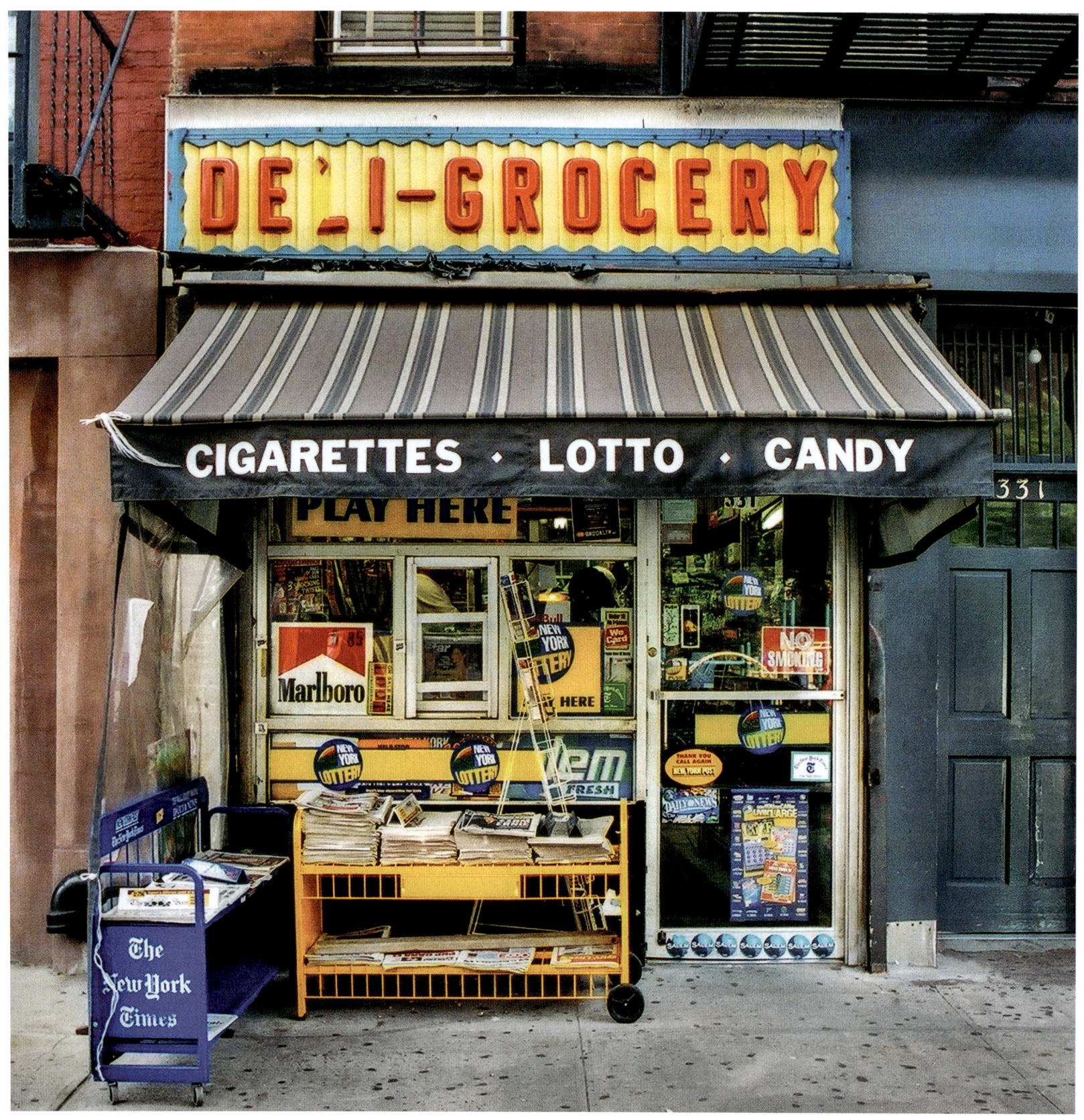

184 HENRY STREET DELI
Henry Street near Atlantic Avenue, Cobble Hill, 2004

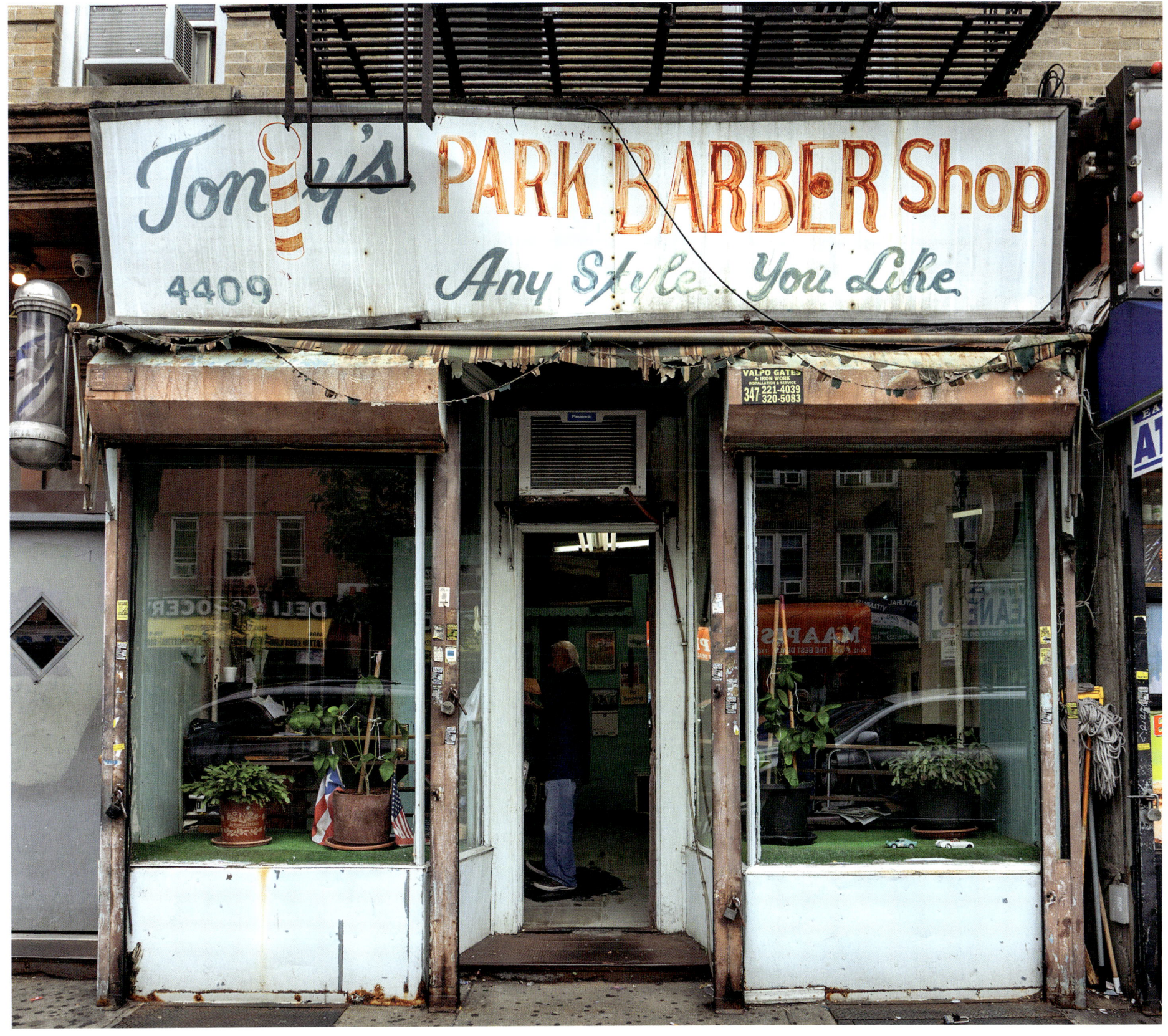

TONY'S PARK BARBER SHOP
5th Avenue near 44th Street, Sunset Park, 2006

BROOKLYN

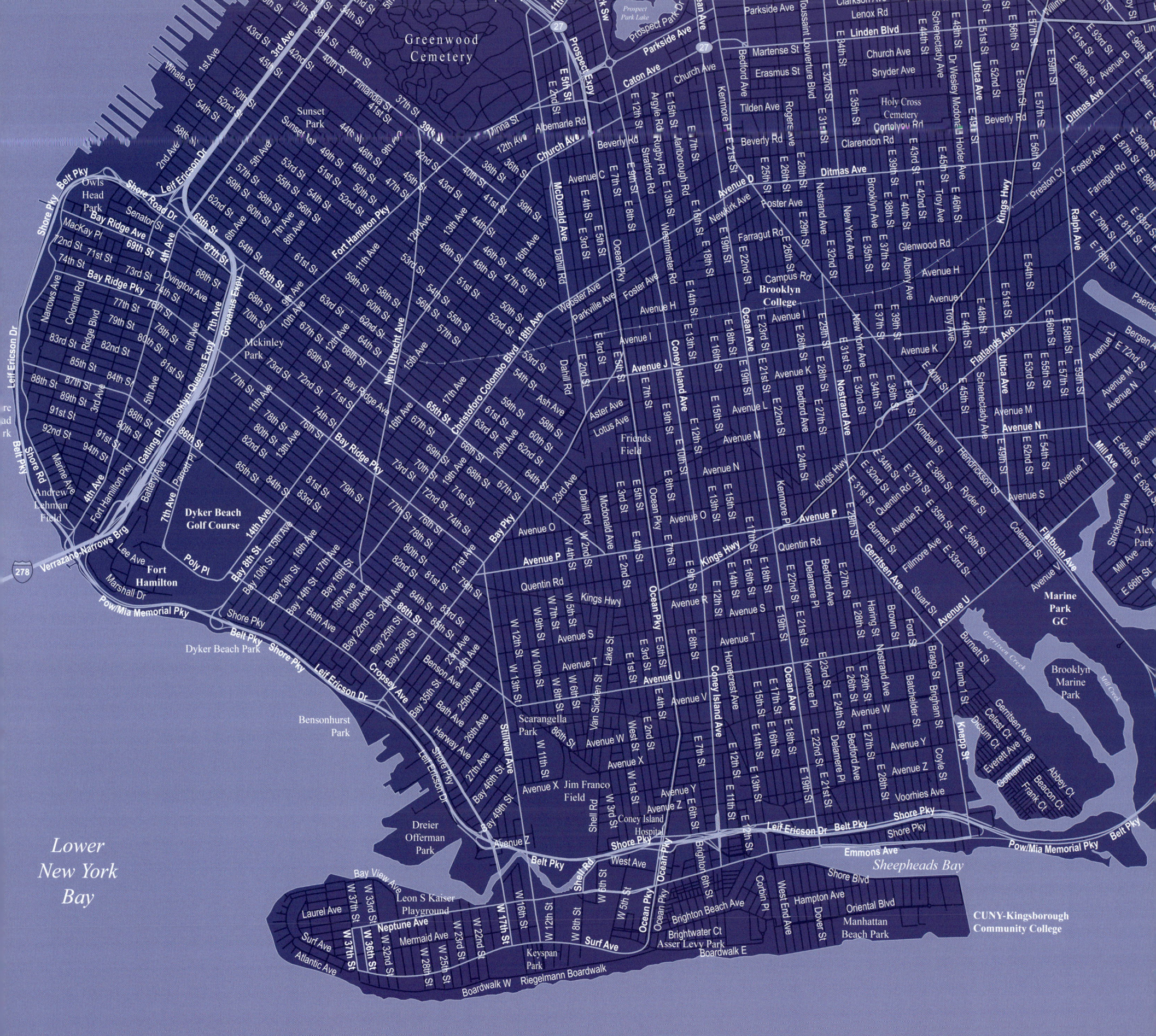

SOUTHERN BROOKLYN

BOROUGH PARK — DYKER HEIGHTS — BENSONHURST — MIDWOOD — GRAVESEND — CONEY ISLAND — HOMECREST — SHEEPSHEAD BAY — FLATLANDS

Borough Park is bounded to the north by 37th Street, to the east by McDonald Avenue, to the south by around 62nd Street, and to the west by 8th Avenue. Beginning in the 1920s, Jews and Italians began to settle there. Many Reform Jewish residents left the area in the 1960s, but Orthodox Jews, originally from Williamsburg and Crown Heights, took their place. Hasidic Jews from other parts of the world settled there too.

Dyker Heights is bounded to the north by 8th Avenue and 62nd Street, to the east by New Utrecht and 18th Avenues, to the south by Gravesend Bay and Fort Hamilton, and to the west by 8th Avenue and Fort Hamilton Parkway. It remained mostly rural until the early 1900s, when developers built single- and two-family homes there. The population to this day is predominantly Italian, with many families having lived there for four or five generations.

Bensonhurst is bounded to the north by 61st Street, to the east by McDonald Avenue, to the south by Gravesend Bay, and to the west by 14th Avenue. Italians and Jews moved there after 1915, when the subway reached the area. In the 1950s, thousands of immigrants from southern Italy settled there. Beginning in the 1980s, people from Asia and Russia began to move in.

Midwood is bounded to the north by Avenue H and the campus of Brooklyn College, to the east by Flatbush Avenue, to the south by Avenue T, and to the west by Coney Island Avenue. It remained largely unpopulated until the 1920s, when apartment buildings and detached houses were built and settled by people of mainly Italian and Jewish descent. It is still heavily Jewish, but has grown more diverse in recent years.

Gravesend is bounded roughly to the north by Avenue P, to the east by Coney Island Avenue, to the south by the Belt Parkway, and to the west by Stillwell Avenue. The area was mainly farmland until 1875, when three racetracks, as well as nearby Coney Island, were developed. The

population increased after the electrification of the rail lines in 1898 reduced travel time to Manhattan. Gravesend is now home to recent immigrants from many parts of the globe.

Coney Island is bounded to the north by Coney Island Creek and the Belt Parkway, to the east by Ocean Parkway, to the south by the Atlantic Ocean, and to the west by Norton's Point. Between 1880 and World War II, the neighborhood was a major summer resort. After the subway reached the area in 1920, over a million people visited every weekend. Coney Island's popularity declined after World War II—however, through redevelopment efforts that began in 2001, it is slowly being restored to its former glory.

Homecrest is bounded to the north by Avenue U, to the east by East 21st Street, to the south by Avenue W, and to the west by Ocean Parkway. It began to be developed in the early 1900s. Today its population is diverse, and includes Chinese, Russian, Korean, Italian, Israeli, Egyptian, and Lebanese residents.

Sheepshead Bay is bordered to the north by Marine Park, to the east by Shell Bank Creek, to the south by Manhattan Beach, and to the west by the neighborhood of Gravesend. It remained undeveloped until the 1870s, when the extension of several railroads and boulevards enabled easier access. By the early 1990s, the population was mostly Italian and Jewish, but increasing numbers of immigrants from other parts of the world began moving in in the 2000s.

Flatlands is bounded to the north by Flatlands Avenue, to the east by Paerdegat Basin, to the south by Avenue U, and to the west by Flatbush Avenue. The area became developed when horsecar service reached it. Although the Interborough Rapid Transit rail line was extended there too, the neighborhood remained difficult to reach until the automobile became more popular in the early 1920s. Today, Flatlands remains mostly an Italian, Irish, and Jewish area.

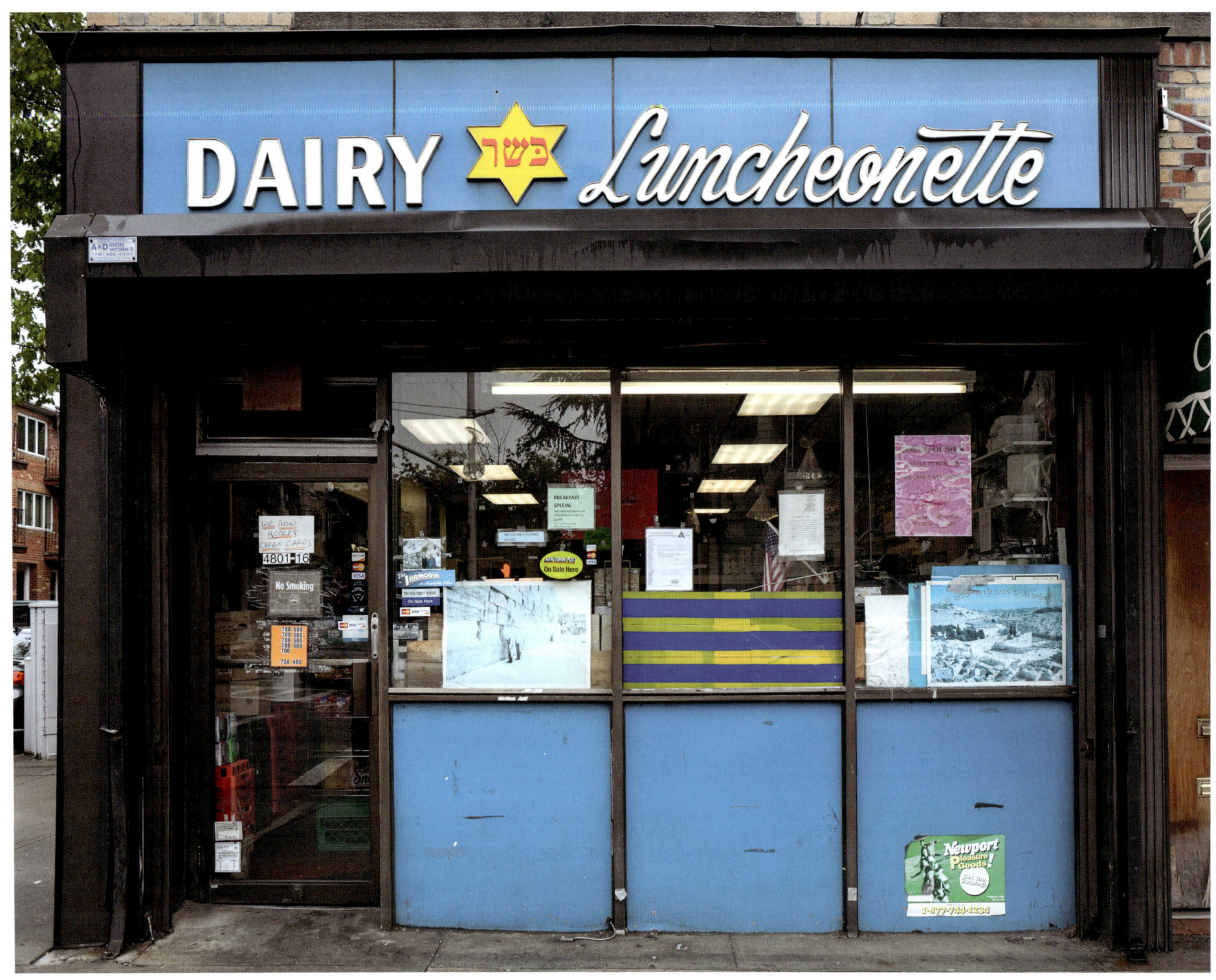

DAIRY LUNCHEONETTE
16th Avenue at 48th Street, Borough Park, 2010

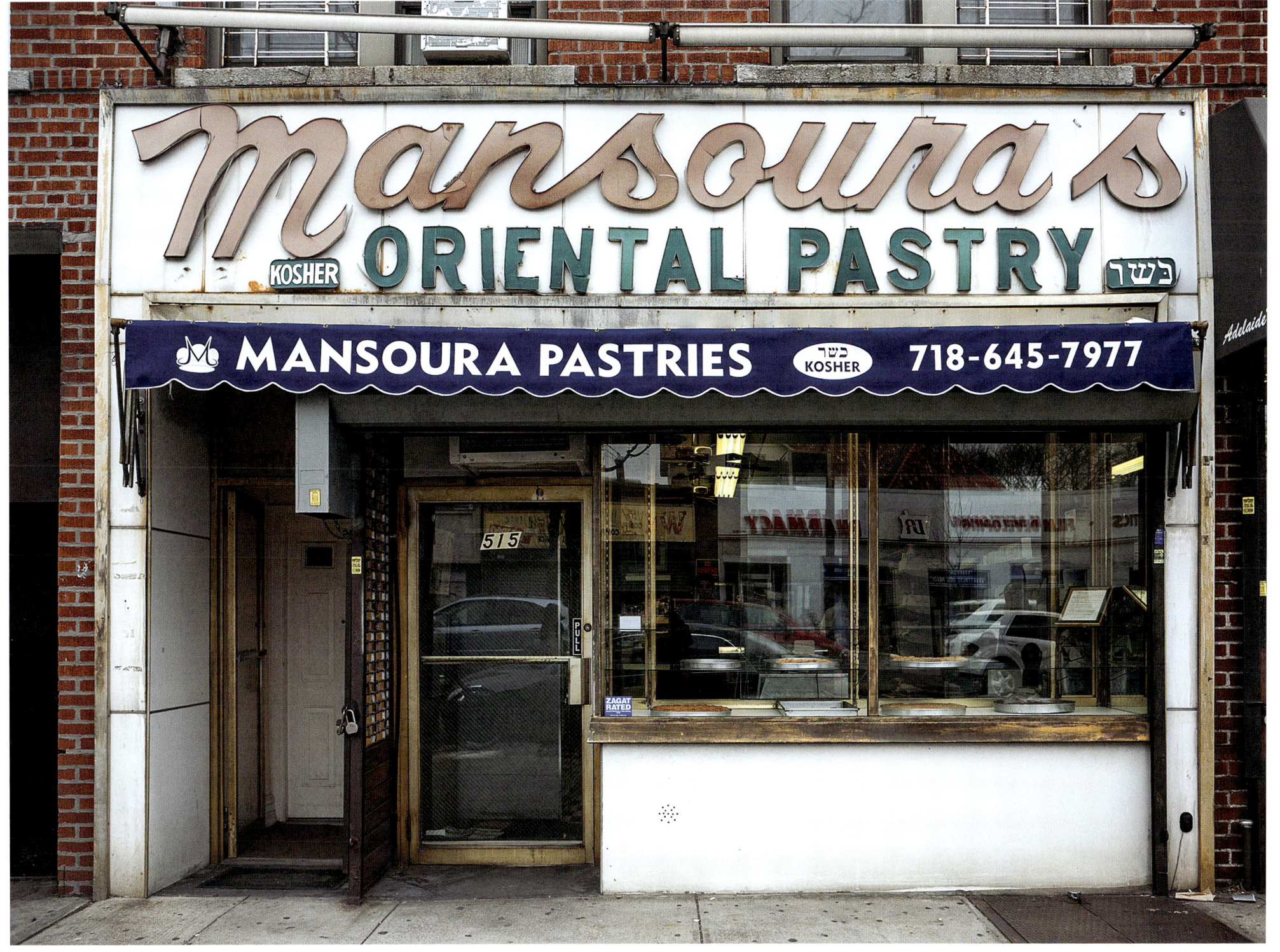

MANSOURA'S BAKERY
Kings Highway near East 3rd Street, Gravesend, 2009

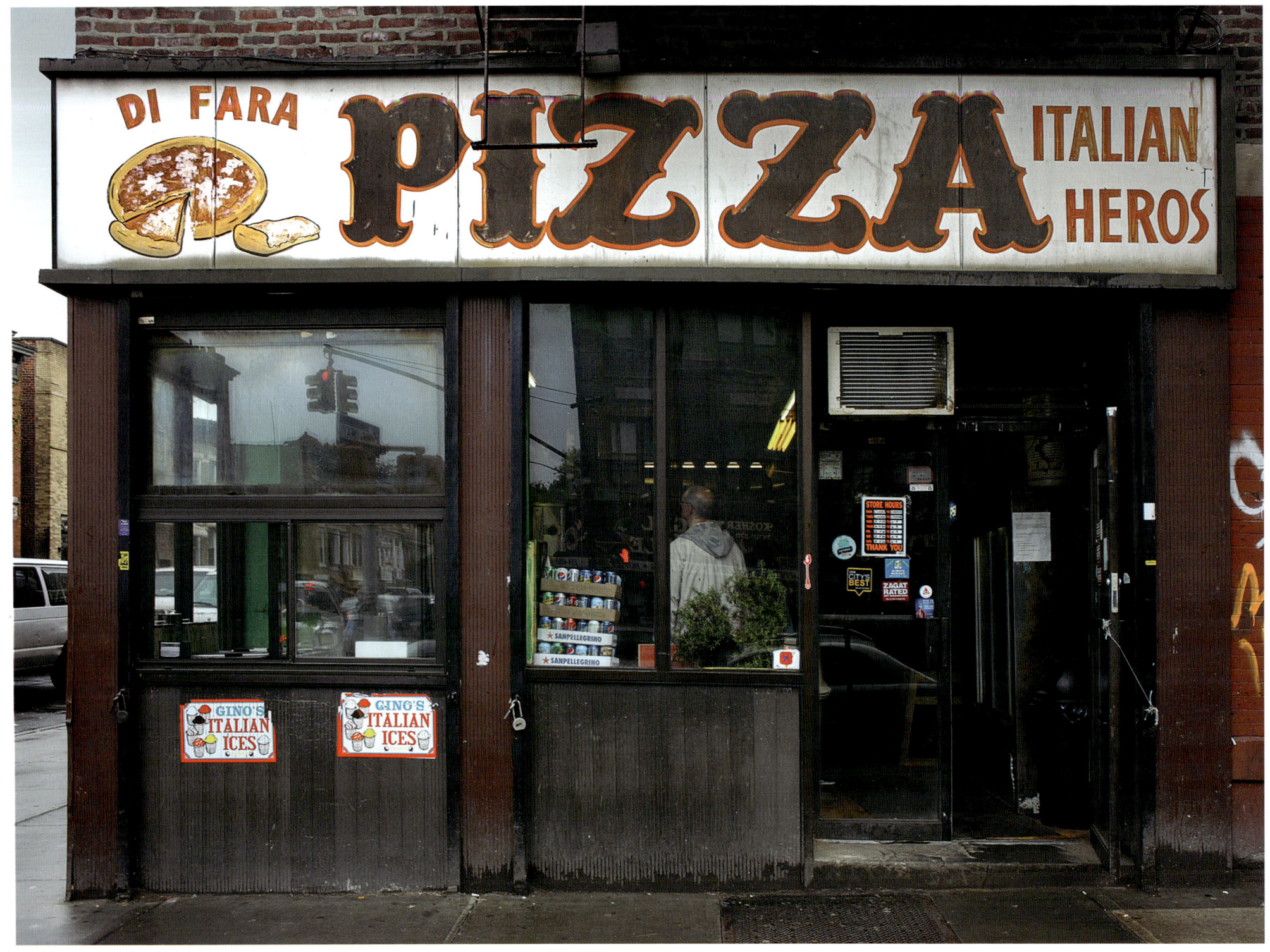

190 DI FARA PIZZA
Avenue J at East 15th Street, Midwood, 2010

DITMAS MEATS & POULTRY
Ditmas Avenue near East 5th Street, Borough Park, 2004

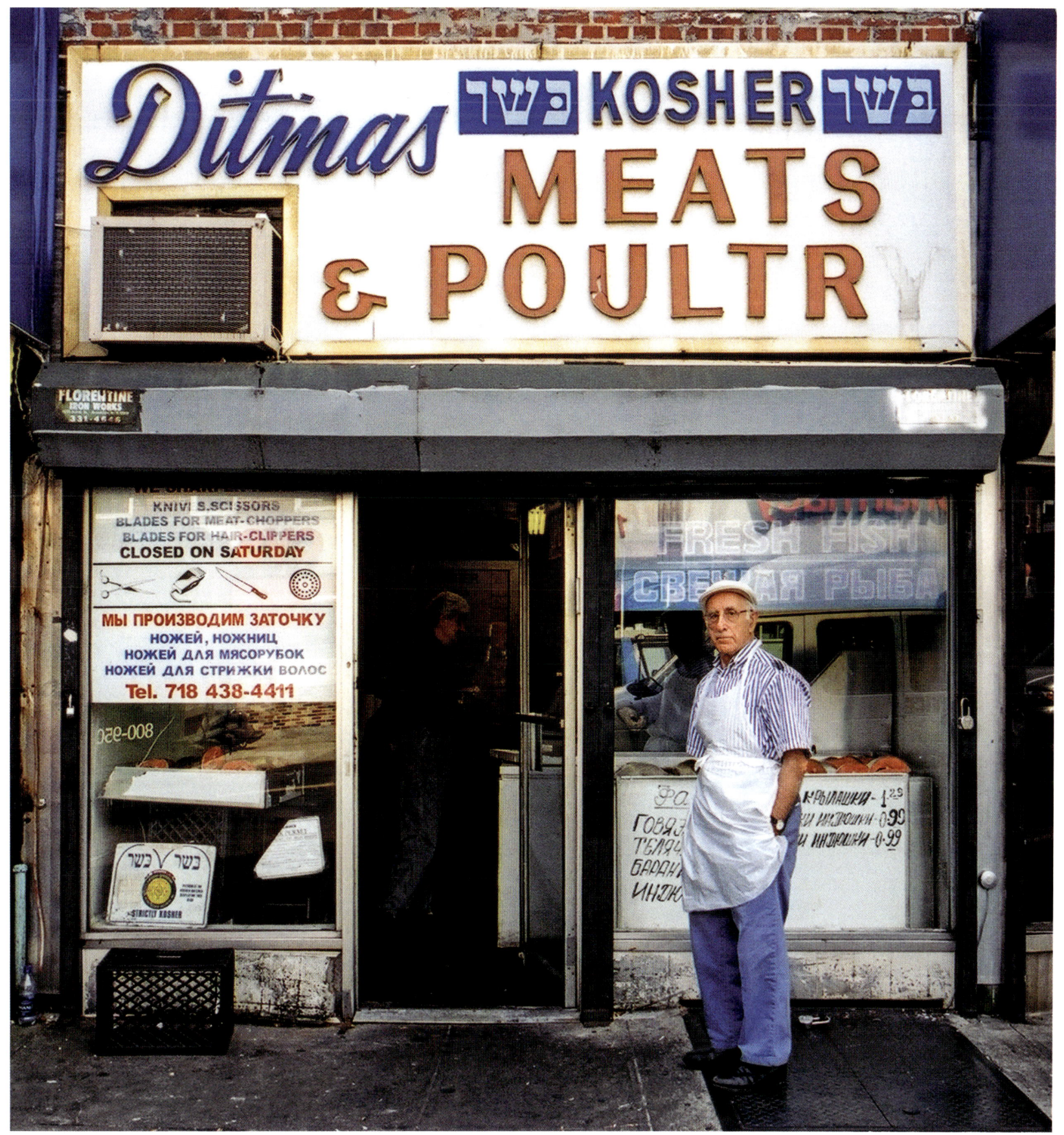

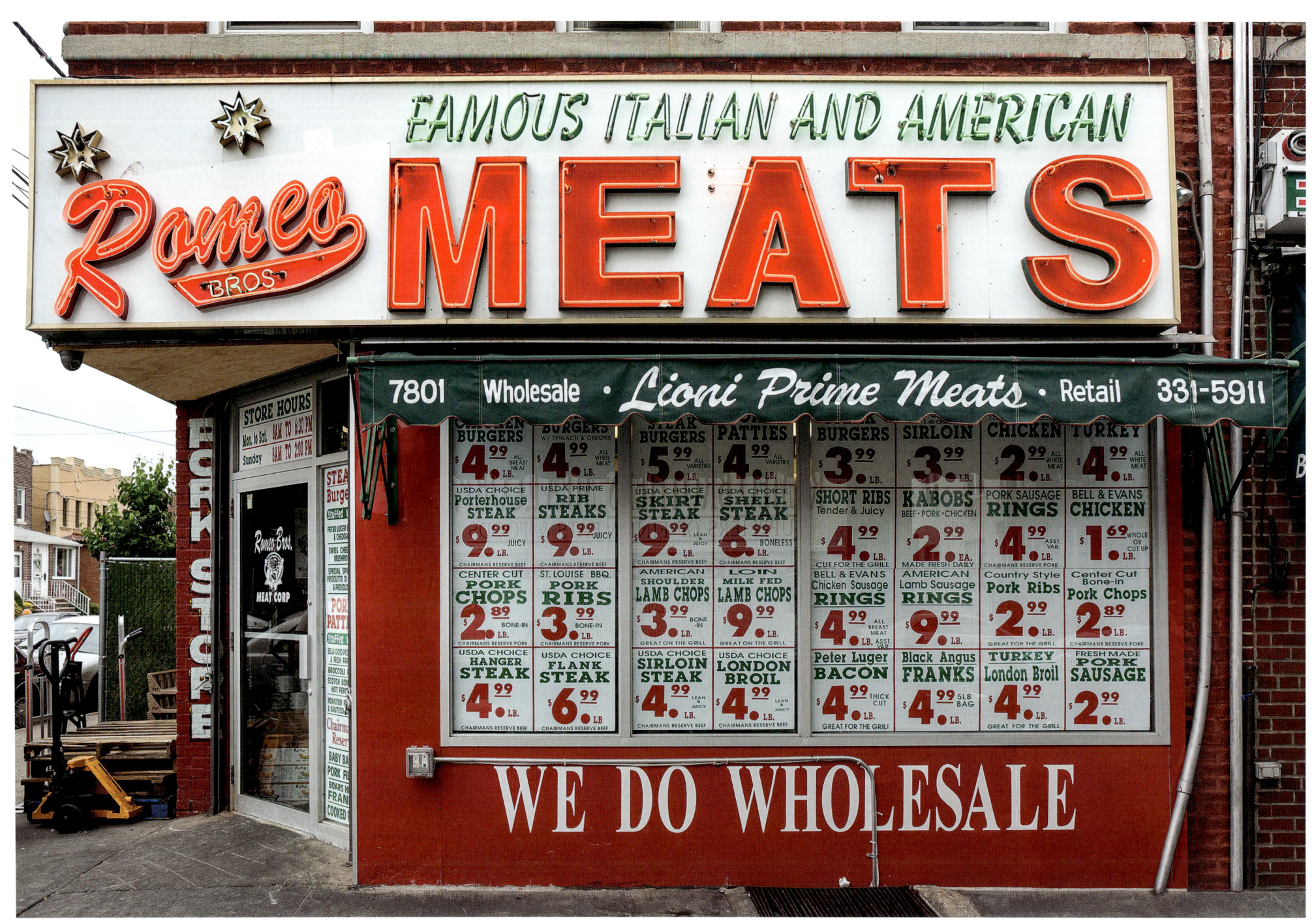

192 ROMEO BROTHERS MEATS
15th Avenue at 78th Street, Bensonhurst, 2012

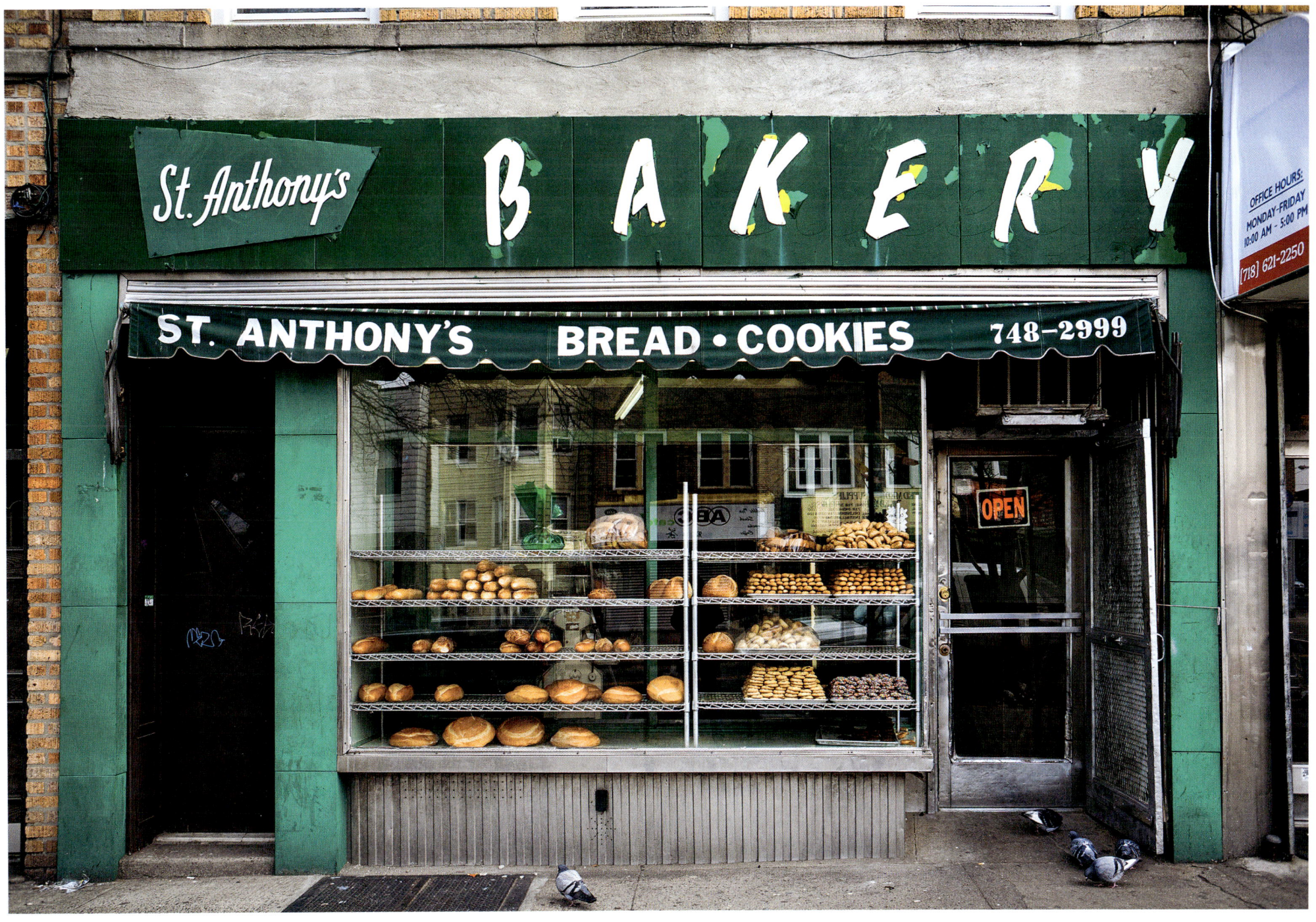

ST. ANTHONY'S BAKERY
Fort Hamilton Parkway near Bay Ridge Avenue, Dyker Heights, 2009

→
LANDI'S PORK STORE
Avenue N near East 59th Street, Flatlands, 2009

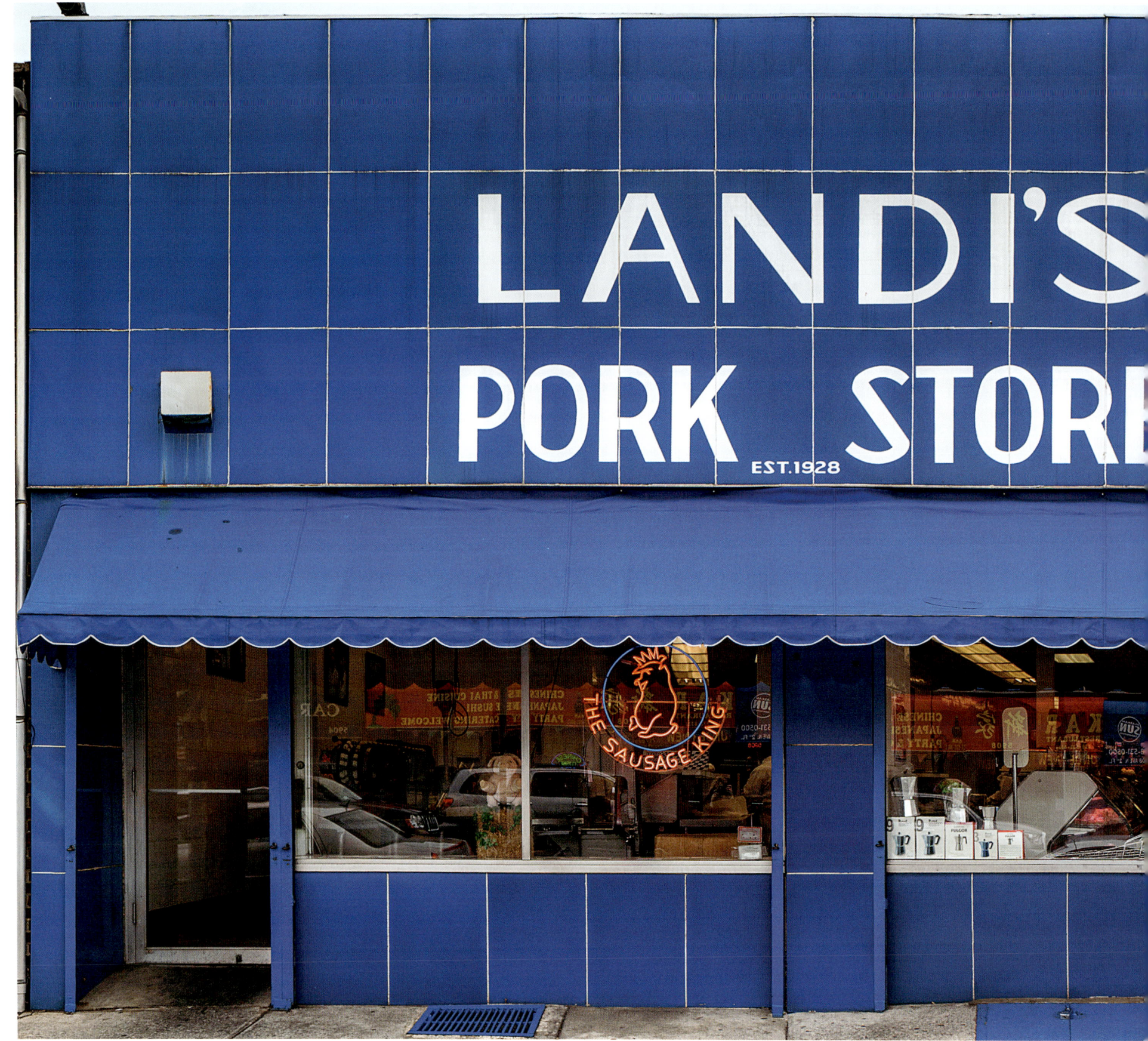

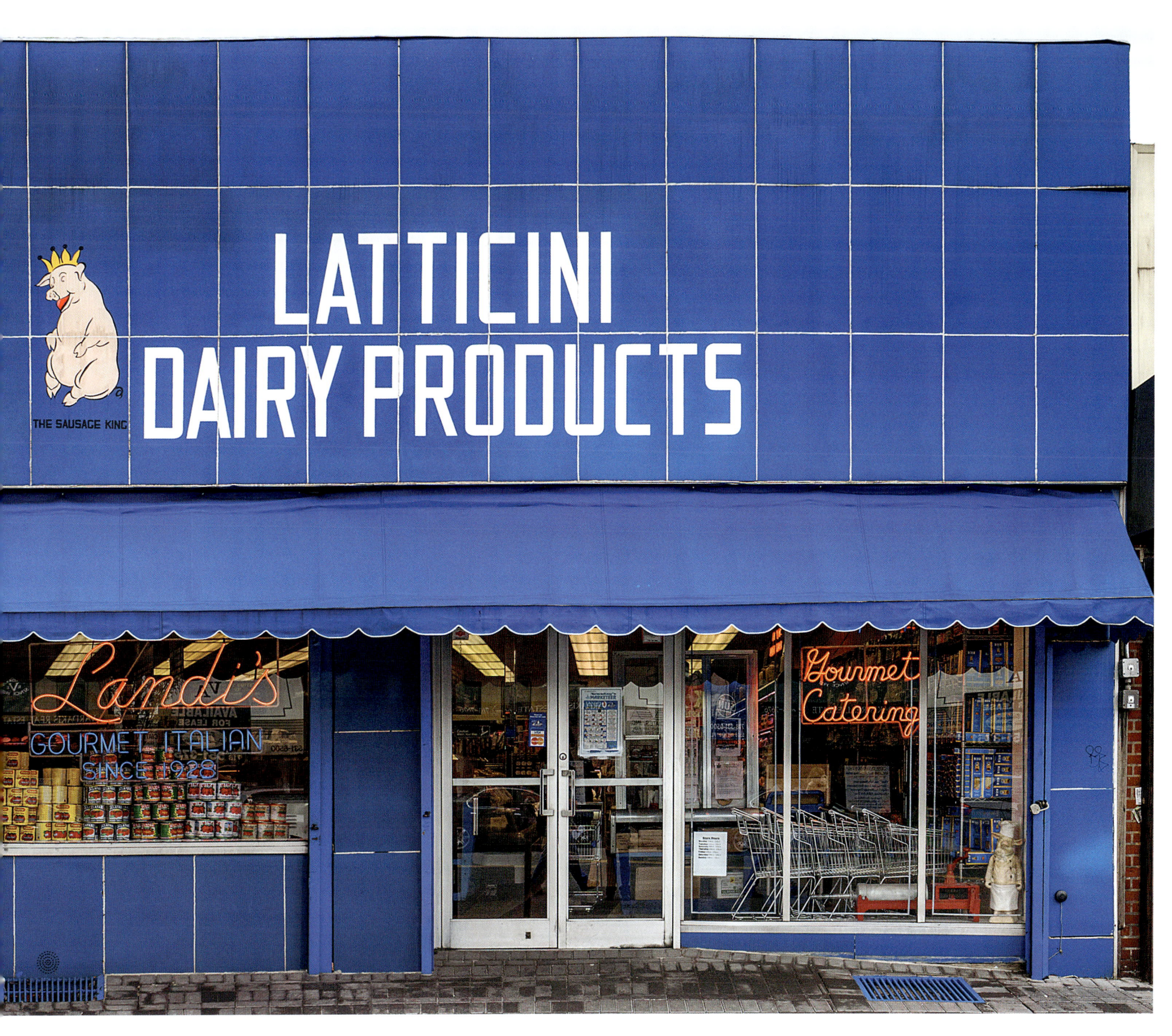

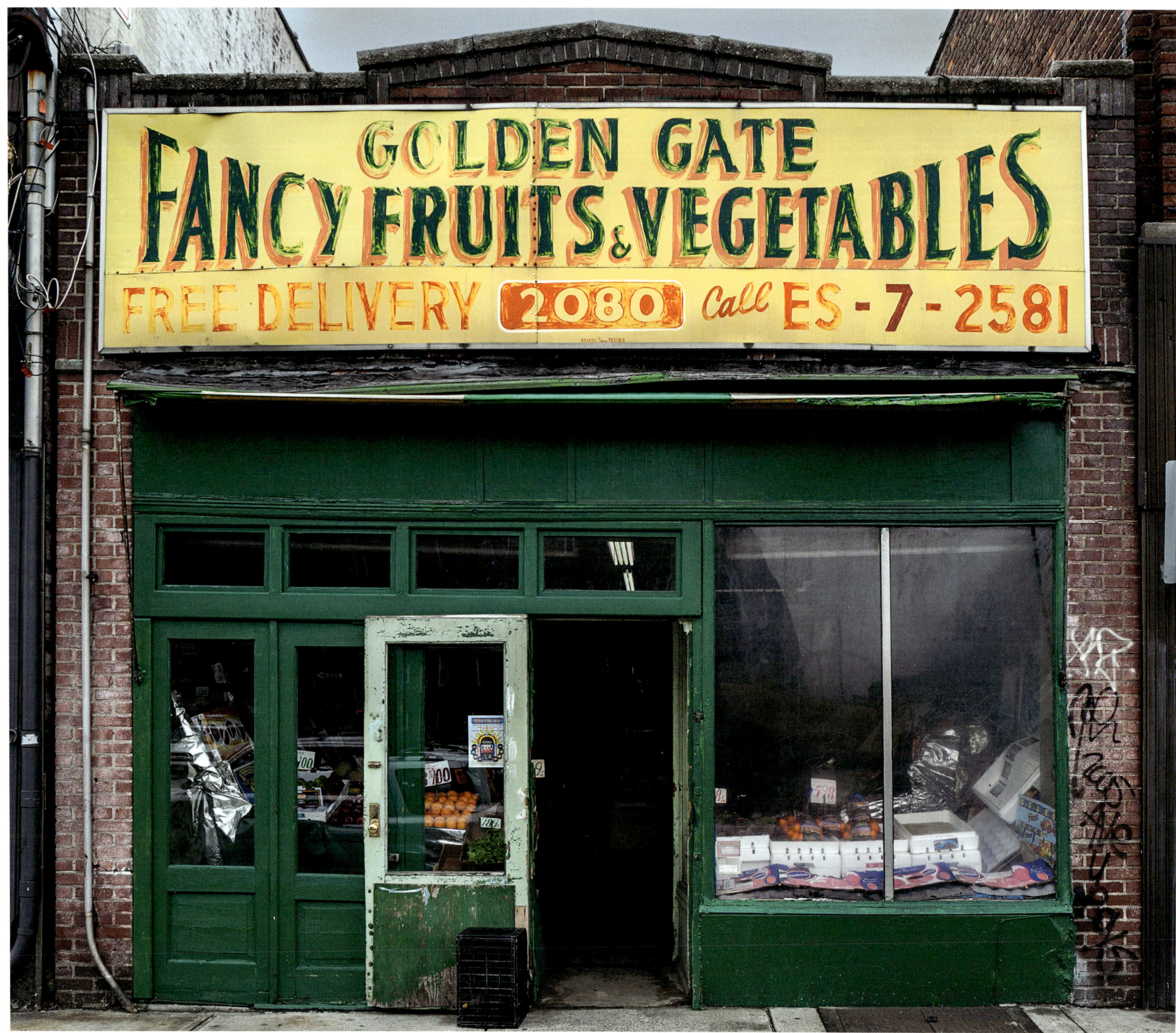

←

GOLDEN GATE FANCY
FRUITS & VEGETABLES
Flatbush Avenue near Troy Avenue,
Flatlands, 2009

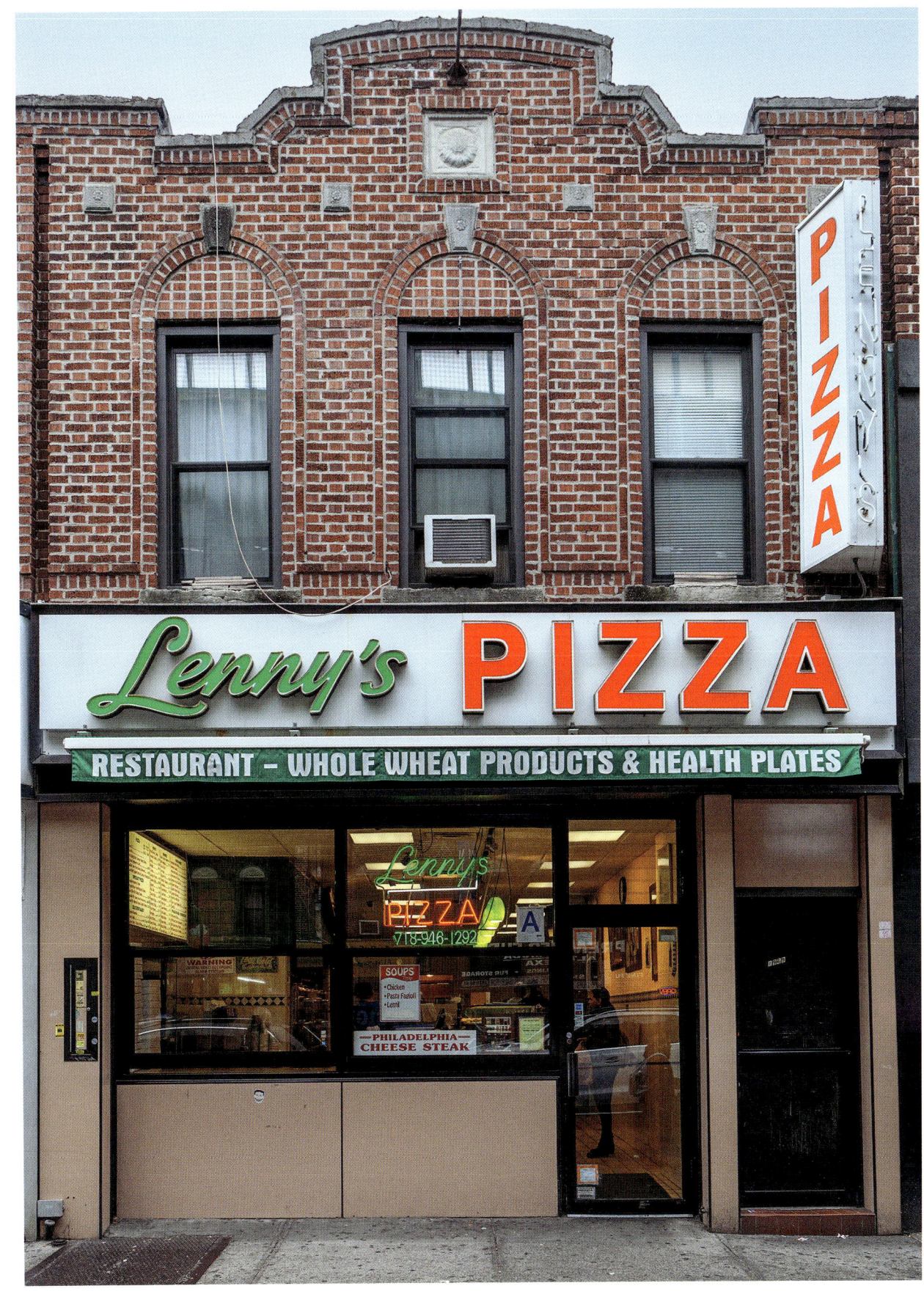

LENNY'S PIZZA
86th Street near 20th Avenue,
Bensonhurst, 2018

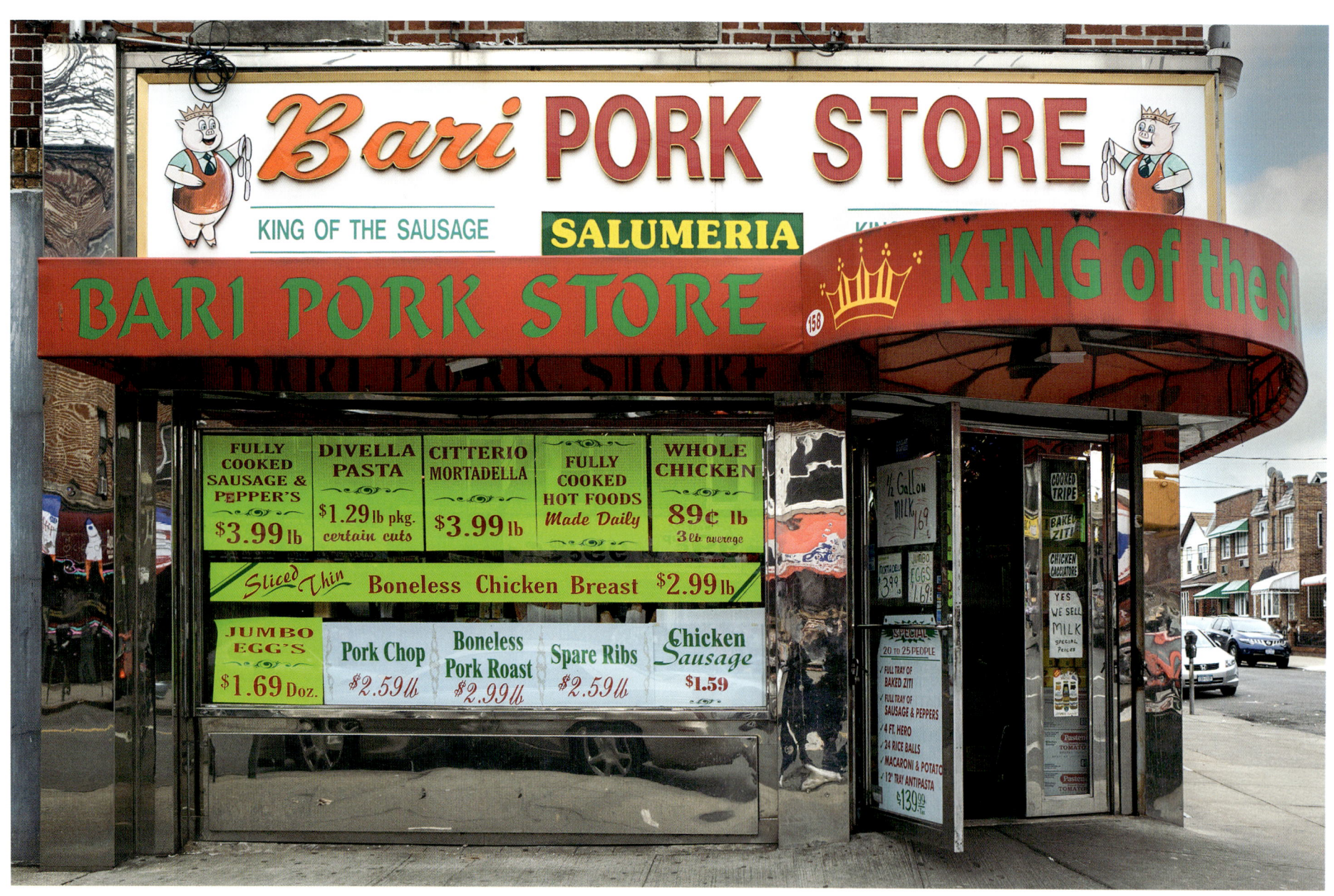

BARI PORK STORE
Avenue U at West 7th Street, Gravesend, 2009

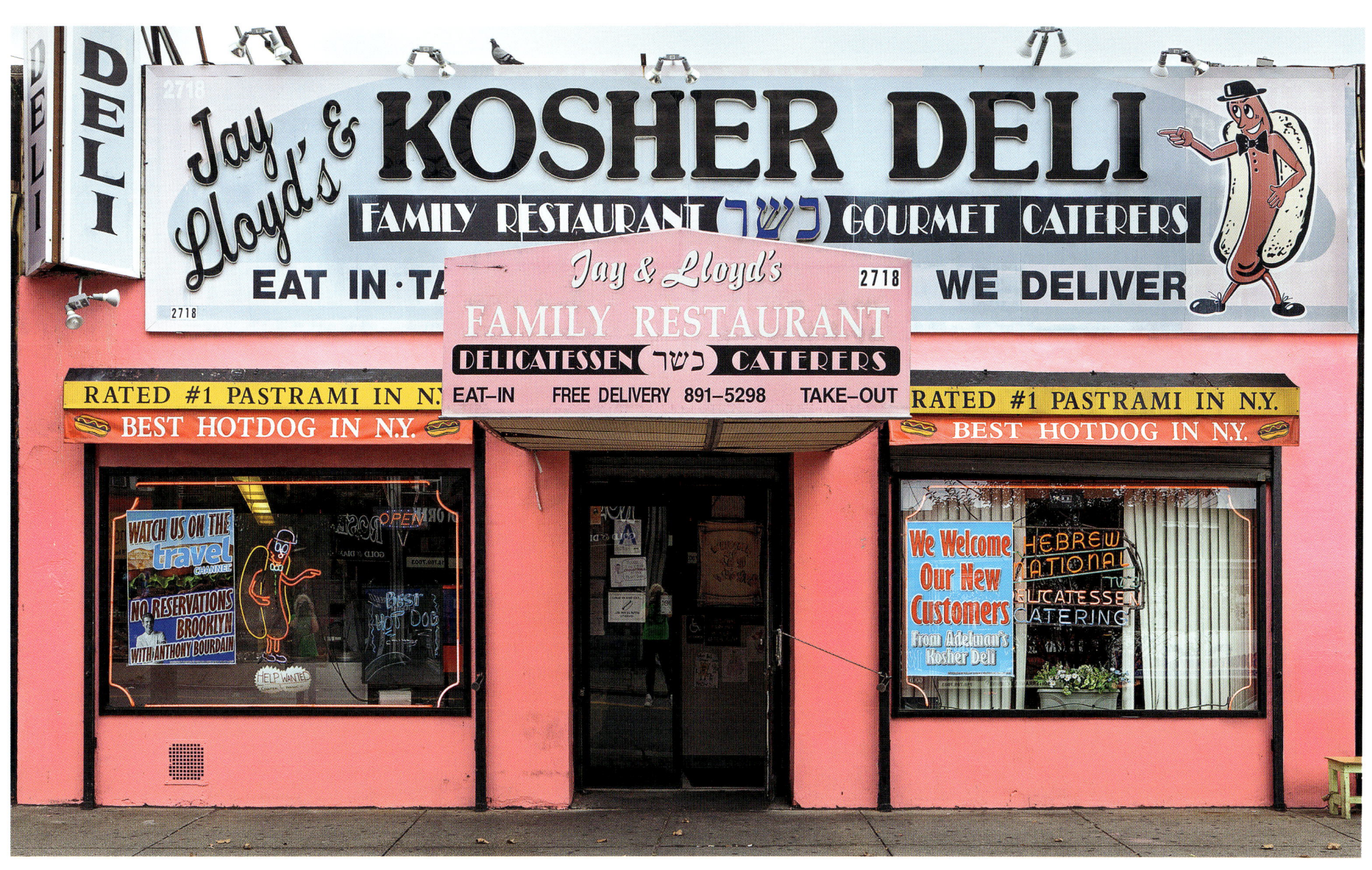

JAY & LLOYD'S KOSHER DELI
Avenue U near East 28th Street, Sheepshead Bay, 2013

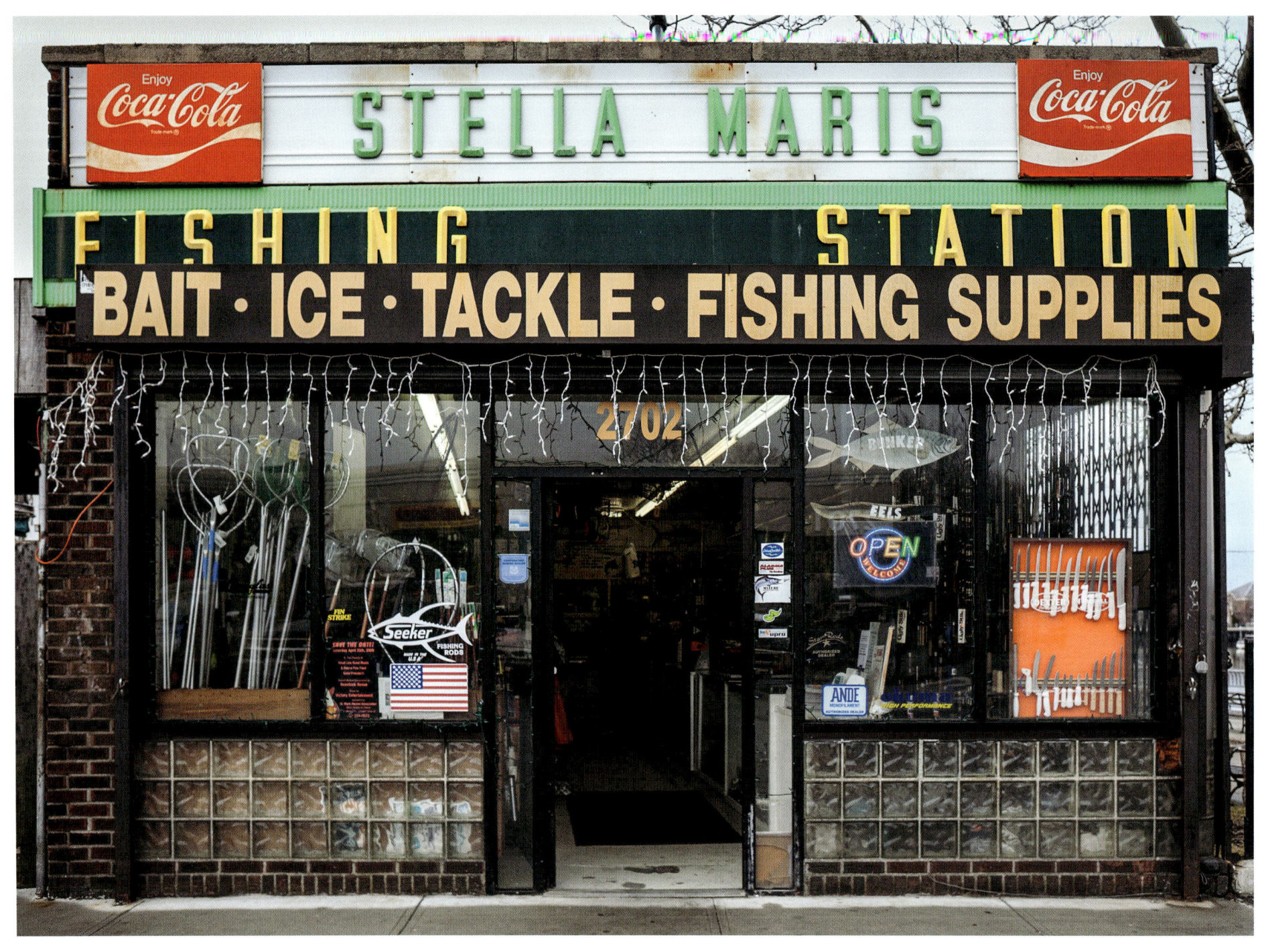

200 STELLA MARIS BAIT & TACKLE
Emmons Avenue at East 27th Street, Sheepshead Bay, 2009

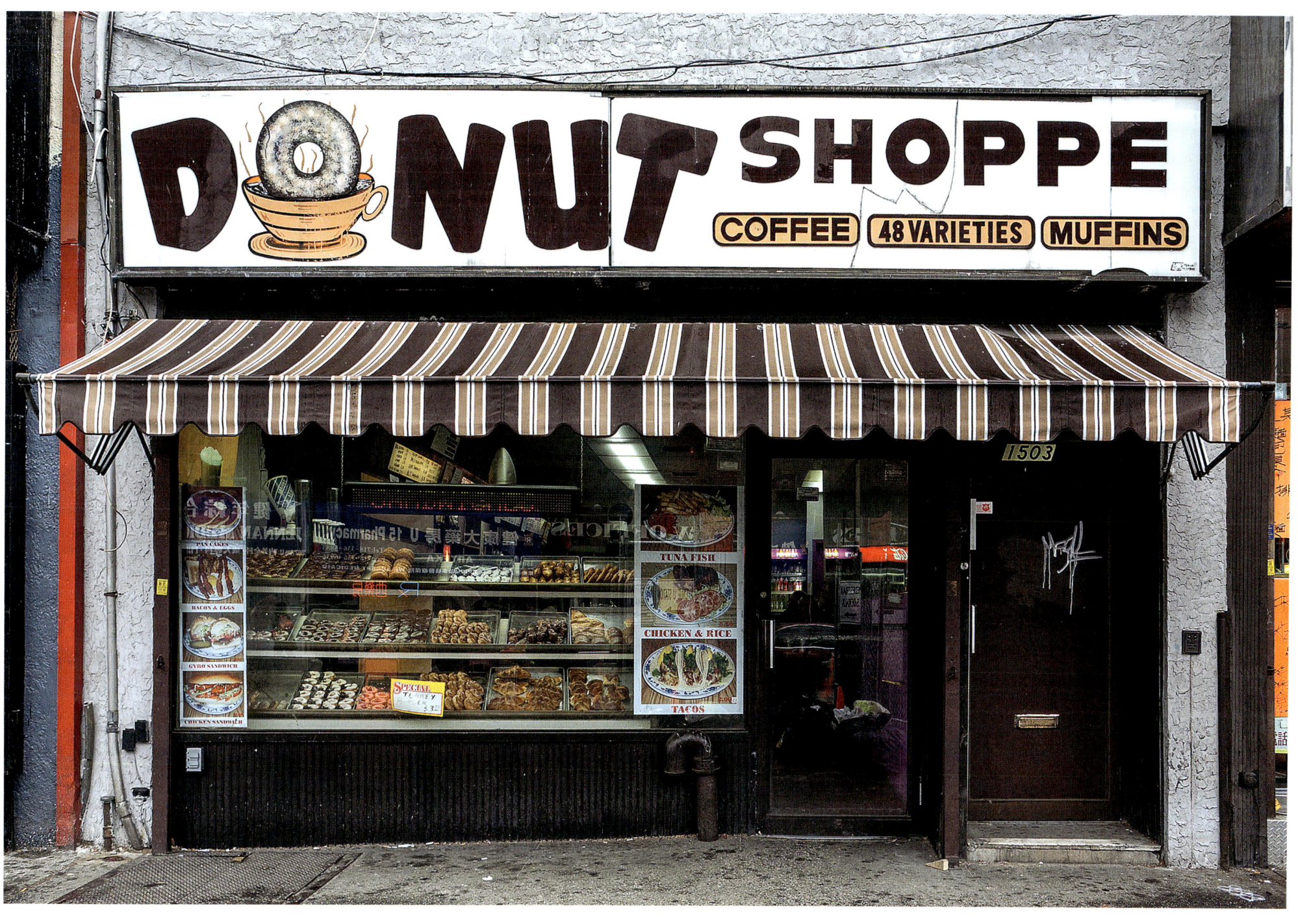

DONUT SHOPPE
Avenue U near East 15th Street, Homecrest, 2009

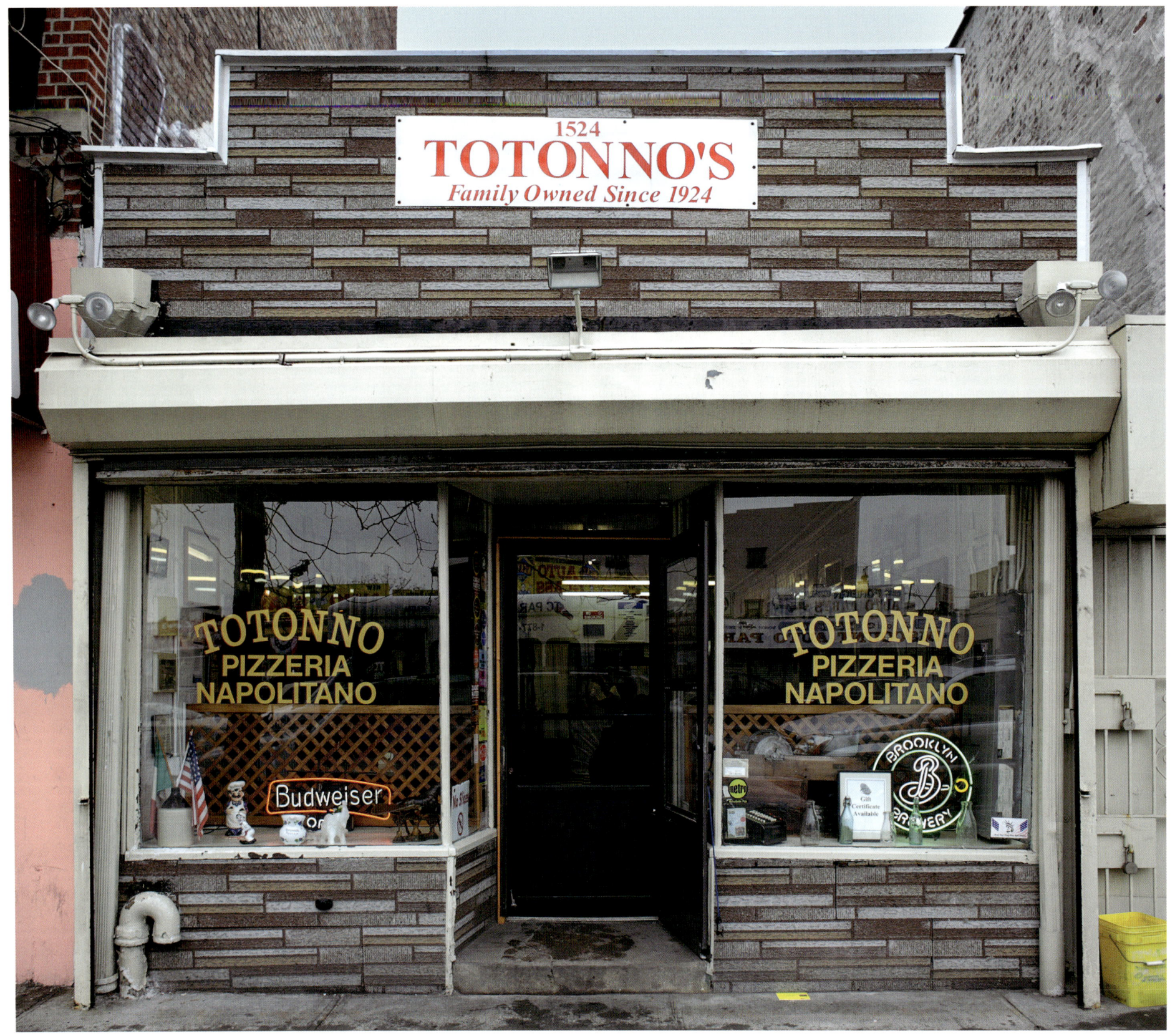

202

TOTONNO'S
Neptune Avenue near West 16th Street, Coney Island, 2009

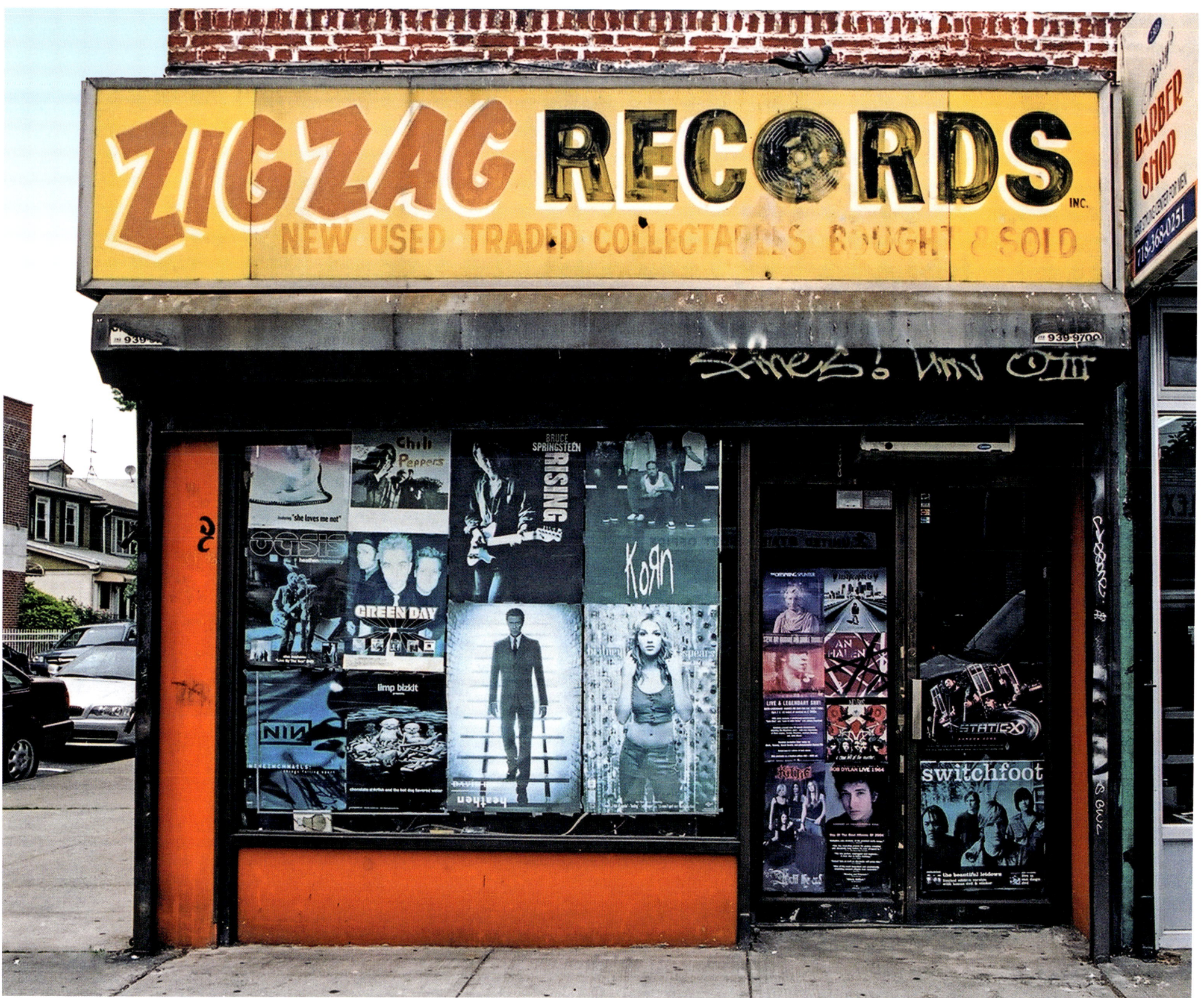

203 ZIG ZAG RECORDS
Avenue U at East 23rd Street, Sheepshead Bay, 2005

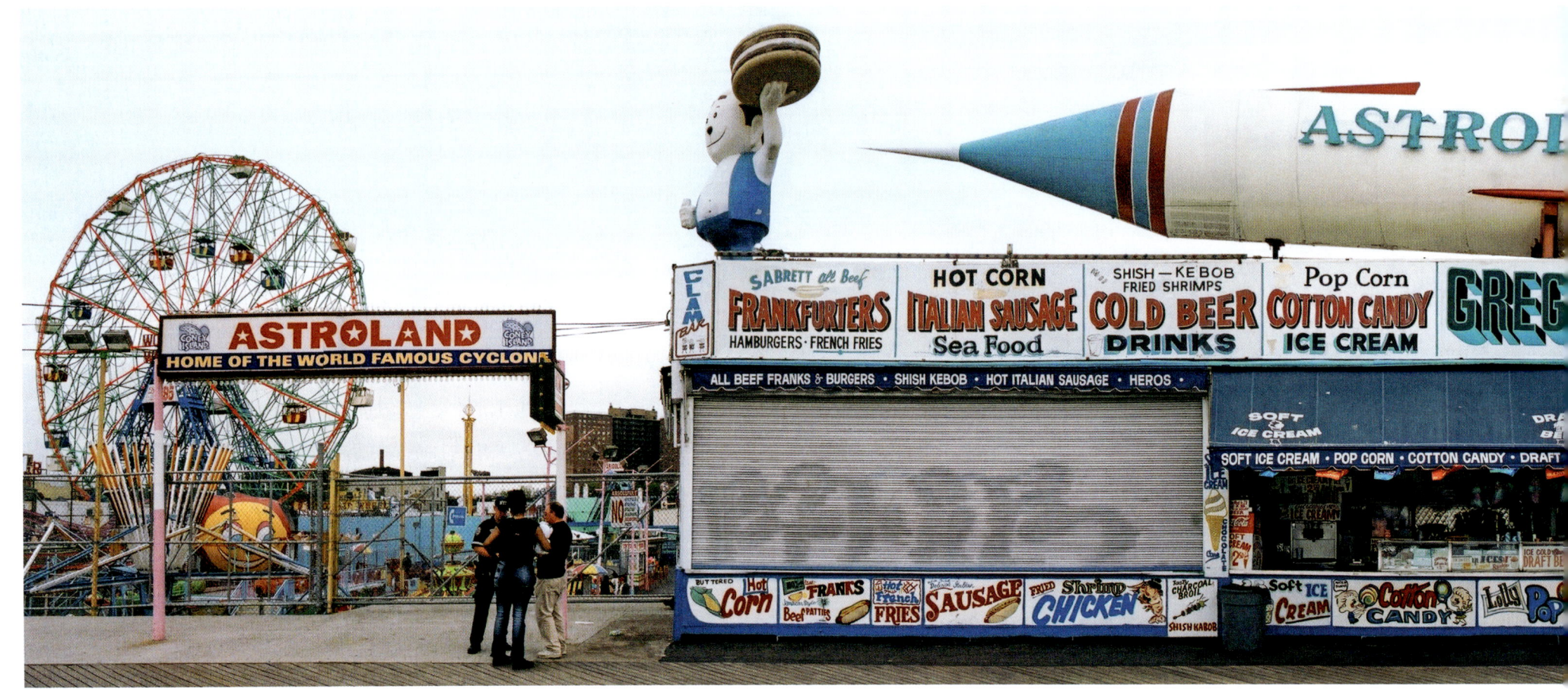

204 ASTROLAND
Boardwalk at West 10th Street, Coney Island, 2005

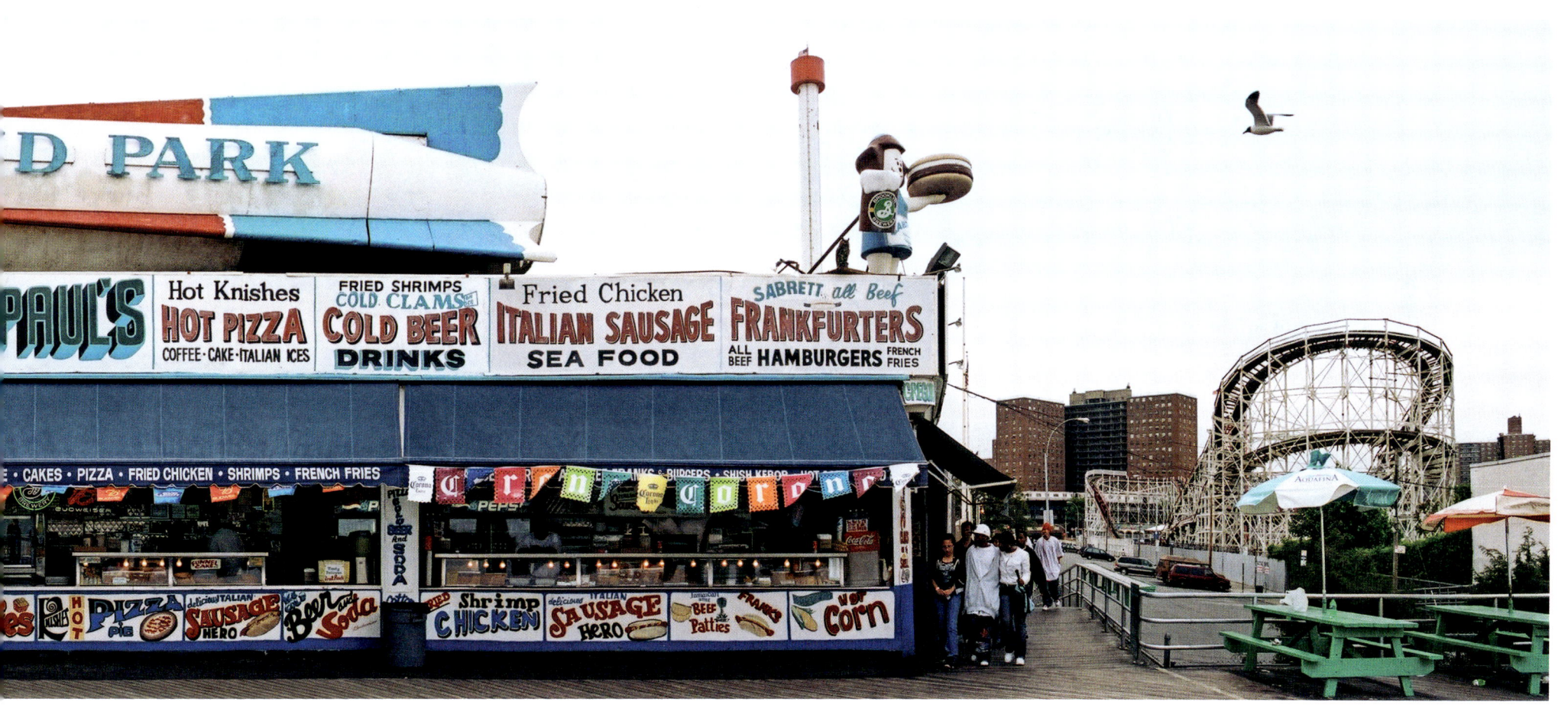

QUEENS

Queens is New York City's biggest borough. At 109 square miles, it's almost as large as Manhattan, the Bronx, and Staten Island combined. It is bounded to the north by the East River, to the east by Long Island's Nassau County, to the south by the Atlantic Ocean, to the southwest by Brooklyn, and to the west by the East River. Queens was originally settled as farmland, but became more populated when railroads reached the area in the mid-1800s and thousands of immigrant families moved there from Manhattan.

With the expansion of the subway system in the early 1900s and the opening of the Queensboro Bridge in 1909—which connected Manhattan to Queens—the population grew rapidly, and distinct shopping districts were created. After immigration laws were changed in 1965, many new immigrants settled in Queens, especially people from Asia and Latin America.

The borough is famous for its diversity: there are more languages spoken in Queens than anywhere else in the world. The 7 train, which spans the length of the borough, is nicknamed the "International Express," running through one ethnic community after another. Residents of Queens often closely identify with their neighborhood. Even postal addresses are written with the neighborhood rather than the borough or city. Each area in Queens is home to a variety of shopping and dining options.

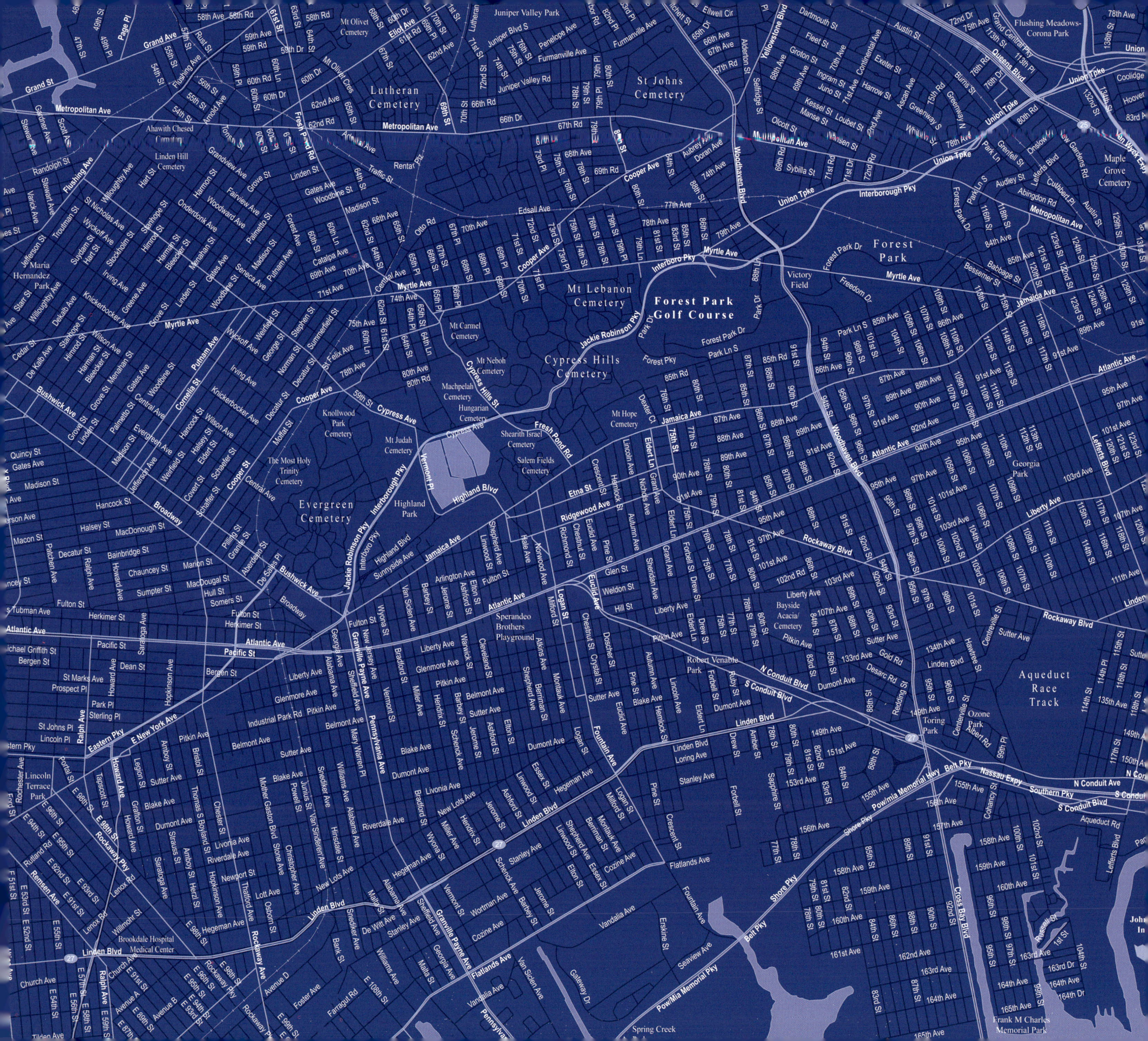

SOUTHWESTERN QUEENS

RICHMOND HILL — WOODHAVEN — RIDGEWOOD

Richmond Hill is bounded to the north by Myrtle Avenue and Hillside Avenue, to the east by the Van Wyck Expressway, to the south by Linden Boulevard, and to the west by 100th Street. Until the area was developed in the late 1860s, it was mostly farmland. The population was mainly of German and Irish descent until the mid-1970s, when Latino immigrants began moving in. Close to 40 percent of those settling in Richmond Hill in the 1980s were from Guyana, with others from the Dominican Republic, Colombia, Ecuador, India, and Jamaica. Today, the neighborhood remains mostly residential, with many elegant houses and structures.

Woodhaven is bounded to the north by Park Lane South, to the east by 106th and 107th Streets, to the south by Atlantic Avenue, and to the west by the Brooklyn border. The area was undeveloped until a racetrack called Union Course was built in 1821; many wealthy northerners and plantation owners from the South raced their horses there. Development increased in the mid-1850s as a railroad station was built and tinware and stamping works factories were erected. Elevated rail lines were extended along Liberty Avenue in 1915 and Jamaica Avenue in 1917, bringing thousands of Italian and Irish people to settle in Woodhaven. After 1970, the neighborhood became more diverse, attracting African Americans and Latinos as well as immigrants from Guyana, Jamaica, and China.

Ridgewood is bounded to the north by Metropolitan Avenue, to the east by the tracks of the Long Island Railroad and Conrail, to the south by Central Avenue, and to the west by Flushing Avenue. German middle-class residents chose to settle there beginning in the late 1800s and supported its numerous knitting mills and breweries. A large population of Romanians, Italians, and Slovenians moved in after World War II. Until the late 1970s, Ridgewood was considered part of Brooklyn. But in 1979, local residents voted to officially change the postal zone to one in Queens in order to disassociate themselves from the negative perceptions of nearby Bushwick, Brooklyn. While still largely a German community, during the 1980s many more immigrants from Eastern Europe, especially from Romania as well as the former republics of Yugoslavia, and from Poland, began to settle in the area. By the 1990s, the demographic continued to shift with a large influx of Latinos from the Dominican Republic and Ecuador as well as immigrants from China and Korea. Ridgewood today remains a working-class neighborhood. It has also attracted young artists and students seeking affordable housing.

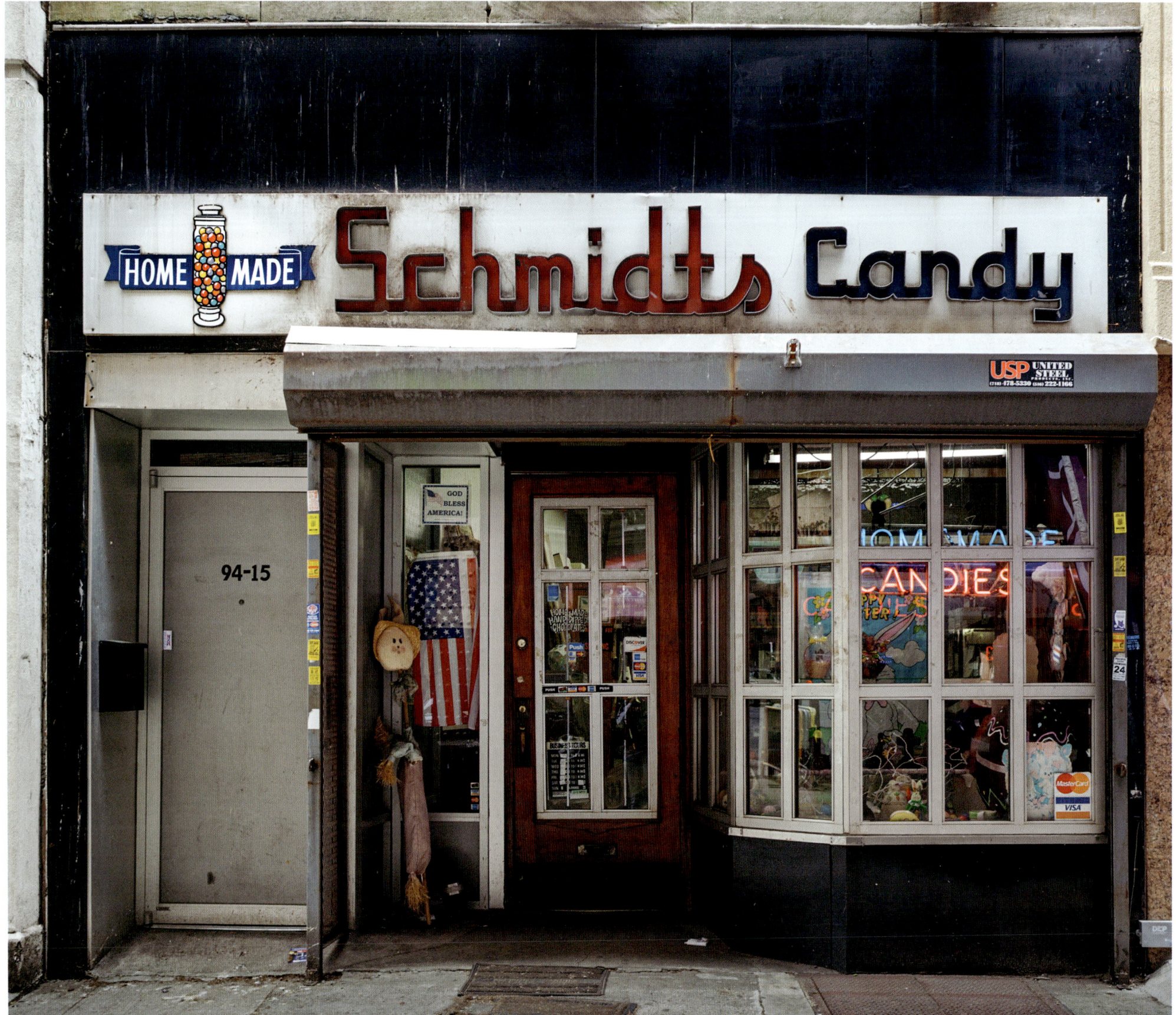

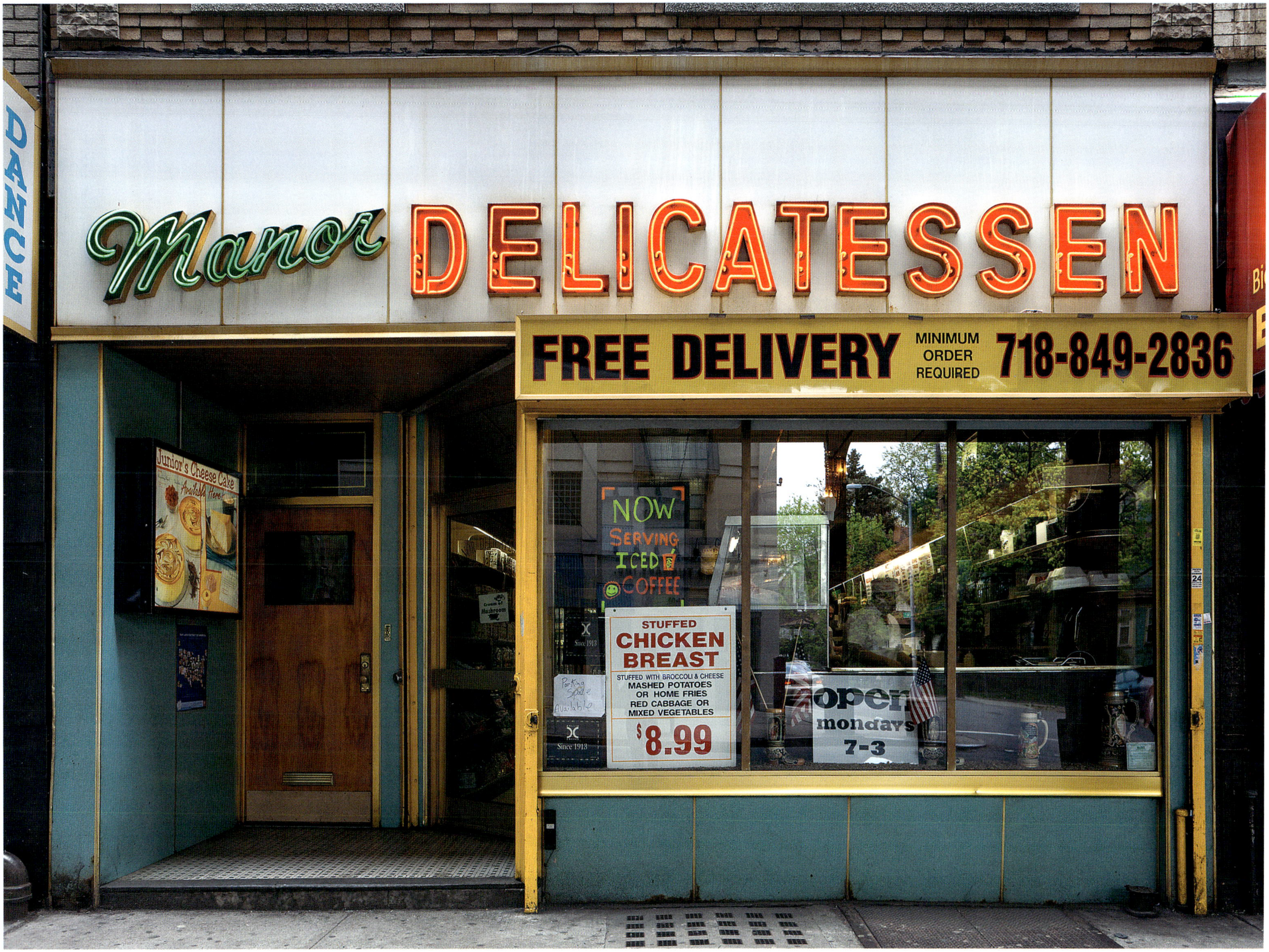

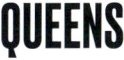

211   **SCHMIDT'S CANDY**
Jamaica Avenue near 94th Street, Woodhaven, 2010

MANOR DELICATESSEN
Jamaica Avenue near 94th Street, Woodhaven, 2010

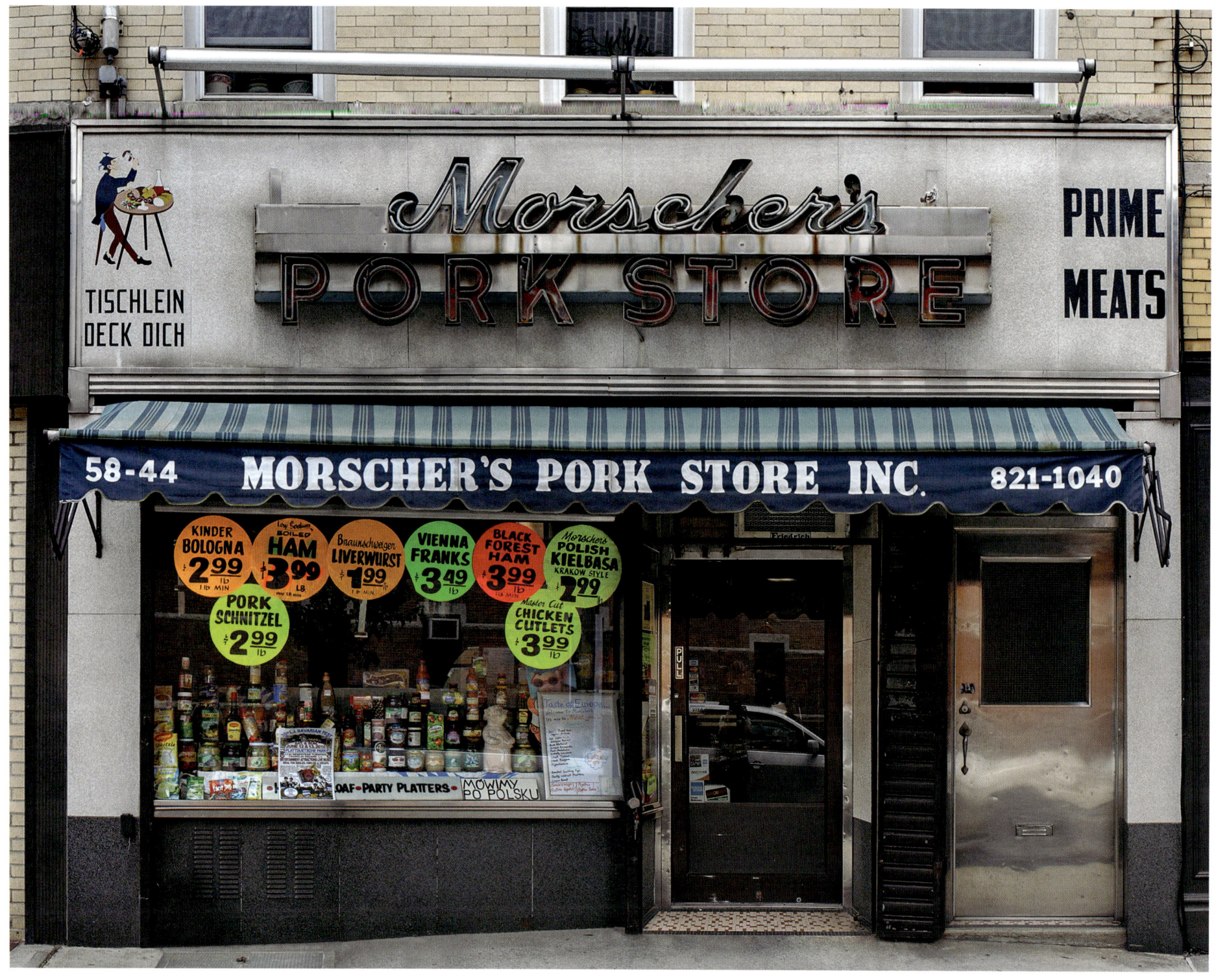

212 MORSCHER'S PORK STORE
Catalpa Avenue near Woodward Avenue, Ridgewood, 2009

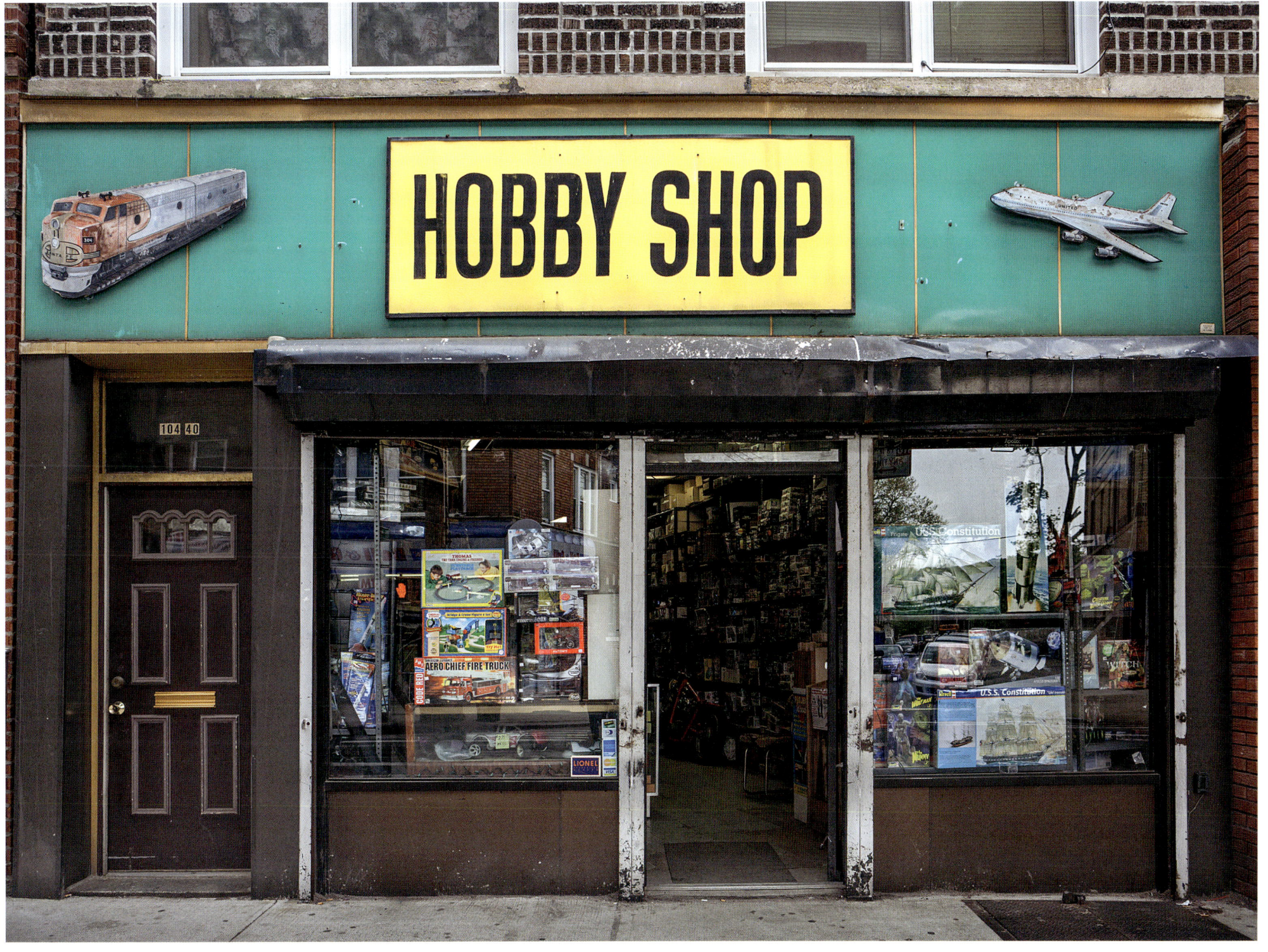

HOBBY SHOP
Jamaica Avenue near 105th Street, Richmond Hill, 2010

→
JOE & JOHN'S PIZZERIA
Myrtle Avenue at Stephen Street, Ridgewood, 2009

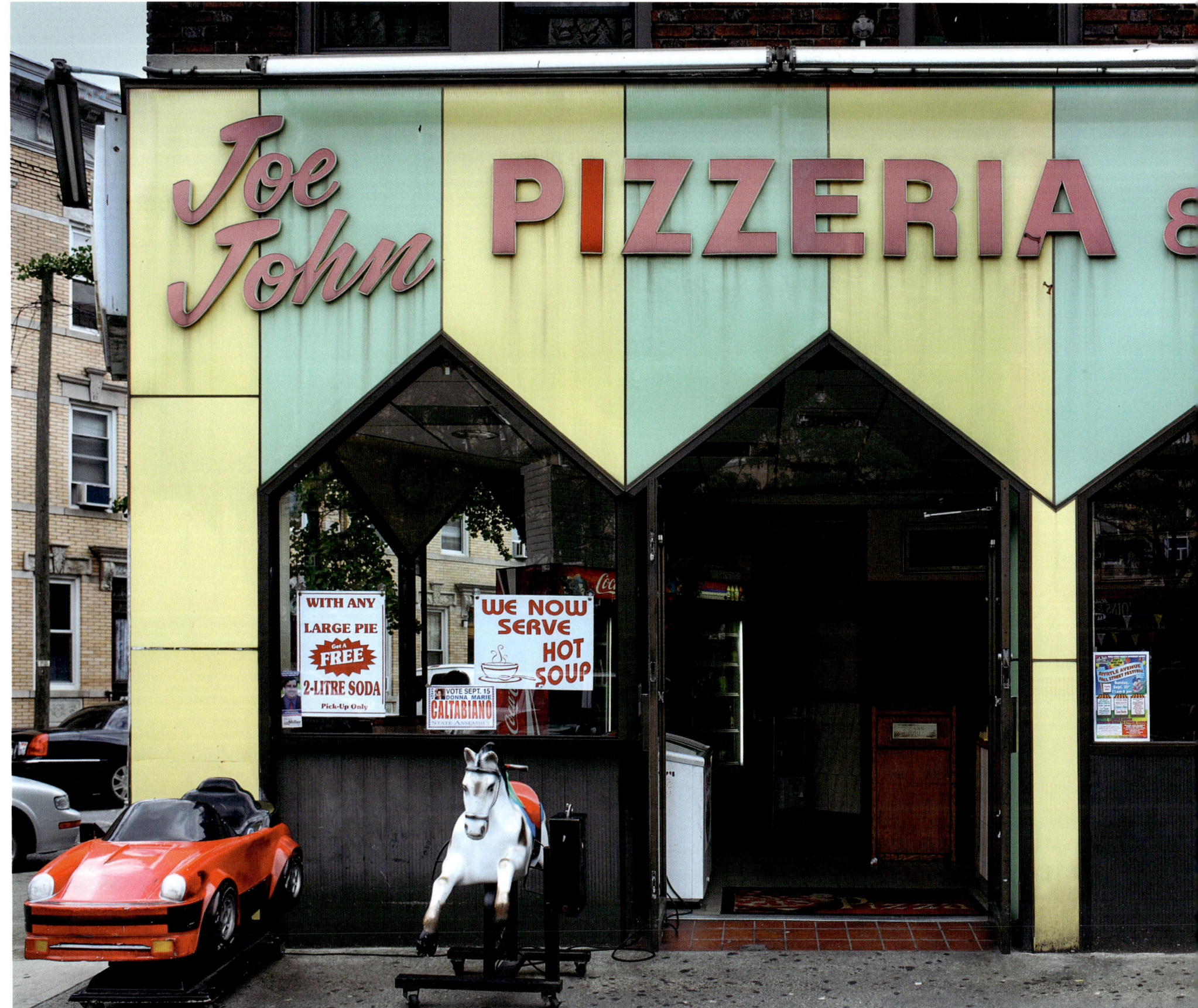

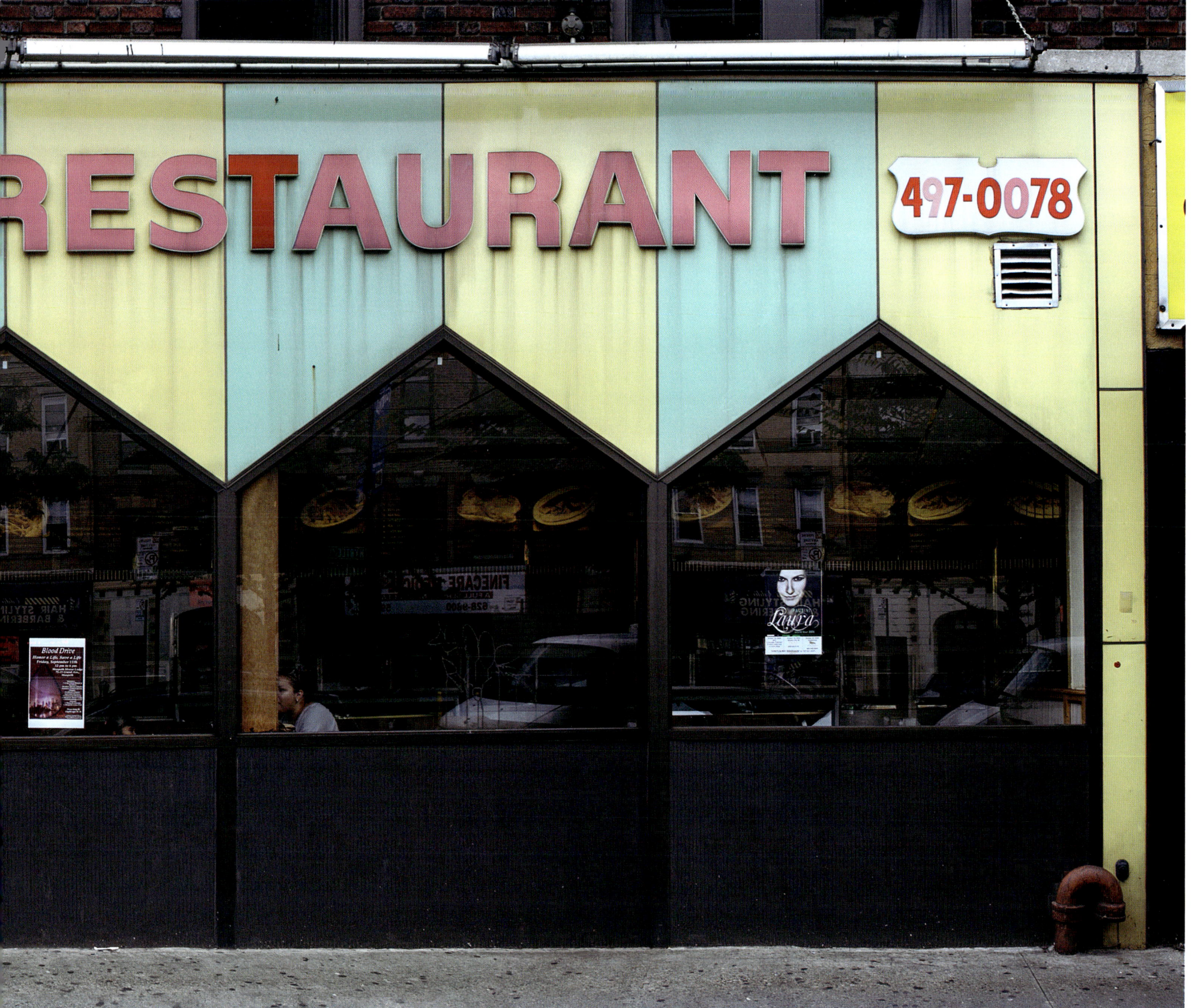

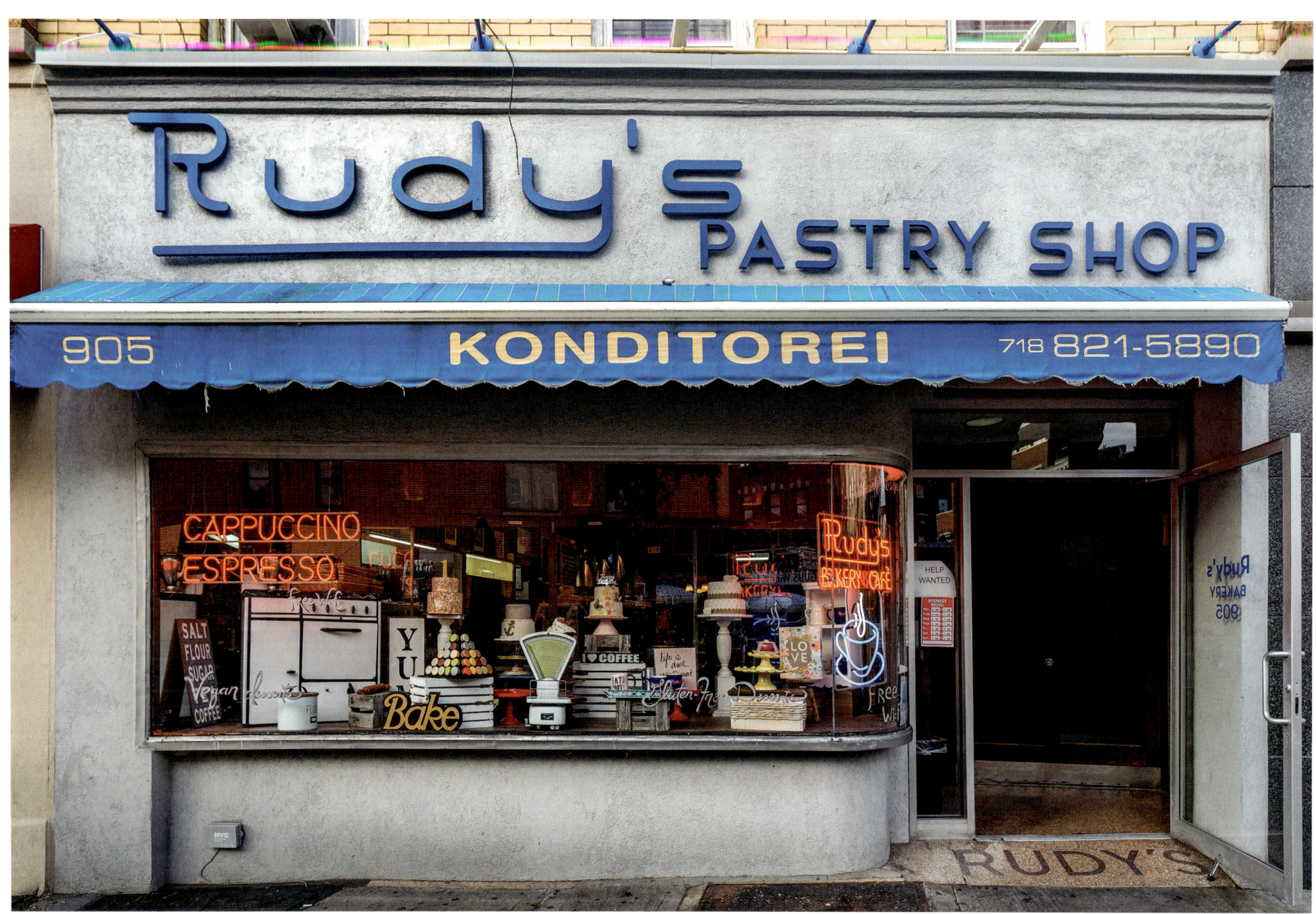

216 RUDY'S PASTRY SHOP
Seneca Avenue near Catalpa Avenue, Ridgewood, 2021

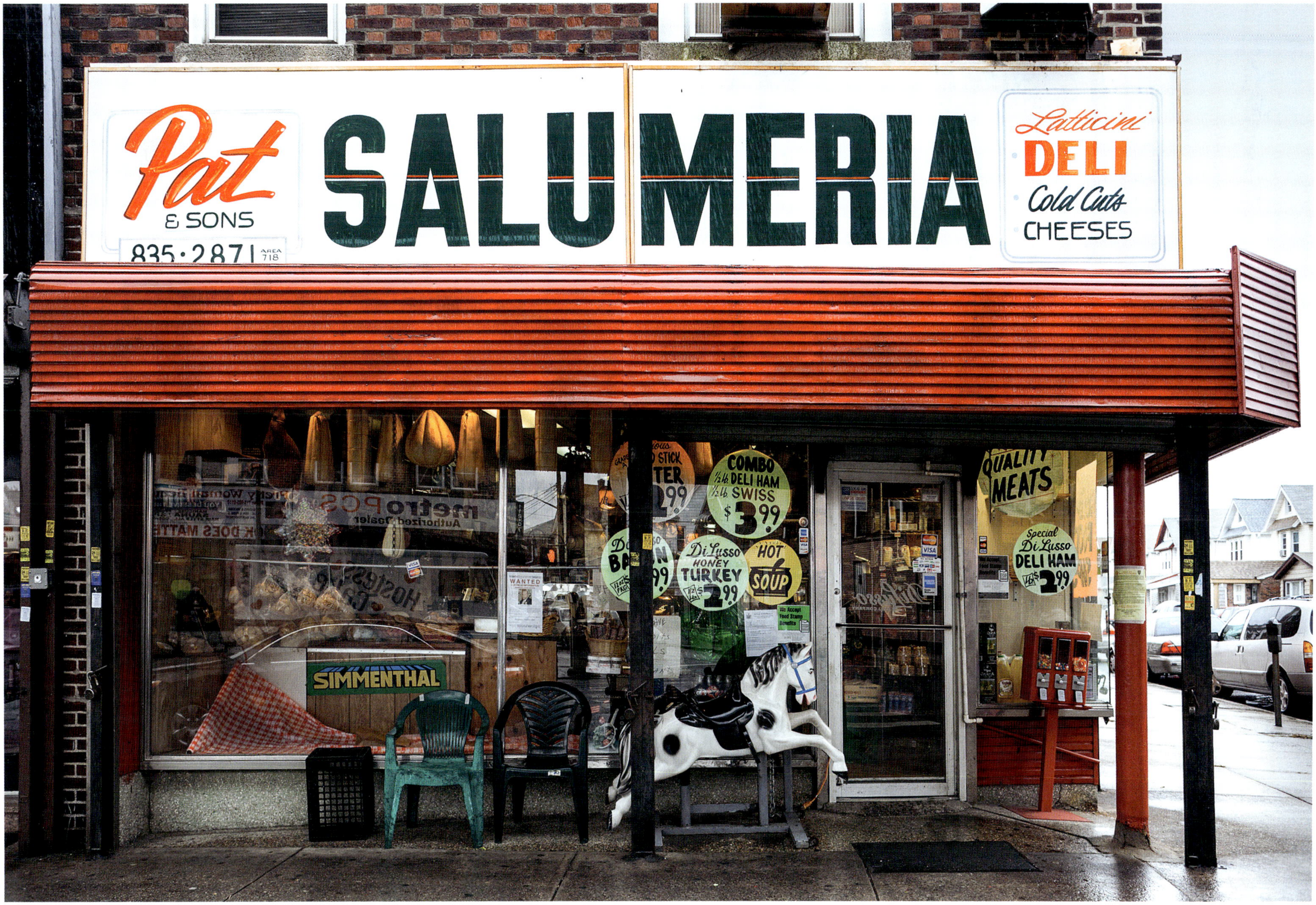

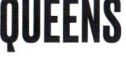

217 PAT & SONS SALUMERIA
Liberty Avenue at 112th Street, South Richmond Hill, 2009

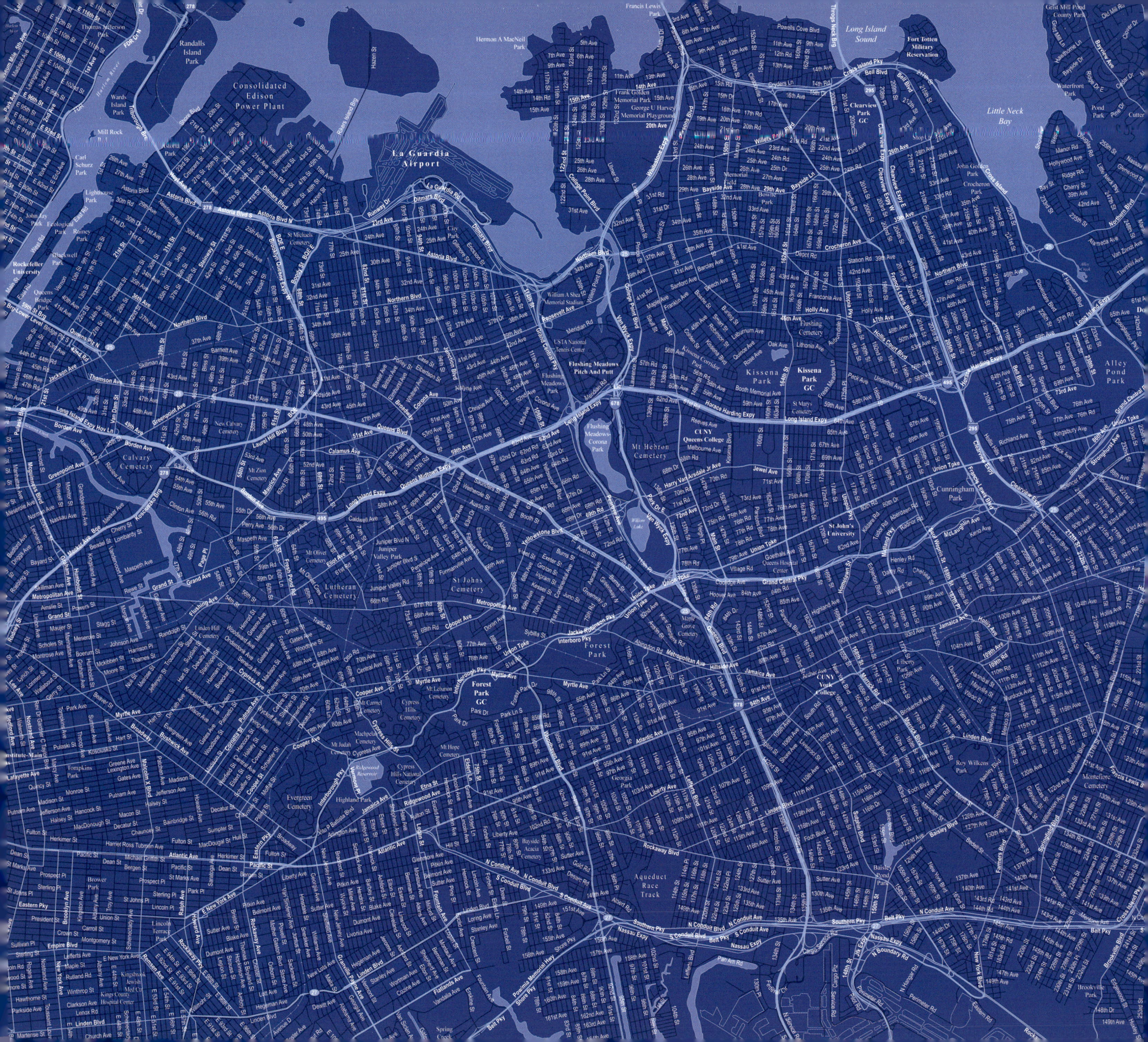

NORTHERN AND CENTRAL QUEENS

ASTORIA — ELMHURST — CORONA — FOREST HILLS — DOUGLASTON — FRESH MEADOWS

Astoria is bounded to the north and west by the East River and to the south by Broadway. It was founded in 1839 by Stephen A. Halsey, a fur merchant who named the community for the wealthy fur trader John Jacob Astor (with the hope that he would be inspired to invest in the area). Astor lived across the ferry landing in Manhattan, and although he did not invest, Astoria became a home for wealthy New Yorkers who built mansions there. In 1870, William Steinway bought a large section of land on both sides of Steinway Street, from Astoria Boulevard to the East River. He set up piano factories and a village with houses for the workers. After rapid transit reached Astoria in 1917, large numbers of apartment buildings were constructed. A connection to the Bronx was provided via the Triborough Bridge in 1936. Greek immigrants settled in the neighborhood after World War II, yet the population remained largely Italian. In the 1990s, immigrants from Lebanon, Egypt, Tunisia, Yemen, and Morocco moved in. By 2000, Astoria's population became more diverse as people from Brazil, Colombia, Bangladesh, China, Guyana, and Korea settled there.

Elmhurst is bounded by Roosevelt Avenue to the north, Junction Boulevard to the east, the Long Island Expressway to the south, and the New York Connecting Railroad to the west. It was founded in 1652 as Newtown but was renamed Elmhurst in 1896 to avoid negative associations with the heavily polluted Newtown Creek. By the early 1900s, the population was composed almost exclusively of Jewish and Italian middle-class residents, but after World War II, the neighborhood became more ethnically diverse. Today it remains a melting pot, with immigrants from more than one hundred nations residing in the neighborhood, including many Latinos and Chinese Americans.

Corona, in north-central Queens, is the "crown of villages" of Long Island. It is bounded by 45th Avenue to the north, Flushing Meadows Corona Park to the east, 62nd Avenue to the south, and Junction Boulevard to the west.

The neighborhood was largely Italian and Jewish with some African American residents until World War II, when the ethnic makeup became more diverse. In 1964, Flushing Meadows Corona Park was host to the New York World's Fair. The population is now largely Latino with some Italian Americans, African Americans, and Asian Americans.

Forest Hills is bounded to the north by the Long Island Expressway, to the east by Flushing Meadows Park, to the south by Union Turnpike, and to the west by Junction Boulevard and the disused tracks of the Long Island Railroad. The neighborhood was developed in the early 1900s with many elegant single-family homes, including a planned community of Tudor style homes and buildings called Forest Hills Gardens, which was designed to feel like an English-style village.

Douglaston is located on a peninsula and is bounded by Little Neck Bay to the north, the New York City–Nassau County border to the east, Grand Central Parkway to the south, and the Cross Island Parkway to the west. Although the area was first settled in 1656 by Thomas Hicks, much of the land was bought in 1835 by George Douglas. Douglaston became a desirable place to live, with quaint, hilly streets in park-like settings, a yacht club, and abundant shopping options.

Fresh Meadows is bounded to the north by the Long Island Expressway, to the east by Francis Lewis Boulevard, to the south by the Union Turnpike, and to the west by 182nd and 185th Streets. It is mainly a residential community. The neighborhood's name was taken from the Fresh Meadows housing development, which was built in 1946 on the site of a golf course by the New York Life Insurance Company. The population was almost exclusively white until a discrimination suit was filed in 1983 by the National Association for the Advancement of Colored People. The NAACP was successful, and the area gradually became more diverse.

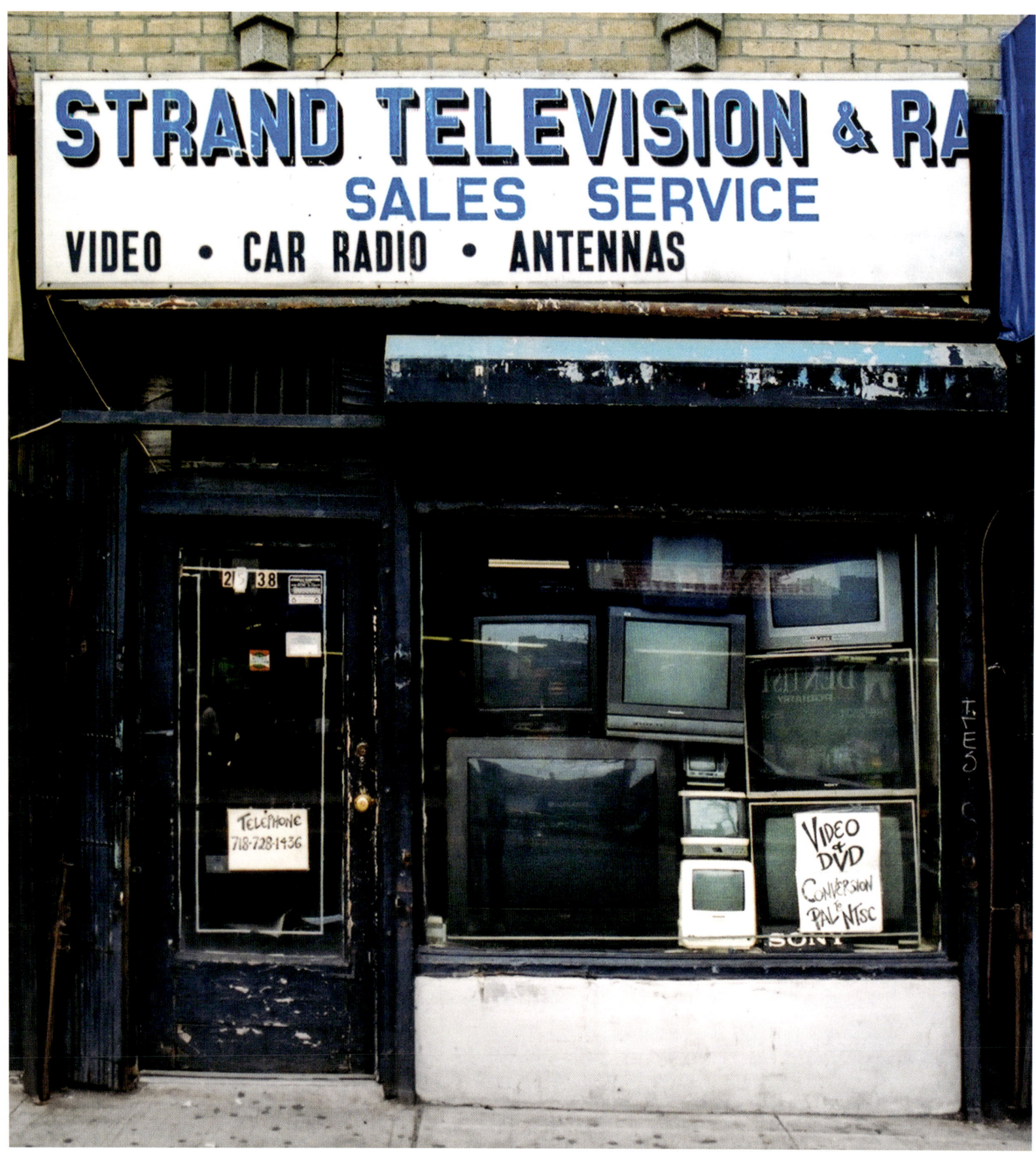

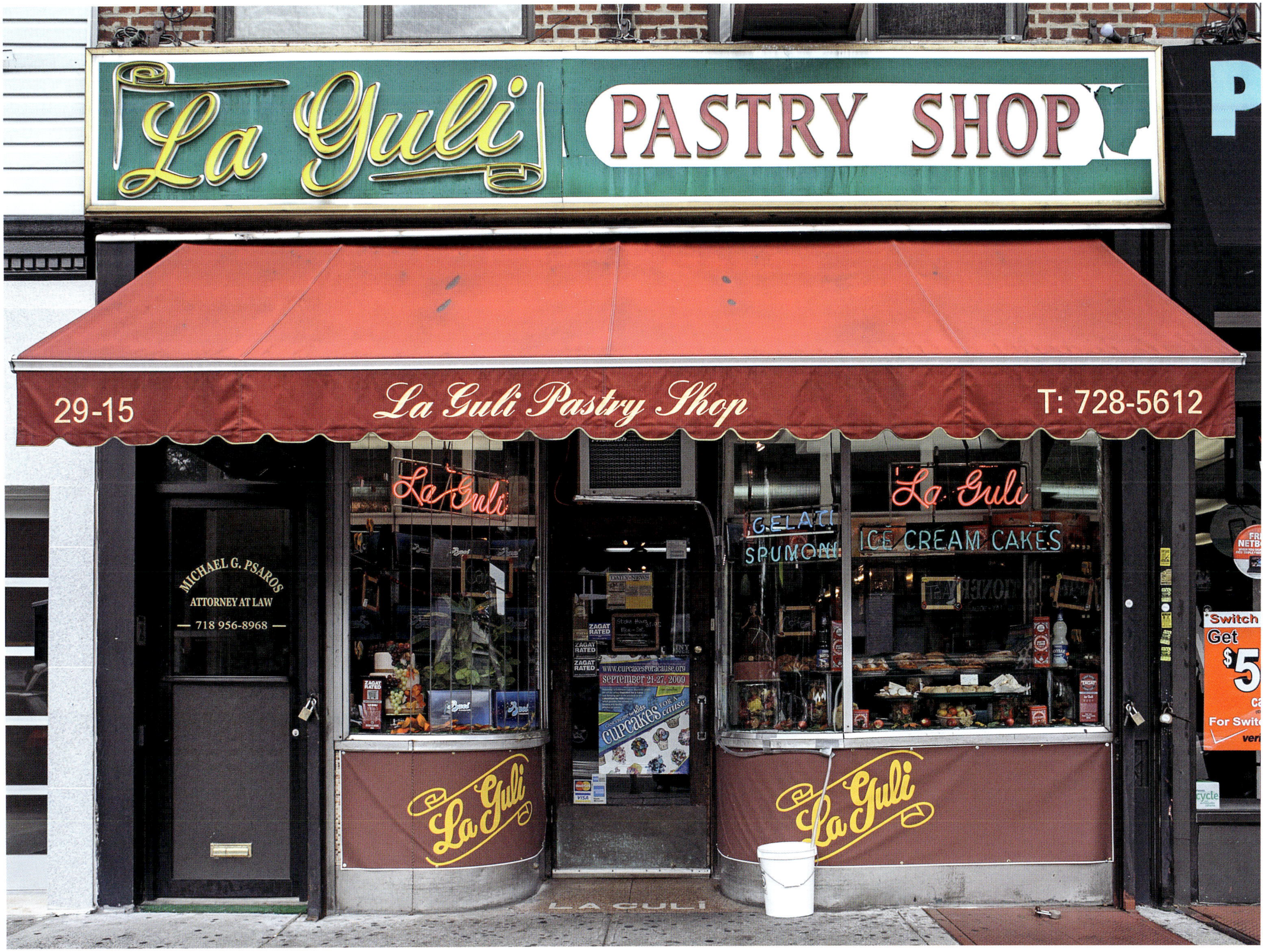

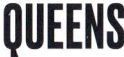

STRAND TELEVISION & RADIO SERVICE
Broadway near 29th Street, Astoria, 2006

LA GULI PASTRY SHOP
Ditmars Boulevard near 29th Street, Astoria, 2009

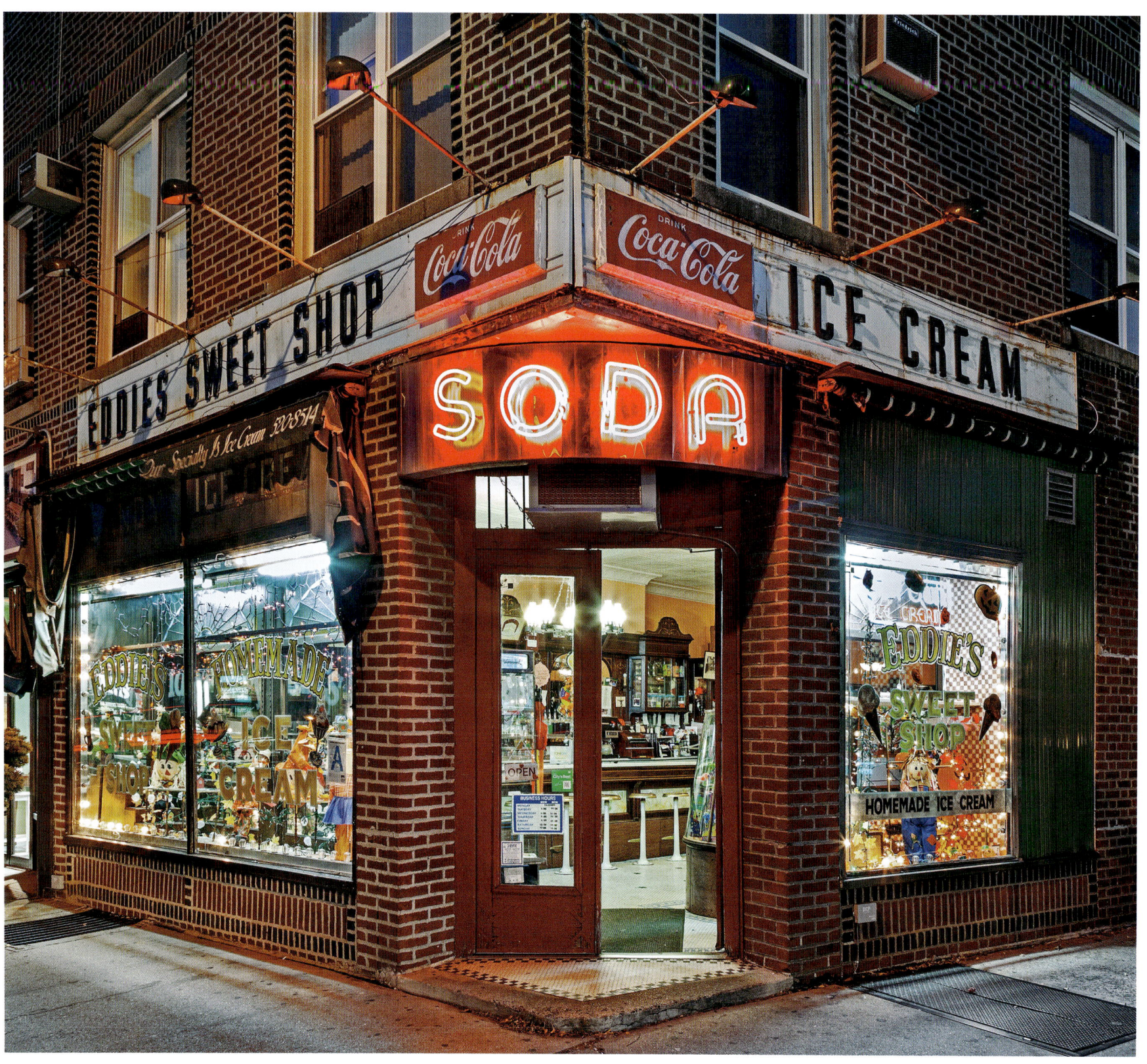

222 EDDIE'S SWEET SHOP
Metropolitan Avenue at 72nd Road, Forest Hills, 2017

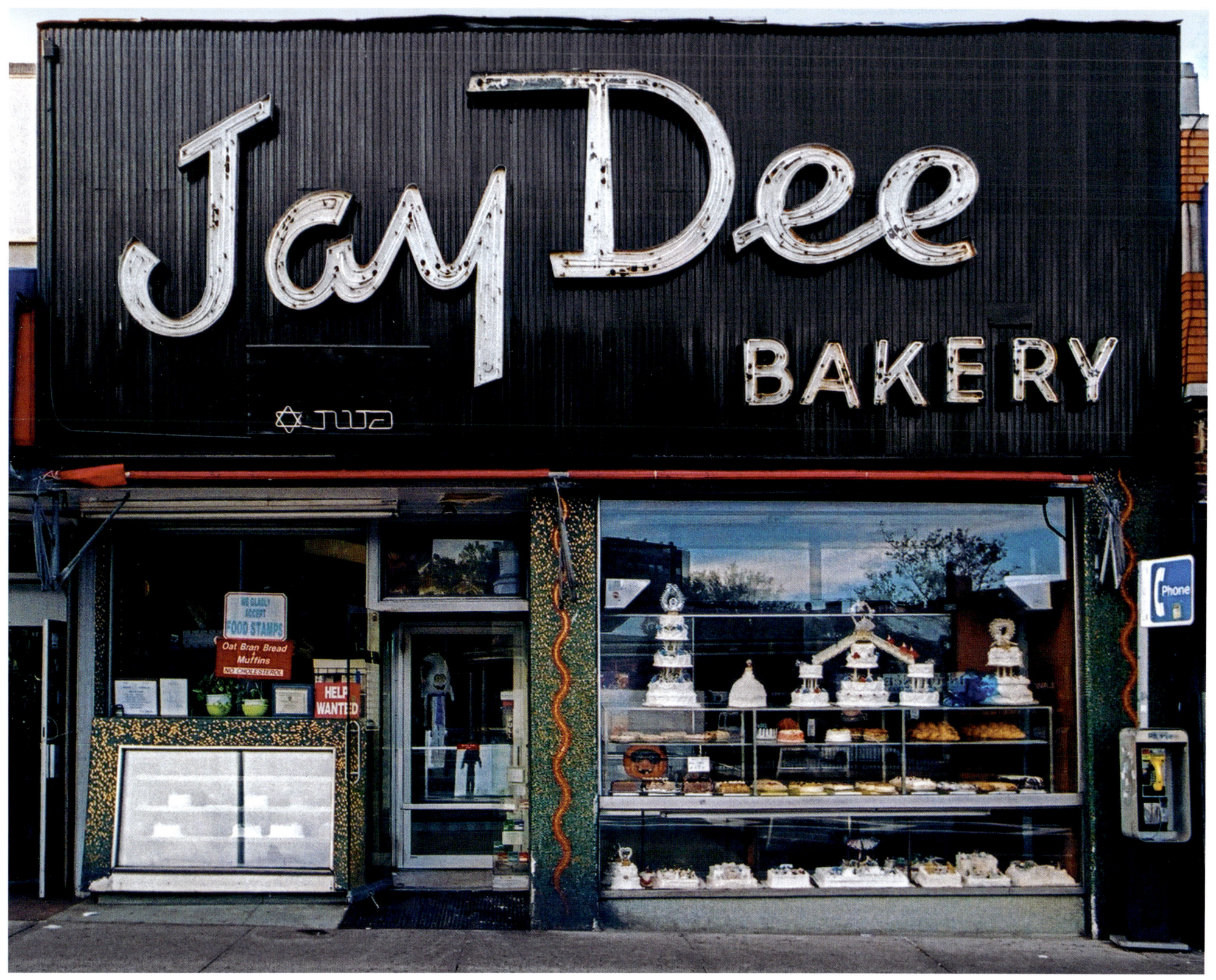

223 JAY DEE BAKERY
Queens Boulevard near 66th Avenue, Forest Hills, 2005

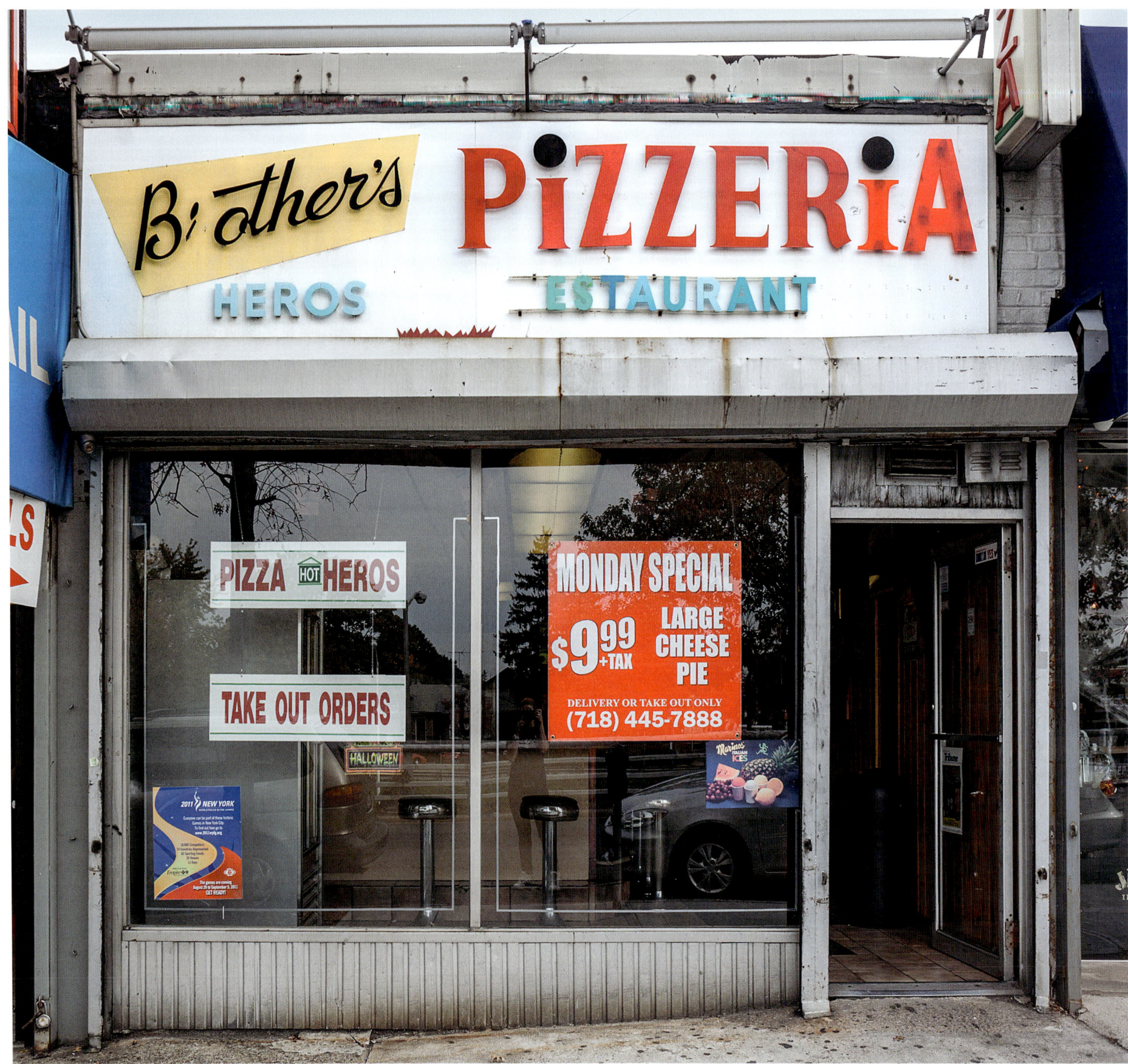

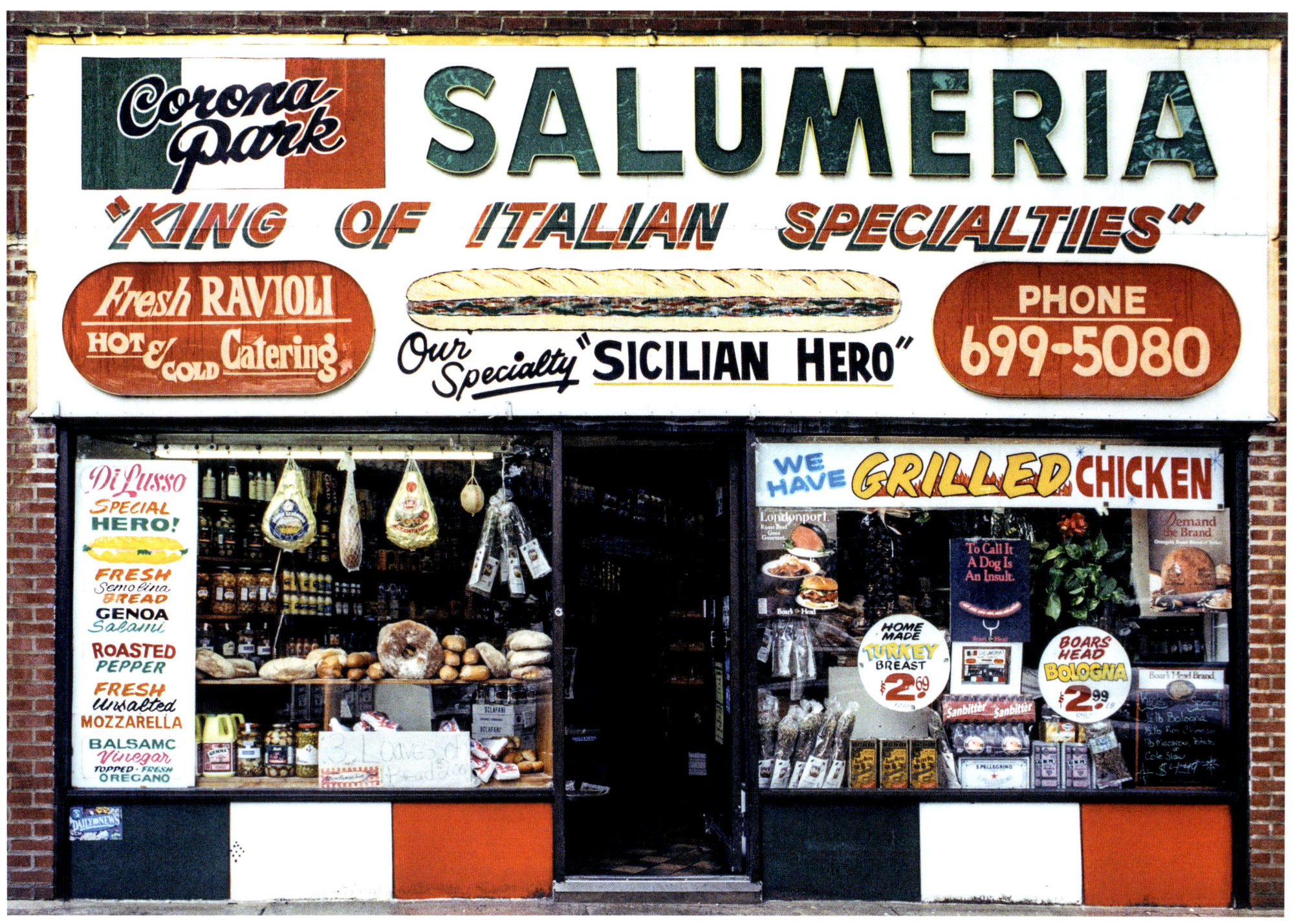

BROTHER'S PIZZERIA
Horace Harding Expressway near 185th Street, Fresh Meadows, 2010

CORONA PARK SALUMERIA
Corona Avenue near 52nd Avenue, Corona, 2004

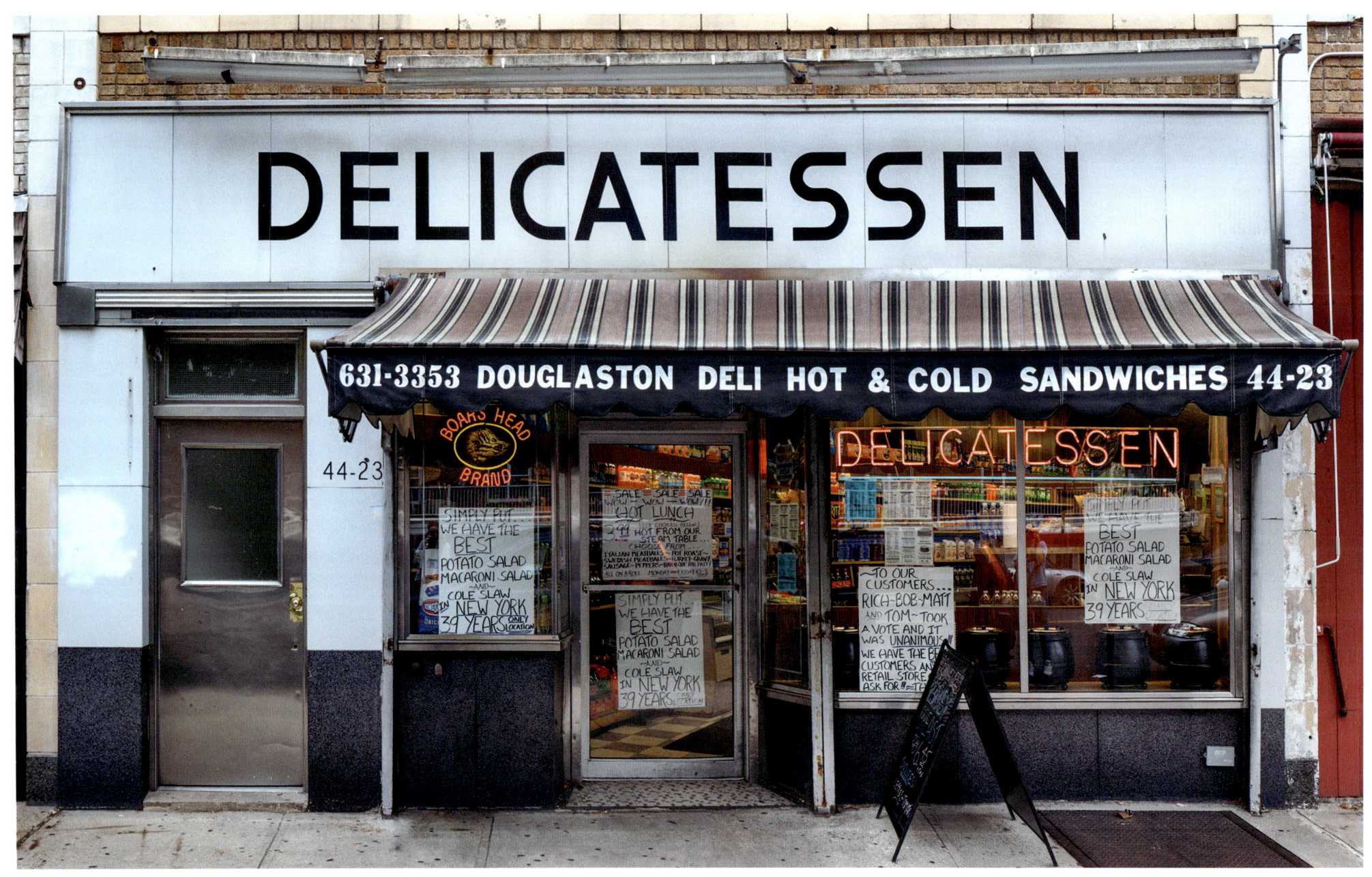

DOUGLASTON DELICATESSEN
Douglaston Parkway near Church Street, Douglaston, 2011

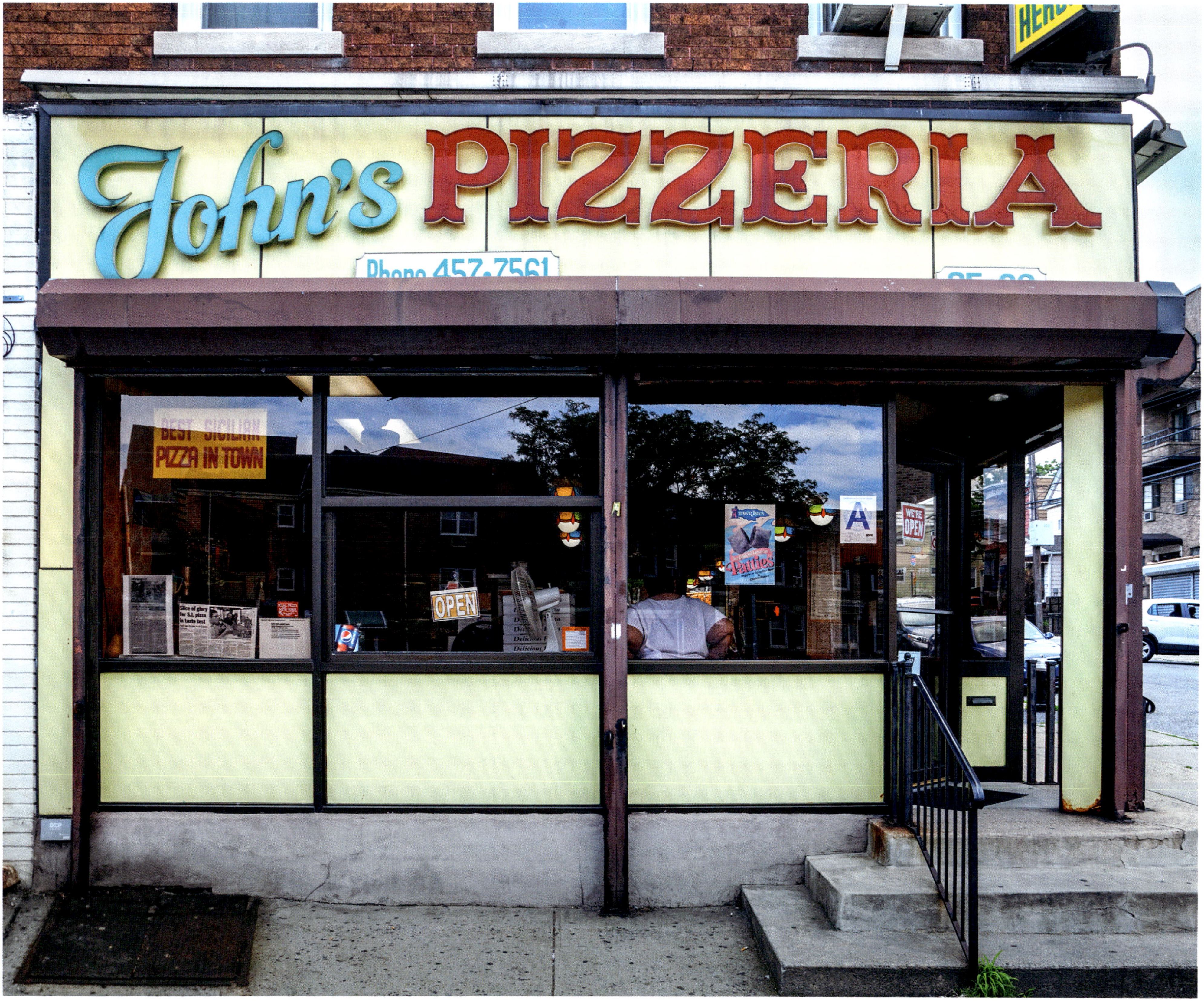

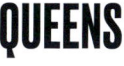

227   JOHN'S PIZZERIA
Grand Avenue at Haspel Street, Elmhurst, 2018

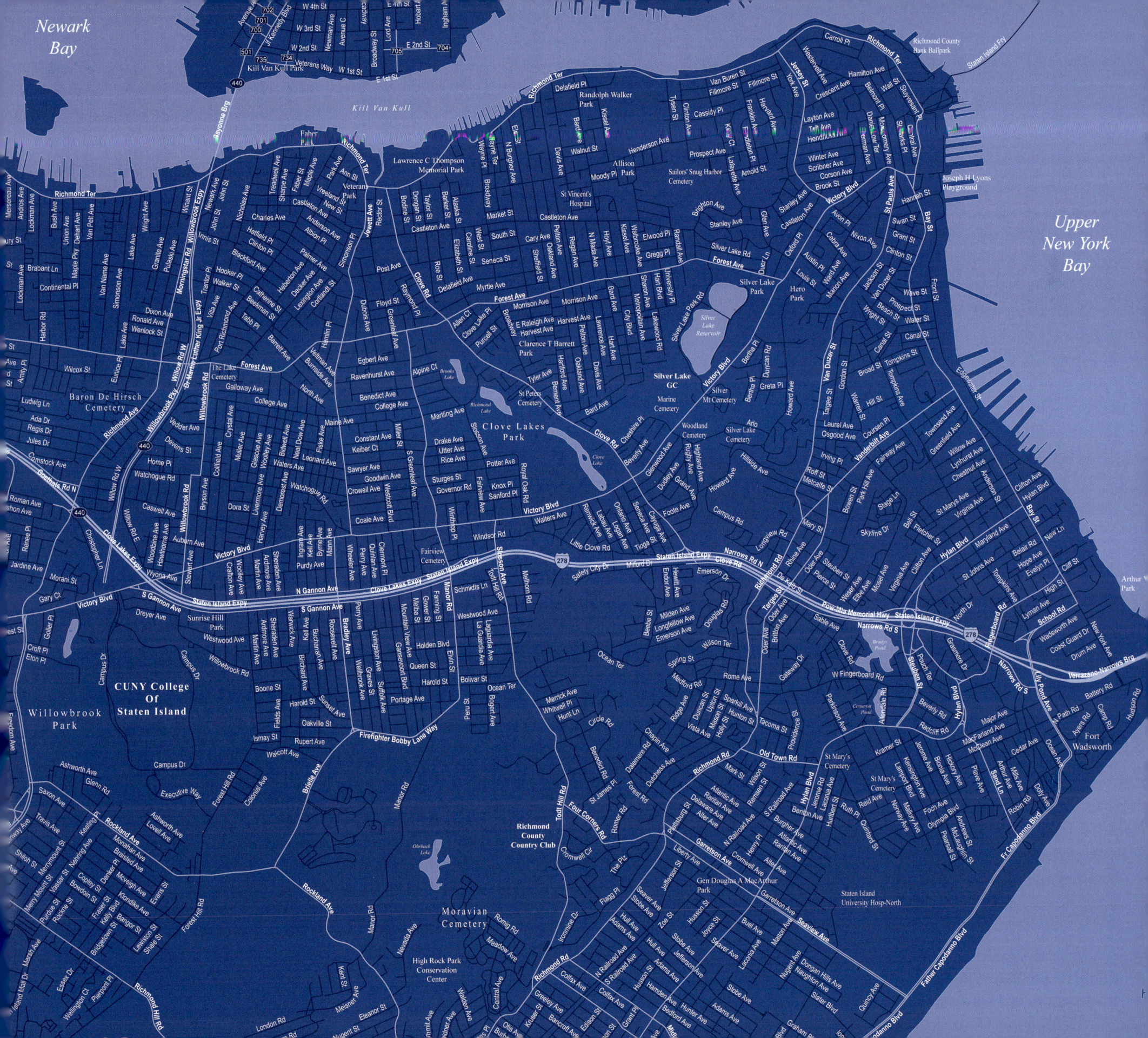

STATEN ISLAND

The borough of Staten Island is located at the juncture of Upper and Lower New York Bay. It is the third largest borough in sheer area, but the least populated. It is also the borough farthest from Manhattan, separated by a roughly 5-mile stretch of water. It can be reached from Manhattan only by the world-famous Staten Island Ferry. The passenger ferry, which runs twenty-four hours a day, is a lifeline for the large number of Staten Island residents that commute daily. Its free fare and amazing views of New York Harbor, including the Statue of Liberty and Lower Manhattan, have also made the ferry a popular tourist attraction.

Staten Island was settled by the Dutch in the early 1700s as a coastal fishing community and agricultural area with vast farmland. The growth of Manhattan and Brooklyn in the 19th century spurred residential development, but the borough remained relatively undeveloped, except the areas along the harbor. It became a borough of New York City in 1898, and in the 1920s saw a building boom that was sparked by plans for a system of bridges to New Jersey and a (never realized) subway connection with the city. Staten Island was promoted as a borough of homes, ideal for commuting, similar to Queens.

The opening of the Verrazano–Narrows Bridge in 1964 connected Staten Island with Brooklyn and led to more growth in the 1970s and '80s. There are more Italian Americans living on Staten Island than in any other county in the United States. It remains a largely residential borough, with the highest proportion of single-family and owner-occupied housing in the city.

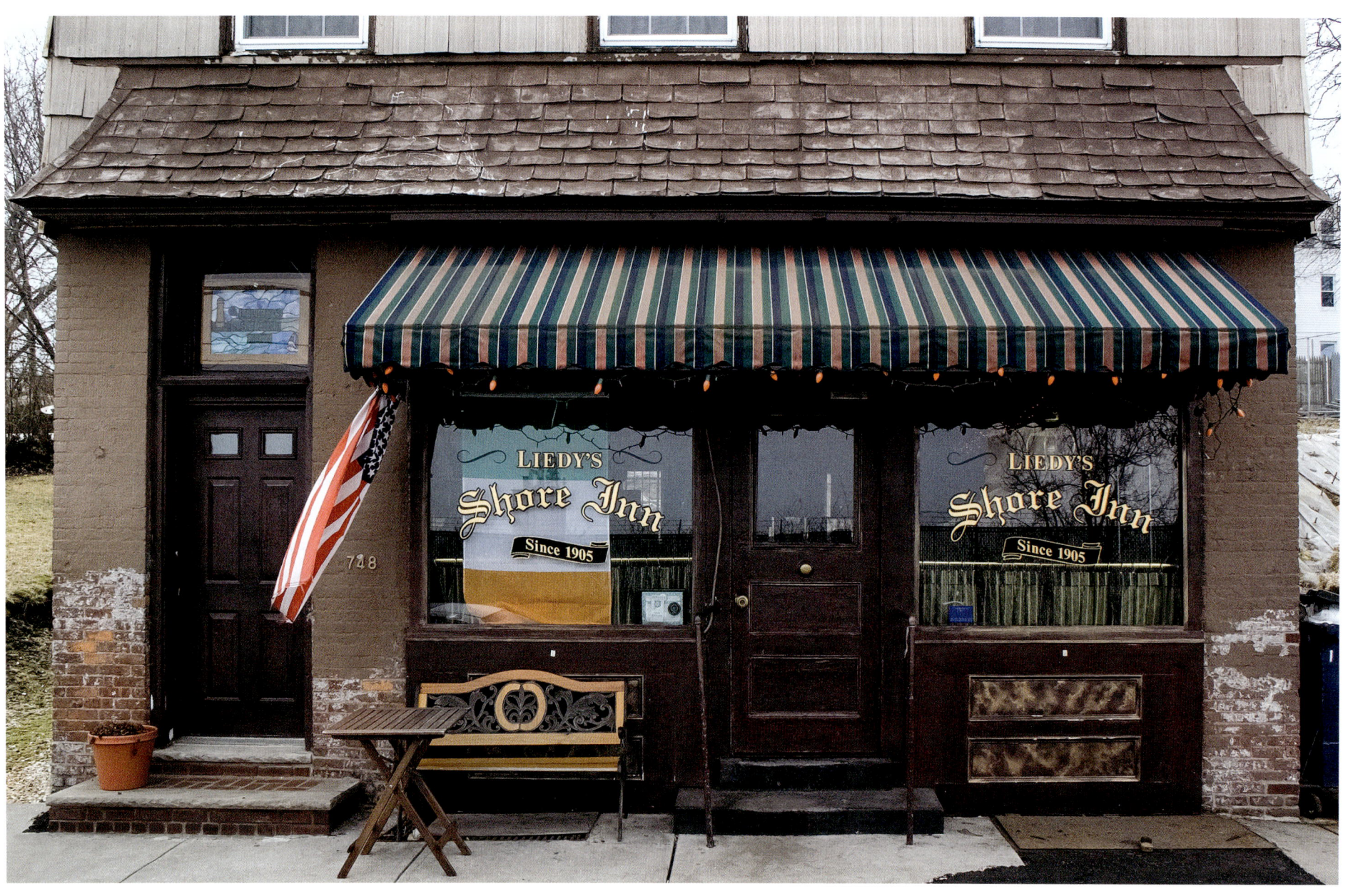

230   LIEDY'S SHORE INN
Richmond Terrace near Lafayette Avenue, Randall Manor, 2007

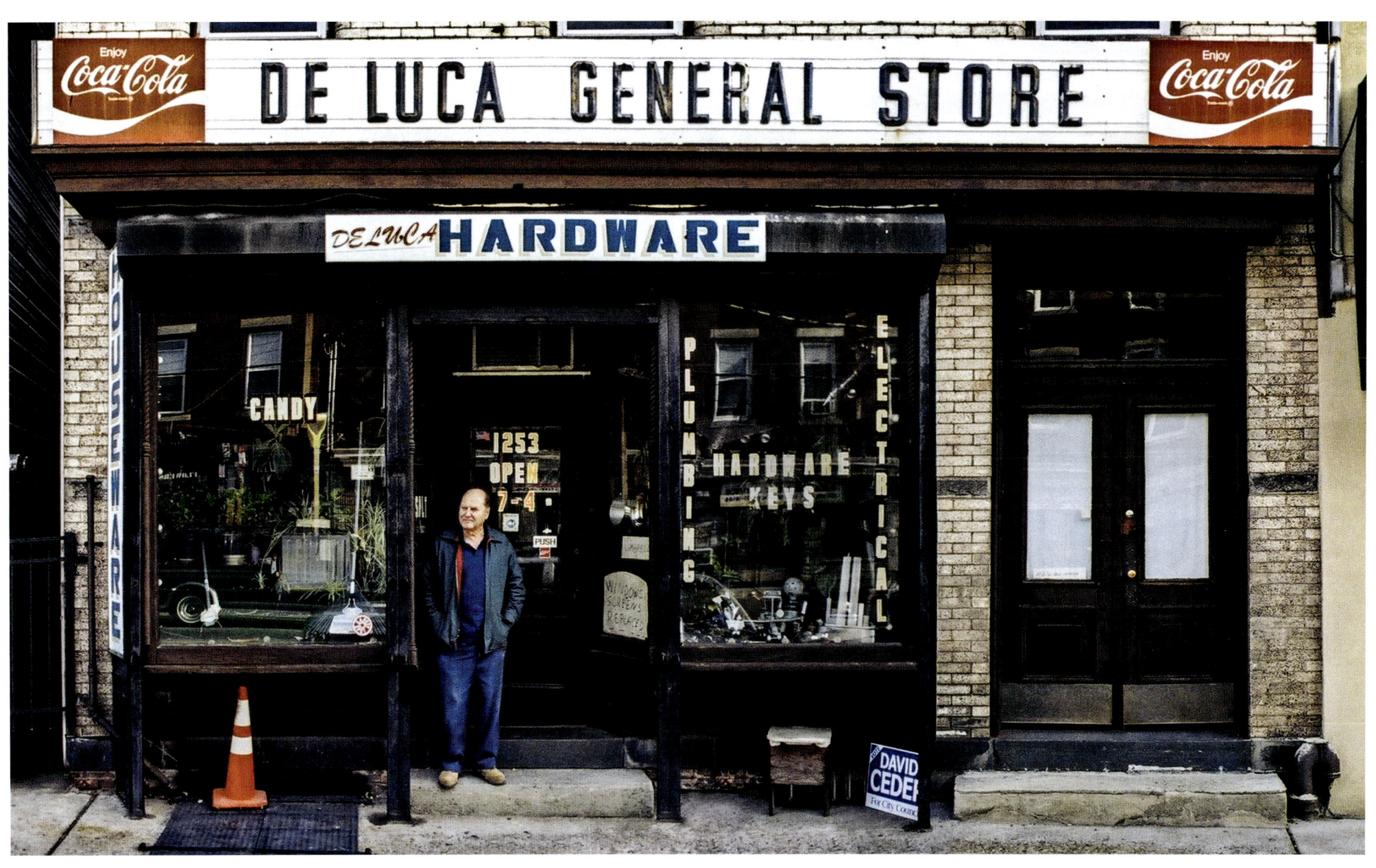

231 DE LUCA GENERAL STORE
Bay Street near Maryland Avenue, Rosebank, 2005

STATEN ISLAND

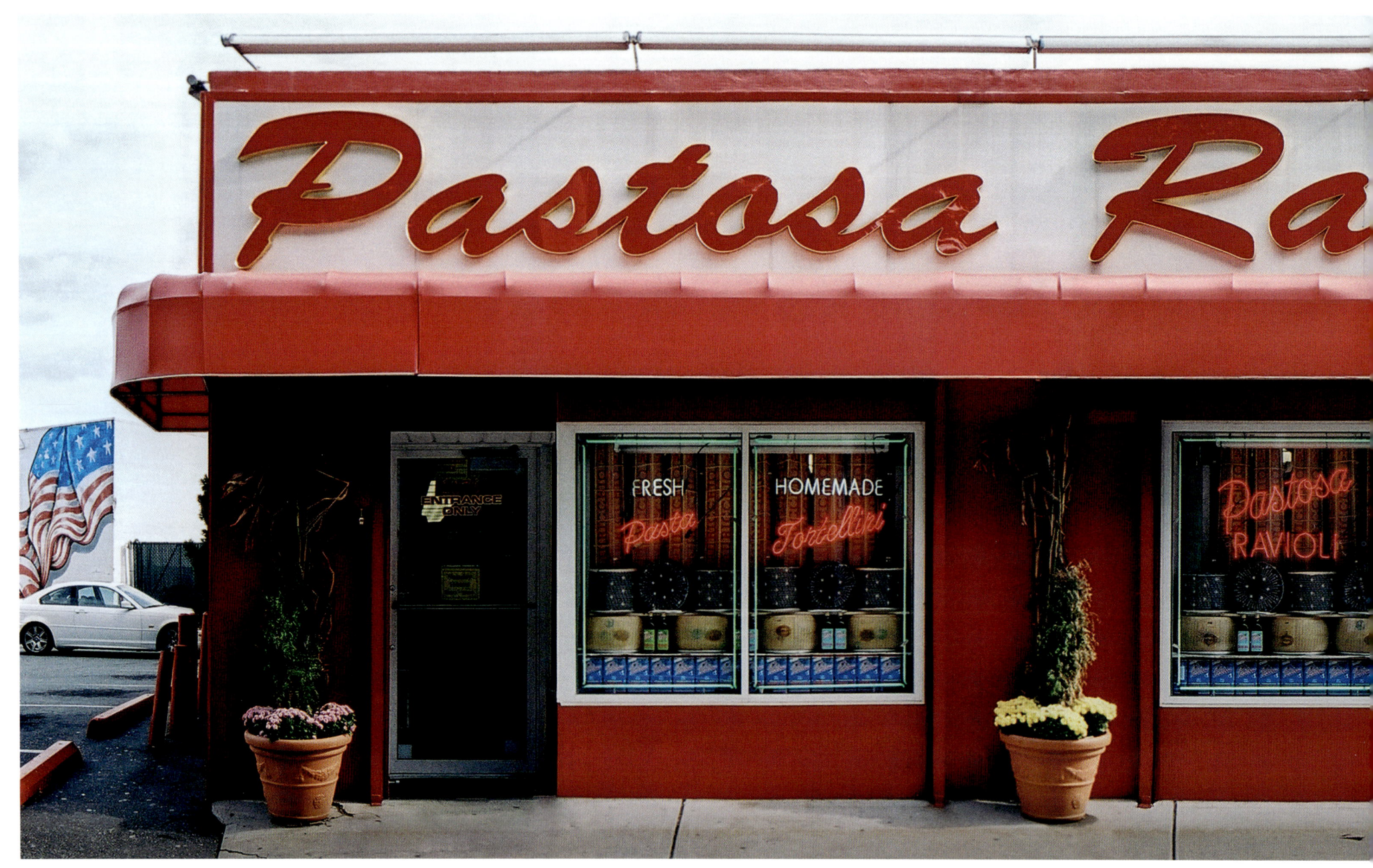

232 PASTOSA RAVIOLI
Richmond Road near Columbus Avenue, Todt Hill, 2005

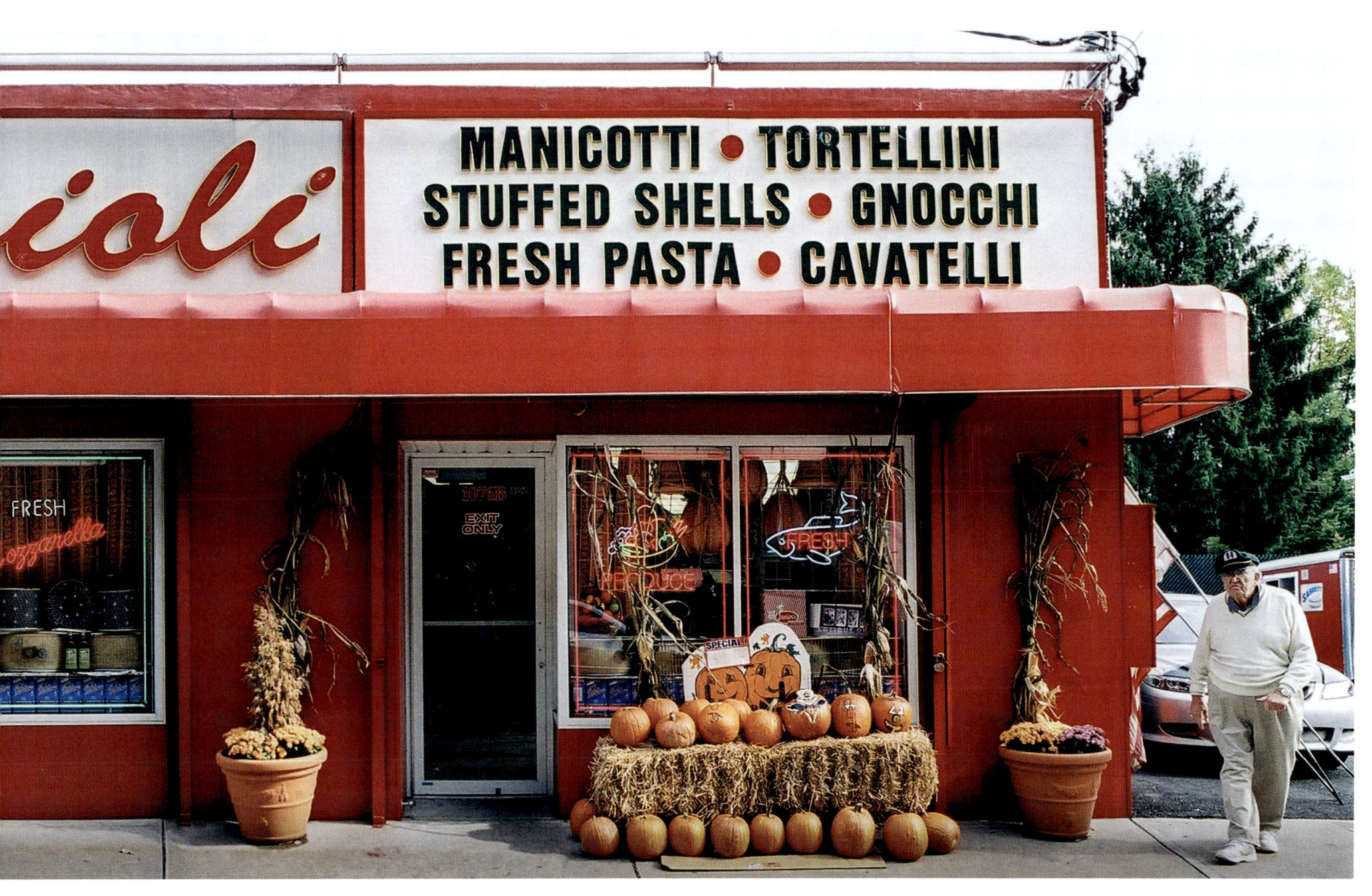

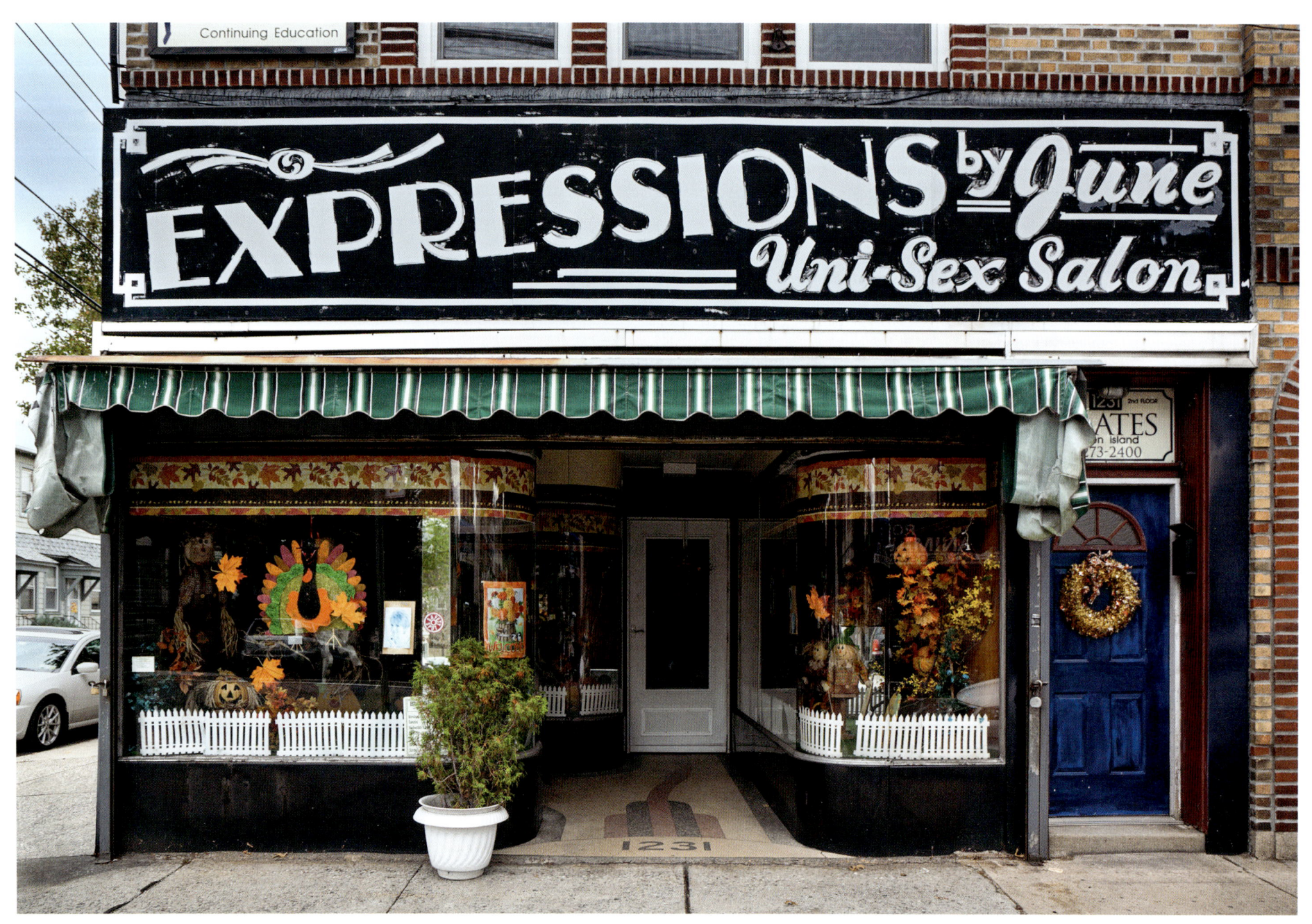

234

EXPRESSIONS BY JUNE UNI-SEX SALON
Bay Street at Maryland Avenue, Rosebank, 2014

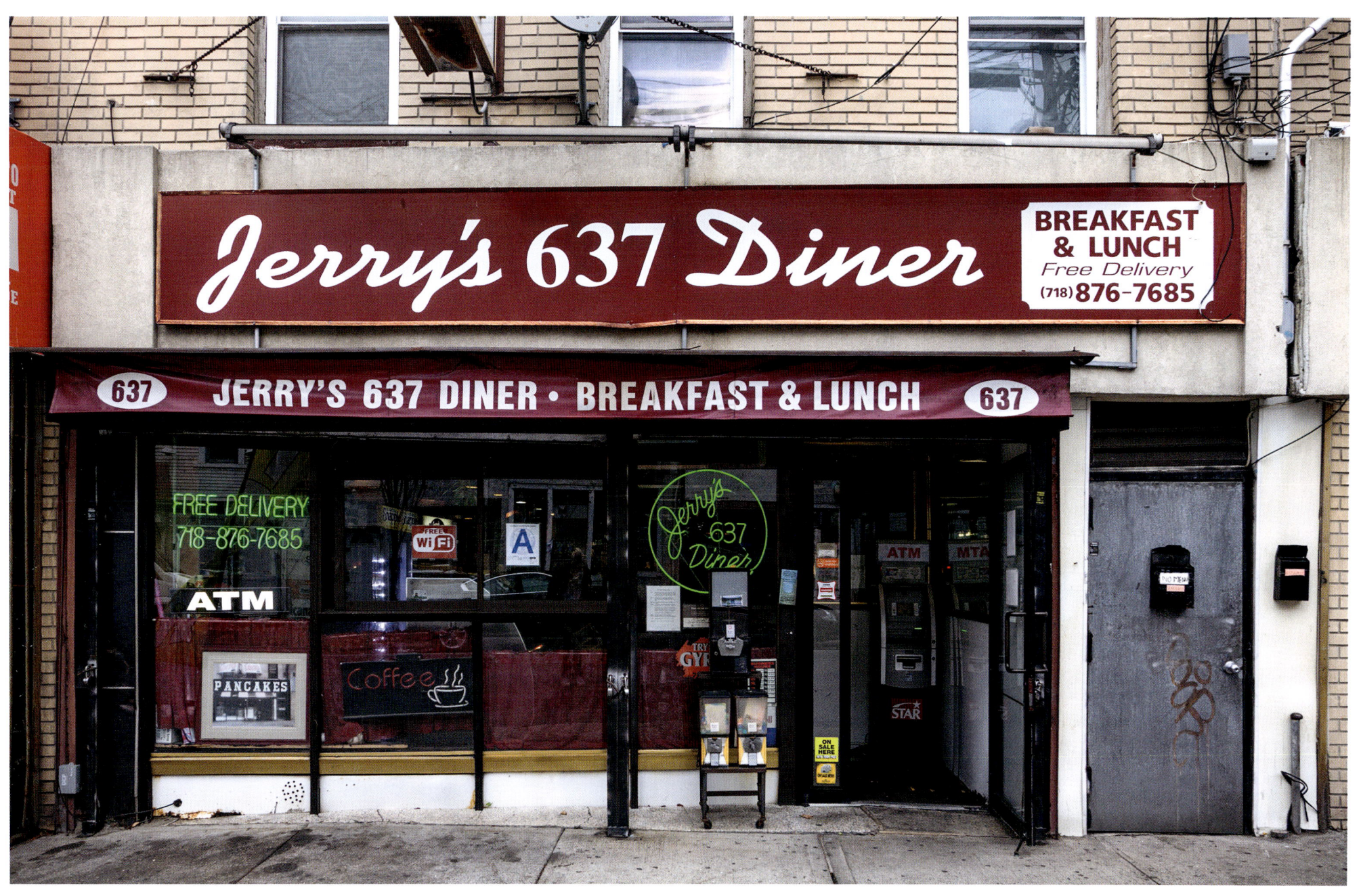

JERRY'S 637 DINER
Bay Street near Canal Street, Stapleton Heights, 2014

INDEX OF STORE FRONTS

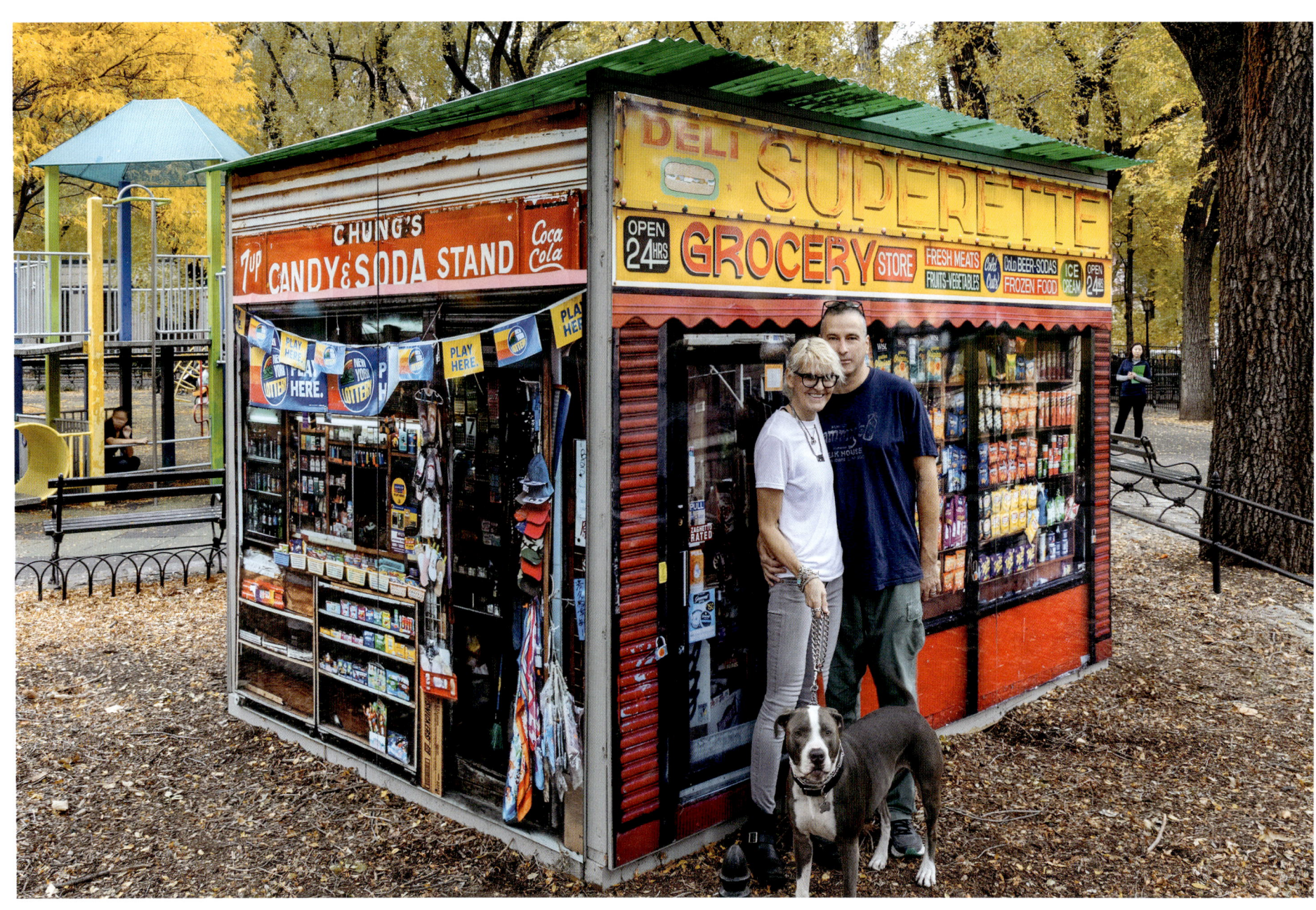

JAMES & KARLA MURRAY
WITH THEIR DOG, HUDSON

ABOUT THE AUTHORS

James and Karla Murray are husband-and-wife architectural and interior photographers and videographers based in New York City. Since 1997, they have focused their lens on the streetscape through portraits of store fronts and shop owners, seeking to capture the spirit, energy, and cultural diversity of individual neighborhoods through their work.

James and Karla's critically acclaimed books include *Store Front: The Disappearing Face of New York*, *New York Nights*, *Store Front II: A History Preserved*, and *Broken Windows: Graffiti NYC*. Their work has been widely exhibited around the world, including in solo exhibitions at the Brooklyn Historical Society, Clic Gallery, and the Storefront Project Gallery in New York City, and Fotogalerie im Blauen Haus in Munich, as well as group shows at the New-York Historical Society and the Museum of Neon Art in Glendale, California. Their photographs are included in the permanent collections of major institutions including the Smithsonian Center for Folklife and Cultural Heritage in Washington, DC, the New York Public Library, and NYU Langone Medical Center.

Their photography has appeared in numerous publications including the *New York Times*, the *London Telegraph*, the *Wall Street Journal*, the *New York Post*, *New York* magazine, and the *New Yorker*. James and Karla were awarded the 2015 Regina Kellerman Award by the Greenwich Village Society for Historic Preservation (GVSHP) in recognition of their significant contribution to the quality of life in Greenwich Village, the East Village, and NoHo. In 2017–20, they were awarded Creative Engagement Manhattan Arts Grants by the New York State Council on the Arts and administered by the Lower Manhattan Cultural Council. They received the prestigious Art in the Parks: UNIQLO Park Expressions Grant in 2018 for their public art installation, *Mom-and-Pops of the L.E.S.* (pictured at left).

James and Karla live in the East Village of Manhattan with their rescue dog, Hudson. Their work can be viewed at jamesandkarlamurray.com, and on their Instagram and YouTube accounts @jamesandkarla.

ACKNOWLEDGMENTS

This book would not have been possible without the help of many people. We particularly want to thank all of the business owners whose establishments appear in this book. We would also like to acknowledge Kenneth Jackson's *The Encyclopedia of New York City*, a book we used extensively while researching this project. Finally, we gratefully acknowledge our editor, Ali Gitlow, and the team at Prestel Publishing; our copy editor, Ryan Newbanks; and our designer, Benjamin Wolbergs.

© Prestel Verlag, Munich · London · New York, 2023
A member of Penguin Random House Verlagsgruppe GmbH
Neumarkter Strasse 28 · 81073 Munich

© for the photographs by James T. & Karla L. Murray, 2023
© for the text by James T. & Karla L. Murray and Chris Stein, 2023
produktsicherheit@penguinrandomhouse.de
(The above information is mandatory according to GPSR)

Reprinted 2025

Library of Congress Control Number: 2022952039

A CIP catalogue record for this book is available from the British Library.

Editorial direction: Ali Gitlow
Copyediting and proofreading: Ryan Newbanks
Design and layout: Benjamin Wolbergs
Production management: Luisa Klose
Separations: Reproline Mediateam, Munich
Printing and binding: TBB, a.s., Banská Bystrica
Paper: Profisilk

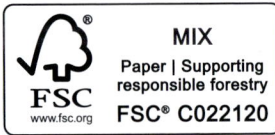

Penguin Random House Verlagsgruppe FSC® N001967

Printed in Slovakia

ISBN 978-3-7913-8964-6

www.prestel.com